Praise for Robert Kuttner's

"Robert Kuttner h̲a̲s̲ ... ̲plan̲ations of the complex de̲... ̲ its knees. *Debtors' Prison* ta̲... ̲omic history, using the le̲n̲... ̲st boom-and-bust cycles ar̲... ̲in current economic debates. Kuttner's impressive history also catapults the reader into the future, providing critical insight on strengthening the financial system. A must-read for anyone interested in our economic future." —Senator Elizabeth Warren

"Kuttner's thesis is girded to a historical narrative that yields a coherent, readable and highly impassioned book. . . . The charge that 'austerity mongers' on the Continent have been standing guard over a new debtors' prison cannot be easily dismissed." —*The New York Times Book Review*

"No topics in modern political life have spawned more confusion, misdirected effort, and overall malarkey than 'deficits' and 'debt.' Robert Kuttner does us the enormous service of explaining which kinds of debt we should worry more about, and which kinds less—and how to manage public and private debt so as to sustain an age of broadly shared prosperity rather than of austere decline." —James Fallows, author of *China Airborne*

"[I]nformed, passionate, at times angry. . . . The breadth of Kuttner's review of the politics of credit and debt through American history is impressive." —*Dissent*

"This timely, thought-provoking book will add valuable insight to ongoing fiscal policy debates." —*Booklist*

"*Debtors' Prison* is more than a devastating brief against the trans-Atlantic pursuit of austerity. It is a magisterial retelling of our history through the prism of the struggle over credit and debt. Navigating between countries and eras with the authority of a scholar and the narrative skill of a journalist, Robert Kuttner has written the authoritative guide to economic recovery and financial reform."

—Jacob S. Hacker, coauthor of
Winner-Take-All Politics: How Washington Made the Rich Richer—And Turned Its Back on the Middle Class

"[T]imely. . . . An insightful and relevant look at the topic of debt in the United States and abroad."   —*Library Journal*

"[C]ontribute[s] a much-needed historical perspective that explores, as Kuttner puts it, 'how the bad economic advice of the austerity lobby became the prevailing view.' . . . Arrive[s] at an opportune time. . . . [Kuttner] hold[s] out the possibility of a different future."   —*Democracy*

ROBERT KUTTNER

DEBTORS' PRISON

Robert Kuttner is cofounder and coeditor of *The American Prospect*, as well as a professor at Brandeis University's Heller School. He was a longtime columnist for *Businessweek* and continues to write columns in *The Boston Globe*, *The New York Times Global Edition*, and *The Huffington Post*. This is his tenth book.

ALSO BY ROBERT KUTTNER

A Presidency in Peril:
The Inside Story of Obama's Promise, Wall Street's Power
and the Struggle to Control Our Economic Future

Obama's Challenge:
America's Economic Crisis and
the Power of a Transformative Presidency

The Squandering of America:
How the Failure of Our Politics Undermines Our Prosperity

Everything for Sale:
The Virtues and Limits of Markets

The End of Laissez-Faire:
National Purpose and the Global Economy After the Cold War

The Life of the Party:
Democratic Prospects in 1988 and Beyond

The Economic Illusion:
False Choices Between Prosperity and Social Justice

Revolt of the Haves:
Tax Rebellions and Hard Times

Family Re-Union:
Reconnecting Parents and Children in Adulthood

DEBTORS' PRISON

THE POLITICS OF AUSTERITY
VERSUS POSSIBILITY

ROBERT KUTTNER

Vintage Books
A Division of Penguin Random House LLC
New York

FIRST VINTAGE BOOKS EDITION, JUNE 2015

Copyright © 2013, 2015 by Robert Kuttner

All rights reserved. Published in the United States by Vintage Books,
a division of Penguin Random House LLC, New York, and distributed
in Canada by Random House of Canada, a division of Penguin Random
House Ltd., Toronto. Originally published in hardcover in the United
States by Alfred A. Knopf, a division of Penguin Random House LLC,
New York, in 2013.

Vintage and colophon are registered trademarks of
Penguin Random House LLC.

The Library of Congress has cataloged the Knopf edition as follows:
Kuttner, Robert.
Debtors' prison : the politics of austerity versus possibility / Robert
Kuttner.
p. cm
1. Debt.   2. Budget deficits.
3. Government spending policy.   4. Consumption (Economics)   I. Title.
HG3701.K88 2013   339.5'2—dc23   2012036230

Vintage Books Trade Paperback ISBN: 978-1-101-91052-8
eBook ISBN: 978-0-307-95981-2

Book design by M. Kristen Bearse
Author photograph © Michael Lionstar
Cover design by Linda Huang
Cover illustration by Thomas Colligan

www.vintagebooks.com

Printed in the United States of America
10 9 8 7 6 5 4 3 2 1

For Joan

I will have my bond.

—Shylock, in William Shakespeare's
The Merchant of Venice

Contents

The Real Debt Problem

THE FIRST EDITION OF *Debtors' Prison* appeared in mid-2013. At that point, both the United States and the European Union were pursuing policies of budgetary austerity. This strategy was billed, improbably, as the cure for prolonged economic stagnation resulting from a financial crash. Since then, the United States has partly moved away from austerity and begun a partial recovery. But the benefits have gone mainly to the very top and have not yet translated into broadly shared prosperity. The EU continues its tragically misguided course of austerity and stagnation.

I titled this book *Debtors' Prison* to suggest an analogy. In the era when it was common to throw people in jail as a punishment for debts they could not pay, the result was perverse for both debtor and creditor. The debtor's economic life ended—in prison there was no way the inmate could earn money to repay debt; thus there was no way the creditor could be made whole.

The invention of bankruptcy in England in 1706 during the reign of Queen Anne offered an ingenious solution. A magistrate would evaluate the assets of the bankrupt party; creditors would be repaid at so many pence in the pound; the debt would be considered discharged and the debtor could get on with his life. This was the origin of the modern US Chapter 11 bankruptcy, in which a corporation is able to settle old debts for pennies on the dollar and then begin again with a clean slate. Even the statute of Queen Anne was a variation on a more ancient, now abandoned, concept—the biblical Jubilee, in which debts were forgiven after fifty years. Bankruptcy reform was a significant breakthrough because it de-linked what was presumed to be a moral imperative from what was economically sensible. It was widely deemed immoral not to pay debts. Further, if profligate behavior had caused the crippling debt, foregiveness would be that much worse. Yet economic theory deems bankruptcy efficient, because it allows commerce to proceed; it allows entrepreneurs to take risks knowing that they will not face total ruin if they miscalculate. It writes off yesterday's debt for the sake of tomorrow's growth. Even financiers (who want to be paid back) accept the occasional corporate bankruptcy as the price of enterprise. There is a broader analogy here.

Although the notion that debts must be repaid has moral overtones, in this case pragmatic economic logic trumps conventional moral wisdom. When a bankruptcy judge approves a settlement allowing old debts to be written off, the behavior that wrecked the company is not at issue unless it is criminal. The only question for the judge to decide is whether the company can survive if it gets debt relief. Otherwise, it is liquidated and the creditors share the remains.

Ever since 1706, however, bankruptcy law has been replete with double standards. At its inception, bankruptcy was only for the commercial class. Merchants worth more than one thousand pounds could get relief. Ordinary deadbeats stayed in jail. In recent decades, the double standards have only worsened.

Consider the situation facing several indebted nations today. They are being punished for past behavior deemed profligate—even if the government responsible for the debts is long gone; even if the citizens who suffer the consequences were not party to the government's schemes; even if the nation is the victim of generalized depression that it did not create. But there is no Chapter 11 for nations, even though the investors in their sovereign debt took the same kind of knowing risks as investors in corporate bonds. Yet nations such as Greece are being pressed so hard to pay back debts that their economic life is strangled. Like the bankrupt merchant of Queen Anne's day, the more they are squeezed, the less capacity they have to repay debts.

The effort of a new government in Greece to win some debt relief, and the response of the European elite, shows just how potent and foolhardy is this policy consensus. Europe's elite would rather crush Greece than agree to debt relief that contradicts their pre-1706 conceits about the morality of debt repayment. The new government of Greece, elected in January 2015 on a commitment to renegotiate debt, and win relief, was given only a few months reprieve. The larger austerity program was unrelenting.

A similar reality rooted in similarly perverse concepts and policies still confronts millions of American homeowners whose houses are worth less than the mortgages on them. In the vast majority of cases, this is not the fault of the homeowners. Most were innocent bystanders with the bad luck to get caught in a general economic downdraft that depressed property values. Some were cheated by subprime swindlers. But Congress, presented in 2010 with a bill to create a new category of bankruptcy to give underwater homeowners the same sort of relief available to corporations, voted it down under pressure from Wall Street.

A third category of people sandbagged by crushing debt before their economic life has even begun is recent college graduates. Their parents and grandparents were able to attend public universities essentially for free. A summer job would easily cover the cost of very modest tuitions and fees. Today, young adults are saddled with debts totaling over $1.2 trillion—not because they were profligate in their consumption of lattes and smartphones, but because the system changed the rules on them.

Just to tighten the noose, Congress in 2005 changed the bankruptcy laws to make it far more difficult for individuals to declare bankruptcy and get a fresh start.

Corporations are still able to declare bankruptcy, write off old debts, and resume their business operations. Often the same executives who drove the business into the ground are able to keep control. Indebted former students, on the other hand, are explicitly barred from using the bankruptcy laws. They may never get out from under their debts, which potentially follow them to their graves—a minor exception being partial forgiveness for public service.

In each of these cases—country debt, underwater homeowner debt, student debt—the crushing debt load functions like a lead weight on economic possibility. Yet the harsh morality of the creditor class overrules common sense. I wrote this book in order to connect the dots between seemingly different kinds of debts and to make the case for more sensible economics.

One remarkable and long-forgotten example of debt forgiveness is cited in chapter 4 of this book. The most fiscally profligate nation of all time was Nazi Germany. In addition to his other misdeeds, Hitler ran up debts equal to about 675 percent of GDP. Greece is being kept in debtors' prison for a debt level of less than 200 percent of its GDP. Whatever Greece's sins, it's fair to say that Hitler's were worse.

So what did the victorious Allies do after World War II? Did they strangle the postwar German economy either as retribution or in order to try to collect debts that could not be paid? That was the catastrophic mistake the Allies made after World War I in the punitive reparations terms of the Treaty of Versailles, which in turn seeded the German economic crisis of the 1920s, Nazism, and a second world war.

Instead, the Allies actually learned from history—perhaps helped along by the threat of Stalin's presence on West Germany's borders—and wrote off nearly all of Germany's Nazi-era debt. By the early 1950s, Germany enjoyed a debt ratio of about 10 percent of GDP. America had a debt ratio of more than 100 percent; Britain, more than 200 percent. *The German postwar economic miracle was built on debt relief.* But Greece, which suffered one of the most brutal German occupations of any European nation, is being denied relief, primarily by Germany.

This is the real debt problem—the merciless and economically stupid failure to write off old debt. It is the opposite of the story that is relentlessly promoted by conservative groups, who tell a story of debts that must always be paid and of public debt burdening future generations. The reality is the opposite. It is growth that tames debt and makes it less burdensome; sometimes it takes debt relief to restore growth.

Here in the United States, the Peter G. Peterson Foundation and a variety of front groups that it has created have spent more than one billion dollars to propagate the story of public debt destroying America's economic future. In this view, only austerity—budget cuts intended to pay down debt—can spare America from this fate.

This view violates the most basic logic of economics. If an economy is in a deep recession, balancing the budget is the worst policy that can be pursued, because fiscal contraction during a downturn reduces the rate of growth. The government's books may eventually balance, but at a needlessly depressed level of economic output. This is what has occurred in Greece, where forced austerity has caused the economy to shrink by more than 25 percent and the budget is still not in balance.

A deep recession is a time of depressed private sector activity. Notwithstanding high preexisting public debt, a recession is the right time for government to borrow, invest money publicly, create jobs, and restore growth. As GDP increases, the debt ratio comes down. This is precisely what occurred during the long economic boom in the twenty-five years after World War II. The huge wartime borrowing had pushed the debt ratio to more than 120 percent—far higher than today's. But that debt ratio gradually came down, to less than 30 percent by the

1970s, not because we tightened our belts and paid off old debt, but because of an expanding economy.

Peterson and the deficit hawks have continued to warn that deficits and debts are courting sky-high inflation, on the theory that government borrowing crowds out business borrowing and pushes up rates. But in a subpar economy, demand for credit is depressed and the inflation never arrives. That the austerity mongers have been proven wrong again and again has not diminished their puritanical crusade.

President Obama needlessly succumbed to the allure of the deficit hawks in 2010. He defined America's prime economic problem not as prolonged stagnation but as excessive public debt. He appointed a bipartisan commission inspired by the Peterson Foundation, chaired by Erskine Bowles and Alan Simpson, to come up with a belt-tightening program. Mercifully, the commission could not agree on a plan that met its required supermajority. But Obama's embrace of austerity rather than recovery cost Democrats the 2010 mid-term election. Republicans went on to enforce deep budget cuts through other means such as the budget "sequester."

Only when the Federal Reserve embraced heroic monetary policies of bond purchases on a scale unknown since World War II—more debt!— did the economy begin a real recovery. The debt-to-GDP ratio began coming down faster than projected—not mainly because of the budget cuts but because growth was resuming. Obama finally abandoned austerity economics in his 2015 State of the Union Address. By then, the political damage was done. Republicans controlled both houses of Congress and his proposals for increased public investment were dead on arrival.

Europe, meanwhile, continued on a much more austere course— demanding budget cuts, resisting debt relief. Only in late 2014 did the European Central Bank, after years of capitulating to resistance from Chancellor Angela Merkel, begin a program, modeled on the Federal Reserve's, of large-scale bond purchases as a form of long-overdue stimulus. But the bond purchase program initiated by Bank President Mario Draghi is probably too little and too late. It was initiated only after Europe was in a deflationary spiral, and it will not be sufficient as long as Europe continues to impose fiscal headwinds.

Needless to say, these austerity policies are politicians playing with fire. The combustible mix of high unemployment, fear of terrorism, and backlash against immigrants in general is energizing far-right nationalist parties on a continent that has had more than its share of them. In Greece, the new leftist government offers policy proposals far more sensible than those of European elites. Greece has a small neo-Nazi party, but its own firsthand experience with actual occupying Nazis during World War II inoculates the country from embracing Nazism.

In the United States, we have our own version of this dynamic. A prolonged period of stagnation, with too little help from the government and an uneven recovery that benefits mainly the top one percent, has led to widespread pocketbook frustration. That frustration, in turn, has inspired the Tea Party movement and pushed the Republican Party to the far right. Republican obstruction and antigovernment sentiment in turn blocks the recovery policies that the economy needs.

The remedy for debtors' prison is both intellectual and political. We need to appreciate that austerity is no cure for depression. We need a Chapter 11 for countries, to write down the burden of old debt. In the same spirit, we need debt relief for students and for underwater homeowners. And on both sides of the Atlantic we need large-scale programs of public investment—yes, some of it financed by debt—in order to restore growth, create jobs, and thereby reduce the debt ratio as time goes on. The choice is whether to reduce the burden of past debt by austerity, or by expansion. The preferred course ought to be obvious.

When the first edition of *Debtors' Prison* was published two years ago, I hoped that the weight of evidence, the power of argument, and the failure of conventional policies would lead to a course correction. There has been partial change in the United States, but hardly any in Europe. So the potential of our economies remains behind bars at terrible human cost, and the political stakes only grow. Tragically, far too many people are still wedded to a pre-1706 ideology that conceives of debt as a moral question rather than one of pragmatic economics. What is good enough for corporations, which use Chapter 11 to get a fresh start, should be good enough for the rest of us.

—ROBERT KUTTNER, June 2015

DEBTORS' PRISON

Introduction

ON OCTOBER 29, 1692, DANIEL DEFOE, merchant, pamphleteer, and future best-selling author of *Robinson Crusoe,* was committed to King's Bench Prison in London because he owed more than 17,000 pounds and could not pay his debts. Before Defoe was declared bankrupt, he had pursued such far-flung ventures as underwriting marine insurance, importing wine from Portugal, buying a diving bell used to search for buried treasure, and investing in some seventy civet cats, whose musk secretions were prized for the manufacture of perfume.

In that era, there was no Chapter 11, no system for settling debts and getting a fresh start. Bankruptcy, formally defined in an English statute of 1542, was nothing more than legally recognized insolvency, with harsh consequences. For hundreds of years, bankrupts like Defoe ended up in debtors' prison, a medieval institution that would persist well into the nineteenth century. Often the entire family joined a destitute breadwinner in jail, where the warden attempted to collect fees for food and lodging. Inmates with means could obtain better quarters. Children and wives were sent out to work or to beg. At London's notorious Marshalsea Prison, on the south bank of the Thames, a parliamentary committee reported in 1729 that some three hundred inmates had died in a three-month period, mainly of starvation.

Typically, creditors obtained a writ of seizure of the debtor's assets. (Historians record that Defoe's civet cats were rounded up by the sheriff's men.) If the assets were insufficient to settle the debt, another writ would send the bankrupt to prison, from which he could win release only by coming to terms with his creditors. Defoe had no fewer than 140 creditors, but he managed to negotiate his freedom in February 1693, though he would continue to evade debt collectors for the next fifteen years. His misadventures later informed *Robinson Crusoe* (1719), whose fictional protagonist faces financial ruin and expresses remorse at pursuing "projects and undertakings beyond my reach" and ending up "the willful agent of all my own miseries."

The banking system of seventeenth-century England was rudimentary. Easy credit was broadly available to the merchant class, and it financed England's commercial expansion. As we may recall from Shakespeare's *Merchant of Venice* (set in Italy but depicting English commercial practice around 1600), traders typically got credit not from banks but from one another. If a merchant was ruined by foolish optimism or bad luck (as the eponymous merchant, Antonio, was when his ships were presumed lost), he would be unable to repay his guarantor (Bassanio), known as a surety, who was often ruined in turn. At the end of this chain was the moneylender (in this instance, Shylock), who might also face insolvency (or, in Shylock's case, retribution). In a general downturn, the system imploded, and large segments of the merchant class ended up in jail, further contracting the supply of credit and worsening the slump.

Thus did the primitive credit system reinforce the cycle of booms and busts. The chartering of the Bank of England in 1694 helped only marginally. The institution was more concerned with financing the military needs of the British Crown—and, later, with adjusting the bank rate to protect the gold standard—than with advancing commercial liquidity to prevent periodic depressions. As a guardian of sound money, it had a deflationary bias. Banking is far more sophisticated today and has the further backstop of central banks as lenders of last resort. But in the absence of vigorous government countermeasures both to prevent excessive speculation before the fact of a collapse and to halt the deflationary spiral afterward, the financial system is still, in modern economic parlance, "pro-cyclical." In a boom, financial engineering underwrites euphoria. In a downturn, credit contracts. Harsh treatment of debt and debtors only exacerbates the general deflation.

In late seventeenth-century England, the commercial class came to appreciate that jailing bankrupts was self-defeating. As the legal historian Bruce Mann observed, "It beggared debtors without significantly benefiting creditors." Once behind bars, a debtor stripped of his remaining assets had no means of resuming a productive economic life, much less of satisfying his debts. In this insight was the germ of Chapter 11 of the modern U.S. bankruptcy code, the provision that allows an insolvent corporation to write off old debts under the supervision of a judge and enjoy a fresh start as a going concern.

As early as 1616, a failed playwright and jailed bankrupt named Thomas Dekker wrote a reformist pamphlet contrasting the "infortunate Marchant, whose estate is swallowed by the mercilesse Seas" with the wily "politick bankrupt" who deliberately seeks to defraud his creditors. But the first critic to successfully alter the Crown's policy was Daniel Defoe.

Reflecting on his own bitter experience, Defoe became England's leading crusader for bankruptcy reform. In 1697, he published the book-length *Essay upon Projects,* in which he proposed a novel solution. Rather than throwing the debtor to the mercy of his creditors, a "Court of Inquiries" could make an assessment of the bankrupt's assets, allocate them to creditors at so many pence in the pound, and leave the debtor with enough money to carry on his business. This legal action, undertaken with the cooperation of the debtor, would result in the full "discharge" of any remaining obligation to creditors. Defoe's reasoning cut to the essence of the problem: "After a debtor was confined in prison both he and the creditor lost through his prolonged distress."

Fortuitously, London in the 1690s was dealing with the aftermath of both bubonic plague and commercial losses due to the recent wars with France. Debtors' prisons were overflowing not only with sundry speculators and deadbeats but with solid businessmen whose enterprises had been ruined by the era's economic dislocations. A terrible storm in November 1703 that devastated merchant shipping added to the economic misery. In 1705, with the support of Queen Anne's ministers, Parliament took up a bankruptcy reform act, introducing for the first time the concept of discharge.

Defoe's thrice-weekly newspaper, *A Review of the State of the English Nation,* reported on the progress of the bill and served as its most authoritative advocate. The government, looking to drum up support, purchased and distributed copies, increasing its paid circulation to fifteen hundred. The act was understood as an emergency measure to restore commerce; it was to remain in force for just three years.

The legislation drew two key distinctions. It differentiated between honest bankrupts who were victims of financial circumstances beyond their control and perpetrators of fraud, who were to be treated as criminals. The act, moreover, was aimed at providing relief for merchants. Ordinary bankrupts, fraudulent or just unlucky, stayed in prison.

The new law, enacted in 1706 after extensive debate, fell far short of what Defoe had urged. It required the consent of four-fifths of a bankrupt's creditors before a certificate of discharge could be issued. The law was written primarily to protect creditors, not debtors. Ironically, though his pamphleteering had inspired the reform, Defoe could not qualify, and he temporarily fled to Scotland. Nonetheless, an important conceptual breakthrough had occurred.

———

Revisiting the bankruptcy reform of 1706 from the vantage point of the current economic crisis, one is struck by three recurring themes. First, the history of debt relief is one of double standards, which fill the chapters that follow. Even though debt can destroy the productive potential of ordinary people as well as elites, it is typically the merchant class that gets relief, just as in Defoe's day. Corporate executives can use bankruptcy to write off past debts and then continue operations. Homeowners and small nations cannot. Governments cover the losses of large banks whose indebtedness rendered them insolvent. Smaller banks just go bust.

Second, moral claims keep getting conflated with practical economic questions. Repayment of debt is assumed to be a moral obligation, though there are plainly circumstances when debt relief is an economic imperative. Yet austerity and "shared sacrifice," even when economically irrational, are commended almost as if suffering were a necessary form of redemption for past sins.

Third, our debates focus obsessively on the wrong debts. Today, private debts are strangling the recovery—young people weighted down with college loans, homeowners whose mortgages are worth more than the value of the house, consumers who turn to credit cards when wages lag behind the cost of living or medical bills overwhelm savings. Yet the national conversation is all about reducing public debts.

Listening to our national arguments about debt, a reader might reasonably assume that a book titled *Debtors' Prison* would be all about how Social Security and the national debt ratio are destroying the economy that we will leave to our children. But a closer look at these issues suggests that rising public deficits did not cause the financial collapse; the collapse caused the higher deficits. The prospects of our children depend on whether our economy can produce better job opportunities and less of a private debt burden in the immediate future, not on Social Security's projected finances decades from now. The public debt, in truth, finances outlays that help revive a wounded private economy. There is a case that it should be even larger.

As Defoe's contemporaries recognized, there are times when debts cannot be paid no matter how much creditors squeeze. A market economy thus finds it expedient to relieve indebted merchants so that they can have a fresh start, leaving aside whether recklessness was implicated in the insolvency. This is deemed economically efficient. Rather than allowing creditors to liquidate productive assets, the settlement provides for partial payment and gives the enterprise a second chance. Legal historians have observed that, for capitalism to proceed, it was necessary to shift debt from a moral issue to a merely instrumental one.

But in the recurring double standards of debt relief, the use of Chapter 11 bankruptcy enables corporations to shed pension plans that are debts to their workers and retirees. Bankers get bailed out in their role as debtors, while protected in their capacity as creditors. In a corporate bankruptcy, bankers usually get in line to be repaid ahead of pensioners. Recent changes in the U.S. bankruptcy code have stacked the deck against insolvent families, even though the leading cause of consumer bankruptcy is not spending sprees but medical debt. In a corporate restructuring under Chapter 11, new loans go not to service old debts, but for expansion. In the treatment of small, heavily indebted nations, new credits are targeted to allow payments to old bondholders, leaving the nation further in debt and less able to rebuild its economy.

Victorious nations are periodically able to write off massive debts. America's first Treasury secretary, Alexander Hamilton, lionized in the textbooks for "funding the national debt," actually paid off Continental Congress war bonds at one cent on the dollar. More vulnerable nations are often held to onerous terms, as is the case with Greece today. The same bankers and corporations that benefit from trillions of dollars in public aid, and the easy debt relief of the bankruptcy code, lobby against relief for homeowners or small countries, even though the mortgage crisis and the sovereign debt panic are serious drags on the recovery.

These double standards are more about political power than economic efficiency. Debtors' prisons have mostly been abolished, but the mentality lives on. Indeed, despite formal abolition of imprisonment for debt in the nineteenth century, under recent laws judges throw tens of thousands of Americans in jail for failure to pay debts on motor vehicle fines and child support.

Take a good look at what passes for public debate today, and you will see a great inversion. While public debt dominates political discourse, it was private debt that caused the crash—and prolongs its aftermath. Banks borrowed heavily in short-term credit markets to finance speculation that created a housing bubble. Families whose incomes did not keep pace with the cost of living borrowed against the inflated value of their homes. Because of bad education policy, young people have incurred a trillion dollars of student loans and begin their economic lives as debtors. In this inversion of sensible policy, the commercial sector has offloaded its debts onto the government and families, while the government has converted public responsibilites into private burdens that destroy the economy's potential and the dreams of citizens. Rightwing ideologues then use the public debt load as a rationale for further cuts in government. But in a deep slump, cutting public deficits that are sustaining purchasing power will only deepen the economic depression.

The late financial bubble was, in the useful phrase of the political economist Colin Crouch, *privatized Keynesianism*—unsustainable borrowing in the private sector. Debt pumped up the economy—but it was speculative rather than productive debt. That sort of private debt is procyclical. It is excessive in booms and then evaporates just when it is needed, in busts. By contrast, genuine Keynesianism—public spending financed by deficits—can be used as the economy requires. Today, in the aftermath of collapse, we need more public borrowing to jump-start a depressed private economy. Once we get a real recovery, higher growth will pay down the debt ratio as it did after World War II.

The devastation of Hurricane Sandy suggests that we should be spending hundreds of billions of dollars on seawalls and surge barriers, as well as improvements to subways, power stations, and water and sewer systems. In addition, we need public outlays to mitigate further global climate change. If the destruction of Sandy had been caused by a war, we'd have no hesitation. Indeed, in the aftermath of the attacks of 9/11, we increased military spending by more than three trillion dollars over a decade. A massive outlay to protect our coastal areas from the effects of climate change could do double duty as economic stimulus.

But even after the re-election of a Democratic president, public debate has emphasized less public investment, not more. The discourse has obsessively focused on deficit reduction rather than economic recovery. The dominant narrative is topsy-turvy. A Washington echo chamber denounces public debts that are in fact entirely manageable, while the real economic damage comes from everything from mortgage debts to student debts to corporate defaults on pension debts.

Today, future economic activity is held hostage to past debts that cannot be repaid, no matter how harsh the terms. There is much truth to the old saw that you can't get blood from a stone. That's why debtors' prison was such a ruinous idea and why my title is more than just a metaphor. To add insult to injury, it is widely held that in a deep slump the main goal of fiscal policy should be austerity. This perverse combination—the overhang of debt, the unevenness of relief, and the enforcement of belt-tightening—keeps our economy in a prison, where it cannot realize its potential. Despite differences of institution and history, the self-defeating essentials are the same in Europe and America. The European Union, now back in recession, provides a laboratory case of why austerity is the wrong cure for the aftermath of a financial collapse.

If the dominant counsel prevails, nations on both sides of the Atlantic will suffer a protracted and needless period of economic stagnation. There is no good theory of economics that explains how universal belt-tightening expands a deflated economy in the wake of a financial bust. As austerity causes an economy to contract, slower growth increases the weight of past debt. Instead of getting closer to fiscal balance, the economy enters a downward spiral of prolonged deflation. The alleged benefit of fiscal discipline to business confidence fails to materialize, because businesses hesitate to invest in a depressed economy even with interest rates at historic lows. With enough austerity, we may eventually reach the dismal grail of budget balance, but at a reduced level of economic output. The privations will be distributed in the usual fashion, falling disproportionately on the needy, the young, and the jobless. The risks of social upheaval will increase.

Ours turns out to be a venerable story with a recurring set of arguments. Such contemporary questions as relief for underwater mortgage holders in the United States and debt restructuring for Greece evoke the three centuries of struggle over bankruptcy terms in Anglo-American law and, long before that, the politics of whether Hebrew kings would proclaim debt forgiveness in Jubilee years. The "money issue" that dominated the politics of nineteenth-century America was about whether credit would be cheap or dear, reliable or capricious, for ordinary farmers, artisans, and small merchants. It was a conflict between haves and have-nots but also a battle between past claims and future possibility.

Before there were debtors' prisons, there was indentured servitude. In traditional societies, personal bondage was often the consequence of debt. Sometimes the involuntary nature of debt peonage was flagrantly explicit. If a free farmer or artisan caught in a general downturn could not satisfy creditors, he landed in servitude or prison. Other times these debts were ostensibly incurred "freely," as when a father financed a dowry by binding over a son or nephew to serve a creditor in lieu of cash payment; in some cultures, this debt was considered satisfied when the creditor magnanimously spent a few nights with the bride. However, behind the illusion of choice were the constraints of the economic situation. For a poor man with a marriageable daughter, the effective choice was to leave her without a husband and heirs or to consign another family member to bondage. These agreements were what legal scholars would later call contracts of desperation.

The economic anthropologist David Graeber exaggerates only slightly when he writes: "For thousands of years, the struggle between rich and poor has largely taken the form of conflicts between creditors and debtors—of arguments about the rights and wrongs of interest payments, debt peonage, amnesty, repossession, restitution, the sequestering of sheep, the seizing of vineyards, and the selling of debtors' children into slavery."

———

Debtors' Prison addresses the current crisis and the history of debt and debt relief. The book unpacks the different kinds of debt—national debt, corporate debt, financial speculator debt, consumer debt—that tend to be conflated in the conservative story of general ruinous borrowing.

Part 1, focusing on the United States, tells the story of how austerity has become the conventional wisdom. It explains how the political dominance of finance is undermining both sensible recovery policies and reforms of the financial system needed to prevent future cycles of bubble, collapse, and induced depression.

Part 2 addresses the European variation, beginning with the contrast between the ruinous aftermath of World War I, an era of creditor rule, and the enlightened relief and recovery policies that followed World War II. The current austerity regime being inflicted on the European Union's heavily indebted member nations ignores those lessons and deepens the Continent's distress.

Part 3 revisits the politics of credit, debt, property, and the cycles of boom and bust throughout modern history. This account finds that creditor interests tend to dominate, but with instructive exceptions.

Indeed, these exceptions to the pattern are the most interesting part of the story—notably those of the middle third of the twentieth century in America and Europe. The Great Depression, World War II, and the postwar anticommunist alliance produced striking political and ideological shifts. Coalitions came to power in the West determined to harness capitalism in a broad public interest. These in turn undergirded a managed form of capitalism that allowed the productive potential of the economy to surmount narrow claims of creditor supremacy. That era was also a period when finance was well regulated so that the rest of the economy could thrive. There is nothing about the evolution of markets or the speed of electronic communication that prevents us from applying those lessons in the current crisis, though globalization makes the politics more difficult.

A disclaimer: This book should not be read as an exercise in conspiracy theory. In a capitalist economy with extremes of inequality, it is only natural that owners or manipulators of vast pools of capital should enjoy outsize political power. But one can be heartened by history's intermittent exceptions. They suggest that the hegemony of finance is not an iron law, only a predisposition. In a democracy, an activated citizenry can contest that dominance and channel finance to a role more conducive to broad prosperity and less prone to periodic disaster.

Today, a deflationary legacy of financial excess is depressing not just the economy but also the political imagination. Most commentators accept the story that the road to recovery must be paved with sacrifice and that in a computer-driven global economy speculative finance cannot be contained. Center-left parties are too intimidated to propose bold recovery programs. The immodest hope of this book is to alter how we think about the relationship of debt to economic recovery and to rekindle a politics of alternatives.

PART ONE

Chapter 1

Agony Economics

IN THIS, THE FIFTH YEAR of a prolonged downturn triggered by a financial crash, the prevailing view is that we all must pay for yesterday's excess. This case is made in both economic and moral terms. Nations and households ran up unsustainable debts; these obligations must be honored—to satisfy creditors, restore market confidence, deter future recklessness, and compel people and nations to live within their means.

A phrase often heard is *moral hazard*, a concept borrowed by economists from the insurance industry. In its original usage, the term referred to the risk that insuring against an adverse event would invite the event. For example, someone who insured a house for more than its worth would have an incentive to burn it down. Nowadays, economists use the term to mean any unintended reward for bad behavior. Presumably, if we give debt relief to struggling homeowners or beleaguered nations, we invite more profligacy in the future. Hence, belts need to be tightened not just to improve fiscal balance but as punishment for past misdeeds and inducement for better self-discipline in the future.

There are several problems with the application of the moral hazard doctrine to the present crisis. It's certainly true that under normal circumstances debts need to be honored, with bankruptcy reserved for special cases. Public policy should neither encourage governments, households, enterprises, or banks to borrow beyond prudent limits nor make it too easy for them to walk away from debts. But after a collapse, a debt overhang becomes a *macroeconomic* problem, not a personal or moral one. In a deflated economy, debt burdens undermine both debtors' capacity to pay and their ability to pursue productive economic activity. Intensified belt-tightening deepens depression by further undercutting purchasing power generally. Despite facile analogies between governments and households, government is different from other actors. In a depression, even with high levels of public debt, additional government borrowing and spending may be the only way to jump-start the economy's productive capacity at a time when the private sector is too traumatized to invest and spend.

The idea that anxiety about future deficits harms investor or consumer confidence is contradicted by both economic theory and evidence. At this writing, the U.S. government is able to borrow from private money markets for ten years at interest rates well under 2 percent and for thirty years at less than 3 percent. If markets were concerned that higher deficits five or even twenty-five years from now would cause rising inflation or a weaker dollar, they would not dream of lending the government money for thirty years at 3 percent interest. Consumers are reluctant to spend and businesses hesitant to invest because of reduced purchasing power in a weak economy. Abstract worries about the federal deficit are simply not part of this calculus.

"Living within one's means" is an appealing but oversimplified metaphor. Before the crisis, some families and nations did borrow to finance consumption—a good definition of living beyond one's means. But this borrowing was not the prime cause of the crisis. Today, far larger numbers of entirely prudent people find themselves with diminished means as a result of broader circumstances beyond their control, and bad policies compound the problem.

After a general collapse, one's means are influenced by whether the economy is growing or shrinking. If I am out of work, with depleted income, almost any normal expenditure is beyond my means. If my lack of a job throws you out of work, soon you are living beyond your means, too, and the whole economy cascades downward. In an already depressed economy, demanding that we all live within our (depleted) means can further reduce everyone's means. If you put an entire nation under a rigid austerity regime, its capacity for economic growth is crippled. Even creditors will eventually suffer from the distress and social chaos that follow.

Take a closer look at moral hazard *ex ante* and *ex post* and you will find that blame is widely attributed to the wrong immoralists. Governments and families are being asked to accept austerity for the common good. Yet the prime movers of the crisis were bankers who incurred massive debts in order to pursue speculative activities. The weak reforms to date have not changed the incentives for excessively risky banker behaviors, which persist.

The best cure for moral hazard is the proverbial ounce of prevention. Moral hazard was rampant in the run-up to the crash because the financial industry was allowed to make wildly speculative bets and to pass along risks to the rest of the society. Yet in its aftermath, this financial crisis is being treated more as an object lesson in personal improvidence than as a case for drastic financial reform.

AUSTERITY AND ITS ALTERNATIVES

The last great financial collapse, by contrast, transformed America's economics. First, however, the Roosevelt administration needed to transform politics. FDR's reforms during the Great Depression constrained both the financial abuses that caused the crash of 1929 and the political power of Wall Street. Deficit-financed public spending under the New Deal restored growth rates but did not eliminate joblessness. The much larger spending of World War II—with deficits averaging 26 percent of gross domestic product for each of the four war years—finally brought the economy back to full employment, setting the stage for the postwar recovery.

By the war's end, the U.S. government's public debt exceeded 120 percent of GDP, almost twice today's ratio. America worked off that debt not by tightening its belt but by liberating the economy's potential. In 1945, there was no panel like President Obama's Bowles-Simpson commission targeting the debt ratio a decade into the future and commending ten years of budget cuts. Rather, the greater worry was that absent the stimulus of war and with twelve million newly jobless GIs returning home, the civilian economy would revert to depression. So America doubled down on its public investments with programs like the GI Bill and the Marshall Plan. For three decades, the economy grew faster than the debt, and the debt dwindled to less than 30 percent of GDP. Finance was well regulated so that there was no speculation in the public debt. The Department of the Treasury pegged the rate that the government would pay for its bonds at an affordable 2.5 percent. The Federal Reserve Board provided liquidity as necessary.

The Franklin Roosevelt era ushered in an exceptional period in the dismal history of debt politics. Not only were banks well regulated, but the government used innovative public institutions such as the Reconstruction Finance Corporation* to recapitalize banks and industrial enterprises and the Home Owners' Loan Corporation to refinance home mortgages. Chastened by the catastrophe of the reparations extracted from Germany after World War I, the victorious Allies in 1948 wrote off nearly all of the Nazi debt so that the German economy could recover and then sweetened the pot with Marshall Plan aid. Globally, the Bretton Woods accord created a new international monetary system that limited the power of private financiers, offered new public forms of credit, and biased the financial system toward economic expansion. This story is told in detail in the chapters that follow.

In 1936, John Maynard Keynes provocatively called for "the euthanasia of the rentier." He meant that once an economy was stabilized into a high-growth regime of managed capitalism, combining low real interest rates with strictures against speculation, and using macroeconomic management of the business cycle to maintain full employment, capital markets would efficiently and even passively channel financial investment into productive enterprise. In such a world, there would still be innovative entrepreneurs, but the parasitic role of a purely financial class reaping immense profits from the manipulation of paper would dwindle to insignificance. Legitimate passive investors—pension funds, life insurance companies, small savers, and the proverbial trust accounts of widows and orphans—would reap decent returns, but there would be neither windfalls for the financial middlemen nor catastrophic risks imposed by them on the rest of the economy. Stripped of the hyperbole, this picture describes the orderly but dynamic economy of the 1940s, 1950s, and 1960s, a time when finance was harnessed to the public interest, true innovators were rewarded, most investors earned merely normal returns, and windfall speculative profits were not available— because the rules of the game gave priority to investment in the real productive economy.

In today's economy, which is dominated by high finance, small debtors and small creditors are on the same side of a larger class divide. The economic prospects of working families are sandbagged by the

* The RFC was launched by President Herbert Hoover in 1932, but dramatically expanded under Roosevelt.

mortgage debt overhang. Meanwhile, retirees can't get decent returns on their investments because central banks have cut interest rates to historic lows to prevent the crisis from deepening. Yet the paydays of hedge fund managers and of executives of large banks that only yesterday were given debt relief by the government are bigger than ever. And corporate executives and their private equity affiliates can shed debts using the bankruptcy code and then sail merrily on.

Exaggerated worries about public debt are a staple of conservative rhetoric in good times and bad. Many misguided critics preached austerity even during the Great Depression. As banks, factories, and farms were failing in a cumulative economic collapse, Andrew Mellon, one of America's richest men and Treasury secretary from 1921 to 1932, famously advised President Hoover to "liquidate labor, liquidate stocks, liquidate farmers, liquidate real estate . . . it will purge the rottenness out of the system. High costs of living and high living will come down. People will work harder, live a more moral life." The sentiments, which today sound ludicrous against the history of the Depression, are not so different from those being solemnly expressed by the U.S. austerity lobby or the German Bundesbank.

THE GREAT CONFLATION

Austerity economics conflates several kinds of debt, each with its own causes, consequences, and remedies. The reality is that public debt, financial industry debt, consumer debt, and debt owed to foreign creditors are entirely different creatures.

The prime nemesis of the conventional account is *government debt*. Public borrowing is said to crowd out productive private investment, raise interest rates, and risk inflation. At some point, the nation goes broke paying interest on past debt, the world stops trusting the dollar, and we end up like Greece or Weimar Germany. Deficit hawks further conflate current increases in the deficit caused by the recession itself with projected deficits in Social Security and Medicare. Supposedly, cutting Social Security benefits over the next decade or two will restore financial confidence now. Since businesses don't base investment decisions on such projections, those claims defy credulity.

Until the collapse of 2008, most government debts were manageable.

Spain and Ireland, two of the alleged sinner nations, actually had low ratios of debt to gross domestic product. Ireland ran up its public debt bailing out the reckless bets of private banks. Spain suffered the consequences of a housing bubble, later exacerbated by a run on its government bonds. The United States had a budget surplus and a sharply declining debt-to-GDP ratio as recently as 2001. In that year, thanks to low unemployment and increasing payroll tax revenues, Social Security's reserves were projected to increase faster than the claims of retirees. (More on Social Security in chapter 3.)

The U.S. debt ratio rose between 2001 and 2008 because of two wars and gratuitous tax cuts for the wealthy, not because of an excess of social generosity. The deficit then spiked mainly because of a dramatic falloff in government revenues as a result of the recession itself. The sharp increase in government debt was the effect of the collapse, not the cause.

The United States and other nations had far higher ratios of public debt to GDP at different points in their histories, and those debts did not prevent prosperity—as long as other sensible policies were followed. Britain's debt was well over 200 percent of GDP after the Napoleonic Wars, on the eve of the Industrial Revolution. It rose to more than 260 percent at the end of World War II, a period that ushered in the British economy's best three decades of performance since before World War I.

Along with government borrowing, *consumer* debt is the other villain of the orthodox account. Supposedly, people went on a borrowing binge to finance purchases they couldn't afford, and now the piper must be paid. This contention is a half-truth that leaves out two key details.

One is the worsening economic situation of ordinary families. In the first three decades after World War II, wages rose in lockstep with productivity. As the economy, on average, became more prosperous, that prosperity was broadly shared. American consumers took out mortgages to buy homes (with very low default rates) but engaged in little other borrowing. However earnings stagnated in the 1970s, and that trend worsened after 2001. Nearly all the productivity gains of the economy went to the top 1 percent.

Wages began to lag because of changes in America's social contract. Unions were weakened. Good unemployment insurance and other government support of workers' bargaining power eroded. High unemployment created pressure to cut wages. Corporations that had once been benignly paternalistic became less loyal to their employees. Deregulation undermined stable work arrangements. Globalization on corporate terms made it easier for employers to look for cheaper labor abroad. (See chapter 2 for more on lagging wages.)

During this same period, housing values began to increase faster than the rate of inflation, as interest rates steadily fell after 1982. Many critics ascribe the housing bubble to the subprime scandal, but in fact subprime loans accounted for just the last few puffs. The rise in prices mostly reflected the fact that standard mortgages kept getting cheaper, thanks to a climate of declining interest rates. Low-interest mortgage loans meant that more people could become homeowners and that existing homeowners could afford more expensive houses. With 30-year mortgages at 8 percent, a $2,000 monthly payment finances about a $275,000 home. Cut mortgage rates to 4 percent and the same payment buys a $550,000 home. Low interest rates bid up housing prices. And the higher the paper value of a home, the more one can borrow against it. (It's possible to temper asset bubbles with regulatory measures, such as varying down-payments or cracking down on risky mortgage products. But the Fed has resisted using these powers.)

The combination of these two trends—declining real wages and inflated asset prices—led the American middle class to use debt as a substitute for income. People lacked adequate earnings but felt wealthier. A generation of Americans grew accustomed to borrowing against their homes to finance consumption, and banks were more than happy to be their enablers. In my generation, second mortgages were considered highly risky for homeowners. The financial industry rebranded them as home equity loans, and they became ubiquitous. Third mortgages, even riskier, were marketed as "home equity lines of credit."

State legislatures, meanwhile, paid for tax cuts by reducing funding for public universities. To make up the difference, they raised tuition. Federal policy increasingly substituted loans for grants. In 1980, federal Pell grants covered 77 percent of the cost of attending a public university. By 1012, this was down to 36 percent. Nominally public state universities are now only 20 percent funded by legislatures, and their tuition has trebled since 1989. By the end of 2011, the average student debt was $25,250. In mid-2012, total outstanding student loan debt passed a trillion dollars, leaving recent graduates weighed down with debt before their economic lives even began. This borrowing is anything but frivolous. Students without affluent parents have little alternative to these debts if they want college degrees. But as monthly payments crowd out other consumer spending, the macroeconomic effect is to add one more drag to the recovery

Had Congress faced the consequences head-on, it is hard to imagine a deliberate policy decision to sandbag the life prospects of the next generation. But this is what legislators at both the federal and state levels, in effect, did by stealth. They cut taxes on well-off Americans, and increased student debts of the non-wealthy young to make up the difference. The real debt crisis is precisely the opposite of the one in the dominant narrative: efficient public investments were cut, imposing inefficient private debts on those who could least afford to carry them.

During this same period, beginning with the Reagan presidency, other government social protections were weakened and employer benefits such as retirement and health plans became less reliable. People were thrown back on what my colleague Tamara Draut calls "the plastic safety net" of credit card borrowing. In short, debt became the economic strategy of struggling workaday Americans. For the broad middle class, the ratio of debt to income increased from 67 percent in 1983 to 157 percent in 2007. Mortgage debt on owner-occupied homes increased from 29 percent to 47 percent of the value of the house. When housing values collapsed, debt ratios increased further.

From the 1940s through the 1970s—a period when real wages and homeownership rates steadily rose—the habit of the first postwar generation had been to pay down mortgages until homes were owned free and clear and then to use the savings to help finance retirement. By contrast, the custom of the financially strapped second postwar generation, who came of age in the 1970s, 1980s, and 1990s, was to keep refinancing their mortgages, often taking out cash with a second mortgage as well.

Increasingly, young adults facing income shortfalls turned to credit cards and other forms of short-term borrowing. By 2001, the average household headed by someone between twenty-five and thirty-four carried credit card debt of over $4,000—twice as much as in 1989—and was devoting a quarter of its income to interest payments. As Senator

Elizabeth Warren of Massachusetts has documented, most of the debt increase went to life's basic necessities, not luxuries. As health insurance coverage dwindled, the biggest single category was medical debt.

As a matter of macroeconomics, the practice of borrowing against assets sustained consumption in the face of flat or falling wages—until the music stopped. When housing prices began to tumble, the use of debt to finance consumption did not just halt; the process went into reverse as households had to pay down debt. Rising unemployment compounded the damage. Consumer purchasing power took a huge hit, and the economy has yet to recover from this.

According to the Federal Reserve, household net worth declined by 39 percent from 2007 to 2010. The ratio of debt to household income has declined from a peak of 134 percent in 2007 to about 114 percent in 2012, and it is still falling. Borrowing to sustain consumption is no longer viable.

After the fact, it is too facile to cluck that people who suffered declining earnings should have just consumed less. As a long-term proposition, stagnant wages and rising debts were a dubious way to run an economy, but in a short-run depression, paying down net debt only adds to the deflationary drag. The remedy, however, is not to redouble general austerity but to restore household purchasing power and decent wages with a strong recovery.

The real villain of the story is *financial industry debt*. During the boom years, investment banks, hedge funds, commercial banks with "off-balance-sheet" liabilities, and lightly regulated hybrids such as the insurance giant American International Group (AIG) were typically operating with leverage ratios of 30 to 1 and in some cases of more than 50 to 1. "Leverage" is a polite word for borrowing. In plain English, they borrowed fifty dollars for every one dollar of their own capital. They incurred immense *debts*, substantially in very short-term money-market loans that had to be refinanced daily. In the case of AIG, which underwrote credit default swaps (a kind of insurance but with no reserves against loss), the leverage was literally infinite. When panic set in, the access to credit dried up in a matter of days.

With the collusion of credit rating agencies that blessed their opaque and risky securities with triple-A ratings, these financial engineers sold their toxic products to investors around the world. Sometimes the financial engineers even borrowed money to bet against the same securities they created—marketing them as sound investments while they shorted their own creations. When the boom turned out to be a bubble, the highly interconnected financial system crashed, with trillions of dollars in collateral damage to bystanders.

INNOVATION, INVESTMENT, AND SPECULATION

Apologists for the recent crash argue that all financial innovations are virtuous and that all investments are in a sense speculative. An entrepreneur, after all, is defined as someone who takes a risk. An investor gambles that an enterprise will flourish. Damp down speculation with financial regulation and you will snuff out innovation. As Edward Chancellor, the historian of speculation, archly observed, "The line separating speculation from investment is so thin that it has been said both that speculation is the name given to a failed investment and that investment is the name given to a successful speculation."

However, a closer look reveals that speculation is not the same as ordinary enterprise. Three telltale features differentiate speculation, especially the most toxic kind, from productive forms of investment. First, speculation is typically done with borrowed money. In finance, there is nothing new under the sun. The financial innovations of recent decades were all variations on techniques that were familiar in thirteenth-century Venice, the Dutch Republic, Elizabethan England, and early America—and all involved very high degrees of borrowing. The degree of leverage was typically concealed or disguised, and for good reason. If the pyramiding and true risks had been understood by investors, they would not likely have parted with their money.

Second, speculations are usually bets on short-term fluctuations in prices or temporary asset inflation (or, in the case of short-selling, temporary deflation). Often the speculation itself is designed to promote that inflation. This is known in the trade as "pump and dump."

Third, speculation is all about quick killings. The speculator is often a middleman positioned to exploit privileged knowledge or an outsider with a very short time horizon hoping to game market trends. As Keynes astutely noted, productive investment entails "forecasting the prospective yield of assets over their whole life," while speculation is merely "forecasting the psychology of the market." A popular expression on Wall Street during the last financial bubble was "IBGYBG," which stood for "I'll Be Gone, You'll Be Gone"—meaning "Let's do this deal before the rubes figure out the game, then quickly cash in and get out before it collapses."

Nearly all of the supposedly innovative abuses that crashed the financial system in 2008 had antecedents in earlier centuries: extreme leverage, collateralized debt obligations, speculation in derivatives, insider trading, off-balance-sheet special purpose vehicles, and shadow banks not backed by deposits or proper equity. The schemes just went by different names.

Government bond futures were traded almost as soon as the Venetian Republic issued debt securities, before 1300. These were the first derivatives, and like all derivatives, they provided an opportunity for concealed leverage and insider trading. On seventeenth-century financial exchanges in Amsterdam and elsewhere, options and futures in products as diverse as whale oil, sugar, silks, and herring were used both to hedge investments and to speculate in paper. Securitized loans appeared in the 1600s and regularly recurred. Off-balance-sheet vehicles would have been familiar to William Duer, the failed speculator in Bank of the United States shares, who financed his stock manipulations in the 1790s with personal notes of credit totaling some $30 million. In the 1920s, bank loans to foreign governments were regularly converted to bonds and sold off to unsuspecting clients, often with the sponsoring banks betting against them.

More than 170 years ago, American speculators like Jacob Little, the original Great Bear of Wall Street, and Daniel Drew, known as Ursa Major, were selling stock they didn't own, hoping to drive down the price so they could then buy it back at a profit—recognizable today as short-selling. They were called bears because they "sold the skin of the bear before they caught the bear."

Little and Drew were simply employing a technique whose first recorded use was on the Amsterdam stock exchange in 1609 by a Flemish speculator named Isaac Le Maire. The twenty-first century's shadow banks, unregulated hedge funds, and outfits like AIG had exact counterparts in nineteenth-century financial institutions known as agency houses, which made loans but took no deposits, thus evading reserve requirements. This practice was refined in the 1890s with the invention of trust companies, which did most of what banks did but without federal or state charters or reserve requirements. Call loans from brokers to investors who played the stock market on margin date to the 1830s. All of these schemes recurred with new creative concealment in the 1920s. The common elements were extreme leverage, insider trading, misrepresentation of risks to investors, and manipulation of prices.

Defenders of speculation contended that the fruits of the financial engineering of the 1980s and 1990s—which would lead to the collapse of 2008—were valuable innovations that increased the liquidity (a polite word for leverage) of financial markets and hence made the economy more efficient. The extensive technical literature on the market-enhancing benefits of liquidity was ignorant of economic history and attributed the latest forms of disguised risk to the marvels of the computer. But these techniques were not novel at all: each was an Internet-age variation of centuries-old scams. As former Fed chairman Paul Volcker—no radical—observed, the last useful financial innovation was the ATM.

It's true that all participants in a market economy take risks. But nonspeculative investments are of an entirely different character. Patient investors may hope for asset inflation in the sense of capital gains, but they typically anticipate merely a normal rate of return, not a windfall. If investors guess wrong and the investment loses money, they are not contributing to a wider financial disaster. The loss is simply their own. An ordinary manufacturer, wholesaler, or proprietor of a small business may borrow money to finance inventory or expansion, but not to play financial markets. All businesses face risks, say, of a bad year or an innovative competitor. But these are fundamentally different from the risks of highly leveraged financial speculation.

Even the occasional outlier entrepreneur, such as a Steve Jobs or a Bill Gates, may earn immense profits, but these derive from genuine productive innovation, not financial speculation. A true venture capitalist who invests his own money in the hope that an innovator will yield high returns is another creature altogether from the leveraged buyout artist looking for a fast gain and tax breaks by using borrowed money to flip control of a company to which he adds little or no value.

By the same token, ordinary commercial bankers never got filthy rich and never crashed the economy. A bank that pays its depositors 4 percent and charges its business borrowers 7 percent will hire loan officers who extend credit with great diligence and care, not traders operating on inside tips and formulas. A bank seeking a normal rate of return to meet the expectations of its shareholders and pay for its operating costs cannot afford more than an occasional loan loss. If the bank conducts its business prudently, it has a reasonable expectation that most of its commercial loans will be repaid. Commercial banks typically have leverage ratios of 8 or 10 to 1. Their own capital cushions their lending and tempers their recklessness. Their actions are straightforward and transparent to bank examiners. Even though the business of taking deposits and making commercial loans is leveraged and incurs risks, it is not speculative. If anything, it is rather humdrum. The trouble began when ordinary bankers started envying hedge funds.

Homeowners, likewise, may hope that the value of their houses increases faster than the general rate of inflation. If it does, that is frosting on the cake. But the cake is what economists call the use value of having an investment that accumulates equity and is also a place to live. Financial speculators—the inventors of the subprime daisy chain—spoiled this system of slow, steady, and broadly distributed property wealth accumulation for at least a generation of Americans.

The Glass-Steagall Act of 1933 was a work of political genius and financial radicalism because it separated the speculative part of the economy from the real part. The law constructed a wall between commercial banking and investment banking. Speculators were free to gamble to their hearts' content, as long as they put only their own money at risk. The rest of the financial economy was freed to perform its essential but less lucrative daily functions of channeling capital to productive investment. With a well-regulated banking sector doing its job, the real economy of the regulated era had no difficulty financing its expansion.

Since the inception of modern capitalism, the central challenge of financial policy in a market economy has been to keep capital costs low for the real economy of factories, farms, consumers, and entrepreneurs without allowing that same cheap money to promote asset bubbles and other forms of purely speculative windfall gain. More often than not, financial policy has failed that challenge. Either it has allowed or promoted cheap credit, but without adequate controls on excessive leverage and speculation, or it has kept credit too tight generally, constraining speculation but choking off the productive economy. Often it has oscillated between those two poles.

Many commentators contend that the great policy error of the decade before the collapse was to allow interest costs to drop to very low levels. That climate of cheap money supposedly bid up asset levels, engendered speculative uses of credit, and fairly invited the crash. That, however, is exactly the wrong lesson to draw. The real economy—as opposed to the financial one—needs cheap capital in order to grow. The lesson of the era of managed capitalism is that the economic sweet spot is the combination of *plentiful credit and tight regulation*, so that low interest rates finance mainly productive enterprise. The mistake of Federal Reserve chairman Alan Greenspan and chief economic advisers Robert Rubin and Lawrence Summers and others was not to loosen money; it was to loosen regulatory constraints on its speculative use. And this was no innocent technical mistake. It was the result of relentless industry pressure for deregulation coupled with the financial sector's success in installing allies in key government posts, regardless of whether the administration was nominally Republican or Democrat.

Today's fiscal alarms are less a legitimate economic concern than an expedient way to starve and stifle government, preserve a lucrative if toxic business model, and ensure that even minute amounts of inflation do not disturb the comfort of creditors.

The core claim is that budget discipline is the royal road to recovery. However, in a deflated economy, recovery is the *precondition* for fiscal balance. In the usual framing of the debate, not only are the cause and effect backward, but several distinct issues are deliberately blurred. They are:

- How to bring about a rapid and sustainable economic recovery
- How to relieve private debt burdens that are prolonging the downturn, such as mortgage debt and student debt
- How to achieve an acceptable level of public debt once the crisis is behind us
- How to set a level of public spending adequate to address social needs that have only been intensified by the recession's hardships and budget cuts
- How to finance those social needs
- How to best address projected imbalances in our two largest and most redistributive programs of social insurance, Social Security and Medicare

- How to restore adequate regulation so that the productive economy can have the low interest costs it needs to encourage growth without promoting the next round of reckless financial speculation

The austerity scenario blurs the short term with the long term, confuses the issue of social insurance reform with the question of the best recovery strategy, makes improbable claims about what is depressing business and consumer confidence, and inverts cause and effect. The level of public spending and the degree of budget balance are two entirely separate issues. A mistaken premise is that high levels of public spending produce high deficits. But a government can have declining domestic spending and rising deficits, as Ronald Reagan showed. Conversely, a country can opt for high spending and low deficits. The Nordic nations, for instance, have prudent fiscal policies yet devote almost half of their GDPs to social spending. They pay for that spending with taxes. The real issues are the best path to recovery from crisis, the desired levels of budget balance and social spending for the long term, and how that spending is paid for. In a deflated economy, an increase in the short-term deficit to finance investment is better medicine than austerity.

GENERATIONAL JUSTICE RECONSIDERED

At stake in these debates is our economic future. A huge part of the austerity crusade has been based on moral claims of generational justice. We are said to be selfishly passing along massive public debts to our children and grandchildren. As these debts come due and payable, interest rates and taxes will rise, and future generations will suffer reduced living standards because of our own profligacy and shortsightedness. This story has become a staple of popular imagery and political rhetoric. Even the relatively liberal *New Yorker* magazine, on the cover of its October 8, 2012, issue depicted an elderly rich man literally taking candy from a baby. As Judd Gregg, a former senator from New Hampshire, warned, "This issue [debt] represents the potential fiscal meltdown of this nation and it absolutely guarantees if it's not addressed that our children will have less of a quality of life than we've had; that they will have a government they can't afford, and that we will be demanding so much of them in the area of taxes that they will not have the money to send their kids to college or buy that home or just live a good quality life."

The economics of this story are just about backward. The well-being of our children and grandchildren in 2023 or 2033 is not a function of how much deficit reduction we target or enforce in this decade but of whether we get economic growth back on track. If we cut the deficit, reduce social spending, and tighten our belts as the deficit hawks recommend, we will condemn the economy to stagnant growth and flat or declining wages. That will indeed leave the next generation a lot poorer. The existing debt will loom larger relative to the size of the real economy, and there will be too few public funds to invest in the education, employment, job-training, and research outlays that our children and grandchildren need.

In the absence of these social supports that gave earlier generations the American promise of upward mobility, young adults will be thrown back on a private, familial welfare state. As Mitt Romney recommended during the 2012 campaign, more young people will borrow from their parents—a splendid strategy if you have affluent parents. Family financial help already gives the children of the affluent a big head start and leaves others either to do without or to incur debts that indeed lower living standards by burdening young families with interest and repayment obligations. As social resources are starved for funds, the private welfare state enables the affluent to pass along economic advantages to their children in everything from the schools they attend and the enrichment programs in which they partake to the gift of graduating from college debt-free, the subsidy of unpaid internships that give a boost up the career ladder, and help with down payments on starter homes. Class lines harden, and the children of the nonrich become increasingly disadvantaged. A starved public sector further reduces society's opportunity institutions.

As noted, the financing of higher education—the great equalizer—has been shifted dramatically from grants-in-aid and cheap public universities to high tuitions and burdensome student loans. The jobs available to the young today are far less likely than a generation ago to include good benefits such as health insurance and pensions. With two-tier wage systems, the incomes of the young are disproportionally lower than those of workers generally. Even though low interest rates seemingly make homeownership a bargain, the inflation in housing prices that occurred in previous decades puts housing out of reach for many young families. Recent graduates carrying large student loans have difficulty qualifying for mortgages. Even during the boom years, while homeownership rates were rising generally, they were declining for young adults. Between 1980 and 1990, the homeownership rate for people aged twenty-five to thirty-four fell from 52 percent to 45 percent. It rebounded slightly in the hot housing market of the 2000s, only to fall back after the crash. What is destroying the living standards and life prospects of young adults (at least those without rich parents) is not the current deficit or the projection of Social Security costs two or three decades into the future but the bad policies of the present and recent past and the failure to pursue recovery policies.

The effects of prolonged recession extend from young parents to their own children. The work of the Harvard pediatric researcher Jack Shonkoff and others demonstrates the cascading impact of unemployment, income loss, and the juggling of multiple jobs on child rearing and on children's well-being. Parents are less available to be with children and less effective when they are present, and older children are pressed into service to care for younger siblings. Parents are less likely to read to children, to be consistent and loving role models and disciplinarians, to work closely with schools, to be attentive to children's health and wellness issues, and to be emotionally at peace themselves. There are predictable and documented increases in child abuse and domestic violence.

This is the first postwar recession in which all levels of government have cut rather than increased the countercyclical outlays necessary to serve both social and economic purposes. The effect has been concentrated on low-income families. The bipartisan welfare reform program Temporary Assistance for Needy Families, approved by Congress and signed by President Clinton in 1996, was intended to push welfare recipients into work. But it was enacted when the economy was at close to full employment and assumed the availability of jobs. Today, with unemployment around 8 percent (and the real number double that when we count people who have dropped out of the workforce and part-timers who want but can't find full-time jobs), welfare no longer provides aid on the basis of need to all who qualify. Only about a quarter of people who are eligible for the program actually get benefits.

Young families are being denied access to the asset accumulation that their parents and grandparents enjoyed. Asset poverty, in turn, affects economic well-being throughout the life course. It means less of a savings cushion for temporary reverses, less money to help one's children get a good education, and less socked away for a decent retirement. This is the real generational injustice of the current crisis. None of it has anything to do with the national debt or the projected shortfall in Social Security. The budget cutting demanded by deficit hawks deprives government of the resources necessary to improve the lives of young adults and families right now.

Despite the scapegoating of Social Security and Medicare, the failure to apply the right remedies to the crisis also harms the older generation. The Federal Reserve is using very low interest rates to keep the economy from sliding further. But near-zero interest rates leave the elderly with almost no return on their savings. Meanwhile, the fiscal crisis has caused state and local governments to cut or underfund pensions for civil servants, while private industry has been trimming its labor costs for two decades by phasing out traditional pension plans in favor of plans in which all the risk is borne by workers. The typical worker near retirement age has 401(k) savings sufficient for only a few years of retirement. Though labor force participation rates have generally declined in a climate of high unemployment, increasing numbers of Americans in their seventies are taking typically low-wage jobs just to make ends meet.

The median income of elderly Americans in 2010 was just $25,704 for men and $15,072 for women. Almost two-thirds of Americans over age 65 rely on Social Security for at least 70 percent of their income. If Social Security and Medicare are cut, this hardship will only increase. Poverty rates among Americans over age 65, after declining steadily since the 1960s, are now once again higher than among the working-age population. Decent treatment of the elderly is also a form of generational justice. Despite a lot of rhetoric about "greedy geezers" harming the young, both generations are victims of bad economics. The real conflict is not old versus young but the top 1 percent versus the rest of society.

THE CHOICES WE FACE

The received wisdom today is deeply conservative in distinct and mutually reinforcing respects. The orthodoxy is conservative in the political sense in that creditor self-interests predominate; conservative as a perverse pre-Keynesian economics that ignores the lessons of the past eighty years and promotes self-perpetuating deflation; and conservative in that most of the proposed remedial measures would balance accounts by undermining the public programs necessary for a more egalitarian form of capitalism.

In principle, we could restore economic growth and fiscal equilibrium with a restructuring of past debts, higher levels of taxing and spending, constraints on the speculative license of creditors, and expansions of the public realm. This alternative is largely absent from the discourse. For financial elites, the splendid irony of the current austerity crusade is that the very people whose financial engineering caused the collapse— people who never much liked an effective public sector or programs like Social Security—are now using the ensuing recession to justify a severe assault on the countervailing public institutions needed to keep their own immense economic and political power in check.

So the world faces a momentous choice: austerity or recovery. Unfortunately, the debate is mostly the sound of one hand clapping. Creditor self-interest dominates public discourse to an extent not seen since the period after World War I, when the victorious nations imposed punitive reparations on Germany and inflicted tight monetary policies on their own citizens, condemning Europe to two decades of economic misery and seeding a second world war. (Today's German government, oblivious to the irony, is taking its revenge.) Center-right governments and their business allies are using the alleged fiscal crisis as a pretext for long-sought cuts in social spending that have nothing to do with the causes of the collapse or with its cure. Meanwhile, as the real economic crisis deepens, center-left parties seem unable to propose anything better than a little less of the retrenchment advocated by their political adversaries.

Cut through the welter of detail and the enduring questions are these: After a financial catastrophe, will unrealistic creditor claims be permitted to hobble the future, or will policies emphasize economic recovery? Will defaults on debt be disorderly, inflicting wider economic damage, or will debt relief be carefully restructured in service of efficient renewed growth? Will there be double standards, as in bailouts for banks and corporations but not for homeowners? And will rules be put in place both to ensure wide availability of credit at moderate interest costs and to prevent future abuses so that we get restored growth without repeating the cycle of speculation, bubble, and collapse?

If the austerity-mongers prevail, we will be condemned to debtors' prison. If we can understand and act on these challenges, we can surmount the current bout of deflation, restore broad prosperity, and prevent recurring crises.

Chapter 2

The Great Deflation

THE WEEK OF SEPTEMBER 15, 2008, America's largest financial institutions began collapsing. The venerable investment firm Lehman Brothers, with $639 billion in assets, went bankrupt. An insolvent Merrill Lynch was sold to Bank of America in a shotgun merger arranged by the Treasury and the Fed. AIG reported losses of tens of billions of dollars in its credit default swap operations and was taken over by the government. Citigroup was effectively broke and required hundreds of billions in aid from the Treasury and the Fed to survive. The nation's largest savings and loan association, Washington Mutual, was insolvent and was taken over by the Federal Deposit Insurance Corporation before being merged into Wells Fargo. It looked as if the two remaining large investment banks, JPMorgan Chase and Goldman Sachs, could be next to fall.

The free market had disgraced itself in practice and in theory. Only massive emergency financial support, frantically improvised by the Federal Reserve and then legislated by a reluctant Congress in the $700 billion Troubled Asset Relief Program of October 2008, prevented the entire banking system from seizing up. The Fed, using emergency powers granted during the Depression, immediately began buying securities and advancing trillions of dollars to banks and to firms like AIG that were not even part of the Federal Reserve System. Until the government acted, banks literally stopped lending to each other because nobody was sure who would survive to repay the loans. Ben Bernanke would testify that "out of maybe 13 of the most important financial institutions in the United States, 12 were at risk of failure within a period of a week or two." Five years later, the world continues to suffer from depressed output, slow growth, and a debt overhang.

The purely financial part of the crisis had several immediate causes, but they all reflected a speculative business model based on too little transparency, too much leverage, and pervasive regulatory corruption.

At the core was the creation of exotic financial securities financed by pyramids of short-term debt misrepresented on the balance sheets of banks. These opaque and toxic securities were diffused throughout the system, a process advertised as "spreading risk." Mainly, they spread risk the way an epidemic spreads typhoid.

The financial collapse, abetted by regulatory default, has been the subject of dozens of books, including one of mine. This is not our primary topic here, though it is necessary prologue to appreciate what followed. Our main subject in this chapter is the prolonged aftermath of the crash and its relation to deficits, debts, income distribution, and austerity politics. Financial abuses are at the center of the story.

WHY THIS RECESSION IS A DEPRESSION

The collapse of 2008 triggered a broader economic recession, but it was unlike other postwar slumps. The dynamics, though less devastating, were more like those of the Great Depression of the 1930s. What the two have in common is *debt deflation,* a condition in which past debts overwhelm the productive power of the economy. If debt obligations are fixed but wages are falling, then the real cost of debt increases relative to people's capacity to pay—and debt service costs crowd out other economic activity. When a crash in asset prices causes private debts to exceed the market value of their collateral, then people lose homes, banks suffer losses on mortgages as homes are unloaded at fire-sale prices, and the entire economy goes into a downward spiral. This collapse depresses purchasing power, creating a prolonged, self-reinforcing depression in economic activity. Depressions, as opposed to recessions, are nearly always the result of a speculative financial collapse.

The Great Depression was a massive debt deflation. The current crisis is a partially contained one, but with many of the same dynamics. The financial bust of 2008 traumatized banks, households, owners of commercial real estate, and other business firms. In the spiral that followed, companies laid off workers, consumers were hesitant to spend or borrow, businesses deferred investments, and banks were reluctant to lend. A variant of the same cascade starts to occur in milder recessions but is soon halted by government intervention—cuts in interest rates or increased spending—and by the market's own natural tendencies to rebound from a modest slump as costs fall. Other postwar recessions did not experience debt deflation because they were not supercharged by a collapse of heavily leveraged and interconnected assets. So public intervention to cure a debt deflation needs to be on a much larger scale.

During the Great Depression, prices of a broad range of assets, products, and services fell, including the price of labor, while the cost of debt service remained fixed. All this had the effect of increasing the real burden of the debt and deflating the purchasing power of consumers. That is the very definition of a debt deflation, first identified by Irving Fisher in a classic article from 1933. In a debt deflation, falling prices also lead people to put off purchases because products will likely be cheaper tomorrow. Businesses hesitate to buy raw materials because retail prices may be lower than wholesale ones. Economic activity simply stalls.

Consumers and businesses overwhelmed by debts face an invidious choice. They can tighten their belts and reduce other purchases in order to keep current on the debt payments. Or they can default on the debt, losing their collateral and causing a fire sale of assets into a down market, reducing prices still further. Either way, their actions constrain demand and worsen the economy's general deflation.

The crash of the dot-com bubble in 2000, by contrast, was not a debt deflation. It wiped out some $8 trillion in paper stock values, about the same scale of loss as the decline in housing prices after their peak in 2006. But the dot-com crash involved only the stock market, with little leverage. The collapse of 2008 brought down a whole secondary pyramid of securities propped up by borrowed money, which wiped out much of the equity of the banking system. While the economy recovered quickly from the dot-com bust, the secondary damage from the financial collapse creates a persistent and continuing drag. This is a less extreme variation on what occurred in the 1930s.

In the collapse of 2008, the most direct debt deflation was confined to housing, commercial real estate, and securities backed by mortgages. Thanks to the unprecedented intervention by the Federal Reserve, which bought trillions of dollars of securities, we narrowly avoided a general price deflation. But the wider damage, though not at Depression levels, was still massive. The largest single asset of most Americans is their homes. The total value of residential real estate in the United States was just over $24 trillion in 2006. The crash and the ensuing decline in housing prices wiped out about $9 trillion of that household wealth, while mortgage debt hardly fell at all. Counting the additional hit to pension savings, 401(k) plans, and other forms of household assets, the consumer sector at the pit of the slump was out about $13 trillion in net worth.

Since the peak in housing values in 2006, average home equity per homeowner has declined from $200,000 to $78,000 in inflation-adjusted dollars, the lowest level since 1968. The decline in equity reflected not just the unprecedented drop in housing values but the fact that strapped wage earners during the quarter century before the crash increasingly borrowed against their homes. Once prices crashed, this form of economic artificial respiration could not continue.

In the bubble economy of the early 2000s, savings rates turned negative. At the peak, the consumer sector as a whole was borrowing about 6 percent more than it was earning. Once the crash came, savings turned positive again, both because families grew more anxious and because they had far less to borrow against. Since 2008, households have been paying down debt. This shift, though desirable for the long run, has functioned as another drag on the recovery. Debt service as a percentage of consumer income is down from a peak of about 19 percent in 2007 to under 16 percent today. This is good news to the extent that consumers were overburdened with debts, but it is bad news because that borrowing was sustaining demand and disguising the weakness of wages. With earnings still deeply depressed, the economy has no good substitute for that consumer borrowing. Public borrowing invested in new economic activity could play that role, but the conventional wisdom says public deficits need to shrink.

Despite a feeble recovery and a stock market rebound, housing prices have continued to sag. At this writing, the gap between the value of underwater homes and the mortgages on them is estimated at $700 billion. As millions of homeowners suffer foreclosure, their homes are sold into a depressed market, creating a supply glut and reducing housing prices still further—classic debt deflation. Throughout 2011 and into early 2012, housing prices in seventeen of the nation's twenty largest housing markets continued to fall. By the fall of 2012, the decline was bottoming out and real estate prices were rising in most metro areas, but housing values were still down about 30 percent from their 2006 peak.

A PERSISTENT DOWNDRAFT

The housing drag reinforces a broader deflationary psychology. In formal economics, this is called a liquidity trap. The term simply means that consumers prefer to "stay liquid"—namely, to hold on to their money. They are too traumatized to spend at a rate sufficient to purchase all the goods and services that the economy can produce. Since the value of their assets has declined, they also have reduced capacity or desire to borrow. In a deep downturn where worse may be yet to come, this behavior can be rational for a prudent individual, but it is dysfunctional for the economy as a whole. Businesses, likewise, are hesitant to invest. And banks are reluctant to lend to any but the safest borrowers. In a liquidity trap, the economy gets stuck at a level of output well below its potential. This is another case of a free market not optimizing outcomes.

In such circumstances, a tight monetary policy by the Federal Reserve would only make matters worse, but very low interest rates don't solve the problem. Since 2009, the Fed has flooded the economy with cheap money, despite criticism that it is courting inflation. The Fed increased its balance sheet—the measure of its net borrowing and lending—from several hundred billion dollars before the collapse to almost $3 trillion at the peak of its interventions. In effect, it created that additional money. The Fed has advanced funds to banks at interest rates of effectively zero and has kept the government's borrowing costs low by buying federal bonds as necessary. It has even invested in depressed mortgage-backed securities held by banks in order to replenish their cash.

The Fed's loose monetary policy has produced the cheapest mortgages in two generations. But credit created by the Fed is only "money" to the extent that banks lend it. If consumers are anxious about losing their jobs or their homes and don't want to spend, and businesses don't borrow because they don't see enough customers, and banks are hesitant to lend, then cheap money doesn't cure deflation. Banks are now sitting on about $1.8 trillion in cash or government securities because they can't imagine where to profitably invest it. About 70 percent of bank profits come from securities creation and trading. In comparable conditions in the 1930s, the failure of low interest rates to end the Depression was likened to "pushing on a string." It was the wrong policy instrument, or at best not a sufficient one.

In a protracted deflation, there is a right instrument: fiscal policy. When nobody else is willing to spend and invest at sufficient levels, the government can step in. It can borrow the money that the private sector is reluctant to spend and invest, and it can use the proceeds to create public improvements and jobs, which in turn can restore purchasing power and confidence more broadly. The government can also tax idle wealth and invest the proceeds socially, so that its spending is not entirely dependent on borrowing. Most of the outlay, in the form of wages and government contracts with businesses, cycles right back into the private sector.

But today's consensus view holds that the last thing the government should do is borrow more money. So despite a fragile economic recovery, the deflationary trap continues. President Obama's Recovery Act, approved by Congress in February 2009, spent about $721 billion over three fiscal years. During the same period, state and local governments cut spending by more than $450 billion. So the net government stimulus was slightly less than 1 percent of GDP per year, better than nothing but not nearly enough to escape the trap. The benefits of that stimulus are now used up.

This is the only economic slump in nearly a century in which the government shed jobs rather than adding them to offset the private sector's employment shortfall. Since August 2008, all levels of government actually cut about 680,000 jobs. The vast majority of these were in state and local governments, which were reeling from lost revenues, were constitutionally prohibited from running deficits, and were often in the grip of far-right governors and legislators who welcomed the opportunity to slash government. The weakened spending of the public sector added to the downward drag.

"The Great Recession," a term popularized by *The New York Times,* is a misnomer. We should stop using it. Recessions are mild dips in the business cycle that are either self-correcting or soon cured by modest fiscal or monetary stimulus. Because of the continuing deflationary trap, it would be more accurate to call this decade's stagnant economy The Lesser Depression or The Great Deflation.

Ever since the National Bureau of Economic Research (a private organization despite the name) nominated itself back in the 1950s to be the official arbiter of when recessions start and end, the generally accepted definition of a recession has been two consecutive quarters of negative GDP performance. By that criterion, the recession officially began in December 2007 and ended in June 2009. But four years later, a deflationary depression continues. It's worth recalling that in the depressed 1930s, economic growth turned positive in late 1933. For the remainder of the decade, GDP grew in all but one year, often impressively so. The economy grew at a rate of 11 percent in 1934, 9 percent in 1935, and 13 percent in 1936—far faster than in the current decade. Yet the Great Depression persisted, with unemployment in excess of 12 percent and the economy clearly performing far below its potential, until World War II. Using the NBER definition, *it is possible to be out of a recession and still be in a deflationary depression.*

The current economy displays the weakest post-recession recovery on record. Even in mild postwar recessions, the annual growth rate in the years immediately following was typically 5 or 6 percent as the economy gained back the recession's losses and more. Though the recession following the 2008 collapse officially ended in mid-2009, when GDP performance turned positive, growth for 2010 was a modest 3 percent, and then an anemic 1.7 percent in 2011. The growth rate for 2012 was around 2.2 percent. This performance is not sufficient to blast out of the deflationary trap.

Both the nonpartisan Congressional Budget Office and the White House's Office of Management and Budget, wishfully seeing "green shoots," have been using overly optimistic projections of when robust growth will resume. The president's budget for the fiscal year 2011 projected a growth rate of 4.3 percent in 2011 and 4.3 percent in 2012. The actual numbers were barely half that. Assuming an unrealistically high growth rate, they then made sanguine projections about the deficit. The deficit for 2011, they forecasted, would fall to 8.3 percent of GDP. In the event, it was 10.1 percent. For 2012, they projected a further decline in the deficit to just 5.1 percent. The actual number was 7.0 percent. Why the sloppy optimism? Amazingly, when the CBO and OMB project growth two years into the future, they assume a "return to trend"— that the economy will just revert to normal—without any plausible set of assumptions to back up the projection.

These agencies keep getting forecasts wrong because they fail to acknowledge the depth of deflationary forces and assume a normal recovery from a normal business cycle recession. To budget hawks, the higher-than-projected deficits are reason to redouble our efforts to cut public spending. But at this stage of a very weak recovery, that course would only further retard growth, reduce tax receipts, and worsen deficits.

In the president's budget for fiscal year 2013, the White House corrected the figure projected for 2011—actual growth turned out to be just 1.7 percent—but persisted in the wishful projections of the near future: real GDP would increase by 3 percent in 2013, 3.6 percent in 2014, and 4.1 percent in 2015. But if Congress and the president pursue belt-tightening fiscal policies, GDP will do nothing of the sort.

THE REAL DEBT PROBLEM: DECLINING INCOMES AND SQUEEZED CONSUMERS

The housing bubble and the related creation of toxic securities were one large symptom of a deeper malady. For more than a quarter century *before* the crash, the real wages of most American workers had been flat or declining, as most of the economy's gains went to the very top. Between 1973 and 2007, on the eve of the crash, the earnings of the median family hardly budged. The top 1 percent took about 60 percent of all income gains. The productivity of the economy grew by 80.4 percent between 1973 and 2011, but the real hourly pay of the median worker rose by only 10.7 percent, and nearly all of that gain occurred in a short period of full employment during the late 1990s. Today's median household income is back to the level of 1995, according to the Census Bureau. People kept pace with inflation by working longer hours and by borrowing.

Beyond the problem of declining real wages, the typical working family of the twenty-first century was less likely to have employer-provided pensions or health insurance and more likely to be paying a larger share of health premiums and co-pays. Workers were less likely to have a standard salaried job and were more at risk of layoff. Economic risks that had been borne by large, stable employers or by the government— the loss of a job, health insurance, income in old age, or the death or disability of a breadwinner—were increasingly shifted onto families. Social buffers such as unemployment insurance or job-training funds were weakened.

This trend worsened after 2000, and worsened again after the 2008 financial collapse. In the decade since 2002, median wages have fallen about 10 percent. In 2008 and 2009, some fourteen million people lost their jobs. Unemployment peaked at 10.2 percent. The high unemployment exacerbated the trend of falling wages. Between 2009 and the end of 2011, worker productivity increased by 8 percent, but median wages fell by 2 percent. Even skilled workers at the ninetieth percentile of the income distribution had no gains in earnings.

In early 2012, there was guarded optimism about the recovery because the economy began producing jobs at the rate of slightly more than 200,000 a month. Despite the creation of more than 3.6 million jobs since the pit of the slump in 2010, the economy had still lost a net 5.2 million jobs and needed another 4.7 million just to accommodate population growth. It was by far the weakest recovery of the postwar era.

Job creation even at the rate of 200,000 a month is not sufficient to fill the gap. The unemployment rate has held steady around 8 percent only because large numbers of people exit the labor force. The labor force participation rate has shrunk to below 64 percent, down from a level of over 68 percent in the late 1990s. And it has not improved despite the supposed recovery. The percentage of adults working or seeking work has not been so low since the 1970s, a period when far fewer women were in the labor force. The share of workers with standard full-time jobs has also plummeted. We are in the fifth year of this crisis, and at the current rate of recovery, it will take another decade to return to the low unemployment and high labor force participation rates of the 1990s. Even the Great Depression only lasted for eleven years.

Today's pace of job creation is also too weak to restore the purchasing power of wages. The increases in both corporate profits and windfall gains to the very top, however, have been prodigious. Top hedge fund sponsors routinely take home over a billion dollars a year. Despite the weakness of their balance sheets, the profits of banks rebounded to their precrash levels by 2010. According to the economist Andrew Sum, during the first nine quarters of economic recovery from the recession of 2007 to 2009, "real corporate profits increased by $611 billion, accounting for 83 percent of the growth in real national income." Sum reports that this share of corporate profits in national income growth "was the largest by far in any of the six past recoveries and the largest in any national recession recovery since the official statistics start in 1929."

Widened income inequality is not just socially unattractive or morally repugnant. It has real macroeconomic effects. As wealth concentrates, the very rich can't possibly spend it all. Much of their income is saved or invested. The rest of us, meanwhile, have deficient purchasing power relative to the economy's capacity. As wages are constrained, the economy remains in a self-reinforcing slump. The idea that raising taxes on wealthy "job creators" would be bad for employment has it backward. Those revenues, spent socially, would create far more jobs.

LOW INFLATION, LOOSE MONEY, AND HIDDEN BUBBLES

Why was inflation low and declining for the past quarter century? The process began with the disinflation of the mid-1980s, after the Federal Reserve reversed its earlier policies of very high interest rates that had been used to tame the inflation of the 1970s. Then, increasingly, cost-of-living adjustments were squeezed out of the economy as unions were steadily weakened and production moved offshore. Wages lagged well behind productivity growth for the entire period. Workers had progressively less bargaining power, except during the brief period of full employment in the late 1990s. In addition, cheap imports from China and other low-wage producers meant that the price of a broad range of consumer goods actually declined. A decent suit or a high-powered computer cost less in 2012 than in 1992, and a car that cost the same price was a lot more car.

Falling prices and stagnant real wages in turn changed the thinking at the Federal Reserve. Until the mid-1990s, Alan Greenspan and most of his colleagues held that if you lowered interest rates to allow the unemployment rate to fall much below 6 percent, the economy would overheat and inflation would result—the supposed trade-off described by the Phillips curve. But in the late 1990s, Greenspan himself became a convert to the view that something structural had changed in the economy. Labor's power to bargain for wage increases had been broken. A cornucopia of cheap products was coming from abroad. Productivity was on the rise. Global savings were plentiful. Thanks to high rates of financial savings around the world, loans from China and other Asian nations, and financial "innovations" created on Wall Street, capital scarcity had ceased to be a problem. In this climate, the Federal Reserve could confidently take its foot off the monetary brake and let prosperity ensue. The combination of low capital costs and high growth was known in policy circles as the great moderation. Greenspan's successor, Ben Bernanke, embraced this entirely mistaken view in a paper given in 2004. In fact, purchasing power and economic growth were sustained by a steadily inflating bubble economy.

In the two decades prior to the crash, the Fed had another motive for shifting to low interest rates. Deregulation and speculative practices by banks regularly got the financial industry into severe trouble well before the big bust of 2008. Had the Fed enforced the letter of the law and required accurate valuation of their nonperforming loans, losses on loans to Third World countries in the early 1980s would have rendered most money center banks technically insolvent. The banks then incurred huge losses in the Mexican and East Asian crises of the 1990s and in the 1998 collapse of the mammoth hedge fund Long-Term Capital Management. Lowering interest rates nearly to zero gave the banks access to very cheap funds and helped them recapitalize their balance sheets. In effect, the Fed was using cheap money to compensate for earlier failures of regulatory policy—and seeding the next failure.[*]

As Greenspan himself famously pointed out in 1996, cheap money fed "irrational exuberance" in stock market speculation, but shaky banks needed that cheap money, and he did not act to raise rates until 1999, helping to burst a bubble in technology stocks (which also reflected phony accounting and unpoliced conflicts of interest on Wall Street). Discouraging the purely speculative use of cheap money was beyond Greenspan's imagination or ideology. In the aftermath of the dot-com crash, the Fed pushed interest rates even lower to prop the economy back up.

After 2000, subprime loans added more air to what was already a housing bubble. For better than two decades, the combination of inflated housing prices, rock-bottom interest rates, lax financial regulation, and increased borrowing allowed the economy to disguise an unsustainable imbalance: the steady decline in the incomes of working- and middle-class Americans and the substitution of debt for lost earnings.

---

[*] This policy was known on Wall Street as the Greenspan put. A put is an option to sell a security at a price guaranteed in advance. By analogy, banks could freely speculate, assuming that the Fed would make them whole by lowering rates as necessary, to prop up the market.

TOO BIG TO LEND

Despite its emergency rescue, the banking sector has remained deeply dysfunctional. The government, beginning in 2008, propped up failing banks by pumping in capital and then merging them with other banks, leaving an even more concentrated industry. The too-big-to-fail banks, whose misadventures in exotic off-balance-sheet securities caused the collapse, are now bigger than ever. In 2002, as the big banks were creating the preconditions of the crash, the top ten banks controlled 55 percent of all U.S. banking assets. By 2011, after several failures and mergers, they controlled 77 percent. Although the Dodd-Frank Act of 2010 purports to end too-big-to-fail, if any of the large banks were on the brink of failure, the government would bail them out again.

With concentrated economic power has come immense political influence. The large banks have used their political power to water down Dodd-Frank's practical impact and to preserve their business model. Notwithstanding the inclusion of the so-called Volcker rule limiting the ability of banks to engage in speculative securities trading for their own accounts, lobbying by the big banks has marginalized the rule's practical effect. The provisions requiring more transparent trading of derivatives have also been gutted by the regulatory agencies.

In the government's bailout of the banks, there was a gross regulatory double standard. The Treasury and the Federal Reserve gave priority to saving the largest banks, whose failure could have brought down the whole system. In this exercise, smaller banks were an afterthought. By definition, they were not "systemically significant." They were too small to bail. If some failed, it was no big deal. Fully 97 percent of the $205 billion in TARP capital infusions went to the very largest banks. Only 3 percent went to the community banks that do more than 60 percent of America's small-business lending. At the end of June 2008, just before the crisis hit, America's largest banks, those with assets of at least $100 billion, had outstanding commercial and industrial loans of $962 billion. By the end of 2010, that had dropped more than 28 percent, to $693 billion, according to the FDIC. Smaller community banks, despite having something like 60 percent of their lending collateralized by some form of real estate (whose value was plummeting), also cut back, but by only about 9 percent.

Since the repeal of the Glass-Steagall Act in 1999, a large money center bank still makes commercial loans but looks to investment banking, the creation of complex securities, and proprietary trading for its major profits. Traditional commercial banks are in a very different line of business. Unlike the biggest money center banks, community lenders do not pursue investment banking. Mainly, they lend to local enterprises and households. In a recession, some of their loans fall behind, and their balance sheets weaken. With reduced capital and earnings to leverage, they tend to tighten their lending standards, even for their most reliable customers.

Several Federal Reserve regional bank presidents, including Thomas Hoenig of the Federal Reserve Bank of Kansas City (now FDIC vice chairman), echoed the complaints that they were hearing from local businesses and bankers in the heartland: the regulatory double standard was favoring Wall Street and harming small-bank customers on Main Street. For the largest banks and their exotic securities business, regulatory standards were substantially relaxed during the crisis. The too-big-to-fail banks got whatever level of government support they needed. Regulators conspired in the fiction that complex securities with a very depressed market value could be carried on the bank's books at or close to their nominal par value. But for smaller community banks, it was regulatory business as usual. If an examiner found nonperforming loans in a bank's portfolio, the bank would have to either come up with additional capital—very difficult in a recession—or cut back on lending. Forcing a bank to rebuild capital at the expense of lending in a deep recession is "pro-cyclical": instead of countering the downward economic pull, tightened credit worsens it. But as House Financial Services Committee chairman Barney Frank of Massachusetts quipped, "No examiner ever gets fired for a loan that wasn't made."

Sheila Bair, chairwoman of the FDIC, was very much an outlier in the Obama administration. She understood the need to help community banks help the real economy, while her colleagues at the Treasury were more concerned about protecting the largest Wall Street banks. Bair repeatedly tangled with the comptroller of the currency, John Dugan, a Treasury official, over how examiners should treat bank loans in a depressed economy. In February 2010, Bair directed FDIC examiners that even if the value of the collateral backing a commercial loan had dropped below the amount of the loan, the bank should not get a demerit in its examination or be required to reserve additional capital against risk of loss as long as the loan payments were current. Bair also directed that a routine rollover of a commercial loan should be accepted without a new property appraisal so that a temporary downturn in the property's market value would not block the loan or force a distress sale in a down market.

She won the gratitude of small bankers—and criticism from other regulators. "When I would sit in meetings, it amazed me how harsh the comptroller's examiners would be about small banks," Bair told me in early 2012. "John Dugan famously said during one of my open FDIC meetings that small banks were failing and none of his big banks had failed. They didn't fail because they were bailed out!"

Bottom line: Large banks continued to make large profits by acting like investment banks or hedge funds. Small banks were required by regulators to increase capital reserves or reduce lending. Today, the bread-and-butter job of making ordinary commercial loans to small businesses is seen as a low-profit, high-risk line of business. Big banks shun it. So even businesses that would like to expand often find it difficult to raise capital. This further contributes to the prolonged deflationary trap.

The dysfunction of the banking system prolonged the stagnation in one other respect. Bankers refused to address the mortgage crisis. As housing prices fell below the value of the mortgage debt against them and the "reset" provisions of subprime loans kicked in, millions of Americans saw their homes go into default and then foreclosure. Others had to severely tighten their belts in order to make mortgage payments that they could no longer afford. Millions of homes were subject to distress sales, depressing prices still further.

A serious national policy would have given homeowners mortgage relief sufficient to allow them to keep their homes. This would have been good for the economy, since it would have put a floor under housing prices generally and reduced the home equity losses of tens of millions of innocent bystanders to the subprime mess. But big banks used their lobbying muscle to resist such policies. Write-downs of mortgage principal would require them to book losses, while pretending that an underwater mortgage or a distressed mortgage-backed security was worth a hundred cents on the dollar allowed them to simulate healthier books.

The Obama administration, whose main strategy for the banking sector was to prop up the large banks in order to restore confidence, resisted a mortgage relief program that would require banks to recognize their real losses. It instead settled on a series of small-bore programs, voluntary to the banks, that gave a fraction of distressed homeowners modest relief in their monthly payments but did not reduce the principal amounts of their mortgages. So the downward drag of housing prices continued, with scant help from either the banks or the government. (See chapter 8 for more on the housing drag.)

DEFICITS, DEBTS, AND THE AUSTERITY CURE

In sum, a financial crash coupled with a collapse in housing values led to a deflationary depression. High unemployment, lagging wages, and the damage to banks deepened the downturn. The unwinding of borrowing against deflated assets was a further drag on recovery. In a debt deflation, low interest rates were not enough to restore prosperity. Obama's Recovery Act curbed the rate of collapse but was not sufficient to break the deflationary cycle.

Not surprisingly, all these factors worsened the government's fiscal picture. With earnings and other economic activity down, tax receipts fell. Emergency outlays rose, including unemployment compensation, food stamps, Medicaid enrollment, and the one-time stimulus. This widened the federal deficit, which was relatively high to begin with because of the Bush administration's two wars and two huge tax cuts. But paradoxically, the economy needs more deficit spending for several years if it is to escape the deflationary trap.

As a description of historical events, this understanding of a debt deflation reflects a broad consensus on the cause and cure of the Great Depression. Yet as applied to today's economic challenge, the same analysis is far outside the political mainstream. Key figures in both parties, influential commentators in the press, and most business leaders have a diametrically different story. In their narrative, the economy's biggest problem is not depression and debt deflation but public deficits. They view deficits not as an effect of the prolonged downturn but as the cause. Hence, the primary task of public policy is not to produce an economic recovery directly but rather to reassure financial markets by acting to cut the deficit.

The large deficits and the increasing ratio of debt to GDP are seen as depressing business confidence and risking inflation. Get the economy on a certain path to a lower debt ratio and confidence will return. Supposedly, if we fail to sharply cut the deficit, foreigners will stop lending us money, the dollar will crash, and the economy will drown in the burden of its debt. As politics, deficit reduction is superficially compelling because voters tell pollsters that they think deficits are too high, and commentators contend that rising debts are the emblem of irresponsible partisan deadlock. As economics, however, the austerity cure is deeply perverse.

Yet a well-funded austerity lobby dominates the debate. Deficit hawks in both parties have called for a ten-year program to steadily reduce the deficit and the ratio of government debt to GDP. The two parties are divided over whether deficit reduction should be based entirely on cuts in public spending (the Republican view) or whether it should also include tax increases (the centrist Democratic position). But both have dutifully put forth multiyear plans that typically cut the deficit by at least $4 trillion over a decade. The intriguing question is how the bad economic advice of the austerity lobby became the prevailing view.

Chapter 3

The Allure of Austerity

SINCE THE EARLY 1990S, a growing network of Washington and Wall Street notables has warned that the nation is overspending and over-promising, putting the solvency of the Republic and the prosperity of the next generation at risk. With the crash of 2008, these groups deliberately blurred the long-term need for adjustments in Social Security and Medicare with the unrelated and urgent question of how to recover from a prolonged deflationary downturn. The budget hawks found a receptive audience among media and political elites. Key commentators and opinion leaders have embraced the story line of the need for shared sacrifice and grand fiscal compromise and the premise that we can somehow deflate our way to recovery.

The career of Peter G. Peterson, a billionaire investment banker and leading tribune of belt-tightening, is instructive. In 1982, Peterson began writing articles and books warning that "unfunded liabilities" of the government, most notably Social Security, would lead to an economic collapse. "To put the matter bluntly," he wrote, "Social Security is heading for a crash. We cannot permit this to happen, because it would put the nation itself in very serious jeopardy." Peterson warned that government debts, explicit and tacit, would crowd out productive private investment, increase interest rates, and reduce confidence in the dollar. This generation of elders was living too well at the expense of their children and grandchildren, he insisted.

Peterson was right about one thing—a crash was coming. But when the collapse came, it had everything to do with the lax financial regulation promoted by Wall Street barons like Peterson himself and nothing whatever to do with budget deficits crowding out productive investment. Indeed, in the run-up to the 2008 collapse, interest rates and capital costs were low and falling, not high and rising.

Over the course of four books and myriad articles and interviews,

Peterson's jeremiads never mentioned the risks of financial speculation—not surprisingly, since he was CEO of Lehman Brothers and later made most of his billions as chairman of the Blackstone Group, a private equity company, one of the most lightly regulated categories of financial firms. It would be wrong, of course, to attribute the austerity crusade to Pete Peterson personally. But in addition to being a well-connected, charming, and highly effective individual willing to spend billions to promote his views, he is emblematic of a creditor class that has become increasingly dominant—hegemonic—in American fiscal politics.

WHY WALL STREET HATES SOCIAL INSURANCE

Financiers like Peterson are averse to deficits and phobic of Social Security for three interlocking reasons. First, there is the genuine though grossly exaggerated worry that very high levels of public debt could raise interest rates and trigger higher inflation. However, recent U.S. government debts and deficits are nowhere near that level. Both interest rates and inflation have remained low, as they typically are after a financial collapse.

Second, a large-scale social retirement system demonstrates the government's efficiency and reliability in providing pensions and reinforces public support for government in general. Third, Social Security means fewer retirement dollars invested through the financial industry. About $800 billion a year flows from payroll taxes to Social Security payouts. Imagine if those funds were invested privately. Private pensions, IRAs, and Keogh accounts have been a bonanza for Wall Street, though they have shifted risks to pensioners (unlike Social Security, whose payments are guaranteed). If Social Security tax receipts went into private brokerage accounts, that would generate massive fee and trading income to middlemen and pump up stock prices. So "saving" Social Security by privatizing it has long been high on Wall Street's wish list; likewise turning Medicare into a voucher program. The claim that both are unsustainable is a key part of the strategy to erode political support for these immensely popular programs, especially among the young.

In 2007, on the eve of the collapse, Peterson cashed out his stake in Blackstone when stock markets were near their peak. He then committed a billion dollars of the proceeds, more than a third of his total fortune, to the newly created Peter G. Peterson Foundation to promote budget austerity and reduced social insurance levels. By 2012, according to tax filings, the foundation had already spent $458 million.

The foundation hired as its president David Walker, the former head of the government's General Accounting Office (rebranded the Government Accountability Office in 2004), a veteran talking head, and a crusader for budget balance. For vice president, Peterson hired a respected mainstream economist, Eugene Steuerle, from the Urban Institute. Both have since departed. The foundation is now run day to day by the benefactor's son Michael, and Pete Peterson retains the title of chairman. The entire board of directors is Peterson, his wife, and his son. Walker, still an adviser to the foundation, ostensibly draws no salary from it. His compensation comes through Peterson Management, the investment arm of the Peterson fortune. As investigative reporters Ryan Grim and Paul Blumenthal pointed out, "Paying [Walker] through the investment fund allows Peterson to obscure his salary and frees Walker from the restrictions on lobbying by nonprofit foundations."

Peterson has formidable financial and political connections in both parties. With his hardscrabble origins in Kearney, Nebraska, as the son of Greek immigrants (the family name was Petropoulos), Peterson retains a folksy manner that doesn't bespeak Wall Street. A former commerce secretary under Richard Nixon, he is personally close to Democratic economic eminence Robert Rubin. The two have long promoted the idea of a grand fiscal bargain in which Democrats agree to cut social insurance and Republicans agree to higher taxes. Peterson served as chairman of the Council on Foreign Relations, and in 2002 he led the search committee that successfully recommended Rubin protégé Timothy Geithner as president of the Federal Reserve Bank of New York. One can assume that Geithner, later Obama's Treasury secretary, returns Peterson's calls.

Peterson has spread his money around, giving over $50 million to the influential Institute for International Economics, long headed by Democrat C. Fred Bergsten. The outfit was duly renamed the Peterson Institute for International Economics, a separate entity from the Peterson Foundation.

AUSTERITY FOR ALL SEASONS

The crusade for fiscal austerity has had three distinct phases. Deficits became a public issue in the mid-1980s after the "supply-side" tax cuts of the first Reagan term failed to deliver the promised revenue increases. The tax breaks, not surprisingly, reduced government income. Deficits, ironically, were disguised by the huge increases in payroll taxes of the 1983 Social Security reform, trillions destined for retirement trust funds—which were then borrowed by the rest of the government, lowering the consolidated government deficit.

Reagan's budget imbalance was further exacerbated by a military buildup. Deficits averaged about 4 percent of GDP throughout the Reagan and George H. W. Bush presidencies, increasing the debt ratio from under 30 percent before Reagan took office in 1981 to over 50 percent at the time of the 1992 election. There were several attempts to put the budget on an automatic path to deficit reduction, using different versions of a "trigger" formula of automatic budget cuts sponsored by Representative Phil Gramm of Texas and Senator Warren Rudman of New Hampshire, both Republicans, and Senator Ernest Hollings of South Carolina, a fiscally conservative Democrat. Though trigger mechanisms were enacted, these efforts did not reduce deficits much, in part because an economic slowdown in the late 1980s reduced revenues. Bush, having sworn "Read my lips, no new taxes" in his 1988 presidential nomination speech, infuriated supporters by signing a 1990 budget deal that included modest tax increases. But the debt remained on an upward path.

By the time of the 1992 election, more than twenty years ago, the rising debt and the political deadlock over how to address it had already become an emblem of dysfunctional government. Ross Perot, running as a third-party candidate, combined deficit reduction and economic nationalism into a weirdly populist crusade. To Perot and his supporters, failure to deal with the deficit symbolized the bankruptcy of the two major parties. For several weeks in the spring of 1992, polls showed that Perot was running ahead of both Clinton and Bush. In early 1992, Peterson founded the Concord Coalition to lobby for a balanced budget, joining with Rudman and Senator Paul Tsongas, a Democratic deficit hawk from Massachusetts. The coalition was substantially underwritten by Peterson.

But an economic boom and President Clinton's politically brave tax increase on the richest 2 percent of Americans nearly put the austerity lobby out of business. In 1993, Clinton struck a famous deal with the chairman of the Federal Reserve to trade smaller deficits for lower interest rates. The two policies had no logical connection, except in Alan Greenspan's ideology. Projected deficits were in fact having no effect on interest rates, which were the province of the Federal Reserve. Cutting the deficit was thus a political imperative, not an economic one. But after the 1993 budget raised taxes, cut spending, and reduced the deficit, Greenspan delivered on his part of the deal. With lower interest rates, growth rebounded throughout the 1990s.

After the strong economic performance balanced the budget in 1999 and endless surpluses were forecasted, the Concord Coalition took down its clock in Times Square that displayed the escalating national debt. Peterson's book *Facing Up* had in 1993 gravely predicted a $300 billion deficit by 2000. That year, the actual budget was in surplus by $236 billion.

Higher growth and reduced unemployment also increased payroll tax receipts and moved the Social Security accounts further into the black. Deficit hawks were fond of pointing to estimates by the Social Security trustees projecting that at some point in the 2030s or early 2040s Social Security would not be able to meet all of its anticipated obligations. The 2012 Trustees' report put the program's long-term deficit at about 1 percent of GDP—something easily solved by modest tax increases on high-bracket wage earners, or better yet, by rising wages.

Social Security is financed by taxes on wage and salary income. It is at risk of incurring a modest shortfall two decades from now only because wages have not kept pace with productivity growth. If wages tracked productivity, Social Security would never be in deficit. In one three-year span during the booming 1990s, the date of Social Security's projected shortfall was pushed back by eight years—from 2029 to 2037—because a high-employment economy meant more payroll taxes coming into the Social Security trust funds. At that rate of improving solvency, Social Security would soon be in perpetual surplus. All it took was decent economic growth with fruits shared by wage earners. The budget hysteria lost its credibility, and the austerity crusaders went into temporary eclipse.

What saved the budget hawks' crusade were two new sets of entirely gratuitous deficits. These were produced first by the tax cuts and wars of the George W. Bush administration and then by a financial collapse created on Wall Street. The budget went moderately back into deficit in

2002. By fiscal year 2008—the last of the Bush presidency—the deficit had increased to 3.3 percent of GDP, enough to give Peterson and company a second wind.

In 2007, David Walker, still head of the GAO, and Robert Bixby, executive director of the Concord Coalition, set out on a Fiscal Wake-Up Tour, which was underwritten by the Peterson Foundation. In 2008, the foundation paid PBS to air *I.O.U.S.A.*, its film covering the tour. In other words, the foundation paid public TV to treat its own event as news. In the film, David Walker warns, "We suffer from a fiscal cancer. It is growing within us, and if we do not treat it, it could have catastrophic consequences for our country." The movie was also shown in some four hundred theaters and broadcast as part of a CNN special on the fiscal crisis that Peterson's people coproduced.

In a depressed economy, fiscal tightening turns deeply perverse. But as the economy went into a debt deflation, the austerity lobby did not alter its message at all. It simply treated the economy's new woes as an ideological windfall, demonstrating the urgency of deeper cuts in a now-larger deficit. In *I.O.U.S.A.*, headlines of a crashing economy are ominously juxtaposed with statistics on rising deficits, as if the deficits had caused the crash, rather than vice versa.

The financial collapse, predictably, caused a sharp deterioration in the nation's fiscal picture. The federal deficit swelled from 3.3 percent in fiscal year 2008 to 10.1 percent in 2009, then declined slightly in 2010 to 9 percent and to 8.7 percent in 2011. Of the projected increase in the deficit between 2010 and 2020, only about 9 percent is the result of deliberate federal stimulus spending.

Nonetheless, the growing deficit was taken as vindication of the hawks' earlier claims, even though that inverted the actual cause and effect. Through some alchemy, progress on long-term deficit reduction would supposedly restore business confidence and thus economic growth—as if entrepreneurs were basing their investment decisions in 2013 on deficit projections for 2023. The economist Paul Krugman aptly termed this wishful claim "the confidence fairy."

PURCHASING CONVENTIONAL WISDOM

Through his foundation and personal donations, Peterson has helped bankroll a large array of nominally bipartisan organizations warning of fiscal Armageddon. The Concord Coalition has now been joined by the Committee for a Responsible Federal Budget, the Peterson-Pew Commission on Budget Reform, the Bipartisan Policy Center, the Moment of Truth Project, Fix the Debt, several campus initiatives, and a fiscal seminar of deficit hawks spanning think tanks from the centrist Brookings Institution to the far-right Heritage Foundation.

Peterson underwrites *The Fiscal Times,* a conservative publication to which *The Washington Post* outsources its coverage of budget issues. The very first story supplied by *The Fiscal Times* and published by the *Post,* on December 31, 2009, was headlined: "Support Grows for Tackling Nation's Debt." The article contended that support was growing across the political spectrum for one of Peterson's pet projects, a bipartisan fiscal commission charged with specifying mandatory budget triggers. The piece prominently quoted one of Peterson's largest grantees, Robert Bixby of the Concord Coalition, without ever disclosing the fact that *The Fiscal Times* and the coalition are underwritten by Peterson:

> "I think there's more interest in the proposal not only in Congress but at the White House because there's a growing realization the deficit and the debt are reaching such levels they can't be ignored any longer," said Robert L. Bixby, executive director of the Concord Coalition, a nonpartisan group that advocates entitlement reform and balanced budgets.

At the end of the piece was this tagline: "This article was produced by the *Fiscal Times,* an independent digital news publication reporting on fiscal, budgetary, health-care and international economics issues." There was no acknowledgment that Peterson was paying the *Post* to provide friendly coverage of his own pet projects and grantees. The *Post*'s ombudsman very delicately criticized the conflict of interest in the piece, but the partnership continued.

Columbia University's Teachers College took $2.45 million between 2009 and 2012 from the Peterson Foundation to develop a curriculum "to help high school students understand the facts, significance and consequences of the US national debt." The curriculum, Understanding Fiscal Responsibility, was unveiled in May 2012 at a ceremony featuring Peter Orszag, the former OMB director under Obama who regularly turns up at Peterson events and is now a senior executive at Citigroup. This is being portrayed as ideologically neutral material, even though it presents a highly alarmist view of the deficit and calls into question the reliability of Social Security. Every high school student in America will receive a copy of the curriculum.

Peterson's foundation gave a group called America's Promise Alliance a million dollars to educate young people on the fiscal crisis, using the film *I.O.U.S.A.* as curricular material. The National Academy of Public Administration received a grant of $783,000 for "development of fiscal learning tool, Budgetball, to bring fiscal awareness to college students and others." Public Agenda, a foundation based in New York, got half a million dollars to promote "college student fiscal awareness."

In November 2010, the Peterson Foundation launched a $6 million media campaign called Owe No! using television spots to educate the public about the consequences of running large deficits and increasing the national debt. The cornball ads featured a fictitious presidential candidate named Hugh Jidette (Huge Debt—get it?) running on a platform of increasing national spending and debt. Peterson said that the aim of the campaign was to "make the threat of unrestrained deficits tangible to ordinary Americans." In March 2012, the foundation put up the funds for a joint venture with the Clinton Global Initiative to engage college students in a "fiscal sustainability" exercise in which teams competed to educate their campuses about the Peterson view of the budget crisis. The foundation even sponsored a national poetry contest on the debt. A sample haiku:

Spend, borrow, repeat
Leave the bills for our children
Too young to object

The foundation's operating principle seems to be: Spend enough money, purchase enough allies, throw enough propaganda at the wall— and some of it may stick. And it has. Though some of these ventures may seem far-fetched, most Washington opinion leaders have bought the basic story that debt is a bigger menace than depression.

At a May 2011 "Fiscal Summit" sponsored by the Peterson Foundation, whose speakers included Bill Clinton and senior Democratic and Republican officials, six groups, ranging from the liberal Economic Policy Institute to the far-right Heritage Foundation, presented budget proposals underwritten by six-figure grants from Peterson. The goal of the project was to show different paths to deficit reduction. The metamessage was that everyone—left, right, and center—agreed that today's deficits were too high and that the Peterson Foundation was interested in soliciting a wide range of views. Peterson got his money's worth. The press coverage was extensive. The insidious part of the exercise was that none of the participating groups could alter the premise and shift the primary focus to the real issue of how to get a robust recovery going. Though EPI's other work has emphasized putting growth first, the meeting reinforced the message that everybody was for deficit reduction.[*]

A repeat Fiscal Summit in May 2012 again included Clinton and also House Speaker John Boehner and Paul Ryan of the Ways and Means Committee, among Republicans, as well as such Democrats as Treasury Secretary Geithner, Representative Chris Van Hollen, and even Xavier Becerra of the House Progressive Caucus, who had been a token liberal on the Bowles-Simpson commission. Peterson succeeded in throwing a party that everyone wanted to attend. Having established the idea that fiscal responsibility is the sine qua non of recovery, the deficit hawks have created a political reality in which major political players feel the need to embrace and thus reinforce that premise.

THE OBLIGING OPINION ELITE

Former Peterson Foundation president David Walker insists that his austerity crusade is "nonideological," as if calls for fiscal restraint in a deep economic slump and for avoidable cuts in social insurance were not one side of an ideological argument. A favorite phrase of both Peterson and Walker is "Washington is broken." This formulation, repeated endlessly by media commentators, is as misleading as it is insidious. It implies politically symmetrical blame and the need for a politically symmetrical remedy: Republicans should agree to raise taxes, and Democrats should cut spending, even though spending has been substantially slashed already and is inadequate to the recovery. Somehow, Washington wasn't broken when President Bush regularly peeled off Democratic votes for his tax cuts. A more accurate characterization might connect the deadlock to the right's tactical games of chicken with the debt ceil-

---

[*] I serve on the executive committee of EPI.

ing and resistance to taxes. But symmetrical blame for fiscal gridlock is a key part of the austerity narrative, and the general tendency is to cut the right a lot of slack.

Though Peterson has occasionally been willing to obliquely criticize Republicans, most of the austerity crowd tends to ignore the inconvenient fact that there would be no fiscal problem but for the Reagan and Bush tax cuts. Maya MacGuineas, the onetime aide to Republican senator Bob Dole who now heads the Peterson-funded Committee for a Responsible Federal Budget, emphasizes spending cuts in her proposed balanced budgets. She once told me that major tax increases were not on her agenda because wall-to-wall Republican opposition made them "politically unrealistic." The narrator of *I.O.U.S.A.*, in order to avoid criticizing Ronald Reagan directly, coyly says of the Reagan "supply-side" tax cuts that massively increased deficits: "The debate over supply-side economics continues to this day, but what is not debatable is that the federal debt exploded in the 1980s."

All of this fiscal propaganda creates what the blogger Greg Sargent calls the Beltway Deficit Feedback Loop—an incestuous Washington echo chamber in which right-thinking people give priority to debt reduction over economic recovery and bemoan partisan gridlock. Both *The Washington Post*'s editorial page and the paper's own beat reporter on tax and budget issues, Lori Montgomery, working in tandem with the staff of *The Fiscal Times,* have been relentless advocates of austerity-first. Montgomery began her gushingly favorable news account of David Walker's Fiscal Wake-Up Tour:

> "I knew there was a problem, but I didn't realize it was this bad," [Joseph] Farrell, 25, marveled after a recent presentation [by Walker] at the University of South Florida, from which he is to graduate in August. "I didn't realize there was no solution in sight. My taxes are going to be *huge.*"
>
> The problem is the skyrocketing cost of government health-care and retirement benefits. By most estimates, they will break the national bank as the baby boom generation retires. If projections hold, Farrell and his contemporaries could face a near-doubling of their income taxes over the next 35 years just to care for the burgeoning ranks of older Americans.

This account is far from economic fact, but it is precisely the austerity lobby's prime pitch to the young. The need to tame the deficit—

rather than acting urgently to generate renewed economic growth—has become a mantra of media commentators. Or consider this profile by Montgomery lionizing the dean of Democratic deficit hawks, North Dakota senator Kent Conrad:

> Sen. Kent Conrad has been the Democrats' balanced-budget guy for more than a decade, and the job takes a toll. His wife paints the North Dakotan as a lonely Cassandra with Power Point slides, warning of a debt-ridden future liberals and conservatives alike would rather ignore.
>
> The past two years have been especially stressful. Conrad almost single-handedly forced President Obama to create the commission known as Bowles-Simpson, which produced a debt-reduction plan now hailed as a model of bipartisan compromise on taxes and government spending. Conrad then spent months working with like-minded senators to build support for the plan and bring it to a vote.

Hailed by whom? By the same club of austerity hawks. The claim of partisan gridlock has become a standard trope, with both parties held equally to blame.

In April 2012, Paul Ryan, Republican chairman of the House Budget Committee, proposed a budget for fiscal year 2013 that would privatize Medicare, reduce overall federal domestic spending to its lowest level since 1953, and cut taxes by over $4.6 trillion on top of making the Bush tax cuts permanent (and then claim deficit reduction by means of unspecified loophole closings). The plan would also remove between fourteen and twenty-seven million Americans from Medicaid coverage. James B. Stewart of *The New York Times* began his laudatory analysis: "This week, President Obama called him a social Darwinist. The conservative Club for Growth criticized him for wimping out on Medicare and military spending, and Ron Paul, the libertarian Republican, blasted him for not cutting tax rates more deeply. I figure Paul D. Ryan, the Wisconsin Republican who is head of the House Budget Committee, must be doing something right."

The channeling of the austerity lobby was pitch-perfect. A politician who proposes sacrifice in a depression is a brave and worthy public figure. The fact that he is criticized by "both sides" proves it. Stewart's piece goes on to approvingly quote Ryan declaring that "the social safety net is failing society's most vulnerable citizens," giving Ryan a free pass on the fact that his budget would destroy most of what's left of the net.

If you look for it, you can find astute criticism of austerity economics in the work of the Nobel laureates Paul Krugman, Joseph Stiglitz, and Robert Solow; on the editorial page of *The New York Times;* and in the efforts of advocacy groups such as the Center on Economic and Policy Research and the Economic Policy Institute, as well as at Demos, where I work, and other think tanks. A great many mainstream economists share Krugman's skepticism that the confidence fairy will somehow restore growth if only Congress would slash the deficit. But the austerity story has nonetheless become the dominant media narrative. The dissenters are treated as quirky outliers, or they are just ignored.

SINS OF COMMISSION: PUTTING GOVERNMENT ON AUTOPILOT

In addition to convincing the public of the gravity of the debt crisis and of the unreliability of social insurance, the austerity lobby's grand strategy is to create bipartisan expert panels of fiscal conservatives to devise automatic triggers that put Congress on a certain path to deficit reduction. The concept, which dates back to the Gramm-Rudman-Hollings formula of the 1980s, invariably includes trading higher taxes for cuts in social insurance. The most impressive convert to this view has been Barack Obama.

In the Obama era, there have been at least six such bodies, both private and official, including a high-profile commission appointed by the president. After the stimulus bill was enacted in February 2009, Obama pivoted from job creation and recovery to the cause of budget balance. On February 23, the president hosted a "fiscal responsibility summit" at the White House, echoing the dubious economic premises of the austerity lobby. He declared:

> If we confront this crisis without also confronting the deficits that helped cause it, we risk sinking into another crisis down the road as our interest payments rise, our obligations come due, confidence in our economy erodes, and our children and grandchildren are unable to pursue their dreams because they are saddled with our debts.
>
> That is why today, I am pledging to cut the deficit we inherited in half

by the end of my first term in office. This will not be easy. It will require us to make difficult decisions and face challenges we have long neglected. But I refuse to leave our children with a debt they cannot repay—and that means taking responsibility right now, in this Administration, for getting our spending under control.

Note these several fallacies. Deficits did not cause the economic crisis. Confidence in the economy has far more to do with whether we are on a path to recovery than with whether we are on a path to reduce debt. The horizons of our children and grandchildren will be more a reflection of the health of the real economy than of the ratio of national debt to GDP (which, remember, was at record levels during the postwar boom, America's greatest era of high growth and shared prosperity). But Obama was now singing from the austerity hymnal, and among the pleased summiteers were Pete Peterson, David Walker, and the Concord Coalition's Robert Bixby. Obama, in fact, did not cut the deficit in half by the end of his term, *because slow growth kept deficits high*. The actual deficit fell by about 31 percent. And it's good that he didn't cut it further. If the president had delivered on his deflationary pledge, the growth rate would have been even lower.

With unemployment exceeding 10 percent in the fall of 2009, it was clear that the February stimulus had been insufficient. The House leadership under Speaker Nancy Pelosi pushed for a second stimulus bill to extend unemployment insurance, increase aid to the states, and directly create jobs. The White House discouraged this new legislation and made no effort to help Pelosi round up the votes. Obama personally urged her to wait for the State of the Union address in January. His chief of staff, Rahm Emanuel, warned the House leadership not to upstage the president. But with members hearing from their hard-pressed constituents, the House Democrats narrowly passed a $154 billion stimulus. The White House was happy to let the measure die in the Senate. In the 2010 State of the Union address, Obama emphasized deficit reduction. After describing the need to increase jobs and business activity, the president declared:

Families across the country are tightening their belts and making tough decisions. The federal government should do the same. So tonight, I'm proposing specific steps to pay for the trillion dollars that it took to rescue the economy last year.

Starting in 2011, we are prepared to freeze government spending for three years. Spending related to our national security, Medicare, Medicaid, and Social Security will not be affected. But all other discretionary government programs will. Like any cash-strapped family, we will work within a budget to invest in what we need and sacrifice what we don't. And if I have to enforce this discipline by veto, I will.

Obama's analogy rightly caused groans among economists, including those on his own staff. Generations of economics students have learned that the government has a macroeconomic role to play in a deep downturn. It can't be compared to families, who have no capacity to run a fiscal or monetary policy and whose prudent private behavior in a slump (liquidity preference) tends to reinforce the downturn. In a period of general depression, the government needs to expand economic activity precisely because the private sector is reducing it, not to add to the general contraction.

In the same speech, Obama announced an executive order creating the bipartisan National Commission on Fiscal Responsibility and Reform, as had long been urged by the austerity lobby. The design for the commission was in legislation that would have required an up-or-down vote on the commission's recommendations. But that bill narrowly failed in the Senate in January 2012, after which Obama embraced the commission idea as his own.

Obama named as cochairs Erskine Bowles, a conservative Democrat and investment banker, and former Wyoming senator Alan Simpson, a Republican. In recent years, Bowles has received annual fees ranging from $308,000 to $337,000 for serving as a director of Morgan Stanley, a major beneficiary of the government bank bailouts. In this version of bipartisanship, Bowles represents the Democrats. The party leaders in the House and Senate got to name two-thirds of the eighteen appointees, most of whom turned out to be deficit hawks. The terms required the commission to issue its report by December 1, 2010, safely after the congressional midterm elections. A supermajority of fourteen out of eighteen was required for the recommendations to be official. Obama, modeling the belt-tightening that he commended, gave the commission almost no funding for operations. Staffers were generously donated by the Peterson Foundation.

Austerity advocates inside the administration, led by Peter Orszag, the budget director and a Robert Rubin protégé, had convinced Obama that the commission was a shrewd idea. It would appease fiscal conservatives in Congress while buying some time for the economy to improve. It would associate the president with bipartisanship, please his constituency on Wall Street, and act on the premise that getting serious about deficit reduction would restore confidence and investment and spur recovery. The recommendations of the commission would conveniently come after the 2010 midterm election; in the meantime, it would provide "cover" for Obama's sin against the fiscal orthodoxy of having spent close to a trillion dollars in the deficit-widening February 2009 stimulus.

But key members of Obama's economic team, including Christina Romer, chairwoman of the Council of Economic Advisers, and Jared Bernstein, the vice president's chief economist, were appalled. With the economy still deep in recession and the stimulus of 2009 plainly inadequate, Obama was calling for a government spending freeze and appointing a commission certain to recommend the Social Security and Medicare cuts that Obama himself was ducking for the moment, putting new pressure on the president to accept deeper cuts later on. The economic advisers were overruled by the political team.

The pivot to fiscal conservatism turned out to be a disastrous miscalculation, economically and politically. It was premature macroeconomically, and it sent the public a mixed message about the administration's goals. With a weak recovery, the 2010 midterm election was the worst repudiation of congressional Democrats in more than seventy years. Washington opinion leaders, Wall Streeters, and some Tea Party activists may have been obsessed with deficits, but most voters cared more about jobs and recovery.

Having appointed the Bowles-Simpson commission, Obama painted himself into a corner: he was obligated to accept either its conservative belt-tightening recommendations or something very much like them. On three separate occasions after the midterm elections—when the commission's majority report came out in December 2010; when Republicans created an entirely artificial crisis by blocking a routine extension of the national debt ceiling in the summer of 2011; and when Obama personally sought to make a budget deal with House Speaker John Boehner in the fall—the president was fully prepared to sacrifice Social Security and to take deep cuts in domestic spending in order to get a bipartisan agreement. Only the Republican refusal to entertain any tax increases under any circumstances saved the Democrats from even worse policies—at least so far.

The terms of the Bowles-Simpson commission required fourteen of its members to embrace its recommendations for them to be official. The commission fell short, voting 11–7 to approve its majority report. But the report, and Bowles and Simpson personally, have enjoyed an afterlife, funded, of course, by the Peterson Foundation. In 2011, the austerity lobby came up with yet another variant of the autopilot idea: a supercommittee of Congress. The supercommittee would recommend a mandatory path to deficit reduction, subject to a fast-track up-or-down vote. But like other efforts, the supercommittee foundered on the Republican refusal to entertain new taxes.

In mid-2012, the Peterson Foundation underwrote yet another effort to promote an automatic debt reduction formula. This one, with leading corporate executives playing key roles, is called the Fix the Debt campaign. Besides Bowles and Simpson, it features Democrats Alice Rivlin and Ed Rendell and Republicans Judd Gregg and the irrepressible Pete Peterson. The business leaders include Dave Cote of Honeywell, Sandy Cutler of Eaton, Gregg Sherrill of Tenneco, Marty Flanagan of Invesco, Gary Loveman of Caesars, Thomas Quinlan of RR Donnelley, the investment banker Steven Rattner, and Jamie Dimon of JPMorgan Chase. By the end of 2012, they had raised $60 million to beat the drums for budget balance. Steven Pearlstein, in an effusive *Washington Post* column, praised the effort as a belated effort by corporate executives to be the long-missing "grown-ups in the room" of squabbling children. Not surprisingly, the corporate grown-ups would support an extremely conservative fiscal agenda.

ENDLESS FISCAL CLIFFS

In mid-2012, one more bizarre inversion occurred. As the two parties girded for the next election-year budgetary impasse, it became evident that the budget was already on a doomsday course for a disaster nobody wanted. A fiscal train wreck was programmed for January 2013. For starters, the Bush tax cuts expired on January 1. Democrats wanted to extend them for all but the top 2 percent; Republicans wanted to extend them for everybody. The temporary two-percentage-point cut in the payroll tax was set to expire as well. But the parties were deadlocked, and in the absence of a deal, a still-weak economy would face a huge tax hike for everyone that would be felt immediately in payroll deductions.

To add to the contractionary pressure, January 2 was the day the dreaded "sequester" would hit. When the parties had failed to agree on a long-term budget deal back in 2011, the Republicans' price in the Budget Control Act of 2011 for funding the government was an automatic trigger to take effect if Congress did not agree on its own deficit reductions. The act, approved after agonizing negotiation, provided for $55 billion of cuts in domestic spending and another $55 billion in defense outlays to begin January 2, 2013, with a total of $1.2 trillion in automatic cuts over a decade.

The Congressional Budget Office calculated that the combined effects of the end of the tax cuts plus the automatic budget reductions mandated by the sequester would be a fiscal contraction of some $607 billion in a single fiscal year, or about 4 percent of GDP. According to the CBO, this abrupt budget tightening in a still-weak economy would kick the fragile economy back into recession in 2013. Fed chair Ben Bernanke implored Congress to act so that the recovery would not go off a cliff.

Media commentary treated the fiscal cliff as some kind of natural calamity, like a comet headed for earth. In fact, the cliff was precisely the creation of one of those automatic budget triggers long promoted by the austerity lobby. Yet as the phrase "fiscal cliff" seeped into alarmist media and political commentary, the risk of an abrupt fiscal contraction became still more grist for the people promoting . . . an abrupt fiscal contraction! Erskine Bowles, David Walker, and company began using worries about the fiscal cliff in their materials urging a grand budget bargain—that would also slow down the recovery. If a $607 billion cut in one year is a cliff, a $4 trillion cut over a decade is a chasm.

With Obama's re-election in November, the president reiterated his call for a balanced program of deficit reduction. Obama took a hard line only on the issue of tax policy. Taxes had to be increased on the wealthiest 2 percent, he insisted, so that the bottom 98 percent could continue to get the lower rates from the Bush tax cuts. In his first weekly address after the election, Obama declared: "I refuse to accept any approach that isn't balanced. I will not ask students or seniors or middle-class families to pay down the entire deficit while people making over $250,000 aren't asked to pay a dime more in taxes."

On New Year's weekend 2013, just hours before taxes were due to increase for all, Congress passed a bill raising taxes to pre-Bush levels on roughly the top one percent. The dreaded sequester of automatic spending cuts was deferred for two months, as were other budget decisions. The action headed off the "fiscal cliff" only temporarily. It handed President Obama a tactical victory by forcing Republicans to raise taxes on the wealthiest. But the entire framing of the debate and Obama's continuing embrace of the premise that confidence and growth require deficit reduction guaranteed that Americans would continue debating the wrong questions about the connection between debt and economic recovery. With a depressed economy generating about $1.5 trillion per year less than its potential GDP, political elites of both parties continued to debate how to cut the budget rather than how to strengthen economic performance.

There is a better path to recovery and fiscal responsibility. The economy needs deficit-financed public outlay during the next few years, and then very gradual budgetary restraint as the recovery strengthens. Deficit-narrowing built on increased revenue collections that reflect an improved economy is far superior to budget balance that comes from belt-tightening.

I argued in my book *Obama's Challenge,* published in August 2008, that the economy needed to permanently increase its federal spending by about four percentage points of GDP, to around 24 percent, up from a pre-recession average of just under 20 percent—and that the budget should move close to balance only once the worst of the slump was behind us. That's about $600 billion of additional spending a year.

In the short run, that additional expenditure should be financed by deficit, I urged, because the economy needed the fiscal stimulus. Once the economy reached a sustainable recovery, this outlay would still be necessary to meet long-deferred social needs. Taxes on the wealthy could be increased, so that federal revenue totaled about 22 percent of GDP, leaving a deficit of just 2 percent. At that level, the ratio of debt to GDP would gradually come down, as it did after World War II. (The deficit would not always be precisely 2 percent of GDP; it would be lower in boom years and higher in recessions.) But this formula would accelerate a recovery, would meet public needs rather than shortchange them, and would moderate the debt ratio over time.

Writing five years ago, I proposed the following annual increases in public spending:

Permanent investment in public infrastructure	$200 billion
Energy independence	$100 billion
Active labor market policy (training and subsidy)	$100 billion
Aid to states and localities	$100 billion
Professionalization of human services work	$100 billion
Universal prekindergarten and child care	$50 billion
Housing relief	$50 billion
Cuts in military outlay	–$100 billion
Net annual spending increase	$600 billion

This is still a pretty good list.

Note that the Obama administration, six months later, did enact a stimulus of $787 billion—but only as a one-time event. Pundits have argued about whether Obama could have gotten more. Some say Congress would not have approved an additional nickel. Others contend that as the recession worsened, a still-popular Obama could have appealed to public opinion and pressed the Democratic Congress for more. But the White House slogan calling for a "timely, targeted, and temporary" stimulus was mistaken economics and set the stage for blockage of additional recovery spending. In fact, the stimulus needed—and needs—to be a multiyear affair to fill a persistent shortfall in demand, restore middle-class jobs, and rebuild a crumbling public household.

Revising the bill of particulars today, I would add more intergovernmental aid and more funds for mortgage refinancing, as well as relief of student debt. I would also add a long-term program of investment in infrastructure to protect our coasts from rising sea levels. But a four-percentage point increase in public outlay, largely financed by taxes, is the right order of magnitude. With interest rates exceptionally low, this is precisely the moment for the government to borrow large sums to finance multiyear public investments that will pay great dividends. If we ever get to single-payer health insurance, we would need to move a lot of money out of employer-financed coverage and onto the books of the government, though this would be held in a separate trust fund.

In their own version of how to stabilize public finances, the deficit hawks invariably get to budget balance at a much lower level of taxing and spending. This conflates an *ideological* goal—smaller government, reduced social insurance and public services, lower taxes on wealth—with a supposed *fiscal* goal of deficit reduction. But these ideological choices need to be unpacked and debated rather than blurred.

SCAPEGOATING SOCIAL SECURITY AND MEDICARE

The claim that we need to reduce Social Security benefits because Americans are living longer and the huge baby boom generation is retiring seems to make a certain intuitive sense. But the coming retirement of the boomers was not exactly a surprise. The Social Security trustees and their actuaries were well aware back in the 1970s that baby boom retirement was coming, and the system planned for it. The last great Social Security overhaul, enacted in 1983 and signed by President Reagan, raised the retirement age by two years, reduced the cost-of-living adjustment very slightly, and increased the tax rate and the cap on income subject to Social Security taxes.

The higher taxes enacted in 1983 very deliberately created an immense surplus in the Social Security trust funds to cover the anticipated costs of boomer retirement. Working people took large tax increases that prepaid their retirement benefits. Even with the reduced employment levels of the deep recession, Social Security will continue to be in surplus every year until 2021, when it will slowly begin drawing the surplus down to meet payouts. So the idea that the Social Security surplus is fair game for general deficit reduction is outrageous. Yet deficit hawks are fond of quoting Willie Sutton: we need to go after Social Security reserves, they say, because "that's where the money is." The notorious Depression-era bank robber provides a more apt analogy than they intend. That money was paid in by working Americans to help finance their retirements. Diverting it for other uses is plain robbery.

Had it not been for the divergence of wages from productivity growth that began in the 1970s and widened after 2000, compounded by the effects of a once-in-a-century financial collapse, the adjustments of 1983 would have kept Social Security solvent for the indefinite future. The fact is that America's retirement benefits are very modest compared with those of other advanced nations. We rank twenty-sixth out of thirty Organization for Economic Cooperation and Development member countries in our social outlays overall, and our ratios of retirement income to lifetime work income are well below average. Because of the later retirement age that was part of the revisions of 1983, the lifetime ratio of work income to retirement income is already declining. If anything, pension policy in the United States needs to increase the security and generosity of retirement income, not reduce it further. We are also in somewhat better shape demographically than most European nations, in that our population is not as old and we have a higher birth rate, more immigration, and thus relatively more young workers paying into the system.

The private retirement plans that complement Social Security are steadily becoming less reliable as more companies shift from traditional pensions, which guarantee set monthly payments, to systems such as 401(k)s in which all of the risks and most of the costs fall on workers and retirees. State and local pension plans are also under fiscal and political assault and are underfunded because of the right's relentless attack on adequate taxation. Social Security is the one part of the system that is guaranteed by the federal government, is not subject to the vagaries of the stock market, is indexed to the growth of the economy, and is highly efficient compared with all possible private substitutes.

Despite all of the scaremongering, the assaults on workers' pay, and the negative effects of a prolonged and unanticipated slump, the Social Security program faces a relatively small projected seventy-five-year shortfall. It was estimated by the Congressional Budget Office in 2010 at 0.49 percent of GDP. That was increased to 0.80 percent in 2011 because of falling wages, protracted unemployment, slower growth, and revisions in assumptions about longevity. Even so, the projected gap between taxable payroll and Social Security's long-term obligations is better than what it was in 1997. To put these figures in perspective, the total projected shortfall almost exactly equals the cost of the Bush tax cuts of 2001 and 2003 on the wealthiest 2 percent of Americans.

The economic assumptions used to project the gap include a very low rate of long-term GDP growth (just 2.1 percent after 2020) and slow wage growth (which we will surely get if we pursue austerity). Even if it turns out that the projected deficit is real, very small modifications in income or payouts could return the system to surplus. For instance, if we restored the income subject to payroll taxes to its historical level, where 90 percent of all income was taxed (because of widening income disparities, only 83 percent is currently taxed), that alone would make up more than half the gap. If we taxed capital income as well as wage income, that change would produce indefinite surplus.

The fiscal challenges facing Medicare are another story entirely. Medicare will go into deficit within a decade if nothing is done. As critics from all points on the political spectrum have observed, we don't have a budget crisis so much as a medical inflation crisis. Total annual Medicare spending is projected to increase from $523 billion in 2010 to $932 billion by 2020. When you add expected increases in Medicaid costs, nearly all of the projected net increase in the budget deficit are the result of rising health care costs.

Some of these increases reflect an aging population and increased costs of medical technology. However, Medicare's cost inflation is mainly the consequence of the extreme inefficiency of the larger health system of which the program is a part. (Since 2000, Medicare's inflation rate has been lower than that of the private parts of the system.) The fact is that nations with universal health insurance cover everyone for about 9 percent of GDP, while we spend nearly twice that—and leave tens of millions without insurance, even after the Obama reforms.

While all societies have had to deal with an aging population and costly advances in medical technology, ours has uniquely high health care costs and a higher-than-average rate of cost increases mainly because of the commercial domination and fragmentation of our system. That reality, in turn, leads to a seeking of profit centers (which are someone else's cost centers) rather than the most cost-effective use of medical outlays. More than thirty years of private sector solutions, such as the use of HMOs and incentive compensation for physicians, have not been able to alter this dynamic. With the Obama plan reliant mainly on private for-profit insurers, it is not likely that the latest reform proposals will fundamentally bend the cost curve either, except at the expense of care.

Within the federal budget, Medicare bears the brunt of this larger systemic inefficiency. If we do not convert to universal health insurance and make the structural reforms needed to contain health care inflation, Medicare is on a relentless path to reduced benefits. Republicans let the cat out of the bag in 2010, when Paul Ryan, as the ranking Republican on the House Budget Committee, proposed converting Medicare into a voucher program. Ryan stuck to his guns, but after becoming the vice presidential nominee in 2012, he sought to fudge the impact on the existing public program. Under the voucher plan—rebranded "premium support"—people sixty-five and older would get a fixed sum with which to buy whatever private insurance they could afford. People would have to pay several thousand dollars a year out of pocket to get decent coverage. This approach, inevitable in the absence of basic structural reforms to the health system, has huge class implications. The more affluent will be able to supplement bare-bones coverage, while ordinary Americans will not. How to achieve universal coverage, as decent health policy and as a more efficient use of scarce resources, must be the subject of an urgent national debate. But this alternative is simply not addressed by the austerity hawks.

The United States now spends 17 percent of GDP on health care, and nearly 60 percent of that is already contributed by some level of government. (The CBO places the figure at just over 50 percent, but its computations exclude employers' federal, state, and local contributions to the coverage of public employees and their families.) Costs are rising overseas, but more slowly than in the United States. Other advanced nations have healthier populations with longer life spans because they treat health care, including preventive care, as a social good rather than as a commercial product. We already spend about 9 percent of GDP socially in the government-funded parts of our patchwork system, but because of the private domination of our system, we leave some fifty million people without insurance and cover the remaining 85 percent with great inefficiency. If employer premiums to private insurers were shifted to a Medicare-for-all system, we could gain the cost efficiencies of a single-payer system and cover everyone without additional cost to the public. And we could restrain Medicare's inflation rate far more effectively than we would by retaining Medicare as an island of single-payer coverage in a sea of fragmented commercial insurance.

TRANSATLANTIC AUSTERITY

Austerity politics in the United States reflects a witches' brew of Wall Street conservatives who want to reduce social insurance, political moderates who mistakenly believe that deficit reduction will restore business confidence, economic innocents who view belt-tightening as the road to prosperity, far-right conservatives who want to use deficit reduction to further starve government, and Democrats without the confidence to challenge the conventional wisdom. Oddly enough, Europe, despite its quite dissimilar governmental institutions and recent political history, is also in the grip of economically self-defeating austerity fever.

As part 2 of this book suggests, Europe has been wrestling with austerity and its alternatives for a century. The excessive reparations imposed on Germany after World War I helped create a chronic debt crisis all over Europe and ultimately fed into the forces that produced the Great Depression and Hitler. After World War II, the policy of the victors was diametrically opposite. Though even more drastic reparations might have been justified by the far greater damage done by the Nazis, the victorious Allies recognized that an economically healthy Germany was the best protection against a lapse back into fascism. The postwar recovery program included not just Marshall Plan aid but massive debt relief.

Yet today, Europe is embracing austerity even more fervently than is the United States. Dangerously oblivious to the brutal lessons of the past century, the nation most fervently promoting belt-tightening and a policy of no mercy for debtors is Germany. Where austerity in the United States invites merely protracted stagnation, in Europe the austerity consensus risks a deeper depression, the loosing of dark nationalist forces, and the destruction of the sixty-year project of European unification.

PART TWO

Chapter 4

A Tale of Two Wars

WORLD WAR I UPENDED the global financial system and left all of the war-ring European nations with huge debts, both to their own citizens and to each other. France and Britain hoped that they could pay down these debts by squeezing a defeated Germany to collect reparations for war damage. This policy only prevented Germany from recovering and set loose social forces that led to a worse conflict. At least one official of the wartime British government, John Maynard Keynes, thought the policy insane. "If Germany is to be 'milked,'" he wrote in an internal memo of November 1919, "she must not first of all be ruined."

In 1919, Keynes, then thirty-six, was His Majesty's Government's leading expert on wartime finance. The precocious son of a Cambridge don, Keynes had read mathematics at King's College but was soon drawn to economics. Graduating in 1902, he contemplated a civil service post at the Treasury, but he placed second in the highly competitive exam for the position. Ironically, the man who got the job, a graduate of Oxford's Balliol College named Otto Niemeyer, would be Keynes's nemesis in the 1920s and 1930s as one of the Treasury's chief exponents of financial orthodoxy.

Keynes returned to Cambridge as a fellow and in 1907 settled for the consolation prize of a position in the government's India Office. There he became an expert on Indian currency and finances and on money, banking, and financial economics generally. He also became active in literary and journalistic circles, serving as editor of the prestigious *Economic Journal* and publishing in popular outlets such as *The Economist*. He continued commuting from Bloomsbury to Cambridge to teach. By the time the war broke out, he was well known in Cambridge and London as a brilliant student of monetary policy and was soon called to the center of policymaking.

When Britain declared war on August 4, 1914, its financial system was unprepared. Fully half of all world trade was financed in London by short-term bank credits. At the end of July, about $1.5 billion in bills of exchange—loans to finance foreign transactions—had been due and payable at London banks. With the outbreak of war, payments were disrupted. Panicky bankers, in turn, began calling in other loans, creating runs on more banks and brokers, who had to sell stocks to meet collateral demands. Within days, the whole financial system was unwinding. The government, urged on by the big banks, initially responded by keeping money very tight. The Bank of England's lending rate to other banks was briefly raised to a punitive 10 percent. To buy time, the government declared a short bank holiday and a one-month moratorium on payments of bills of exchange.

Keynes was appalled by the government's recourse to tight money, and said so. He was invited by senior government officials to advise the Treasury, and he reported for duty on August 6. Keynes immediately wrote a memo to the chancellor of the exchequer, David Lloyd George, urging that the Bank of England advance funds to banks, using frozen bills of exchange as collateral—in effect guaranteeing all bills of exchange for the duration of the war. He further counseled that conversion of gold to cash be suspended domestically but honored internationally to lubricate payment flows. Keynes's position carried the day. Writing about the episode in *The Economic Journal* that December, Keynes was scathing on the subject of the behavior of the bankers who had needlessly caused a run and on the foolishness of the proposition that official gold stocks should be hoarded to maintain confidence. If that were the function of gold, Keynes wrote, why not just "melt the reserve into a great golden image of the chief cashier and place it on a monument?"

In January 1915, Keynes got his long-sought official post at the Treasury. He was given a relatively junior job, but he soon became a major player. At the recommendation of Montagu Norman, governor of the Bank of England, Keynes—after just a month on the job—was added to the British delegation to a secret conference in Paris on interally war credits. Keynes not only was a brilliant economic theorist but was exemplary at the more humble and often more useful pursuit of collecting and analyzing statistics. In early 1916, he led a team that began pursuing the question of a postwar indemnity payment by Germany.

THE ROAD TO REPARATIONS

Payment of tribute by losers in wars dates to ancient times. In 241 B.C., when Rome defeated Carthage in the First Punic War, the people of Carthage were required to pay the Romans thirty-two hundred talents and to cede the provinces of Sicily and Sardinia. After the Second Punic War, in 202 B.C., Carthage had to pay ten thousand talents—much of it borrowed from the Romans—over a period of fifty years. It is difficult to translate this sum to a share of modern GDP, but the burden was sufficiently crushing to destroy Carthage as a commercial as well as a military power.

In the century before World War I, France had twice been on the losing end of reparations agreements. After the Napoleonic Wars, the French had to pay an indemnity equal to about 15 to 21 percent of GDP, and when France lost the Franco-Prussian War of 1870–71, the victorious Germans extracted not only the industrial provinces of Alsace and Lorraine but also a reparation payment of five billion francs, or about a billion 1870 dollars. This had the precise effect that German chancellor Otto von Bismarck desired: weakening France as an industrial power relative to Germany. So as the Allies savored their impending victory over the Germans in 1918, reparations were on the agenda. In France, there were calls for a Carthaginian peace.

In November 1918, Keynes prepared the first comprehensive assessment of war damage. He pointed out the fallacy of assuming that the Allied claims necessarily matched Germany's capacity to pay. He noted that any reparations must not be so severe as to impair Germany's productive capacity, adding that the country's ability to finance reparations was dependent on its export earnings.

The maximum conceivable claim for actual civilian war damage, Keynes calculated, was $20 billion, far more than Germany could pay. A feasible demand, he wrote, was $10 billion paid out over time, no more than $500 million a year. That sum was approximately 5 percent of German GDP. Keynes had another ingenious and unorthodox idea. The war debt among the Allies, who had made a complex series of loans to each other, should simply be canceled. That would leave the Americans as net creditors, to the tune of some $12 billion. This residual debt could be converted to long-term bonds, to be repaid by the

Germans. All parties would benefit. The European recovery would not be undermined by war debts, the Americans as creditors would be none the worse, and a more productive postwar Germany would be better positioned to pay off the bonds over time.

Following the armistice of November 11, Keynes had reason to be hopeful. America's president, Woodrow Wilson, had persuaded the Allies to accept a generous peace settlement based on the principles of his Fourteen Points. The Germans had agreed to lay down their arms on the basis of a November 5 letter from Wilson providing that Germany would pay indemnities only for civilian war damage, as well as cede lands back to France and to the newly created Polish Republic. The spirit of Wilson's diplomacy was one of peace, disarmament, and reconstruction, not retaliation.

Lloyd George, now prime minister, seemed to share the views of Keynes and Wilson. Punitive reparations were not on his agenda. "We must not allow any sense of revenge, any spirit of greed, any grasping desire to over-rule the fundamental principles of justice," he declared. His coalition war cabinet included leaders of his own Liberal Party, plus those from the Conservative Party and the Labour Party. At the peak of his prestige following the armistice, the prime minister decided to call a snap election. The coalition election manifesto of November 22 declared: "Our first task must be to conclude a just and lasting peace, and so to establish the foundations for a new Europe that occasion for further wars may ever be averted." Keynes later wrote, "I do not believe that, at the date of the Armistice, responsible authorities in the Allied countries expected any indemnity beyond the cost of reparation of direct material damage which had resulted from the invasion of Allied territory and from the submarine campaign."

But the quick election turned out to be a disastrous miscalculation. Revenge was exactly what the British and French citizenry sought. Throughout the short campaign, opponents accused Lloyd George of wanting to "let the Hun off." In the three weeks between the dissolution of Parliament on November 26 and the election of December 16, British public opinion hardened, and with it the hopes of a generous, durable peace.

On November 26, Lloyd George appointed an official committee to determine how much Germany should pay. In deference to hardening public sentiment, he named two extreme hawks to the three-man committee: Lord Cunliffe, former governor of the Bank of England, and William Morris Hughes, the Australian prime minister who had been serving in Lloyd George's war cabinet as a representative of the colonies. Another member of Lloyd George's war cabinet, Sir Eric Geddes, campaigning in Cambridge on December 9, declared, "The Germans, if this Government is returned, are going to pay every penny; they are going to be squeezed as a lemon is squeezed—until the pips squeak." The phrase delighted the London tabloids and soon became a jingoist rallying cry.

Following an election defeat from which the Liberal Party never recovered, Lloyd George stayed on for three more years as coalition prime minister. But a large majority in the House of Commons now belonged to the ferociously anti-German Tory Party. As Keynes archly wrote, "Shortly after their arrival at Westminster, I asked a Conservative friend, who had known previous Houses, what he thought of them. 'They are a lot of hard-faced men,' he said, 'who look as if they had done very well out of the war.'"

In December 1918, public opinion in France and Britain decisively shifted to the fantasy that squeezing Germany could accomplish, in a stroke, two goals: compensating the Allies for the horrific costs of the war and so weakening the Germans that they would never again make war. With our knowledge of Hitler's rise and of the enlightened policies following World War II, it seems preposterous that French and British leaders of 1918 and 1919 could have held such self-defeating views. Given that today's economic questions are not complicated by national demands for vengeance, future historians may look back at early twenty-first-century austerity politics with the same bewilderment.

A SCENE OF NIGHTMARE

In January 1919, on the eve of the Paris Peace Conference, the Hughes Committee recommended German reparations of $120 billion. It was an absurd number. German annual GDP just before the war had been about $12 billion. While Lloyd George sidestepped the recommendation, he did name Hughes and Cunliffe to serve as senior British representatives to the reparations commission at Versailles, along with a third hard-liner, Lord Sumner.

As the national delegations gathered, their French hosts were even more determined than the British to exact disabling retribution. Prime Minister Georges Clemenceau persuaded the other leaders to treat Germany as if it had unconditionally surrendered. One of the first decisions of the Allies was to constitute a committee of four as the peace conference directorate: Clemenceau, Lloyd George, Wilson, and the Italian prime minister Vittorio Emanuele Orlando. The Germans were pointedly excluded from discussions of their fate.

Early in the deliberations, the Inter-Ally Supreme Council for Supply and Relief, chaired by Herbert Hoover, proposed supplying 270,000 tons of food to starving German civilians if the Germans ceded their merchant marine to the Allies. The French finance minister, Louis-Lucien Klotz, resisted even this act of mercy, contending that anything of value given up by the Germans should first be used for reparations. The Germans, understandably, were unwilling to transfer the ships. Negotiations deadlocked. The American delegation wanted a reparations settlement in the range of $10 billion to $20 billion. But the Americans were outmaneuvered by Clemenceau and the British hard-liners. Lords Cunliffe and Sumner, known as the Heavenly Twins, refused to go below $55 billion. In late March, the Allies resolved to buck the reparations question to a committee, with instructions to report back by 1921, so that the rest of the peace process could go forward.

When the text of the Treaty of Versailles was finally made public in May 1919, the reaction throughout Germany was shocked outrage. Germany was to lose more than 12 percent of its territory, as well as all of its colonies. An independent Poland was in part carved from its eastern lands. Alsace and Lorraine, ceded in the Franco-Prussian War, reverted to France, along with the Saarland's coal mines. The French were to take over the Ruhr's coal production for fifteen years. None of these losses, valued well into the tens of billions of dollars, were to be credited to reparations payments. The Rhineland was to be permanently occupied, and the German army limited to a hundred thousand troops. The German navy was abolished, and most of the merchant marine transferred to the Allies. Five thousand locomotives and 150,000 railway cars were to be surrendered. Germany was expected to make a down payment on reparations by May 1921 of $5 billion, a sum equal to about half of one year's GDP. There was no postwar recovery program for Germany itself. Despite broad public opposition, and with the

German army demobilized, the new government fragile, and the civilian population experiencing starvation and disease, the German representatives had little alternative but to sign the treaty on June 28.

Somehow, amid the human misery compounded by Allied reparation demands, a fragile democracy had emerged. The kaiser had fled and revolution had broken out all over Germany in early November. In February 1919, as the Allies were dictating the defeated nation's economic fate, German democrats were gathering in Weimar to create a parliamentary republic. As Berlin's financial delegation wrote in its bitter response to the draft treaty: "German democracy is thus annihilated at the very moment when the German people was about to build it up after severe struggle—annihilated by the very people who throughout the war never tired of maintaining that they sought to bring democracy to us."

Keynes was already gone. He had witnessed the deliberations first-hand and had tried and failed to alter the disaster in the making. In his short letter of resignation to Lloyd George, dated June 5, he wrote:

Dear Prime Minister,
I ought to let you know that on Saturday I am slipping away from the scene of nightmare. I can do no more good here. I've gone on hoping even through these last dreadful weeks that you'd find some way to make of the Treaty a just and expedient document. But it's apparently too late. The battle is lost. I leave the twins to gloat over the devastation of Europe, and to assess to taste what remains for the British taxpayer.
Sincerely,
J. M. Keynes

Departing for Cambridge, Keynes turned his well-documented indignation into the book that made him a celebrity intellectual, *The Economic Consequences of the Peace,* published in November 1919. It displayed both his statistical and his analytic genius, as well as his humanity and deep foreboding about what was to come.

Of the French prime minister's wish to restore the balance of economic and political power between Germany and France to what it was in 1870, Keynes wrote that apart from the issue of whether such a goal was desirable, the "Carthaginian Peace is not *practically* right or possible." Writing as if he were addressing Clemenceau personally, Keynes warned, "You cannot restore Central Europe to 1870 without setting up such strains in the European structure and letting loose such human and spiritual forces as, pushing beyond frontiers and races, will overwhelm not only you and your 'guarantees,' but your institutions, and the existing order of your Society."

If he viewed Clemenceau as cynical and perverse, Keynes considered Wilson merely ineffectual. The American president had more cards than any other leader at Versailles, but he was thoroughly outplayed. Though he admired Wilson's magnanimity and intellect, Keynes wrote, "There can seldom have been a statesman of the first rank more incompetent than the President in the agilities of the council chamber."

Keynes considered the French dangerously delusional. In a laborious tally of war damages, he calculated that the French claims of $26.8 billion were at least six times actual damages. For the fiscal year that began in June 1919, Keynes noted, the French budget was about $4.4 billion (or twenty-two billion francs). French tax revenues were only half that amount. To make up the rest, the French had either to rely on the printing press or to indulge preposterous fantasies about the magical intercession of reparations payments from Germany. Keynes reported on the September 5, 1919, speech that Klotz gave to the Chamber of Deputies, explaining that the Germans would pay thirty-four annual installments of about $5 billion each, of which France would receive about $2.75 billion a year, slightly more than sufficient to fill the hole in the French budget. That payment, however, would amount to nearly half the total German output, an inconceivable sum. Keynes acidly commented: "So long as such statements can be accepted in Paris without protest, there can be no financial or economic future for France, and a catastrophe of disillusion is not far distant."

Keynes's central point was that Europe, reeling from the financial and physical ruin of war, above all needed a recovery of its economy. The prewar European economy was integrated and highly interdependent, with nations heavily reliant on their trading partners for both imports and exports. There was a dense web of financial flows from capital-surplus nations such as Britain and Germany to countries in eastern and southern Europe that imported capital. The war—Keynes aptly termed it the European civil war—disrupted all of this. Before the war, he noted, "Germany was the best customer of Russia, Norway, Holland, Belgium, Switzerland, Italy, and Austria-Hungary; she was the second best customer of Great Britain, Sweden, and Denmark; and the third best customer of France." Germany, with only a modest trade surplus, was also a leading exporter to these same nations, as well as a prime source of their investment capital. So a hobbled Germany would hobble her trading partners.

Keynes tallied up all the possible sources of reparations that could conceivably be paid by May 1921 and came up with $1.25 billion to $1.75 billion. Once again, he was right on the money. In the event, Germany paid $2 billion, at severe cost to its own recovery.

Noting that the German mark had fallen to a seventh of its prewar value and was destined to fall further, Keynes warned, "Business loses its genuine character and becomes no better than a speculation in the exchanges, the fluctuations in which entirely obliterate the normal profits of commerce." He would later make precisely the same point in his *General Theory of Employment, Interest, and Money:* "Speculators may do no harm as bubbles on a steady stream of enterprise. But the position is serious when enterprise becomes the bubble on a whirlpool of speculation."

Though it would be seventeen years until Keynes would write that masterwork, and a quarter century before he offered his design for the post–World War II reconstruction, the clarity of his thinking on debt relief and economic revival, and on the relationships between speculation and enterprise and between the claims of the financial economy and the revival of the real one, was already evident in his farsighted work on German reparations in 1918 and 1919.

At bottom, his message was that Europe needed recovery, not retribution. In some circumstances, cancellation of old debts is a far sounder policy than coerced payment. The gold standard is a millstone, and efforts to maintain unrealistically high currency values lead to mutually disabling contests to needlessly raise interest rates and hence capital costs. Currency instability rewards only speculators. These policies help the rentier class, at grave expense to the rest of society and to the productive potential of the real economy. Germany was now a fledgling democracy. What sense did it make to punish the German people for a war prosecuted by a regime that no longer existed? "The policy of reducing Germany to servitude for a generation," Keynes argued, "of degrading the lives of millions of human beings, and of depriving a whole nation of happiness should be abhorrent and detestable,— abhorrent and detestable, even if it were possible, even if it enriched ourselves, even if it did not sow the decay of the whole civilized life of Europe."

THE DEBT OBSESSION

In April 1921, the reparations commission belatedly set a final figure of $33 billion. With Germany reeling from postwar economic distress and dislocation, it was already clear that this amount was wildly unrealistic, and the Germans resisted accepting it. The sum was reduced to $12.5 billion, with annual payments in the range of $600 million to $800 million, not far off what Keynes had proposed in 1918. But in the meantime, more than two years had been wasted and immense damage had compounded.

Combined with the reparations burden, the havoc wreaked on its export capacity meant that Germany could not earn the foreign exchange needed to pay for vital imports. The complete absence of recovery aid ensured that Germany's economy would stay in ruins, seeding the hyperinflation that followed and demolishing what was left of the savings of Germany's middle class.

Adding to the impending political catastrophe was the fact that key diplomats on the receiving end of the Allies' humiliating *diktat* were Jews. A senior member of the German financial delegation, Carl Melchior of the banking firm M. M. Warburg, was Jewish, as was Walther Rathenau, foreign minister of the new Weimar Republic. In May 1921, it fell to Rathenau to accept the much-reduced reparations terms on behalf of his government. A year later, he was assassinated by a right-wing proto-Nazi gang. Kurt Eisner, the Jewish social democrat who led the revolution that overthrew the monarchy in Bavaria and established a republican government in November 1918, was also murdered. Hugo Preuss, principal architect of the constitution of the Weimar Republic and later its interior minister, was a Jew; so was the first Weimar minister of justice, Otto Landsberg. The involvement of prominent Jews in these humiliating negotiations and in the weak regime they produced would feed the "stab in the back" story of the Nazis.

Following Rathenau's murder in 1922, financial panic gripped Germany, driving the mark from 190 to 7,600 to the dollar. In early 1923, when Germany was late on a scheduled reparations payment, French and Belgian troops invaded its industrial belt in the Ruhr Valley, as permitted by treaty. Local workers went on strike, and the German government encouraged a strategy of passive resistance to the occupation, paying workers unemployment benefits. The Ruhr crisis worsened government finances. The deficit doubled, and officials turned to the printing press. By August 1923, a dollar was worth 630 billion marks.

Some latter-day historians have contended that the reparations ordered at Versailles were wrongfully blamed for Weimar Germany's economic ruin. They make two arguments: that the actual reparations were much reduced from those initially decreed and that one can't quite draw a linear connection between the reparations demands of 1919 and 1920 and the German hyperinflation of 1923. But in fact, the obsessions throughout the early 1920s with reparation payments, debt obligations, and gold parities were all of a piece and crowded out the more urgent business of creating the conditions for a durable recovery of Germany and of Europe. As an extensive study by the Yale economist Timothy W. Guinnane concluded:

> The damage to Germany came as much from uncertainty about reparations as from any payments burden. Business investment requires a stable, predictable environment. In the absence of a fixed plan for dealing with the reparations matter, investors, both German and foreign, had to worry that the government would increase taxes to meet the obligation, or that Allied countries would simply confiscate German assets.

Given that the Weimar government was both fragile and democratically elected, it is impossible to imagine it responding to the dire circumstances of the early 1920s by raising additional taxes or further cutting back public spending. Foreign lending—a much less durable or reliable form of investment—tended to be speculative. The recourse to the printing press was all that the government had left. The extent of monetary excess and the hyperinflation that followed were perhaps not inevitable, but both were logical consequences of the punitive policies of Versailles.

The financial politics of the 1920s were an extension of Versailles into peacetime. As the economic historian Liaquat Ahamed observed, "The really pernicious effect of war debts was that they made it hard, if not impossible, for Britain to forgo collecting its own debts from France and Germany, made France all the more obstinate in its efforts to collect reparations from Germany, and led Europe into a self-defeating vicious cycle of financial claims and counterclaims." Fiscal conservatism and a debt collector mentality trumped the urgent need to promote a durable recovery.

AUSTERITY AT HOME

In Britain, the government, the financial elite, and the Bank of England did exactly what Keynes had warned against: they tried to turn back the clock. Specifically, they sought to restore Britain's preeminence as a financial capital by restoring the prewar value of the pound. But the weakened state of Britain's real economy made this a fool's errand. An overvalued pound meant keeping interest rates artificially high to attract money to London, which in turn raised capital costs to British industry and dampened the recovery. Unemployment remained in excess of 10 percent for the entire interwar period.

As the economic historian Charles Kindleberger later observed, Britain had played the role of monetary hegemon during the several decades before World War I, enforcing a system of fixed exchange rates anchored to the (needlessly deflationary) gold standard, keeping its markets open to imports, freely exporting capital, and serving as a lender of last resort. After World War II, the United States inherited that role. But in the interwar period, Britain was too weakened to play monetary hegemon except at grave cost to its own economy, while the United States had the capacity but not yet the desire. And so the interwar period was marked by chaotic monetary instability, deflationary fiscal policies, backward-looking extraction of debt payments, and speculative excess. It did not end well.

Germany lurched from crisis to crisis. A currency reform managed to stabilize the mark. In 1924, an international conference in London seemed to have solved the reparations problem. An American delegation, chaired by the Chicago banker and former budget director Charles Dawes, who had been a brigadier general in the war, proposed a foreign loan to recapitalize the German central bank and a gentler annual reparations schedule. Money to pay reparations was to be kept in a segregated account at the central bank. The bank, in turn, reported to a supervisory committee, half of whose members were foreigners. In principle, with Germany's internal debt having been deflated away, a larger portion of tax revenues could now go to pay reparations. The foreign loan—the first to Germany since the war—would jump-start the process. With the reparations problem solved, the French would at last leave the Ruhr. When the conference finally approved the plan, the total amount of reparations due was discreetly left ambiguous, but the annual payment schedule appeared to have reduced it from $12.5 billion to under $10 billion.

The plan was not far off what Keynes had proposed in 1918. But more than five precious years had been squandered, during which the European economy sank deeper into deflation, monetary instability, and speculation. The Dawes Plan was barely sufficient to salvage the appearance of national honor, but not the health of the European economy.

The use of new foreign loans prefigured the policies inflicted by the International Monetary Fund and the creditor nations on Third World countries in the 1980s and 1990s and those imposed by the European Union on Greece in the current economic crisis. The new loans merely financed interest on old debts. They did not underwrite the economic growth that these nations needed to escape the cycle of penury. There was a great circular system in which America lent Germany money to pay reparations to the Allies, which in turn made payments on their war debt back to America.

From 1924 to 1929, Germany paid out about 8.5 billion marks, or about $2 billion, in reparations. But during the same period, Germany borrowed more than $3 billion from the capital markets of the United States. Yet another conference (in 1929, chaired by the American businessman Owen Young) produced the Young Plan, which provided yet another loan (of $1.4 billion), moderated the reparations schedule still further, and stretched out payments until 1988, cutting the total German debt to less than what Keynes had proposed at Versailles. But by now, an economically vulnerable Germany was still heavily reliant on short-term speculative borrowing, mainly from the United States. When the crash of 1929 hit America, it doomed Germany. In 1932, debt payments to the United States were suspended by Britain, France, and Germany and then repudiated by Hitler. The emphasis on debt collection as a road to prosperity and peace produced neither.

A SECOND CHANCE

In 1944, Keynes, sixty-one and newly elevated to the peerage as Baron Keynes of Tilton, found himself in precisely the same role he had played at Versailles a quarter century earlier: senior adviser to the British Treasury on war finance and the postwar system. But a great deal had changed since 1919. Keynes was now perhaps the world's most celebrated economist. Far from a voice in the wilderness, he had the grim satisfaction of having seen events vindicate his views. The Carthaginian peace, just as he had feared, had sown the seeds of a second European civil war. The laissez-faire system that Keynes had warned against had produced the greatest collapse in the history of modern capitalism. Keynes recognized that dealing with the indebtedness of the warring countries was essential to economic recovery, prosperity, and the prevention of yet another war.

This time, Keynes was in a unique position to influence events, both as diplomat and as prophet, though in the end the force of his argument mattered less than the fortuitous circumstances. Depression, war, and the incipient Cold War had generated a harmonic convergence of political and economic forces that emphatically rejected laissez-faire. The Roosevelt administration (of which more in chapter 10) had harnessed finance in service of the real economy. Well before Keynes's *General Theory*, Roosevelt had turned to a homegrown form of Keynesian demand stimulus: public works spending. He had taken the United States off the gold standard so that his recovery program would not be constrained by foreign deflation.

The New Deal deficits of around 5 to 6 percent of GDP had been sufficient to restore positive growth rates but not to reduce unemployment much below 12 percent. The far greater deficit spending of the war quickly reduced the effective unemployment rate to zero. In looking forward to the postwar era, the Roosevelt administration emphatically embraced economic planning. The financial and corporate elites had been disgraced by the Great Depression. A trade union movement promoted by government policy served as a further counterweight to organized finance. The success of government—first in surmounting the Great Depression and then in winning the war—left the state with an unusual degree of prestige in what was still a fairly libertarian country.

In Britain, the wartime coalition government led by Winston

Churchill, who at various points in his career had been a Liberal and a Conservative, also looked forward to a much-expanded welfare state. Two reports commissioned by the war cabinet and published in 1942 and 1944 by Lord Beveridge, a Liberal, laid the groundwork for a postwar society of expanded social services and full employment. With the election of a Labour government in 1945, the commitment to a managed form of capitalism and a welfare state became that much more explicit and far-reaching. This was all the more remarkable given that World War II had been an even greater strain on Britain than World War I. The country, as noted, had ended the war with a national debt of around 260 percent of GDP, more than double the record debt levels of the United States. Had the austerity mentality prevailed, Britain would have sentenced itself to devastating economic contraction.

Meanwhile, as European nations that had been occupied by the Nazis restored democratic government, their leaders were typically Christian Democrats and Social Democrats eager to define a managed form of capitalism and a Pan-European politics of reconciliation rather than retribution. An exception was France, which took longer than other Continental nations to abandon the hopes of sizable reparations and a permanently occupied Germany.

Even more than in America, private finance in Europe had been severely weakened as a political force. In occupied nations, much of the business elite and the political right were discredited as collaborators with the Nazis. Whereas European postwar governments in 1919 were the same ones that had led the war effort, the European democratic governments that took office in 1945 and 1946 represented a substantially clean break. In drastic contrast to their dealings with the United States in the 1920s, Europe's leaders now had in Washington a partner fully engaged with the world. Though there were still isolationist tendencies, especially among Republicans, they were soon dispatched by the threat of communism.

There was thus a rare constellation of several forces: a much-weakened private financial elite and rentier class, a domestic politics on both sides of the Atlantic that supported a managed form of capitalism, and a statesmanlike commitment to reconciliation and common reconstruction. Given all this, one would like to report that enlightened self-interest and collective learning from the mistakes of 1919 carried the day. But mostly that was not so.

What finally shifted elite opinion away from reparations and toward Pan-European reconstruction with Germany at the core was the Cold War.

RECONSTRUCTION VERSUS RETRIBUTION

As statesmen gathered in a chain of diplomatic conferences in 1944 and 1945, the interrelated issues included the terms for continuing U.S. financial support to an exhausted and indebted Britain, the plans for the reconstruction of Continental Europe, the role of Germany in that reconstruction, and the architecture of the postwar global financial system. Nazi Germany had been a far more brutal regime than the much-detested semidemocratic Germany of Kaiser Wilhelm. Inevitably, many were inclined to repeat the errors of Versailles.

The U.S. Treasury secretary, Henry Morgenthau Jr., promoted a "pastoralized" Germany stripped of industry. Morgenthau hoped to enlist British support for the idea, since Britain stood to inherit some of Germany's prewar export trade. At the Quebec Conference of September 1944, which addressed mainly bilateral financial issues between Britain and the United States, he personally pitched his plan to Roosevelt and Churchill. Since much of the conference was about the postwar extension of Lend-Lease aid to Britain—an issue whose dominant policymaker was Morgenthau—there was the tacit implication of a quid pro quo. Churchill was initially supportive.

But the State Department and the British Foreign Office resisted, and the decision would later be reversed. With the Russians occupying Eastern Europe and poised to fill the vacuum of an enfeebled Germany, Roosevelt began backpedaling from the Morgenthau Plan as early as October. Churchill, satisfied that there was no real link between the pastoralization plan and Lend-Lease, also demurred.

Yet large reparations remained official policy. At the Yalta meeting of February 1945, Stalin pressed for $20 billion from Germany in the form of goods, forced labor, and industrial plants and machinery. The Allies agreed that the Soviets could use German POWs to repair Soviet war damage. By 1947, some four million German POWs and civilians had functioned as Soviet slave labor. Though the issue of other reparations was officially deferred, Russian commanders on the ground began shipping German industrial machinery east. On April 26, 1945, two weeks after Roosevelt's death, Directive 1067 of the Joint Chiefs of Staff declared that Germany "will not be occupied for purposes of liberation, but as a defeated enemy nation." The directive, influenced by the views of Morgenthau, explicitly prohibited military administrators from doing anything "to maintain or strengthen the German economy."

At the Potsdam Conference of July 1945, the Allies agreed to a deliberate policy of scaling back German industrial production. The transfer of German industrial plant and machinery was to generate the equivalent of $23 billion in reparations. The provisional division of Germany into four occupation zones was formalized, and the occupying powers were authorized to remove industrial plants and equipment as a down payment on reparations.

France, hoping to displace Germany as the Continent's leading industrial power, called for a permanent occupation and a severing of the German industrial heartland. It proposed turning the Ruhr into a freestanding neutral state governed by an authority made up of British, French, Belgian, and Dutch representatives, with its independence guaranteed by the United States and the Soviet Union. This idea was supported by the Russians.

Keynes offered the same argument he had in 1918 and 1919. Without industry, Germany could not produce the export earnings needed to feed its people. The Allies and their taxpayers, as occupying powers, had already assumed responsibility for preventing mass starvation. Britain was still rationing bread while spending $80 million a year on occupation expenses and contributing to food relief for Germany. "It seems monstrous," Keynes declared, "that we should first de-industrialize and thus bankrupt the Ruhr to please Russia and then hand over the territory, or at least the industries, to an international body to please France, but that we alone should be responsible for feeding the place." He added that such a policy "might rank as the craziest ever—if one did not remember the last time."

In March 1946, carrying out the terms of the Potsdam Agreement, the Allied Control Council in occupied Germany began issuing "Level of Industry" directives, which required German industrial production to be reduced to 50 to 55 percent of its 1938 level. A report to the commander of the American zone, General Lucius Clay, proposed that German military and other heavy industries be destroyed completely, while chemicals, autos, machine tools, electric power, and steel be controlled and limited, and that German living standards be deliberately reduced to 74 percent of their 1930–38 average. In addition to its industrial machinery, Germany's foreign assets and intellectual property were also confiscated, including patents, licenses, proprietary engineering techniques, and contracts. According to the historian John Gimbel, the "intellectual reparations" of German science and technology appropriated by the United States and Britain totaled close to $10 billion. The Soviets, meanwhile, had removed from their zone entire factories estimated at a quarter of East Germany's manufacturing capacity at the time, as well as every rail car they could commandeer.

All of these punitive policies operated against a background of a German economy in which one person in eight was dead, one housing unit in five was destroyed, and production was barely a third of its prewar level. In June 1945, the official daily ration of food in the American occupation zone was set at 860 calories, less than half of normal consumption.

But by 1947, the Allied view of reparations and industrial dismantling had drastically changed. There were three proximate causes: the bitter winter of 1946–47, which followed a poor harvest and created extensive hardship; the extreme reliance of Western Europe on U.S. exports, which created a dollar shortage and a widening trade gap; and, above all, the increasing tensions between the West and the Soviet Union.

STUMBLING TOWARD THE HIGH ROAD

As early as September 1946, Secretary of State James Byrnes gave a speech in Stuttgart urging the reconstruction rather than the dismantling of German industry. The speech was written by John Kenneth Galbraith, an emergent American Keynesian, who was heading an office at the State Department dealing with the German economy. On June 5, 1947, Byrnes's successor, General George C. Marshall, delivered his famous speech at Harvard calling for a European recovery program, soon to be known as the Marshall Plan. It provided $13 billion over four years and led to the promotion of European economic integration. Joint Chiefs of Staff Directive 1067 was scrapped in favor of Directive 1779, which declared that "an orderly and prosperous Europe requires the economic contributions of a stable and productive Germany." The announcement of the Marshall Plan was followed by a much-delayed currency reform.

For three years, from 1945 to 1948, the circulating currency of Germany was in limbo. The Third Reich was defunct and denazified—but, weirdly, its money lived on, coexisting with Allied occupation marks. The practical value of the Nazi-era reichsmark fluctuated, but it was not totally worthless. In Hamburg in 1948, an egg sold for eight reichsmarks, about a day's pay. In much of Germany, barter filled the vacuum, and cigarettes functioned as de facto currency. A carton of American cigarettes fetched the equivalent of $50 to $150. The cigarettes were exchanged for other goods. In Stuttgart, a bicycle cost six hundred cigarettes. Many American GIs made more money selling cigarettes on the black market than from their official pay. In these circumstances, it is astonishing that the German economy functioned at all.

With the onset of the Cold War, Germany hardened into separate occupation zones. No agreement on currency (or much else) was possible. The United States and Britain combined their zones in 1947. Finally, after several delays, currency reform was at last carried out in the Western zones over the weekend of June 18–20, 1948. About 10.7 billion marks in the new currency had been quietly printed in the United States and were shipped all over western Germany in some twenty-three thousand crates labeled doorknobs. The value was pegged at thirty U.S. cents. Ration offices were used to distribute the bills. Reichsmarks were withdrawn from circulation; a limited number were permitted to be converted to the new currency, the deutsche mark, at the generous ratio of 10 to 1. All Germans were immediately given forty deutsche marks as pocket money. Within days, hoarding largely ceased and commodities that had been available only on the black market began appearing in the shops.

The most remarkable aspect of the currency reform was the outright cancellation of about 93 percent of the Nazi-era debt. Between 1938 and 1944, the German debt rose from 40 billion to 357 billion marks, and money circulation increased from 10.4 billion to 73 billion marks. Hitler ran up a public debt equal to 675 percent of one year's GDP, the modern record for any industrialized nation. In a stroke, most of those debts were simply erased, including the debts of the post office and the state railway system. Had there been no offsetting policies, the commercial banking system would have been destroyed, because much of its capital (in reichsmark securities) would have been wiped out. So reichsmark bonds held by banks were converted to deutsche mark bonds bearing a 3 percent interest rate. The hole in the reserves of commercial banks was made up by grants from the provisional state (*Länder*) central banks that had been created by the Allies, which later were merged into the Bundesbank.

Under the Marshall Plan, other financial claims from the Nazi era were strictly segregated from development aid and from current tax receipts. A bondholder or other creditor from the Hitler period could not go after the assets of the new West German government, and the issue of the Weimar debt was put off, to be resolved at an international conference. As a consequence, reconstruction could move forward without being hobbled by reparations demands or by debt left over from either world war.

Thanks to the write-off of the Third Reich's debt, as the German postwar economic miracle took off, the country's debt-to-GDP ratio in 1950 was under 10 percent, far less than that of the United States or Britain. With memories of the hyperinflation of 1923 still vivid, savings in reichsmarks had been wiped out for the second time in a generation. Universities suffered, as did pension and health plans and other institutions reliant on endowments. These would have to be rebuilt from scratch. But with a highly productive economy, they could be—and soon were. In the 1950s, the West German growth rate averaged 8 percent a year, the most rapid in Europe. Savings rebounded. Unemployment declined to 1 percent, and West Germany began importing workers.

The Marshall Plan, the currency reform, and the miraculous recovery that followed transformed European politics. American aid encouraged a collaborative planning process, whose vehicle was the Organization for European Economic Cooperation. This in turn set in motion the psychology and institutional politics that led to the creation of the European Economic Community in 1957 and the European Union in 1993. It gave the European statesmen of that era a much nobler project than the punishment, containment, or deindustrialization of Germany. Rather, the goal became the anchoring of a democratic Germany in a larger European whole.

As the economic historian Barry Eichengreen has observed:

European integration was a way of reconciling France and other European countries to higher levels of German industrial production and of disarming those, including influential voices in the U.S. government, who insisted on pastoralizing the German economy. By locking Germany into Europe and promoting the development of institutions of shared governance, the Marshall Plan encouraged Paris to agree to the elimination of ceilings on German production. By substituting American aid, it enabled the French and other victors to drop their claim to German reparations.

Eichengreen goes on to observe that the improved atmosphere further compelled the French both to give up their demands for internationalization of the Ruhr and Rhineland, and to accept a fused western zone. This in turn accelerated the end of the occupation and the creation of the German Federal Republic.

DEBT RELIEF AND THE GERMAN MIRACLE

In 1952, after extensive preparation by expert working groups, a conference was convened in London to deal with the question of the pre-Nazi German debt. The Depression had made it impossible for the Weimar government to pay even the reduced international debts, and Hitler had suspended World War I reparations and other obligations unilaterally. Though Europe was now in an entirely new phase of history, that interwar debt was nonetheless treated as a solemn obligation of the new German state, the legal successor to Weimar Germany.

Yet the political and economic objectives of the Allies in 1952 were drastically different from those of the 1920s. The goal was to welcome Germany as a reliable ally and commercial partner, resist the Communist East, and thus limit Germany's debt obligations to something affordable. By now, the provisional occupation had given way to the division of Germany into a federal republic in the west and a Soviet satellite regime in the east.

The issues were exceedingly complex. Not only had the Weimar government incurred extensive foreign debts, but so had German cities and states. Some of these states, including Prussia, no longer existed. Parts of Nazi Germany had been absorbed into Poland and East Germany, which were not party to the negotiations. Hundreds of public and private creditors from twenty-six countries participated directly in the London meetings, which extended over nearly two years. There was also the separate question of indemnities to surviving victims of the Holocaust.

The conference resolved that nearly all of the debt of the Third Reich should be written off. A separate reparation of $1.5 billion was to be made to the State of Israel and to an ad hoc committee to pay claims of Holocaust survivors. The West German chancellor, Konrad Adenauer, eager to normalize his country's role in the world economy, accepted responsibility for the Weimar debts. The Allies agreed to reduce the amount of the debts and to extend the period Germany had to pay them off. Deferred interest was postponed until German reunification, an astute way of recognizing both that West Germany could not be expected to pay the entire debt incurred by what had previously been a much larger country and that reunification was a goal supported by all parties to the talks. In 1990, following unification, a new set of bonds was issued to pay off the remaining debt. Newspaper readers in 2010 were bemused to learn that the German government had retired the last of the Weimar debt, from nearly a century before!

The contrast with the Allied policies after World War I could not have been greater. In the 1920s, reparations functioned as a weight on German recovery—right up until Hitler revived the German economy by repudiating the debt and rearming. Except for intermittent humanitarian relief, there never was an Allied plan for German recovery, much less for reintegration of the larger European economy. Consequently, the weakness of Germany weakened its neighbors. This time—thanks to a farsighted response to the common threat of Stalin—reparation gave way to recovery, and debt collection yielded to debt forgiveness.

What of the rest of Europe? In France, much of the debt was inflated away as the franc quickly plummeted from 119 to the dollar in 1945 to 350 to the dollar in 1949. The debt ratio, mostly to its own citizens, declined from over 200 percent of GDP on the eve of World War II to under 30 percent by the early 1950s. By 1959, the franc was worth just 2.5 percent of its 1934 value. In Italy, the public debt peaked at around 120 percent of GDP, but thanks to massive inflation in 1945 and 1946, the new Italian Republic in 1947 inherited a debt of about 30 percent of GDP. Inflation may not be the most desirable form of debt relief, but in the postwar era it coexisted with an unprecedented economic boom. The creditor class had a large part of the value of its capital wiped out; nonetheless, it gained from a rapidly growing economy, and with a high savings rate the capital stock was rapidly rebuilt. We will return to the salutary role of moderate inflation in chapter 10.

INDEBTED BRITAIN: THE WINNER'S CURSE

Curiously, when it came to debt relief, America's closest ally was treated rather more harshly in the immediate postwar era than either the defeated Germans or the Continental nations formerly occupied by the Nazis. In 1945, Britain was plainly exhausted from the war effort. About $35 billion, or a quarter of its total national wealth, had been lost in the war. Even in its somewhat depleted circumstances after World War I and the Great Depression, Britain had remained one of the world's great creditor nations, with far-flung investments in its empire and elsewhere. To finance the war, it both liquidated foreign investments, to the tune of about $6 billion, and borrowed roughly another $14 billion. In addition, Britain suffered direct war losses of at least $10 billion.

After Continental Europe was overrun in June 1940 and before the entry of the United States into the war in December 1941, the British had almost single-handedly held off the Nazis on the western front. The Soviets entered the war against Germany only in June 1941, when the Nazis breached the Hitler-Stalin pact of 1939 by invading the USSR. Beginning in 1940, well before the United States entered the war, Britain was helped immensely by Roosevelt's shrewd way of getting aid to the British by "lending" destroyers and other war materiel in exchange for long-term "leases" on British bases. Initially an executive action in December 1940 based on Roosevelt's powers as commander in chief, Lend-Lease was formalized in legislation passed by Congress in February 1941. During the war, Britain eventually received almost $27 billion in Lend-Lease military supplies from the United States, in what Winston Churchill characterized as "the most unsordid act in history."

In late 1944, with the war winding down, the British desperately needed an extension of Lend-Lease aid. Britain faced a crushing balance-of-payments deficit, which would entail further debt and a precipitous fall in the already reduced standard of living. The view from London was that Britain had held off Hitler until America was ready to enter the war, that Britain had suffered disproportionately, and that there needed to be "equality of sacrifice." In practice, that meant a write-off of the nominal Lend-Lease debt and an extension of aid into the postwar era of recovery. There were signs that Washington agreed. In September 1943, transmitting a report on Lend-Lease to Congress, Roosevelt had grandly declared that "the United States wants no new war debts to jeopardize the coming peace. Victory and a secure peace are the only coin in which we can be repaid."

However, an increasing number of influential Americans didn't share that magnanimous view. Senator Harry Truman, chairman of the War Investigating Committee, considered Lend-Lease a giveaway. He declared in 1943 that at war's end the United States should receive raw materials as partial repayment. In 1944 and 1945, Congress amended the Lend-Lease Act to drastically limit Roosevelt's ability to extend aid beyond the conclusion of hostilities. Despite the war's tonic effect on the economy, the immense wartime deficits, the rationing, and the loss of life led to a national mood that did not want prolongation for a moment longer than necessary.

As close as Roosevelt and Churchill had been during the war, they found that their national interests diverged in peacetime. U.S. officials, committed to postwar restoration of free trade, demanded that Britain end preferential treatment of imports from the British Commonwealth ("imperial preference"). Britain, wanting to reclaim its role as a great power, desperately needed to retain that perquisite of membership in its former empire. The Americans wanted the British to wind down its "sterling area" and to restore full convertibility of the British pound as soon as possible; the British rightly feared that premature elimination of exchange controls would lead to a run on the pound, a depletion of what remained of British gold holdings, and a forced devaluation.

By mid-1945, Roosevelt and Churchill had been succeeded by Harry Truman and Clement Attlee, men who had no personal relationship forged in wartime. In August, once Japan announced its intention to surrender, Truman abruptly ended Lend-Lease, shocking the British, who had hoped that it might somehow be extended into a "Stage Two" of postwar aid. In these circumstances, Keynes arrived in Washington on September 11, in seriously failing health, as head of a British delegation hoping to negotiate either a grant-in-aid or a zero-interest loan in the amount of $6 billion. In his charming manner, he told the Americans that Britain would prefer to join a postwar multilateral system as early as possible, but that absent additional aid, this would be impossible. His American hosts replied that any aid was out of the question unless Britain firmly committed to multilateralism. In the end, Truman agreed to $3.75 billion—as a loan, not a grant. The loan was also conditioned on an early return to convertibility (allowing pounds to be freely exchanged for dollars), which provoked just the British financial crisis that Keynes had warned against. As part of the December 1945 agreement, $20 billion in Lend-Lease debt was canceled outright. This, however, was long anticipated, and with Britain urgently needing additional credits, any expectation that the British could pay off emergency advances of war materiel was fantasy.

So Britain carried a larger national debt and a more onerous war legacy than any of the other warring powers. It did receive $1.26 billion in aid from the Marshall Plan, a program mainly intended for Continental nations more directly threatened by the Red Army and strong local communist parties. With its huge war debt overhang, which diverted money from modernizing its industrial plants, Britain had a slower rate of economic growth during the postwar boom—about 2.5 percent a year—than any other major Western European country. In 1949, the pound was devalued against the dollar, by 30.5 percent, from $4.03 to $2.80. Inflation slowly reduced the value of Britain's domestic debt, which remained about 100 percent of GDP until 1960, a much larger debt burden than that of Germany, France, or the United States. By 1974, a 3.5 percent British war bond patriotically purchased in 1944 was worth only about twenty pence to the pound.

You might say that the familiarity of the close wartime allies had bred contempt. Or that once the war ended, the commercial and financial rivalry between Britain and the United States came to the fore. You could conclude that since there was no communist threat in Britain, as there was in Germany, France, and Italy, the United States could extract somewhat harsher terms. It would also be fair to observe that prewar Britain had been living somewhat beyond its means, relying on the huge subsidy of an empire that was no longer viable after the war. Yet the British had indeed done more than their share in the early years, when they stood alone against Hitler. The vagaries of debt forgiveness seldom follow purely economic logic. Because nations are involved, there is no escape from geopolitics.

CONSTRAINING FINANCE, PROMOTING PROSPERITY

The elimination of reparations demands after 1947, the write-off of Nazi war debts, the generosity of the Marshall Plan, and the forgiveness or inflating away of the Allies' war debts contributed to a dramatically different economic climate from the one that followed the First World War. Two other factors mattered immensely in undergirding the prosperity of the three-decade postwar boom. First, the major Western nations, faced with large war debt ratios, did not go into austerity mode; rather, they redoubled their public investments. The high rates of growth, helped along by an inflation whose rates moderated in the 1950s, dispatched the debt burden. Second, largely because of the Soviet threat, the United States after World War II was in the role, in Kindleberger's term, of a relatively benign hegemon. It exported dollars, functioned as a lender of last resort, kept its internal markets open, wrote off much of its old foreign sovereign debt, and worked down its immense trade surplus by encouraging American corporations to produce in Europe for European consumption rather than seeking an even larger surplus. The dollar became the de facto common currency.

Keynes had promoted a somewhat different, more internationalized path to the same prosperous result. As a proponent of using the economy's productive potential to its fullest, he was mindful of the tension between keeping the confidence of private speculative money markets and the domestic goal of pursuing high growth and full employment.

Apart from the usual overhang of war debt and war reparations, the interwar period had demonstrated a more general problem with the international financial system. The constraints imposed by private money markets produced systemic deflationary pressures. undermining the goal of achieving a rate of growth consistent with full employment. If a nation grew faster than its neighbors, some of that demand "leaked out" into imports, leaving the high-growth nation with a balance-of-payments deficit. Nations with such deficits typically balanced their budgets by shrinking domestic output, thus exporting deflation to the rest of the world. Nations found themselves in the position of having to raise interest rates in order to defend their currencies, which made capital expensive and slowed growth.

In a general depression, a nation might solve this problem by opting out of the world economy, as the United States did when it raised tariffs and went off the gold standard in the 1930s. Nazi Germany did the same thing when it used rearmament financed by massive borrowing to reach full employment and contained inflation with price controls. These extreme expedients, characteristic of war or depression, were destructive to world trade and unacceptable in peacetime.

Keynes devised a radically ingenious proposal for allowing countries to maximize domestic growth without incurring global financial imbalances. His goal was to keep credit plentiful and global aggregate demand at a high level so that there would be no tension between open trade and domestic full employment. He proposed to achieve this through his International Clearing Union, which would give countries the automatic right to incur overdrafts—a polite term for loans—from a new public international fund that had the power to create financial reserves of $26 billion to $32 billion. It would have its own currency, which Keynes dubbed Bancor, from the French words for bank and gold. Nations with balance-of-payments deficits could borrow almost at will. Even more radically, nations with chronic trade surpluses would automatically have their currencies designated as "scarce," giving other nations the right to discriminate against their exports. This would put pressure on the surplus countries to expand, which would pull in more imports, rather than pressuring the deficit countries to contract. The bias of the whole system would be growth rather than deflation. The system would have fixed exchange rates to ensure predictability and eliminate speculation in currencies. The rates would be maintained by the ability of nations to borrow from the clearing union as necessary.

The goal was to free national economies once and for all from both the deflationary effects of the gold standard and the need to please private money markets, which preferred tight money to economic growth that might risk inflation.

The plan was too radical for its time—orthodox financial critics saw it as an invitation to fiscal profligacy—and it had the further disadvantage of being proposed by the British at a moment when the Americans had the upper hand. A somewhat watered-down version of Keynes's plan was adopted at the Bretton Woods Conference of July 1944. The final plan closely followed the design of the chief American representative at Bretton Woods, Harry Dexter White. Like Keynes, White was a critic of the financial orthodoxy. A left-wing New Dealer, White supported the basic premises of Keynes's Clearing Union, but it was far too expansive, even for the Roosevelt administration, and implied discrimination against the exports of the United States, which stood to come out of the war as the world's leading surplus nation.

As adopted by the Bretton Woods Conference, Keynes's Clearing Union was shrunk into the International Monetary Fund, an ambiguous institution that would gradually mutate from an instrument of growth and national economic autonomy into an agency of austerity on behalf of the world's creditors. There would be no automatic overdrafts. Credits would be approved by a board dominated by the United States and its clients.

Even so, the bias of the postwar system in 1944 was toward growth. As things worked out, the engine of that growth was less the IMF and its sister institution, the World Bank, and more the enlightened self-interest of the United States through the Marshall Plan and other Cold War forms of aid to European recovery. In the postwar era, the world reserve currency turned out to be not Keynes's stillborn Bancor or its weaker IMF counterpart but the U.S. dollar. The system worked until the early 1970s, when the tension between the dollar needs of a growing world economy and the United States' need to resist inflationary pressures became unbridgeable. In 1973, the United States devalued and delinked the dollar from gold, and the system shifted to floating exchange rates set by private market forces—with the very deflationary bias that Keynes sought to avoid. The world economy entered a new phase, one in which the financial orthodoxy returned.

But in the meantime, Europe enjoyed a stunning period of recovery and growth under the auspices of a managed form of capitalism. And European nations that had long been bitter enemies embarked on a far-sighted project of European federalism.

Chapter 5

European Disunion

THOUGH IT IS NOW FASHIONABLE to disparage the European Union as a bureaucratic morass and the euro as a grandiosely naive mistake, one must view the recent missteps against the tragic history of twentieth-century Europe and the postwar political and economic miracle. In that context, the European project should be judged generously. With the exception of a brief and unstable truce between 1919 and 1939, the entire era was marked by intra-European wars, first with Germany as the prime disturber of the peace, then as the Soviet Union occupied half the Continent. In a century that Keynes aptly termed one of European civil war (and that was well before it was half over), the project of European union stands out as an act of rare nobility.

The early postwar era was fortunate in having idealistic leaders who were also effective pragmatists. Because of the thorough discrediting of wartime collaborationist governments, 1945 provided a clean break. A broad vision was shared by a warrior generation sick of militarism and carnage. French Europeanists such as Jean Monnet and Robert Schuman, key architects of the early common market, were determined to end French-German enmity by creating a federalized Europe. In 1943, Monnet told a meeting of the Free French government in exile in Algiers, "There will be no peace in Europe if the States rebuild themselves on the basis of national sovereignty." As prime minister and later foreign minister, Schuman, a French citizen of German and Luxembourger heritage, gave a series of speeches from 1947 to 1951 calling for a European union that included a post-Nazi Germany so that war would become both unthinkable and "materially impossible." Their vision was broadly shared by early postwar national leaders like Alcide De Gasperi and Luigi Einaudi of Italy, Winston Churchill and Clement Attlee of Britain, Paul-Henri Spaak of Belgium, and even the relative nationalist Charles de Gaulle of France. An immensely talented second tier of leaders helped build the common institutions and deepen the common commitment. Germany, too, was blessed with exceptional postwar leaders who fully shared and helped shape this vision. There were no more passionate Europeanists than West German chancellors Konrad Adenauer and Ludwig Erhard among the Christian Democrats and their Social Democratic successors Willy Brandt and Helmut Schmidt. No such statesmen were in evidence after World War I, and precious few are apparent today.

With the nationalist right and the capitalist right both discredited by the chain of events that began in 1929, Christian Democrats and Social Democrats agreed on the need for a Keynesian welfare state, differing only on doctrinal origins and relatively minor practical details. The church and the labor movement shared a long-standing skepticism of market supremacy. Though the Christian Democratic version was rooted in Catholic social teaching rather than in a parliamentary form of democratic socialism, both parties shared views about the need to harness market forces in the common interest, to pursue social justice, and to prevent wars. In the early postwar era, there were hardly any extreme nationalists or extreme advocates of free markets.

At the core of the postwar entente were two grand bargains: a nationalist settlement that contained Germany within Europe and a class settlement that enlarged the realm of the polity and anchored finance in a well-regulated form of managed capitalism committed to full employment and social income. It was a conception of the democratic left initially carried out by the nominally center-right governments of Christian Democrats that dominated Europe in the 1950s.

At just the right moment, the Cold War intervened, bringing the United States as an ally in a surprisingly leftish conception of European union, one that was rather more socialist than the New Deal. This was improbable because in 1945, American public opinion and policy were already shifting to the right. In 1946, the Republicans took back Congress for the first time since 1932. President Truman, more conservative than Roosevelt, was on the defensive. But in the late 1940s, moving to the right, above all, meant combating Stalin. At a time of broad economic suffering in the wake of a devastating war, Western Europe needed a persuasive domestic welfare state to compete with the appeal of communism. Soviet power was not just military; for a time in the late 1940s and 1950s, communists were winning the largest share of the vote in France and Italy. Even American conservatives excused the leftism of European social democrats, as a kind of live-virus vaccine against communism.

The Marshall Plan of 1948, moreover, brought with it not just needed recovery money but the germ of Pan-European planning. NATO, the anti-Soviet alliance established in 1949, created yet another key venue for close collaboration among nations that only yesterday had been bitter enemies. The need to ensure reliable production and access to coal and steel (which had been the source of deep Franco-German enmity in the aftermath of World War I) produced a friendly cartel called the European Coal and Steel Community in 1950. Headed by Jean Monnet, it in turn led directly to the 1956 Treaty of Rome, which created the Common Market, formally known as the European Economic Community.

As national leaders gained practical experience building these Pan-European institutions and collaborating in a remarkable project, they became increasingly committed to the logic of ever-broader European federalism. The EEC created a customs union. That, at least, meant duty-free trade among its six original member nations. But trucks still waited in long lines at national borders for goods inspections and passport checks. Europe still had a patchwork of national currencies, as well as controls on capital and credit movements. Despite the name, Europe was still far from a common market, much less a common polity. The Europeanists passionately believed that if they were to succeed, Europe had to move inexorably toward greater economic and civic union. The strong economic boom of the quarter century after the war gave popular legitimacy to the project. As early as the 1950s, there was talk of a common European defense system, a much deeper common market, a common currency, and common citizenship.

THIRTY GLORIOUS YEARS

From the outset, European union was built on a balance of state and market. The German Christian Democratic term for the postwar class settlement captures the paradox: *soziale Marktwirtschaft,* or a social market economy. After the dislocations of war, a functioning market economy needed to be relaunched. West Germany's first finance minister, Ludwig Erhard, is celebrated for lifting controls and letting market forces rip. Yet even pro-market leaders recognized that to prevent a repeat of the economic calamities that fueled the Second World War, the economy needed social stabilizers as well.

The market part meant overcoming the fragmentation of small national economies with a *common* market. Otherwise, Europe could never hope to compete with the United States or to transcend the legacy of an inward-looking protectionism that was both economically ineffi-cient and politically provocative. The social part contained a number of instruments to promote security, opportunity, and greater equality for ordinary working people. The particulars varied by country, but they included a comprehensive welfare state, substantial government subsidy and planning of industrial recovery, strong unions, and labor market policies that trained workers and provided for public employment. In Britain, France, Belgium, and Italy during much of the early postwar era, the package also included government ownership of key industries and banks. In Italy and Germany, the compromise was initially imple-mented by Christian Democrats looking over their shoulders at strong trade unions, leftist parties, and the nearby Red Army; in France, it reflected the ideal of a benevolent strong state.

Given today's austerity fever, what is all the more remarkable is that social provision was dramatically expanded in Europe at a time when the debt overhang of the war might have led to calls for belt-tightening. Yet the first Labour government after World War II built the National Health Service and expanded other social forms of income at a time when Britain's debt ratio was over 200 percent of GDP. Continen-tal nations still literally digging out from the ruins of war expanded socialized health, retirement, and worker protection systems. Far from hobbling postwar recovery, the social elements of the new European economy energized it. Those who blithely assume that the high Euro-pean growth rates were simply a natural consequence of recovery from war and prewar depression should take a close look at the stunted period after World War I, when no such durable recovery occurred. The success reflected deliberate policies that blended security and growth and constrained private financial speculation. These, in turn, reflected the political base of a strengthened democratic left and a weakened financial and nationalistic right.

In the containment of finance, America, ordinarily the most market oriented of the Western countries, again played an improbable and central role. The postwar Bretton Woods system limited speculative movements of private capital and provided for fixed exchange rates anchored by the U.S. dollar. As trade resumed, dollars soon accumulated in Europe. These so-called Eurodollars became a secondary source for financing European recovery. The normal commercial and financial rivalry between the United States and Europe was more or less suspended, both because the United States was so supremely powerful that it could afford to be magnanimous, and because America needed European recovery as a bulwark against communism.

Thanks to the relatively benign monetary dominance of the United States and a system of fixed exchange rates that lasted until 1972, postwar Europe was spared two financial complications that would come back to haunt the Common Market nations after the early 1970s and, *a fortiori*, in the collapse that began in 2007 and deepened in 2009 with attacks on Eurozone bonds. First, there was no instability caused by fluctuating exchange rates; under Bretton Woods rules, currency values were locked. Nor was there speculation against currencies or sovereign bonds. The pound, artificially strong after the war, did have to be devalued in 1949, and the deutsche mark was revalued upward in 1961, reflecting higher German growth rates. But these one-off events were exceptions in an otherwise stable system. Currency speculation was nonexistent on three counts: with fixed exchange rates, there are no currency movements to bet on; financial controls essentially prohibited it; and the exotic, and ultimately toxic, instruments for speculation that began flourishing in the 1990s had not yet been created.

Yet the real economy grew. In many respects, it grew not despite the constraints on speculative finance but because of them; not in spite of the social complements to the market but as a result of them. In the three decades after the war, the founding nations of the Common Market grew at a rate that has not been matched before or since. Most of Western Europe enjoyed not just full employment but overfull employment. Several nations had to import guest workers to keep up with the demand. Wages rose with productivity, and the income distribution of the Common Market countries became more equal. In France, the postwar boom is remembered as *les trente glorieuses,* the thirty glorious years. In Germany, where the economic miracle was known as the *Wirtschaftswunder,* GDP in the 1950s soon surpassed the pre-1939 peak.

Here is the key institutional fact: The European Economic Community anchored the market part of the grand compromise. Strong nation-states competent to regulate capitalism were guarantors of the social part. But three decades later, as the pro-market European Union assumed more of the role of the state, the bargain would steadily tilt in favor of the market. In the first postwar phase, from 1948 to 1971, tight controls on speculative finance and a stable money system secured a mixed economy and a strong recovery. In the second phase, from 1971 to 1993, monetary chaos led both to a stronger EU and to a resurgence of market forces. And since 1993, as neoliberalism gained ground within Europe's member states, an EU once thought to embody a managed form of capitalism has become an agent of speculation and austerity.

AUSTERITY, EUROPEAN-STYLE

How did the European Union, one of the great achievements of modern statecraft, find itself caught after 2009 in a deepening downdraft of self-destruction? Postwar Europe, the home of advanced welfare states, has long welcomed a constructive role for government in managing the economy and building an equitable society. Yet as the downturn worsened, the response of key European leaders was to drive the Continent further into economic and social breakdown. To understand what has occurred, one needs to appreciate the European crisis as a terrible convergence of several distinct forces, each with its own inexorable momentum.

The first has to do with latent weaknesses in the EU's governing structure. The current European Union was created in 1992, when the eleven member nations of what was then the European Community approved the Maastricht treaty. The new Union gave stronger authority to its executive body, the European Commission in Brussels. It also laid the groundwork for a single currency, the euro. However, the design concealed what was really a fragile confederation. National governments lost power, but the emerging European government remained highly fragmented and too weak to govern in an emergency. Each member state had to concur before major policy changes could be adopted. When agreement could not be reached, the default formula of Maas-

tricht was financial deregulation, market liberalization, and austerity—
the opposite of what was needed in the crisis.

The European Central Bank was established as part of Maastricht,
but without the emergency powers of the U.S. Federal Reserve. At
the insistence of Germany, it was expressly prohibited from buying the
bonds of member states, a strategy that proved crucial in the Fed's containment of the crisis in the United States. The 1993 European Union
had a single monetary policy but eleven different national fiscal policies. By the time of the crisis in 2007, seventeen national governments
used the euro, each with its own national budget. Regulatory authority
was also badly splintered among squabbling national governments and
diverse EU institutions. It was a jury-rigged ship of state, ill equipped to
weather a severe storm.

The structural weakness of the EU is only part of the story. A second problem is the anomaly of the euro, the world's first currency not
issued or backed by an actual state. Never in history had a central bank
reported to seventeen different governments. Had the financial crisis not
come so soon after the euro's introduction in 1999, the new currency
might have had sufficient time to jell. The Continent's fragmented banking system might have matured into a true European one, with common
rules and unified capital markets. Europe might have developed more
consistent tax and fiscal policies and a much larger common budget
to address regional disparities. But before any of this could happen,
the crisis intervened, exposing all of the latent weaknesses of the single
currency. Even so, the euro held up well until speculation began against
Greek government bonds in late 2009.

In addition, there was no provision for an orderly exit from the euro.
So a nation that otherwise might have chosen to devalue was denied that
course. Instead, the hardest-hit nations were compelled by European
Commission policy to pursue "internal devaluations"—namely, cuts in
wages, pension benefits, and public services. These only worsened the
deflationary depression suffered by the EU's peripheral member states.

The third distinct factor reflects the self-centered role of the fiscally
conservative German government. The euro has been very good to Germany. But when the moment came to help other nations, the government of Angela Merkel insisted on severe austerity as the quid pro quo
for mutual aid. Since Maastricht, Germany has been eager to impose its
conservative fiscal model on the rest of Europe. Until the crisis, how-

ever, it lacked the necessary diplomatic leverage, and the common bud-get targets imposed by Maastricht were honored mostly in the breach. The attacks on Greek sovereign debt in 2009 and 2010 provided that leverage—at the worst possible moment for fiscal belt-tightening. The hedge funds and other speculators that took down Greece moved on—to Portugal and Ireland, then Spain and Italy—so that no nation, not even Germany, was entirely safe. It was beyond the ideological imagi-nation of the EU's leaders to grasp that the remedy was to contain the speculators, not to shackle the states.

So despite the very different institutional particulars, the most impor-tant factor in Europe's self-inflicted economic distress is the one that mirrors the American experience: *the political dominance of financial interests*. In Europe as in the United States, the collapse did not lead to greater restraints on speculative finance. On the contrary, the vul-nerability of sovereign debt created new opportunities for speculative windfalls and escalating attacks on government bonds. By 2011, a crisis created largely by private financial excesses had been redefined as a cri-sis of improvident public spending, leading to the self-defeating remedy of general austerity.

After euro notes and coins officially replaced national circulating currencies in January 2002, countries such as Italy, Portugal, Spain, and Greece enjoyed a huge economic lift. When they had borrowed money in lire, escudos, pesetas, or drachmas, they typically had to pay far higher interest rates than the Germans to sell their bonds. The higher rates of return compensated investors for the greater risk of inflation or devaluation. But with a single currency, financial markets were will-ing to buy Greek or Portuguese bonds at near-German interest rates because all bonds were now denominated in euros and there was no risk of devaluation. The markets somehow overlooked the greater risk of default. The willingness of investors to put funds into Portugal for only trivially higher rates of return than those offered by Germany was yet another case of markets mispricing risk. The tacit assumption was that the EU's stronger nations would bail out the weaker ones in a crisis. That premise, needless to say, proved catastrophically wrong.

The euro enhanced economic growth during the boom years, espe-cially in Europe's peripheral countries. But in a crisis, as capital fled weak economies for the safety of Germany, Switzerland, the Nether-lands, and Britain, the psychology went into reverse. In a series of runs on the banks of Greece, Portugal, Spain, and Italy, the wealthy parked their money in London luxury apartments and German government bonds, deepening Europe's regional distortions. Corporations withdrew capital just when vulnerable economies needed it. The less affluent moved euros from banks to mattresses, fearing a return to much weaker national currencies. The single currency coupled with the failure to constrain financial speculation proved to be "pro-cyclical"—exaggerating booms, deepening busts, and widening regional divergences. Even so, Europe's leaders might have acted to counter these trends. Instead, they exacerbated them.

AN INVISIBLE FIST

The evolving role of Germany in the European community is worth closer attention. Unlike the political class of the early 1920s—people who, regardless of party, felt that their homeland had been wrongly singled out for war guilt and brutally punitive reparations—German leaders after World War II were exquisitely sensitive to the need for their country to earn its way back into the company of civilized nations. This meant behavior that was not only scrupulously democratic but, above all, geopolitically restrained. Britain and France got U.N. Security Council seats, not Germany. Whenever NATO called for increases in German military spending at moments of Cold War tension, it was the Germans, not the French or the Belgians, who resisted.

In the cliché of the era, Germany was an economic giant and a political dwarf, the most docile of military allies. And Germans grew to like that role just fine. They had finally found a formula for prosperity and peace—and for considerable influence by indirection. Germany gradually became the dominant power of Continental Europe not through territorial expansion or military might but through its strong economy and anchor currency, the deutsche mark. By being rather inward-looking, Germany could exert quiet external power. This uneasy balance worked well enough until two events late in the twentieth century tipped European hegemony in favor of Berlin: reunification and the creation of the euro. As we shall see, both were closely linked, and both led to a more explicit German preeminence.

In the previous chapter, we encountered Kindleberger's theory of hegemonic stability. These financial hegemons, Britain before World War I and the United States after World War II, were not exactly altruistic. They acquired colonies and protectorates and otherwise threw their weight around, further profiting from the fact that they uniquely incurred foreign debts in their own currency, a status that Valéry Giscard d'Estaing, finance minister and later president of France, decried as an "exorbitant privilege." But on balance, as Kindleberger noted, their hegemony was benign for the global financial and trading system. Indeed, many critics have observed that Britain in the Victorian period and the United States beginning in the 1970s sacrificed their own national economic self-interests for the sake of maintaining a global financial system that served British and American financiers but not their respective economies as a whole. Some historians have contended that post-Victorian Britain and post-1970s America suffered industrial decline under the weight of hegemonic responsibility and the privileging of finance, as they exported capital rather than goods. This contention seems broadly persuasive to me, but it is an argument for another day.

For our purposes here, it could be said, in the spirit of Kindleberger, that after the collapse of the Bretton Woods system in 1971–73, and most emphatically after the introduction of the euro in 1999–2002, Europe entered an unstable financial period unlike either the interwar era of monetary anarchy or the epochs of British or American monetary hegemony. Germany, increasingly, was the financial hegemon of Europe. Other currencies were valued in terms of the deutsche mark. After 2002, Germany was guardian of the euro. But successive German governments did not give priority to their system-maintaining responsibilities. As a hegemon, Germany was not particularly benign. At best, it had a very strained conception of what it meant to be benign— enforcing austerity on the rest of Europe, even in a depression. The Federal Republic's very useful inward-looking habits of the early postwar era persisted long after Germany had become a great power, to the detriment of the rest of Europe.

By the turn of the new century, self-effacement had given way to something like smugness. And in fairness, Germany had much to be smug about. As Chancellor Merkel once told British prime minister Tony Blair, whose government had made what turned out to be a disastrous bet on the primacy of finance over manufacturing, "Mr. Blair, we still make things." Thanks to a kind of soft industrial policy built on labor-management consensus, worker training, regional policies, and technology targeting that added up to a tacit mercantilism, Germany indeed made things. The Germans enjoyed a larger export surplus than the Chinese. With its lopsided favorable balance of trade, Germany could combine an austere budgetary policy with plentiful employment.

However, Germany benefited from an unacknowledged subsidy. Using the euro, Germany had an undervalued currency, which in turn made its goods artificially cheap in world markets. After the introduction of the euro, German exports began rising at a faster clip. Normally, if a nation has a large trade surplus year after year, markets revalue its currency upward; in fact, the old deutsche mark had to be revalued on several occasions. But thanks to its shared common currency with the dissolute "Club Med" nations that the productive Germans love to hate, the currency gets valued somewhere between what's right for Germany and what's right for Italy or Greece. German economists have calculated that if wealthy Germany still had its own national currency, the deutsche mark would be valued at something like 40 percent more than the euro, increasing the price of Germany's goods and reducing its export surplus.

In addition, as speculative pressure after 2009 battered the vulnerable government bonds of nations such as Greece, Portugal, Spain, and Italy, capital fled to Germany, driving down long-term German borrowing costs to well under 2 percent. At this writing, the effective interest rate on German two-year government bonds is negative. The country that gave us the word *schadenfreude* has been profiting from the misfortune of others.

But neither the German public nor leading German politicians experienced reality in those terms. Germans worked hard, played by the rules, and prospered; other nations needed to do likewise. Germany, through labor market deregulation, had moderated its wages to restore competitiveness; others should learn from its example. After a brief use of deficits to finance reunification, Germany ran a tight budgetary policy and had no interest in subsidizing other nations' profligacy.

Never mind that every nation, by definition, could not have an export surplus. Never mind Germany's easy ride on a cheap currency or artificially low interest rates. Never mind that the fiscal policies that served Germany well in normal times were perverse in a Pan-European depression. When the time came to move beyond the self-effacing, inward-looking role it had taken on early in the postwar era, Germany plainly found it hard to act in the broader European interest.

EUROPE'S MONETARY MUDDLE

Decades before the current crisis, the glorious postwar years came crashing to an end, and a lot of the economic downturn had to do with money. In the late 1960s and early 1970s, the United States found itself under inflationary pressure triggered by the cost of the Vietnam War and exacerbated by the first OPEC oil price hike in 1973. Even without these shocks, economists had been warning for more than a decade that the United States could not supply dollars indefinitely both to its domestic economy and to a rapidly expanding Europe without weakening its currency. With the dollar as the world's money, the domestic economy required one monetary policy, and the global economy required another. This increasingly unsustainable straddle was known as the Triffin Dilemma, after Robert Triffin, the Belgian-born Yale economist who had first called attention to the problem in 1947. (Half a century later, the euro would replicate a variant of the dilemma: the same monetary policy could not be right for both Germany and Greece.)

As European nations, led by France, began anticipating a dollar devaluation and exercising their right to exchange dollars for gold, the process fed on itself. The more that the U.S. gold supply dwindled, the more inevitable a dollar devaluation became. In August 1971, Richard Nixon authorized his Treasury secretary, John Connally, to abruptly suspend dollar convertibility to gold. Dollar devaluation came next, followed by a shift to partly floating exchange rates.

There ensued a period of economic and financial instability—the "stagflation" of the 1970s. Growth slowed, unemployment rose, and rising inflation and interest rates followed, slowing growth still further. There was no good substitute for the monetary stability of Bretton Woods, and one casualty was the credibility of the Keynesian welfare state. Conservatives of the sort not elected since the 1920s came to power in Britain and the United States in 1979 and 1981. As the cure for economic malaise, both Margaret Thatcher and Ronald Reagan commended a bracing dose of market fundamentalism, cutting taxes, deregulating finance and other industries, limiting unions, and reducing social outlays. The verdict on this remedy is mixed, at best, especially if we include the financial collapse as a casualty of market excess.

With the ascendancy of Thatcher and Reagan and the weakening of democratic-left parties, the careful balance between state and market in the postwar settlement began shifting ineluctably in the direction of the market. Key leaders of EEC nations now wanted to use the Common Market not to defend managed capitalism but to promote laissez-faire.

The globalization of commerce and finance also weakened the social democratic state, since corporations could increasingly play nations against one another for the most hospitable tax, labor, and regulatory climate. The expansion of global commerce might have operated under rules friendlier to a mixed economy, as Keynes had proposed in 1944, but it did not. The new global trade rules sponsored by the United States under the General Agreement on Tariffs and Trade and ratified in the so-called Uruguay Round of trade negotiations in 1994 went far beyond the reciprocal tariff reductions of the early postwar era and defined all sorts of entirely legitimate economic regulations as "nontariff barriers"—restraints of trade. National controls on financial capital became inconsistent with GATT. A government's subsidies for purposes of regional development and its industrial policies could be challenged as unfair competition. Increasingly, the EU internalized these norms and enforced them on member nations. For the European project, this would have dramatic consequences, tacit at first and flagrant after the crisis of 2008—just when markets needed strong governments to contain and reverse the damage wrought by private market forces run amok.

Throughout the 1970s and 1980s, European leaders, mistrustful of American monetary dominance, searched in vain for a serviceable successor to the stability of Bretton Woods. The shift to floating exchange rates led to competitive outbreaks of beggar-thy-neighbor policies on interest rates and exchange rates, which became a source of economic volatility and diplomatic friction. Thanks to high West German growth rates and the iron hand of a Bundesbank determined to avoid inflation, the deutsche mark was already recognized as Europe's "hardest"—most reliable and trusted—currency. In 1972, the leaders of the European Community created "the snake in the tunnel," a system in which European currencies would fluctuate against each other within a narrow band, with the mark as the snake's head. National leaders and central bankers would intervene jointly (and on the same side) to keep the currencies within the desired zones, plus or minus 2.25 percent.

The system didn't work very well. Almost immediately, currency speculation forced the British pound out of the snake in June 1972, after the Bank of England had haplessly spent more than £30 billion trying to defend its value. This pattern would be repeated in a second crash of the pound in 1993. The Germans were forced to resort to capital controls to keep the strong deutsche mark from rising beyond its target zone. Nixon completed the burial of Bretton Woods by refusing to intervene to prevent dollar devaluation. A conversation caught on one of the famous Watergate tapes in late June 1973 between the president and his chief of staff, H. R. Haldeman, reveals Nixon's disdain for international monetary matters:

> HALDEMAN: [Federal Reserve chairman Arthur] Burns is concerned about speculation about the lira.
> NIXON: Well, I don't give a shit about the lira.

So much for benign hegemony.

In 1973 and 1974, despite some help from the Bundesbank, Italy and France drew down dollar and gold reserves in failed attempts to defend their currency values within the snake. As their currencies floated downward, both nations were accused of lacking a commitment to the European project and of opportunistically wishing to increase exports with cheap currencies. The Germans, meanwhile, were chronically reluctant to revalue the mark upward. In 1978 and 1979, France and Germany jointly sponsored a successor to the snake in the tunnel, the so-called exchange rate mechanism. It used as a reference a basket of currencies known as the European Currency Unit, but it, too, failed to stabilize the system.

The 1970s and 1980s were punctuated by successive European currency crises and an elusive quest for a monetary system that might provide both stability and flexibility. At moments when national central banks raised interest rates to combat inflation or capital flight, currency competition added up to a general climate of tight money, slowing everyone's economic growth. Conversely, there were times when some nations deliberately sought to cheapen their currencies to improve their export positions. Often a nation's central bank would pursue one policy while its Treasury pursued a different one. All around, there were accusations of short-term opportunism and bad faith. Currency instability was destroying the goodwill needed to advance the European project.

PURSUING A MORE PERFECT UNION

It was against this fractious background that Europe's most visionary leaders grew determined to pursue a single currency. In 1985, Jacques Delors, a moderate French Socialist, fiscal hawk, and passionate Europeanist, became president of the European Commission. He set about enlisting other leaders in a project for a much more intimate European union. The first fruit of these efforts was the Single European Act of 1986, creating a single market to become effective in 1990. With this single market, there would no longer be barriers to the free movement throughout the European Community of capital, products, services, and people. This achievement went a long way toward redeeming the promise from three decades earlier of a true common market.

In the meantime, efforts to complement the single market with a single currency were accelerated. In the late 1980s, the leaders of the two strongest Continental economies, President François Mitterrand of France, a Socialist, and Chancellor Helmut Kohl of Germany, a Christian Democrat, threw their support behind the project. In 1988, they appointed a committee of experts headed by Delors and including the European Community's twelve central bank presidents, whose backing would be crucial. But then Kohl, facing domestic political pressures in early 1989, sought to slow down the project. The committee was devising options for a gradual path to monetary union when an entirely unexpected event intervened: the end of the Cold War.

When the Berlin Wall came down in November 1989, Kohl, ordinarily a cautious and plodding leader, made an uncharacteristically impulsive decision. Without asking the consent of key allies inside Germany or out, Kohl concluded that he had a brief window to consummate German reunification. To sweeten the deal, he offered to exchange East German marks for deutsche marks at the stunningly generous rate of 1 for 1 (the black market rate, reflecting actual purchasing power, was between 5 to 1 and 10 to 1), a policy fiercely opposed by the powerful Bundesbank. Eventually, Germany would pump the equivalent of about €2 trillion into the former German Democratic Republic through the currency swap and other forms of subsidy. East Germany officially switched to the deutsche mark in June, and the reunification treaty was signed on August 31, 1990.

Kohl's fateful decision to seize the moment created a crisis for the project of European union. The entire premise of Germany's neighbors (and former victims) had been that European union would both moderate and contain Germany. Now, suddenly, Germany would be that much more powerful; worse, Kohl had acted unilaterally. The British prime minister was apoplectic. But at a dinner of European leaders at the Élysée Palace just a week after the wall fell, Kohl told Thatcher, "You will not stop the German people following their destiny." At various points in early 1990, French, British, Italian, Soviet, and Dutch leaders all warned Kohl against reunification, but he refused to be deterred.

Mitterrand, alternately Kohl's ally and nemesis, was convinced that a grand bargain could yet be had. In exchange for the blessing of very skeptical allies, what if Germany dropped its opposition to monetary union? In a stroke, this would accomplish two goals dear to Mitterrand and Delors: it would accelerate the march to a single currency, which in turn would deepen the integration of Germany into Europe. This was the bargain that was eventually made. In return for the sacrifice of its cherished deutsche mark, emblem of postwar prosperity, the Germans agreed to join the euro. But they insisted on tough fiscal conditions, including a national debt ceiling of 60 percent of GDP and an annual deficit limit of 3 percent, so that the euro would not be an instrument of inflation. This deal became part of the Maastricht treaty defining the next phase of European union.

In retrospect, it's clear that this was far from being a grand bargain in which each party gave something and got something. Germany won in four different ways: very uneasy neighbors accepted the fait accompli of German reunification; the euro became the successor to the deutsche mark, amplifying rather than diffusing Germany's monetary dominance; the terms of engagement imposed Germany's fiscal model on Europe; and, though it was not appreciated at the time, the euro gave Germany a chronically undervalued currency and an artificial export advantage. The €2 trillion cost of reunification to the German Federal Republic increased Germany's national debt and redoubled the German wariness of inflation. Relatively high interest rates imposed first by the Bundesbank and later by the successor European Central Bank left the rest of Europe captive to Germany's tight monetary policy.

REVERSING SOCIAL EUROPE

The postwar European project has always had a pro-market face and a managed-capitalism face. In the 1950s, the original European Economic Community was mainly about getting rid of wartime controls and national barriers to commerce and creating a larger and more efficient market. The social element of Europe, as noted, came from strong nation-states committed to full employment and welfare benefits, as well as from constraints on private speculative capital provided by the Bretton Woods system.

But after the stagflation of the 1970s, neoliberalism—a reversion to a more free-market form of capitalism—became the ascendant ideology. Europe was held by orthodox economists to be the victim of economic sclerosis caused by an excess of social protections and regulatory constraints harmful to entrepreneurship. This contention, shared by political conservatives and diffused by the policy prescriptions of the World Bank, the IMF, the OECD, and the European Commission, is surely debatable. While some European countries, such as Britain and, to an extent, France, had become sclerotic, the Scandinavian social model has proved that a society can combine strong social protections with a flexible and dynamic economy. These small and homogeneous Nordic nations, however, have long-standing traditions of consensual social bargaining, a political model not easily transplanted.

After 1980, many on the European center-left accepted at least some of the neoliberal critique. The Labour and Social Democratic governments that returned to power in the 1990s resolved to fine-tune rather than reverse the pro-market policies of Thatcher, Kohl, and the center-right coalitions that had governed in much of Scandinavia. By the time of the Maastricht treaty, a more powerful EU would serve to reinforce neoliberal policies. These trends had different national particulars but potent common elements.

In Britain, Tony Blair's "New Labour," elected in 1997 after eighteen years of Conservative rule, accepted Thatcher's premise that deregulated finance would reinforce London's role as a global financial center, replacing Britain's reliance on a largely defunct manufacturing sector and producing convenient political alliances between the Labour Party and powerful economic interests. Blair's version of a Third Way between socialism and laissez-faire included a commitment to reduce poverty and improve public services but also substantial deregulation and privatization, as well as a distancing from the unions that had once been the core of the party's constituency. Labour policies liberating finance, euphemistically known as "light touch" regulation, helped seed the conditions for the crisis of 2008. In Britain's version of the collapse, several banks pursued speculative investments, went broke, and had to be nationalized. Britain stayed out of the euro but in the EU. Though it was nominally center-left, the Labour government continued to veto any policies proposed by Brussels to regulate banking excesses.

In Germany, a center-left coalition pursued a variant of the neoliberal formula. Between 1998 and 2005, Germany was governed by a coalition of Social Democrats and Greens led by Chancellor Gerhard Schröder. Reunification had imposed huge costs, unemployment was rising, and neoliberal panaceas were in the air. Schröder made a fateful decision to liberalize both capital and labor markets.

Postwar West Germany had successfully used a "corporatist" model of capitalism, fancifully known as Deutschland AG (Germany Inc.). Banks owned huge blocks of corporate stock that rarely traded, so corporations enjoyed cheap, patient capital and did not have to face shareholder pressures for high quarterly returns. Unions participated in corporate governance through works councils and well-choreographed collective bargaining. They restrained their wage demands to the rate of productivity gains so that German exports would remain competitive. There was generous investment in worker training. The system produced highly competitive industries, decent wages, job security, and good social benefits.

But by the 1990s, shareholder rather than stakeholder capitalism was in fashion. With the pressure to promote recovery after reunification, Germany needed faster growth. Market forces were thought to be the answer. So the Schröder government changed tax and regulatory policy to make the shareholder king. Pressure for high short-term returns increased. Taxes on ordinary citizens were raised, while taxes on capital were reduced. Schröder drastically reduced unemployment benefits and compelled idle workers to take available low-wage jobs or lose social benefits entirely. Industry-wide collective bargaining declined by almost half in just a decade. Union membership dropped by more than 50 percent. Wages lagged behind productivity growth. When unemployment began falling in 2010, these patterns persisted, but German export performance and corporate profits gained.

Even in Sweden, the Social Democrats, who last governed between 1994 and 2006, introduced measures intended to make the welfare state more flexible. Any group of Swedes, for instance, can now organize a local school that receives public funds and competes with the local state school. In principle, the idea was to promote choice and diverse forms of pedagogy. In practice, most of the alternative schools are now for-profit enterprises run by multinational corporations, which leaves the hard cases to increasingly underfunded state schools. Many hospitals have also been privatized. As service providers cease to be public institutions, their employees are less likely to be members of a union. Many government agencies providing services were required to compete with private rivals to win contracts, a competition that battered down wages. Some of these reforms made sense, both to keep the bureaucracy on its toes and as an inoculation against deeper privatization. But the broad formula proved to be a slippery slope that would help conservatives dismantle the political bases of Swedish social democracy.

In the postwar Swedish model, collaborative bargaining between unions and employers, combined with substantial state outlays on job creation and retraining, allowed Sweden to remain at full employment without overheating the economy or causing inflation. As in Germany, unions used centralized bargaining to keep wage gains in line with productivity growth so that Sweden would stay competitive. Nearly every Swedish worker was a member of a union. The unions were key custodians of the model and the soul of the Social Democratic Party, which was the normal party of government for most years between 1936 and 2006.

But the center-right coalition that narrowly won power in the 2006 election, and kept it in 2010, twisted the left's reforms to weaken Sweden's ingeniously efficient full-employment system and undermine the trade unions that form the core of the Social Democratic constituency. In just six years, the Conservative-Liberal coalition government demolished much of this model, drastically cutting outlays on active labor market policy. It shifted to a privatized and voluntary system of unemployment insurance, which used to be obtained through unions. The government also changed hiring rules so that corporations can try out new workers at lower wages for six months, which can be extended to twenty-four, without giving them regular employment. These young workers, marginally attached to the labor force, are harder for unions to reach. The cumulative policy shifts undermined both the high-wage, high-equality, high-productivity Swedish economic model and the Social Democrats' political support. Sweden, long an obligatory pilgrimage for American leftists, has become a destination for the conservative Heritage Foundation.

In the Netherlands, Labor prime minister Wim Kok brokered a grand bargain in 1999. Employers got more discretion to hire temporary and part-time workers, but these workers were supposed to be accorded the same protections as those with regular contracts. In the meantime, "flexicurity," a term coined by a Dutch sociologist to describe the new Dutch model, became a buzzword much promoted by the bureaucrats of Brussels. Workers would trade job security for employment security. Their protections would be social rather than connected to a given job. The state would invest more in worker training. Employers would get more freedom to hire and fire. There was nothing new or centrist about this idea; the Swedes and Danes had been doing it well since the 1960s, under social democratic auspices.

But as events played out all over Europe, flexicurity delivered more on the flexibility than on the security. Employment agencies and corporations gained new powers to keep workers in a long-term "temporary" classification. Collective bargaining was weakened. Changes in labor law interacted with the privatization required by Brussels to promote competition. In the privatized Dutch postal system, self-employed messengers under contract to the new postal companies now deliver the mail at minimum wage—or less. Among young Dutch workers, fully 61 percent have low-wage jobs. On the eve of the financial crisis, even countries that had prided themselves on egalitarian income distributions were approaching American levels of inequality. Most European nations found themselves with large low-wage sectors, something previously unknown.

The one large European nation where social democrats rejected neoliberalism was France. The French economy has been state led since the time of Jean-Baptiste Colbert, court treasurer to King Louis XIV. When François Mitterrand became the Fifth Republic's first Socialist president

in 1981, he moved the Socialist Party's program to the left, national-
izing banks, reducing the standard workweek, and increasing social
outlays. But financial globalization had already reached a point where
Mitterrand could not pursue an expansionary program in one country
without inviting severe capital outflows, thus neatly proving Keynes's
point in the design of Bretton Woods that domestic full-employment
programs required international constraints on capital. Adapting to
the new global environment, Mitterrand's ministers became reluctant
architects of freer global financial markets, with the nominally Socialist
banker Michel Camdessus, newly appointed head of the International
Monetary Fund, leading the way.

Jacques Delors, the father of the post-1993 European Union, had
hoped that a stronger EU could serve as a social bastion on a Continental scale against Anglo-Saxon laissez-faire and global free-market
forces. These hopes were not to be realized. Key member governments
had embraced neoliberalism, and the EU itself was increasingly the
agent of its dissemination. "I succeeded in making a European monetary policy," he told me, "but not European social or economic policy."
The European Union had gained substantial power, he lamented, only
to be the instrument of British policy on financial laxity and German
policy on austerity. It was the opposite of the social democratic entity
that Delors intended. And when the crisis hit, a Pan-European currency
combined with a nation-bound tax and budget policy would prove to
be an impossible straddle.

The next Socialist president, François Hollande, after a seventeen-
year period of conservative rule in France, spoke for the emergent revolt
against failed neoliberal policies. But in the meantime, France also suffered from widening income extremes and declining economic security, while globalization and the EU's new powers narrowed the room
for any one government to choose its own divergent course. Hollande
embraced expansionist policies but had scant capacity to deliver them.

Europe's slide into neoliberal policies had other corrosive consequences. The increased income inequality produced a far less secure
society. The economic deregulation created the preconditions for financial collapse. None of this was necessary economics; it simply reflected
shifting political forces as the power constellation of the postwar boom
was upended. Whatever modest gains to growth might arguably have
been produced by more liberal capital and labor markets were obliterated by the crash and its prolonged aftermath.

Where European nations once had the ability to choose their own national economic strategies, the rules of globalization and the directives of the EU have increasingly enforced a one-size-fits-all regime, and that regime is substantially free-market. In this climate, center-left parties suffered because they could no longer deliver. Social democrat and labor parties lost ground in every nation save France. As social protections were eroded, the remaining benefits of the welfare state came to serve an ever-narrower portion of the population. Europe, in the words of the French political scientist Bruno Palier, became a "society of insiders and outsiders." The insiders still benefiting from the remnants of the welfare state were civil servants, factory workers protected by union contracts, and retirees—a dwindling share of the electorate. Affluent professionals and members of the business elite who could purchase benefits privately were increasingly defecting from the model. The outsiders were young people, immigrants, large numbers of women, and low-wage service-sector workers. Over time, the ranks of the outsiders were growing. The governing center-left parties did little for the outsiders, and under fiscal pressures they were removing benefits even from the insiders. So the broad middle- and working-class coalition that had once supported social democratic parties relentlessly eroded. All of this predated the financial crisis, which only intensified the trends.

Nor could center-left parties other than in France present themselves as a plausible opposition to the increasingly disastrous policies imposed by Berlin and Brussels. The social democrats who had embraced neoliberalism shared responsibility for the financial deregulation that seeded the ground for financial collapse. Since 2008, eleven incumbent European governments have been swept out of office by the voters. There was no ideological pattern—it was simply a vote against a worsening economy. The center-left was voted out in Britain, Spain, Greece, and Portugal. The center-right was voted out in Denmark, France, and Belgium. In the most recent elections in Britain, Sweden, and Germany—nations that were prime architects of Europe's postwar welfare state—the vote for social democrats fell to its lowest level since the 1930s.

AN AMERICAN DILEMMA

With the shift to free-market ideas among the member states, the EU, once criticized by American conservatives as standing for "Fortress

Europe," has become an instrument for further undermining the managed capitalism of the postwar social settlement. While some directives by the Brussels bureaucracy have moderately strengthened a regulated form of capitalism in areas such as antitrust, the environment, and the rights of women, on balance they have severely weakened protections in the core realms of finance and labor.

For example, the Maastricht treaty provides that citizens of member countries are free to take jobs anywhere within the EU. Much of this labor migration, however, is orchestrated by large corporations. The European Commission in 1994 duly issued a directive on workers "posted" (sent by an employer) from one country to another. On paper, the rules seem balanced. The company gets to deploy workers as it pleases; the foreign contract workers get the same minimum rights as local citizens. But in practice, the chain of responsibility is opaque, and the foreign worker often ends up at the bottom of the local labor market, unprotected by unions or regulators. A contractor need pay only the (usually low) social security contributions of the worker's country of origin—giving a further cost advantage to the contract worker over local workers, a gap estimated at around 25 percent in France. The whole process, though seemingly regulated, drags down prevailing wages and contributes to a more laissez-faire labor market.

Even more destructive is the interaction between weak social protections in the new member states and the EU's fundamental doctrine of free movement of capital, goods, services, and people. One recent decision by the European Court of Justice allowed a company based in Estonia to "reflag" a Baltic ferry line that employed Finns and reduce wages to Estonian levels. A second permitted a Latvian construction company to bring workers into Sweden; the company was required to meet statutory wage minimums, but the court held that it could lawfully reject demands of Swedish unions for wages that reflected local collective bargaining norms. A third case denied German state governments the right to set wage standards in government contracting. These rulings are binding as national law. Pan-European regulation of capital has lagged far behind.

Rapid expansion of the EU has also created something close to a permanent center-right majority. There are now twenty-seven member states, and most of the nine former Soviet satellites in the EU have conservative governments. Their ideal successor to Marx is not François Mitterrand but Milton Friedman. In their eagerness to attract Western capital, the center-right governments of Eastern Europe have adopted policies of low taxes, little regulation, and scant social protections. This has helped Poland and other nations achieve good growth rates, but it puts severe pressure on the traditional welfare states of Western Europe to lower their own taxes, reduce social protections, and cut wages, lest they lose market share and jobs.

Even if social democratic national governments won power in every major European nation, they would be stymied by the EU's institutional fragmentation and the ability of a single nation to block major policy changes, as Germany and Britain often do. Where Mitterrand, trying to go it alone three decades ago, had "only" global money markets to thwart his program, a modern successor would also have to reckon with Brussels, at once a bureaucratic force for neoliberal contagion *and* a dysfunctional obstacle to reform of market excess.

The EU, further, is increasingly seen by ordinary Europeans as an elite project. In a time of economic troubles, the popular backlash against an ineffectual but meddlesome Brussels is not unlike the backlash against Washington. A general mood of antigovernment sentiment is a poor climate in which to rebuild a more managed form of democratic capitalism.

Europe, in sum, has managed to back into a quite American dilemma. The Articles of Confederation, which defined the fledgling American republic for its first decade, created a national government that proved too weak to govern. Even the successor U.S. Constitution of 1789, with its separation of powers and supermajority choke points, was deliberately intended to make government action very difficult. Rare bouts of state activism, such as Roosevelt's New Deal and Lyndon Johnson's Great Society, have required either the mandate of large electoral majorities or the emergency executive powers of war.

By contrast, Europe's democracies have historically had parliamentary systems. When a left-of-center party or coalition won a governing majority, it could enact its program. Thus, in the late 1940s, the British Labour government of Clement Attlee could push through socialized medicine despite the fierce opposition of business elites, just as the Mitterrand government of the 1980s could nationalize French banks, and successions of Swedish and Danish social democrats could refine their model of social bargaining to benefit wage workers and export industries.

Now, however, the European constitution is looking more American. It has more fragmentation, more federalism, and more opportunities for vetoes. Yet Brussels has also gained the power to overturn the instruments of managed capitalism that are the handiwork of nation-states, on the premise that these are barriers to the free flow of commerce and capital that is the core principle of Maastricht. Since it takes a strong state to deliver policies to balance powerful business elites, the EU has become a net conservative force. Brussels today is more often in the role of Trojan horse for laissez-faire than of bastion of managed capitalism.

So while laissez-faire capitalism has disgraced itself in both theory and in practice, there is no politically robust opposition on the democratic left. The democratic state, as the instrument of a functioning social contract of security and opportunity, is thwarted both by the EU's own rules and by the political power of finance to set the terms of engagement and to play one state against another.

On reflection, it is not surprising that a far-flung confederation would produce a weaker government with diminished capacity to regulate transnational capitalism. In 1939, the godfather of modern libertarianism, Friedrich Hayek, a proponent of European union, predicted that with a federation "certain economic powers, which are now generally wielded by the national state, could be exercised neither by the federation nor by the individual states." Hayek should be thrilled with the result.

SEPARATED AT BIRTH

The grand bargain that created the euro and the European Central Bank papered over radically differing conceptions of what deeper European union required. The Germans considered fiscal union to be an essential counterpart to monetary union. By fiscal union they emphatically did not mean that richer member nations would aid poorer ones. "Transfer union" is a term of scorn in Germany. Rather, the idea was that other nations should emulate German budgetary prudence.

However, common European budget and tax systems were out of the question in 1993—and still are. So for the Germans, mandatory budget targets were a second best. They believed that rather austere fiscal convergence had to be present from the outset. Otherwise, they feared, there would be political pressures for a lax monetary policy that risked increased inflation.

The French had a completely different conception. Their hope was that as European integration deepened, convergence of economic performance and fiscal policy would come gradually. They favored a kinder, gentler set of budgetary constraints. Since both France and Germany were eager to get the deal done, these differences were glossed over. They came back to haunt the euro's sponsors after 2007, when the crisis hit.

In the early 1990s, when all of Europe was suffering from sluggish growth—in part because Germany raised interest rates to guard against inflationary consequences of reunification and other nations had to defensively raise their own rates—few European nations met the Maastricht budget targets. The French, Germans, and Italians successfully pressured the European Commission not to impose sanctions. But in 2005, when Angela Merkel succeeded Gerhard Schröder as German chancellor, she pressed for a revision of standards to include mandatory penalties for violators.

However, it was not until the crisis of speculation against Greek sovereign debt that the Germans finally succeeded in imposing their fiscal model on the rest of Europe. In exchange for agreeing to a bailout (on draconian terms) for Greece, the German government insisted not only that the Greeks agree to a stringent austerity program but that the rest of the EU finally agree to enforceable deficit and debt targets.

As the impact of these policies unfolded, the very countries most weakened by the recession and by the speculative attacks against their government bonds were required to impose ever more severe austerity programs at a time when demand was already falling. Even the International Monetary Fund, no friend of fiscal profligacy, came to consider these policies perverse and pressed Merkel and the European Commission for easier terms. As economic assistance, the combination of bailout funds to finance old debt plus deeper austerity was self-annihilating.

Despite the euro's latent flaws and the divergent conceptions held by its key sponsors, the single currency in fact performed surprisingly well until the speculative attack on Greek sovereign debt began in late 2009. When it was first launched, the euro was valued at $1.18. For most of 2009, it was trading at above $1.40.

As noted, critics have observed that the euro is a currency without a true state behind it; that absent a central government with substantial transfer mechanisms, the divergences between a Portugal and a Germany are just too wide for the euro to succeed; and that the single currency prevents weaker economies from resorting to the traditional remedy of devaluing. There is a measure of truth to each of these contentions. Since we cannot rerun history, it is hard to know how the euro might have fared had Europe avoided a severe financial crisis for another generation. But it is worth recalling that the single currency nicely weathered the financial crash of 2008—an event whose origins had nothing whatever to do with the euro; that the European financial crisis had two distinct phases; and that the European Central Bank did rather well with the first one, as long as the challenge was providing short-term liquidity to banks.

A TRAVESTY IN TWO ACTS

The first phase began in 2007 with the sudden loss in value of securities backed by subprime mortgages. A full year before the crisis turned acute with the collapse of Lehman Brothers in September 2008, there were severe episodes of financial panic that required prompt and aggressive intervention by central banks. In that phase, the risk was that financial markets were seizing up because highly leveraged banks were incurring losses from investments in mortgage-backed securities; banks did not know which might be the next to go under, and they literally stopped accepting each other's paper.

In the initial round of massive intervention to provide emergency liquidity to markets, most observers credited the European Central Bank with performing at least as well as the Fed. On August 9, 2007, BNP Paribas, one of France's largest banks, announced that three of its hedge funds had incurred huge losses from mortgage-backed securities. This triggered a financial panic, and the ECB moved immediately to pour €95 billion into credit markets in just three hours, and another €109 billion in the next three days. Serving as an emergency lender to financial markets in a liquidity crunch was very much a part of the ECB's franchise, and the bank, untested in a crisis until 2007, did its job well. In late August and September 2007, the ECB, working with the Fed and other central banks, pumped even larger sums into European money markets, using "swap lines" of dollars advanced by the Fed, to be repaid at a later date, to ensure that there would be no runs on European banks.

Jean-Claude Trichet, the ultraconservative president of the ECB until 2011, took great pride that the ECB had moved before and even more aggressively than the Fed. Speaking at a forum in June 2009, he recalled, "We were the first to act back in August 2007, temporarily providing on day one of the turmoil unlimited liquidity to preserve as normal as possible the functioning of the money market." His efforts, he added, taking a poke at the United States, "have yielded one very important result that sometimes seems to be overlooked: there has not been a single failure of a systemically relevant financial institution in the euro area. This is an achievement whose importance cannot be overstated."

By mid-2009, the most dire phase of the first crisis had passed. The ECB, the Fed, and the Bank of England had acted separately and jointly to recapitalize or nationalize failing banks and to flood markets with liquidity. The Fed pursued a policy of aggressive bond purchases, increasing its own balance sheet from about $700 billion to well over $2 trillion. The ECB mounted a parallel operation. Both central banks lowered interest rates. The Obama administration, meanwhile, had launched a $775 billion economic stimulus program, and Britain, Germany, and several other nations pursued antirecessionary policies.

At the G-20 summit in London on April 2, 2009, there was no talk of austerity. Rather, the world's leaders committed themselves to a total of $5 trillion of fiscal expansion, and added an extra $1.1 trillion to the resources of the International Monetary Fund. By late 2009, unemployment was slowly declining in much of the EU, and economic growth had turned positive. Though there were still serious elements of a continuing deflationary drag from the collapse of housing bubbles, notably in the United States, Spain, and Britain, and from the failure of wages to keep pace with productivity, leading to a demand shortfall, there were signs of an economic recovery, albeit a painfully slow one.

Two often forgotten elements of this story are worth underscoring. First, though the ECB was a deeply conservative and inflation-averse institution, its conservatism did not preclude it from pumping short-term liquidity into the banking system in a financial panic. Its leaders had been national central bankers, and they knew what needed to be done. In the first phase of the crisis, aggressive ECB intervention met no significant opposition from either the European Commission or the leaders of the EU's member states. Second, fiscal policy was deliberately *expansionary* in the first phase of the crisis, and Europe and the United States seemed to be emerging from the worst effects of the financial collapse by late 2009, as growth rates rose and unemployment began coming down.

The more dire second phase of the crisis, which has threatened to destroy the euro and the European Union and to condemn the world to depression, did not begin until hedge funds, bankers, and money market funds began speculating against sovereign debt—and neither the ECB nor the European Commission stood in their way. The Germans, by indicating in late 2009 that no help would be forthcoming from Berlin or Frankfurt and that they would veto a rescue by the EU, only fanned the flames. As Europe slid deeper into depression, fiscal policy shifted from expansion to austerity. The catalyst was, of course, Greece.

A SMALL CRISIS IN A SMALL COUNTRY

In October 2009, PASOK, the Greek socialist party, won a resounding victory after having been in opposition for more than five years. The new government soon learned that the public deficit, projected at just 3.5 percent by the previous conservative government that April, was more like 12 percent, or four times the Maastricht limit. Prime Minister George Papandreou's advisers also discovered that the government's books had been manipulated with the help of Goldman Sachs. A special series of complex bonds created by Goldman disguised additional borrowing as merely money management.

After Papandreou made the true budget information public and appealed to Brussels for aid, money markets began betting against Greek bonds. The process quickly fed on itself, increasing Greece's borrowing costs, driving the country deeper into a deflationary depression, and creating a self-fulfilling prophecy of imminent collapse.

At this point, the crisis might have been easily contained. Two policies that were not pursued could have readily stabilized the Greek downward spiral and prevented its spread to other nations.

First, Chancellor Merkel might have agreed to have the EU support a recovery and reform program for Greece, giving the country adequate time for the reforms to be carried out and for revenue collections to be increased while its real economy recovered. Instead, she resisted any aid to Greece until May 2010, after the attack on Greek bonds turned critical—and then imposed devastasting austerity in exchange for loans that did not help Greece but merely repaid its creditors. Had Merkel backed Greek recovery and reform from the outset, or even left open the possibility of aid, there would have been far less downward pressure on the bonds. Instead, she adamantly refused to help, virtually inviting the speculative attacks.

Second, the ECB might have intervened earlier and more aggressively. By purchasing Greek government bonds on the secondary market, taking the opposite side of the bet that the hedge funds were making, the ECB and the other European central banks could have caused the value of Greek bonds to firm and produced instructive losses for the speculators. The hedge funds would have then quit the game, and the run on sovereign debt would not have spread to larger countries. If the European authorities had grasped the potential for broader havoc, they might have taught the speculators a salutary lesson. But the ECB did not pursue this course. Merkel was staunchly opposed, and nobody even seriously debated it. Greece's entire debt was less than €300 billion. Aid in the range of €150 billion would have been sufficient to refinance most of it at low interest rates, squelching speculation, cutting costs, and buying time for the economy to reform and recover. This approach was considered out of the question—by Merkel, by other conservative national leaders, and by the ECB. And so a very modest problem slowly mutated into a threat to the entire European Union as the speculative attack against government bonds spread to Europe's larger economies.

The Greek crisis was treated more as a morality play than as a macroeconomic and regulatory challenge. The Greeks had broken the rules and must pay for their sins. If Greek interest rates were rising, free-market ideology held that this had to be "the market" speaking, providing important information—never mind that the market in this case was traders seeking to create a self-fulfilling prophecy of impending default for short-run profit or that markets had mispriced the risk of investments in Greece during the boom phase. Greece's cooked books were taken as proof of the EU's failure to maintain adequate surveillance and of the need for tougher measures now. It was further pointed out that the ECB was prohibited by its charter from lending directly to governments—this was the no-bailout clause insisted on by the Germans at Maastricht.

The unholy trinity of free-market ideology, German arrogance, and the sheer political power of speculative financial institutions ensured that the crisis would deepen. It was compounded by a European Union with multiple veto points and little room for resolute leadership in a crisis. And so Europe went into a needless depression, causing untold human misery and social instability and placing the entire project of European union at risk.

Chapter 6

A Greek Tragedy

GEORGE PAPANDREOU, SCION OF THE leading family of Greek socialists, saw himself as more of a modernizer than a radical. His father, Andreas, led the first PASOK government in the 1980s. His grandfather Giorgios, for whom he was named, had served in earlier coalition cabinets. Born in Minnesota to an American mother, educated at Amherst College and the London School of Economics, and teased for speaking better English than Greek, the new prime minister permanently settled in Greece only in his twenties. Papandreou was a longtime critic of the corruption in the Greek state, which he described as "clientism."

In Greece, government agencies worked hand in glove with interest groups. It was difficult to enter a profession, start a business, collect taxes, fire people, or make the public sector operate responsibly. Papandreou hoped to change that. "As socialists," he told me, "we need government to be efficient." He was also committed to making the Greek government more transparent and democratic. Taking office in October 2009, he vowed to attack corruption and improve tax collection and public services, as well as to launch an antirecession stimulus program and expand the welfare state. All this would be no small balancing act.

The system of government that Papandreou hoped to reform was in many respects like that of a Third World country. The Greek state was a series of fiefs. The government could not obtain reliable numbers on such basic questions as how many people worked for the civil service, since each agency kept its own records in mutually inconsistent formats. In the spring of 2011, the finance minister ordered all public employees to sign a form before collecting their next paychecks—so that the government could get a comprehensive tally of who was on its payroll. One of Papandreou's first acts was to sign a consulting contract with the German firm SAP to get all of the government's economic data in electronic form. As of this writing, the system is still not fully operational.

Each government agency had its own network of constituencies that resisted change. One of these was the Greek labor movement, a potent element of PASOK. Different departments had separate pension systems, each with its own rules for contributions and benefits. Some allowed employees to retire at fifty. As late as mid-2012, it was revealed that a few semiautonomous state agencies, including public transport and public utilities, had simply ignored the prime minister's orders to cut salaries.

The tax system was famously corrupt. Property tax collection was a sieve because Greece had no national land registry. Commercial enterprises could avoid paying taxes by bribing inspectors. To reform collections, the government had to create a new audit force from scratch. Even so, the government managed to collect about 32 percent of the national income in taxes. Most of these revenues came from value-added and excise levies that fell heavily on low-income consumers, fueling the national wish to avoid other taxes.

Pharmaceutical companies had sweetheart contracts with the Greek health system that resulted in exorbitant charges to consumers, windfall profits to drug companies, and a web of kickbacks. One of Papandreou's early reforms was to require that all prescriptions be computerized, eliminating the overcharges and saving consumers over 30 percent.

In the national health system, salaries were low. When someone from the middle or upper class needed surgery, insurance ostensibly covered the procedure, but it was customary to slip the surgeon a *fakelaki,* a "little envelope" with cash; the patient would then go to the head of the queue. The doctors, in turn, greased the palms of the appropriate hospital administrators. Meanwhile, less affluent Greeks had to wait. In late 2012, the health system, squeezed by budget cuts, failed to pay doctors even their basic salaries. These costs, too, were passed along to patients.

All of this inefficiency and corruption infuriated the minders from the European Commission and the European Central Bank charged with releasing dribs and drabs of loan money as Papandreou sought to carry out reform. The bureaucrats, mostly from northern European nations with a tradition of highly professional civil service, took Greece's slow progress as deliberate foot-dragging or hopeless cultural lassitude. And so austerity demands were redoubled as the Greek economy further sank, losing close to 25 percent of its GDP in four years, the worst loss for any European country since World War II.

The difficulty of Papandreou's task was compounded by the splits in PASOK. Many in the leadership had grown up with the old system of patronage and remained dependent on it. His cabinet was a mix of allies, skilled technocrats, and rivals who could not be excluded. The defense ministry went to Evangelos Venizelos, who regularly undermined Papandreou and later succeeded him as party leader. The new economics minister was Louka Katseli, a Princeton-educated economist and longtime OECD official whose good establishment credentials coexisted with fairly radical views. As finance minister, he selected the British-educated technocrat George Papaconstantinou. But Papaconstantinou could not get other cabinet departments to comply with belt-tightening measures and was replaced in 2011 with Venizelos.

A corrupt system that nevertheless manages to function has potent constituencies resisting change, while only the broadly unorganized public is potentially on the side of drastic reform. Mobilizing public opinion was therefore crucial to Papandreou's prospects of success, and in the second year of a deep recession, there were plenty of public frustrations. He might have made some real headway as a champion of reform and recovery had he not been put in the position of having to simultaneously serve as an agent of brutal austerity. "Our mistake," one of Papandreou's top advisers told me, "was to think that conditions imposed by Brussels would give us leverage to proceed with difficult reforms. Instead, it all associated us with insane policies."

DEBT AND DIGNITY

A few words on Greek history are in order. The Greek national memory is replete with foreign occupations, humiliations, and *diktats*. The Ottoman Turks ruled Greece from the fifteenth century until the nineteenth. Greece declared independence in 1821, a cause broadly supported by European public opinion, though it took six years and the intervention of a French, British, and Russian armada in 1827 to finally oust the Turks. The nascent Greek state took advantage of the broad support for its revolt against the Turks and floated an independence loan. The government defaulted in 1826, even before Greece had fully expelled the Turks, shutting Greece out of European capital markets for the next fifty-three years. The European powers selected a king for newly independent Greece, seventeen-year-old Prince Otto of Bavaria, who spoke little Greek. Otto was expelled in 1862 and replaced by a Dane, George I of Schleswig-Holstein, who reigned until 1913, when he was assassinated.

In World War I, Greece fought on the Allied side against Germany, Austria, and Turkey. After the war, the victorious powers awarded Greece several islands that had been under Turkish control, as well as the predominantly Greek city of Smyrna on the Turkish mainland and a surrounding Greek-speaking enclave. But when the Turks invaded in 1922, the Allies did not come to the aid of the Smyrna Greeks. Hundreds of thousands died, and over a million ethnic Greeks from ancestral homelands in the Asia Minor regions of Ionia, Pontus, and Eastern Thrace were deported to European Greece, where they had never lived. The massacre at Smyrna was second only to the genocide of the Armenians in the catalog of World War I–era Turkish atrocities.

After a period of unstable semi-democracy under a still-influential Greek monarchy, General Ioannis Metaxas, a fascist, seized power in a coup in 1936. When World War II broke out, he sought to keep Greece neutral, but Mussolini demanded the right to occupy several Greek strategic sites. Metaxas refused, leading Italy to invade. The smaller Greek army humiliated the Italians in the war's first defeat of the Axis powers. Hitler rescued his hapless ally with a blitzkrieg attack and invasion in April 1941.

The German occupation of Greece was one of the most brutal in Europe. The local economy was destroyed, and food was in extremely short supply. In Athens alone, at least 250,000 civilians died of starvation. The small Greek Jewish community, dating to antiquity, was all but annihilated. Partisan guerrillas of the Greek resistance made forays from the mountains, and in retaliation Nazis wiped out entire villages thought to harbor sympathizers. The resistance was mostly led by communists, but it included a broad range of anti-Nazis working with British and U.S. intelligence as well as with the Soviets.

The Germans were pushed out of Greece in October 1944, and the aftermath was unlike what ensued in any other occupied European nation. At a Moscow meeting that month, Stalin and Churchill agreed to a pact making the Balkans a Soviet sphere of influence—with the exception of Greece, where the British would be dominant. In the anarchy that followed the German withdrawal, civil war between the resistance and pro-Nazi Greeks broke out in early 1945. To stabilize affairs and prevent a communist victory, the British openly backed right-wing Greeks who had been prominent Nazi collaborationists during the occupation. As the Cold War intensified, the United States, under the Truman Doctrine, provided aid to the anticommunist side, leading to a right-wing victory in 1949.

Elsewhere in postwar Europe, Nazi collaborators were disgraced, imprisoned, and barred from politics. In Greece, they became the ruling elite. A repressive formal democracy was restored in 1949, only to fall to a dictatorship that lasted from 1967 to 1973. Greece at last became an effective democracy in 1981, when the first PASOK government broadly restored civil rights to former anti-Nazi resistance fighters and sponsored a referendum ending the monarchy. Thus Greece has a certain sensitivity to foreign ultimatums and occupations, most notably on the part of Germans.

MERKEL'S MEDICINE

In October 2009, as Papandreou was forming his cabinet, Angela Merkel was in high spirits. Germany's own federal election was held a week before Greece's, on September 27. Merkel's Christian Democratic Union trounced a badly splintered Social Democratic Party (SPD), which was reduced to its lowest level since before the Hitler era, just 22 percent of the popular vote. Merkel, having governed in an awkward grand coalition with the SPD during her first term, now turned to the free-market and antitax Free Democratic Party as her new governing partner, moving her program to the right.

Some of Merkel's posture was a product of her personal history. As a Lutheran minister's daughter raised in the East German state of Brandenburg, Merkel was well suited to the role of fiscal scold. A physical chemistry scholar, she had gotten into politics as communism was collapsing, serving as a press spokeswoman in East Germany's brief postcommunist government. As reunification advanced, Merkel moved over to Germany's governing party, the CDU. She was noticed by Chancellor Helmut Kohl and was named minister of women and sports in his first cabinet after reunification.

Merkel was scornful of the ineptitude of statism and resented the free spending of the Schröder government that she defeated in 2005. But beyond Merkel's own preferences, Germany's perverse role in the crisis reflected its recent history in ways that have not been generally appreciated.

In the 1990s, 4 to 5 percent of German GDP was going every year to subsidize the former German Democratic Republic, where living standards had been less than half those in the West. This income transfer produced higher taxes on West Germans and wider deficits, as well as inflationary pressures that the powerful Bundesbank damped down by raising interest rates.

As the economy sagged and national unemployment rates rose well above 8 percent, Schröder, though a Social Democrat, concluded that a further remedy was to depress wages in the west. He asked Peter Hartz, the labor relations director of Volkswagen, to chair a panel to recommend greater labor market flexibility. The so-called Hartz reforms of 2003–5 weakened trade unions, compelled the unemployed to take low-wage jobs, and created a new category of employment known as "mini jobs," which did not offer normal wages or benefits and from which workers could be fired at will. A major wing of the SPD close to Germany's powerful unions objected. One popular SPD leader, Oskar Lafontaine, quit the government to form a breakaway party, The Left (Die Linke). The reforms were enacted, but the SPD never recovered from the split.

The deficit spending necessary to subsidize reunification widened the German debt ratio from around 40 percent of GDP before reunification to 75.7 percent by 2009, embarrassingly above the Maastricht limit of 60 percent that had been the Germans' own demand. Inflation spiked, then gradually subsided to a relatively low 2 percent by 2009, but it was never far from German consciousness. Aid to other nations, especially aid that might require the printing of money by the ECB, triggers deepseated fears of runaway inflation. In 2012, with inflation almost flat, a major national advertising campaign in Germany warned: "When inflation returns, you'll be glad you're banking with UBS." UBS is a Swiss bank. The message to inflation-phobic Germans: Move your money to Switzerland. It is not conceivable that this slogan would resonate anywhere else in Europe.

Germany, normally a large exporter of capital, turned inward as investment funds flowed to the former East Germany. All of these trends—the higher German interest rates, the reduced German wages, and the diminished capital flows outward—produced a recession in the rest of Europe. They also affected German public opinion.

The heavy costs of reunification were the ultimate transfer union, and they were not popular. After reunification, taxes were raised and wages cut. If West German workers and taxpayers were weary of sub-sidizing fellow Germans who were at least members of a common *volk,* they were in no mood to subsidize Greeks.

Merkel's domestic priority was to get German finances under con-trol. Her major project in this spirit was a constitutional amendment to require near budget balance over the business cycle, limiting deficits to just 0.35 percent of GDP. Such provisions are rare in Europe. Merkel had borrowed the idea from Switzerland. The provision, known as the debt brake (*Schuldenbremse*), was enacted in May 2009. It becomes fully effective for federal budget policy in 2016. By 2020, Germany's states will be prohibited from running any deficits at all. As a constitu-tional provision, the debt brake takes a two-thirds majority to repeal. The weakened SPD was too intimidated to oppose it.

After winning re-election in 2009, Merkel moved to bring German-style fiscal discipline to the entire European Union, expressing her conviction that before deeper integration could proceed (much less a transfer union), the long-deferred terms of Maastricht for common fis-cal discipline had to be enforced throughout the EU. Her vehicle was a "fiscal compact" to finally put some teeth in the still-dormant require-ments of a deficit limit of 3 percent of GDP and a debt limit of 60 per-cent. The pact was approved in January 2012 by all seventeen nations that use the euro and was signed as a treaty by twenty-five of the twenty-seven members of the larger EU in March.

To implement the spirit of the pact, the European Commission issued eight new directives in February 2012, so every member state now gets a detailed report from the Commission on its budget, with explicit requests for fiscal tightening if it is outside the Maastricht limits. This is known as the macroeconomic imbalance procedure. If a country fails to comply, it can be subject to fines equal to one-tenth of 1 percent of its GDP as well as other sanctions.

The Commission reports go far beyond the monitoring of deficits and debts; they also make recommendations and demands in a broad range of other policy areas that reflect the Commission's premise that freer markets will lead to more economic growth. For example, labor markets are supposed to be liberalized for the sake of competitiveness, a polite way of creating pressure for wage reductions. Countries receiving emergency aid, such as Greece, Ireland, and Portugal, get even more explicit direction and in effect become wards of Brussels. In the pursuit of budget balance, Ireland was required to scrap its minimum wage but permitted to keep its low corporate taxes. So the demand for fiscal tightening is far from evenhanded. The entire process functions as a neoliberal hammer.

Thus, when François Hollande became president of France in May 2012, pledging to reject Merkel's fiscal pact (which had been supported by his predecessor, Nicolas Sarkozy), one of the first bouquets sent by the European Commission bureaucracy was a detailed report warning France to reduce its budget deficit or face sanctions. The return address was Brussels, but it might as well have been Berlin. The economic assumptions of these EU reviews are extremely conservative, if not irrational, since fiscal tightening in a recession only makes the situation worse. Yet Chancellor Merkel and the Brussels bureaucracy remain on automatic pilot, stubbornly keeping to a course that was set in the late 1990s, when there was no financial crisis.

The free rein given speculation against the sovereign debt of EU member nations functions as Merkel's enforcer. The message: Tighten your belts or the bond market will get you. (But then, the bond market also reacts against the belt-tightening.) The alternative course of limiting speculation is not part of mainstream debate. As former German chancellor Helmut Schmidt put it, "Thousands of financial traders in the USA and Europe, plus a number of rating agencies, have succeeded in turning the politically responsible governments in Europe into hostages."

If a nation balks at complying with the Commission's demands, it risks a downgrade of its bonds in addition to speculative attacks against them, a twin process that feeds on itself. Though Hollande took office promising to contest the austerity policies, he also pledged that France would hit the 3 percent deficit target in 2013, a deflationary commitment that made no macroeconomic or political sense, except in the context of trying to appease money markets and comply with the arbitrary demands of the Commission.

There is a notable double standard here, in that the European Com-

mission does not press for adjustments on the part of the surplus countries, primarily Germany. Keynes's model for the Bretton Woods system,
by contrast, was intended to put pressure on the surplus countries to
expand so that the deficit countries would not have to contract. But the
current EU procedure puts all the pressure on the deficit countries and
creates a systemic bias in favor of contraction.

German political leaders, bankers, and citizens are also wary
of the direct and indirect exposure of their country to the debt of
other European nations and their banks. In their view, all this debt
is ultimately borrowing against the good credit of Germany. The Ifo
Institute in Munich puts the total German exposure to debts incurred
by other European countries and banks, the ECB, and the new EU
bailout institutions at €778 billion. But the policy of general austerity,
far from sheltering Germany, only risks broader contagion. In September 2012, the OECD projected that even Germany would soon be in
recession.

SPRINGTIME FOR SPECULATORS

In late 2009, against the background of drastically divergent political realities in Athens, Brussels, and Berlin, bets against Greek sovereign debt became a popular hedge fund play in London and New
York. While Papandreou attempted to implement his reform program,
the interest rate on Greek bonds demanded by financial markets kept
relentlessly increasing.

On December 8, 2009, citing worsening fiscal and economic conditions, Fitch Ratings downgraded Greece's credit rating from A– to
BBB+. The action intensified the speculation against Greek government
bonds, and "spreads"—the gap between rates on German and Greek
public debt—began ominously widening. By late January 2009, Greece
was paying a crushing 7 percent interest to sell its ten-year bonds.

Merkel, however, was adamant that Greece needed to get its own
house in order instead of relying on a bailout. Nor did the ECB offer
aid. In early April, depositors began withdrawing large sums from Greek
banks, which were running through their capital reserves. The shares of
other European banks, large holders of Greek bonds, were pummeled
in financial markets. Greek pension funds were also major bondholders.

By April, Greece, on the edge of default, was having to pay upward of 15 percent to market two-year bonds. A default would collapse the Greek economy and set off a chain reaction across Europe. Papandreou, declaring the Greek economy "a sinking ship," formally requested emergency aid from the EC, ECB, and IMF, the so-called troika. A joint delegation of officials arrived in Athens on April 21. After intensive negotiations, Papandreou and his cabinet agreed to further austerity measures, which would be supervised by the troika, in exchange for aid. The terms were to be finalized by European heads of government.

Meeting with European leaders in Brussels on May 7, ECB president Trichet warned that Europe's finances were on the brink of collapse. He had long resisted pressure from the leaders of France, Spain, Italy, Greece, and Portugal to intervene directly in bond markets to purchase government securities, but now there was no alternative, Trichet explained. By purchasing the bonds on the secondary market rather than directly from governments, the ECB would not technically be in violation of the no-bailout clause of the Maastricht treaty. Axel Weber, head of the Bundesbank and a senior member of Trichet's board, strenuously disagreed.

However, ECB intervention to calm the bond markets would not be enough to halt the crisis. The Greek government, facing plummeting revenues and rising interest costs, also needed direct financial aid to help pay its bills. Late on the evening of May 7, Merkel reluctantly agreed both to the ECB bond purchases and to a €110 billion rescue package for Greece. The plan included an €80 billion line of credit from EU member states and an ad hoc €440 billion bailout fund awkwardly called the European Financial Stability Facility. The IMF agreed to contribute to the package, which, all told, totaled €750 billion. The sum was thought large enough to impress markets and to reassure investors not only in Greek bonds but in those of other peripheral nations where spreads were ominously widening. The financial press treated it as a major breakthrough and policy shift.

For Merkel, the timing could hardly have been worse. On May 9, her CDU faced elections in Germany's largest state, North Rhine–Westphalia. If the incumbent center-right coalition lost, Merkel would also lose her working majority in the upper house of the German parliament, which represents the states.

But despite Merkel's political risks, the optimism was premature. The package did not restructure the Greek debt nor provide aid for Greek recovery. It merely lent Greece more money to roll over expiring bonds as they came due and to keep current with interest payments. Since the aid to Greece was in the form of additional loans, not grants, it only increased Greece's overall ratio of debt to GDP. The money went to Greece's creditors, not to the struggling Greek economy. And it came bundled with deeper austerity. This design, repeated by Merkel and the troika over and over again as the sovereign debt crisis worsened during the next three years, would prove to be a fatal flaw.

Two days later, Merkel's center-right coalition was repudiated in the election in North Rhine–Westphalia. The German press, which had generally lauded Merkel as an "iron chancellor" resisting bail-outs, turned on her. The tabloid *Bild*, which plays roughly the role of Fox News in the German media, declared in a headline: "Once Again, We Are the Fools of Europe." The quality press was scarcely kinder. *Frankfurter Allgemeine Zeitung* proclaimed that "a transfer union has effectively been introduced and the central bank is now under political command," leading to the degradation of the euro into a "soft currency and the failure of monetary union."

In exchange for the rescue, Greece had to sign an agreement cutting its deficit by €30 billion in a single year, aiming to reduce the deficit ratio by 5.5 percentage points. To put the scale of this cut in perspective, the comparable figure for the United States would be a staggering $825 billion budget cut in one year, a deflationary policy that no sane economist, left, right, or center, would recommend.

Greece had an ally in Dominique Strauss-Kahn, then head of the IMF (and later disgraced in a sex scandal), who felt strongly that too much austerity was counterproductive. But the ECB, the Commission, and above all Merkel felt that any debt relief for Greece would set a bad example. Strauss-Kahn could not sway Merkel. At one point, she told Papandreou, "We want to make sure nobody else will want this."

Civil servants took an immediate pay cut of 16.7 percent. By long-standing custom, Greek professionals received their yearly pay in four-teen installments. These included one paycheck for each month of the year, then additional paychecks before Christmas and before summer vacation. The annual salary was simply divided by fourteen. But the German and European Commission negotiators treated these two "extra" monthly paychecks as expendable bonuses, and they were called "bonuses" in the official EU documents. They were, in fact, part of the core pay package.

Pensions in excess of €1,200 a month were also cut. In addition, three new tiers of value-added taxes were imposed, on the premise that such taxes were harder to evade. These added as much as ten percentage points to the taxes Greeks paid on retail sales, giving Greece the highest VAT rates in Europe. It was the most deflationary package ever imposed on a member of the EU, and it was guaranteed to intensify the shrinkage of Greece's GDP, make the deficit reduction goal a moving target—and diminish rather than increase the confidence of money markets.

The official European Commission report on Greece published in June 2010 projected, absurdly, that Greece would return to positive GDP growth of 1.1 percent in 2012. In fact, the Greek economy shrank by another 7 percent. Within two months of the deal, money markets had grasped that the austerity and additional debt would only make Greece's economic situation worse, and spreads kept rising again. This pattern would be repeated over the next three years as the crisis widened. By September 2010, spreads were back to their early May peak that had triggered the first aid package. During this period, Greece's actual borrowing came from the troika, at rates of around 5 percent. The spreads were relevant as indicators of the failure of the program to restore market confidence. Except for some short-lived dips, spreads on Greek bonds kept continued to widen, as speculators turned on Portugal, Ireland, Italy, and Spain, a group of nations that, along with Greece, the financial press and political conservatives uncharitably termed the PIIGS.

Eighteen months later, facing a far broader financial emergency, the European Central Bank in December 2011 and January 2012 advanced three-year loans totaling about €1 trillion to Europe's commercial banks, at an interest rate of just 1 percent. Had the ECB made the same deal with Greece in mid-2010, the Greek government could have refinanced its debt at low interest rates, the speculative orgy could very likely have halted, and the crisis would have been contained at a far lower cost.

Greece was subjected to intensive monitoring by a committee of three senior officials representing the European Central Bank, the European Commission, and the International Monetary Fund. The three functionaries who actually negotiated with Greece were Klaus Mazuch of the ECB, a German; Matthias Mors, another German, who served in the

Commission's Directorate-General for Economic and Financial Affairs; and Poul Thomsen of the IMF, a Dane. None had any deep knowledge of the Greek economy. They came at the exercise with budgetary spreadsheets. The three often disagreed on the particulars, with the IMF urging a longer term to reach the deficit-reduction goals. But the rules of the game required unanimity. The entire exercise was in turn closely monitored by the Merkel government, lest any leniency creep in.

The rescue was designed and implemented more to maximize the troika's leverage on the mandated austerity program than to help the Greek economy recover. Emergency loan funds were doled out, a few billion euros at a time, as the Greek deficit cuts were implemented. When the Greek government had difficulty hitting the targets, funds were withheld. This practice reinforced the image of a continuing financial calamity, undermining the beneficial effect of the aid, and whetting the hedge funds' appetite for attacking Greek bonds, which then deepened the crisis.

Week after week, the financial press was filled with reports of the Greek government being right on the edge of default. In the months after the May assistance package, Greek banks and the Greek government grew more dependent on emergency advances from the ECB, and the collapse of the Greek economy continued to deepen. It would be hard to imagine a "bailout" process less conducive to either the goal of reassuring money markets or of inducing the Greeks to combine attainable reform and recovery.

A telling example of the unreality of the exercise was the troika's approach to the privatization of Greek government assets. Papandreou's government had initially proposed privatizing €3 billion to €5 billion euros' worth of Greek government assets. It was no secret that the Greek state was inefficient, and Papandreou and his ministers hoped that some sales could both produce some badly needed revenue and improve the functioning of railways, the gas company, major ports, the postal service, and the state casino monopoly. The port of Piraeus had already been partly privatized, in a deal with the Chinese. The government strategy was to bring in private sector partners to improve management, while retaining a minority stake. In the deal negotiated with the troika in May 2010, the total privatization package was increased to €7.5 billion.

But at a meeting in Athens on February 11, 2011, the troika representatives abruptly declared that the Greeks had to increase the privatized assets to €50 billion, and to sell them off within five years. "There was no economic logic to it; they simply needed to fill a budgetary hole," said the director of the privatization office, George Christodoulakis. For example, they wanted the government to privatize Greece's thirty-eight regional airports, a crucial part of the public infrastructure in an island nation heavily dependent on tourism. Most ran at a loss. "Who would buy them?" Christodoulakis wondered. An economic collapse was the worst possible moment to sell off state assets, which would fetch only fire-sale prices. But the troika refused to back down. When Greece failed to hit the unrealistic targets, this lapse was gravely noted in its next report card, and became more grist for withholding aid.

QUICKSAND

In October 2010, on the eve of a European Summit meeting at the French casino resort town of Deauville, Chancellor Merkel and French president Nicolas Sarkozy had a private chat as they walked along the Normandy beach. There, Merkel enlisted Sarkozy to support a four-part deal devised by her financial advisers, as the centerpiece of the summit. The plan had been under informal discussion since June. Under the scheme, all of Europe would embrace Merkel's proposed fiscal pact. Investors in Greek bonds would be made to accept a reduction in their face value, exchanging them for longer-term bonds partly guaranteed by the European authorities. This was termed, euphemistically, the "Private Sector Initiative." In return for the restructuring of its debt, Greece would undertake even deeper austerity. The deal also included a permanent €500 billion fund, the European Stability Mechanism, to replace the temporary bailout fund.

The idea was to take some of the pressure off Germany, the European Commission, the ECB, and the Greeks, by reducing the face value of Greece's overall debt. It was clear that Greek bonds were never going to be repaid at a hundred cents on the euro. By continuing the pretense that they might be, the authorities were only prolonging the agony. Better for the private investors to take a partial loss up front and use that "haircut" to reduce Greece's total debt exposure, and thus reassure markets that there would be no chaotic default. The Summit leaders accepted the plan. The press referred to the deal as a kind of negotiated partial default. Money markets, however, were not impressed.

The plan backfired in two key respects. Little of the benefit trickled down to the Greek economy, so the net result was to drive Greece even deeper into depression. And if private bondholders were going to take some loss even in the absence of a formal default, they would have even less appetite for holding the bonds of Europe's other peripheral states. Merkel's scheme spread the speculative contagion from Greece to other nations. In the immediate aftermath of Deauville, spreads took a huge leap, not just on Greek bonds but also on those of Ireland, Portugal, Spain, and Italy. Ireland, which could no longer market its bonds, became the second EU nation to officially need a bailout, and Portugal became the third.

At the October 2010 meeting of European leaders, a furious ECB President Jean-Claude Trichet, who had not been consulted on Merkel's Private Sector Initiative, brought a set of charts showing the increasing pressure against government bonds, and lectured Merkel and Sarkozy on the folly of the policy. A shouting match between ECB president Trichet and French president Sarkozy ensued. But the political leaders, led by Merkel, would not be deterred. If states were on the line to underwrite bailouts, the recipient nations had to undergo deeper austerity, and the bondholders had to share in the pain. The alternative course, of direct EU credit support and respite from austerity, was *verboten*.

Hard cases make bad law. Greece, admittedly, had a long record of poor public administration and corrupt government spending. It was difficult for the European public to work up much sympathy for the Greeks; they were widely seen as victims of their own profligacy. But if Greece was the bad boy of the EU, the poster child was Portugal. Since the restoration of its democracy in 1974, Portugal has had a relatively clean and efficient government. The Portuguese enjoyed a solid rate of economic growth in the years before 2000, but the economy faltered even before the crash, pushing unemployment to 7.3 percent by 2007. When Portugal turned to the European powers in April 2011 for aid, it got the same kind of perverse austerity medicine in exchange for loans to prop up its bonds.

In contrast to Greece's Socialist PASOK, which pushed back against the troika's demands, Portugal's newly elected conservative government fairly volunteered for austerity. "We did everything they asked of us, and we even went beyond their demands," Elisa Ferreira, a former cabinet minister and now a senior member of the European Parliament, told me.

Portugal intensified privatization, raised taxes, cut spending, and shaved pensions. Its reduction in the public deficit for 2012 exceeded the targets. The troika showered Portugal with praise. "The far-reaching and ambitious reform agenda is on track in the areas of labor market, health care, housing, judiciary and the insolvency and regulatory framework including competition," exulted the European Commission in its December 2011 report. "Also, privatizations so far have been highly successful. . . . The fiscal adjustment in 2011–2012 is remarkable by any standards."

But austerity didn't work any better as a recovery strategy in Portugal than it did in Greece. Unemployment has risen to 15 percent. The Portuguese economy shrank by 3.3 percent in 2012, one of the worst downward spirals in Europe. Reduced wages and idled workers, not surprisingly, reduce revenue collections. The debt ratio still continues to rise. Portugal still cannot access money markets to roll over its bonds.

The Irish variation on the story was particularly perverse, since Ireland had been a model fiscal citizen with low deficit and debt ratios. As recently as 2008, its debt-to-GDP ratio was just 25 percent. Ireland sank because banks' speculative investments in housing created a massive, debt-financed property bubble that drove its largest banks into insolvency. The foreign borrowings of big banks soared from €15 billion in 2004 to €110 billion in 2008, mostly in the form of ninety-day loans. When the housing bubble popped, and the collateral sank below the value of the debt, the heavily leveraged banks could not roll over their loans and became insolvent. The Irish-American Bank made €72 billion worth of loans on property, and lost €34 billion of that—almost half of what it had lent.

The Irish bank losses did not have to sink the whole economy. But instead of reorganizing failed banks, protecting depositors, and leaving bank shareholders and bondholders to absorb the losses, a corrupted Irish government, with the EU's approval, gave an unlimited financial guarantee to the six major banks, covering their losses with massive state borrowing. Ireland's debt ratio soared, leaving the Irish government unable to access credit markets and entirely dependent on the tender mercies of the troika, which required the usual austerity regimen. By 2012, the Irish public debt ratio was 108.2 percent, right up there with Greece's—but only because a friendly Irish government went broke bailing out foolish bankers. With the austerity medicine imposed by the EU, Ireland's unemployment rate kept climbing, to just under 15 percent by late 2012.

Nor did austerity help Britain. Unlike the weaker peripheral nations of Europe, Britain is a member of the EU but does not use the euro. As a result, it controls its own currency, and has had no runs on its bonds, even though Britain's banking crisis was right up there with those of Ireland and the United States. Like the Federal Reserve, the Bank of England has kept British interest rates near zero—but that has not been sufficient to counteract the government's austerity program.

Prime Minister David Cameron, who took office in May 2010, did not need any troika to impose an austerity program on Britain. In a keynote speech to Conservatives in April 2009, Cameron actually *called for* an "age of austerity." Once in office, Cameron made cutting the deficit his prime policy goal. Public spending was slashed, but in 2012, Britain went back into a double-dip recession. British GDP in late 2012 was 3.1 percent below its level of early 2008. Despite the belt-tightening, Britain's debt ratio has steadily increased—from around 50 percent when Cameron took office in 2010 to nearly 70 percent in 2012—because a deeper recession reduces economic activity and government revenues.

At the end of 2012, independent research institutions such as the nonpartisan Institute for Public Policy Research and the financial press were predicting an unprecedented "triple-dip" recession in 2013. Total employment in the United Kingdom remained well below its 2008 pre-crisis level. Real wage growth of 1.8 percent was lagging behind the inflation rate of 2.7 percent. Despite extensive budget cutting, the government stood to miss its deficit target by at least three years. Conservative austerity policy in Britain provided a real-time experiment in the folly of belt-tightening as the cure for effects of a financial collapse.

ENTER THE PRIVATE GOVERNMENT

After Merkel's October 2010 initiative to press bondholders to share losses, there ensued a revealing set of negotiations with representatives of the banks that wrote credit default swaps. These were the most politi-

cally powerful banks in the world, led by JPMorgan Chase and Goldman Sachs. Their vehicle was a little known lobby and self-regulatory
cartel called the International Swaps and Derivatives Association. The
big banks had created ISDA in 1985 to resist any government regulation of swaps. That way, the swaps could remain lucrative private contracts with terms and conditions defined by the banks.

Now, in 2010, the bankers wanted to be sure that any loss taken by
bondholders would be "voluntary." Since swaps were written as a form
of insurance against default, a voluntary write-down in the value of
Greek bonds would not technically be a default and would not trigger
swaps contracts—and would thus save the big banks billions of dollars.
ISDA has a determinations committee, representing the largest banks,
to decide what constitutes a "credit event" that would trigger payment
of swaps contracts.

The negotiations were further complicated by disagreements among
Greece's European masters. The European Commission, prodded by the
Merkel government, wanted the write-down to be considered a negotiated default. That way, private creditors would absorb more of the
loss, and it would be an object lesson to others. But the ECB, desiring
an orderly process and not wishing to increase the risk of bank runs,
wanted it to be voluntary. The ECB was holding about €100 billion
worth of Greek bonds, bought on the secondary market at below par,
and stood to make a bundle if they were redeemed at face value. As
these convoluted negotiations dragged on for nearly eighteen months,
Greece was more like a spectator than a participant in the bargaining
over its own fate. And with each passing month, Greece sank deeper
into depression.

ISDA epitomizes the power of private regulation. Even though swaps
are issued by regulated banks and have the potential to crash the economy and create massive losses absorbed by taxpayers (as they did when
AIG collapsed in September 2008), they are largely unregulated, even
to this day. In place of transparency and public regulation, the terms are
set by ISDA representing their issuers—a gross conflict of interest.

So while Greece continued to suffer deepening depression and relentless supervision of its austerity program by the troika as a condition
of the release of loan funds, a bizarre private sideshow prolonged the
agony. Would Greece default? Would there be a "voluntary" write-
down in the value of its bonds? Would it be technically considered a

default? A quick resolution might have reduced Greece's borrowing costs. But the protracted uncertainty only widened spreads and worsened Greece's penury.

On October 27, 2011, after a Brussels summit that lasted almost until dawn, Sarkozy and Merkel announced a package intended to stabilize and contain the Greek mess once and for all. EFSF funds would be increased to a formidable €1 trillion. Greek bondholders would accept a 53.5 percent write-down in the face value of their bonds. Existing bonds would be traded for new ones with maturities of at least ten years partly guaranteed by Brussels, lowering interest costs and reducing Greece's overall public debt by about €100 billion. And—inevitably—even deeper austerity would be visited upon the suffering Greeks. There were at least twenty-one different bond issues in the deal, each with different terms. The details were unfathomable to all but a few insiders.

But Prime Minister Papandreou, who supported the deal, now faced a growing rebellion both from the opposition and in his own ranks. Business elites were concerned that the plan would end with nationalization of Greek banks. Louka Katseli, who had been moved to the post of labor minister, voted against a provision of the latest austerity package suspending collective bargaining. She was expelled from PASOK, and the austerity plan cleared the Greek Parliament by just ten votes, 154–144. The terms of the package also included a staggering 22 percent cut in the private sector minimum wage and a provision giving creditors the right to seize gold from the Greek central bank in the event of a default, as well as a requirement that the new debts under the write-down agreement be governed under British rather than Greek law, with terms far more favorable to creditors.

Facing widespread popular opposition, Papandreou began having second thoughts himself. On November 1, he abruptly called for a national referendum on the austerity pact. This produced stunned outrage among other European leaders, bitter divisions within his cabinet, and worsening conditions in the money markets. Though Papandreou insisted that he was calling the referendum in the belief that the Greek voters, most of whom favored staying in the Eurozone, would support the pact, his action was widely viewed either as prologue to a default or as a sign that an exhausted Papandreou was cracking under the strain. Evangelos Venizelos, now finance minister, who stood to gain if Papandreou fell from power, fiercely defended the deal and attacked the referendum. Papandreou then declared that he would not hold the referendum after all, and resigned as prime minister.

After Papandreou's resignation in November 2011, a caretaker government under the former president of the Bank of Greece, Lucas Papademos, assumed power pending elections. Speaking together in Berlin on January 9, Merkel and Sarkozy increased the pressure on both Greece and its creditors. Unless Greece met the austerity commitments, Merkel warned, no aid would be released. And unless the bondholders agreed to a debt restructuring, the European authorities would let Greece default, and creditors would lose everything. In February, a deal was at last struck for the 53.5 percent write-down.

On March 9, 2012, after months of equivocating, ISDA announced that the write-down would be considered a credit event after all. A collective action clause in the Greek bond contracts gave Greek and European authorities the leverage to require most bondholders to accept the write-down. That detail made the loss involuntary, triggering payment of swaps contracts. But because markets had long anticipated and priced in that risk, the actual payment by the banks would be only about $3 billion. Eventually, bondholders representing nearly 97 percent of the value of outstanding Greek sovereign debt agreed to take the deal.

In theory, this restructuring should have benefited Greece. But in practice, when you netted out the savings in interest payments against the increased terms of austerity and absence of recovery aid, Greece stayed in debtors' prison. The Greek government remained unable to access regular credit markets, except on extortionate terms.

One final double standard is worth noting. If 97 percent of bondholders agreed to trade new bonds for old, prominent among the 3 percent of bondholders that refused to trade new bonds for old was a hedge fund called Dart Management, which epitomizes everything unsavory about the unregulated shadow banking system. Dart is run by Kenneth Dart, a U.S. tax exile based in the Cayman Islands who inherited a fortune as heir to the company that makes Styrofoam containers. On May 13, 2012, the hard-pressed Greek government paid €436 million to holdout investors, and a reported 90 percent of that went to Dart, which had been accumulating Greek bonds at around 50 to 60 cents on the dollar. Where other bondholders, including Greek banks, pension funds, and ordinary citizens, took substantial losses,

Dart got paid at 100 cents on the dollar, reaping a windfall gain of hundreds of millions of dollars.

Why did Greece pay Dart? Greece, at the time, was under a caretaker government. Dart had threatened to sue. After the carefully orchestrated write-down deal, the IMF had warned the Greeks that this was no time to roil markets with a default. I was told by Greek officials that an elected government never would have paid.

In the election of May 6, 2012, with Venizelos standing as party leader, PASOK received just 13 percent of the vote. The results were too fragmented to produce a government, and the election had to be repeated in June. This time, there was a narrow working majority for a three-party center-right coalition headed by the right-wing New Democracy Party, the same party that had faked Greece's budget numbers when it led the government between 2004 and 2009.

The tragedy of Papandreou's government was that it very likely represented Greece's best chance of realizing a long-deferred modernization of the Greek state on bearably human terms. Compared to many other Greek politicians, Papandreou was idealistic and uncorrupt. But the austerity demands and the rigid timetable for their implementation made it impossible for a democratic government to combine reform with impoverishment of the Greek economy and still retain the consent of the Greek electorate.

FALSE DAWN

In the late spring of 2012, the crisis intensified. As the cascading impact of the Greek crisis and the terms of Merkel's Private Sector Initiative undermined market confidence in the bonds of one European state after another, Spain and Italy became the latest targets. Spreads on Spanish and Italian government bonds ominously widened.

Spain was particularly vulnerable because its banks had been weakened by the collapse of Spain's housing bubble. Spain's banking system was caught in a circular co-dependency with the Spanish state. The government increasingly depended on the banks to buy its bonds. The banks, in turn, depended on the government to guarantee the bonds. Though Europe's accounting standards defined state bonds as entirely reliable investments, markets believed otherwise. Both the banking system and the state were barely solvent, and commentators regularly compared the situation to two drunks leaning on each other for support. At the same time, Spain was Europe's fourth-largest economy. Unlike Greece, Spain was too big to fail, and it had far more political power within Europe.

In early 2012, as the crisis worsened, Spain had a new prime minister, Mariano Rajoy, whose conservative Popular Party had defeated the Socialist incumbents in November 2011. Rajoy was initially not considered a combative leader, but he was determined that Spain not give up its sovereignty to any foreign troika. Spain, unlike Greece, had a competent system of public administration. Prior to the crisis, Spain had a low debt ratio and a budget surplus, a far better fiscal picture than even Germany's. So as the financial markets battered Spain's sovereign debt, causing spreads to rise and repeating the Greek pattern, Rajoy played a nervy game of chicken. He refused to ask the EU for help, except on entirely different terms from those inflicted on Greece, Portugal, and Ireland.

Spain has a dual banking system comprising commercial banks and *cajas* (savings banks), which supply most of Spain's mortgages. The *cajas* took the worst hit from the aftermath of the housing bubble. In December 2010, several failing regional *cajas* were reorganized into a single larger unit called Bankia. But multiple failures did not aggregate to a success. In May 2012, Bankia, by then Spain's third-largest bank, posted a loss of €4.3 billion and was nationalized, requiring a state bailout of over €19 billion. All told, the Spanish banking system was in a hole approaching €60 billion, and the weakness of Spanish banks was spilling over and driving down the value of the euro and other banking stocks. But Rajoy still refused to request European aid, if that meant taking a deal like the one imposed on Greece.

On June 9, after marathon negotiations, the Spanish economics minister, Luis de Guindos, jubilantly announced that the EFSF would advance the Spanish state a credit line of up to €100 billion to be used to stabilize the banks, with no austerity required in return. The conditions, he declared, "will be imposed on banks, not on Spanish society, nor on its fiscal or economic policy." Details were to be announced later. Rajoy proclaimed victory, Merkel appeared to have backed down on a core principle, and spreads on Spanish bonds narrowed—but it was another false dawn.

It soon became obvious that by lending Spain money to pass along to its banks, the European leaders were repeating the same self-defeating recipe they had used with Greece, Ireland, and Portugal. The Spanish state would be that much deeper in debt, calling its own solvency into question. Even worse, the Germans successfully demanded that the new European credits be "senior" to ordinary commercial credits—the bailout fund would be paid back first—further depressing the appetite of ordinary investors to buy Spanish bonds. Not only did the ratings agencies downgrade Spanish government bonds, but Moody's cut the ratings on twenty-eight leading Spanish banks, citing the fact that Spain's worsening economic picture would harm both the banks and the capacity of the Spanish state to support them.

Spreads increased to record levels. Speculation spilled over onto Italy, where spreads also rose. By June, Spain was paying 7 percent to sell two-year bonds, and Italy only slightly less. Once again, Merkel's medicine had proved toxic. By refusing to permit direct lending to Spanish banks, a non-negotiable bright line that she resolutely refused to cross, Merkel managed to turn an ostensible concession—aid to Spain without austerity—into a deepening of the crisis.

In this deteriorating economic climate, five of Europe's most powerful players resolved that it was time to rein in Merkel. In the preparations for the biennial EU summit of June 28 and 29, the leaders of France, Italy, and Spain, respectively the Eurozone's second-, third-, and fourth-largest economies, formed an anti-Merkel alliance. The move transcended ideology, for they were a socialist (Hollande), a conservative (Rajoy), and a technocrat (Mario Monti of Italy, who publicly vowed to help Hollande contain Merkel). This time, the European Commission's president, José Antonio Barroso, a Portuguese conservative who was ordinarily Merkel's ally when it came to austerity, sided with the growth alliance. So did the European Central Bank, whose president, Mario Draghi, had wanted to end the pretense and have the new European rescue funds lend directly to banks, both as sensible economic policy in its own terms and to take some of the pressure off the ECB.

Under Draghi, the ECB for a time looked as if it might serve as the key counterweight to Merkel. A politically savvy Italian, Draghi had emerged as the consensus candidate to succeed Jean-Claude Trichet in the spring of 2011 after the German heir apparent, Bundesbank president Axel Weber, a very conservative Merkel ally, withdrew. Weber strongly opposed the ECB purchases of European sovereign debt, even on the secondary market, a position that put him at odds with most of the ECB board. As the consensus candidate, the MIT-educated Draghi had punched all the tickets, serving as an EU commissioner, the governor of the Bank of Italy, and a senior executive at Goldman Sachs. He had unanimous support for the job. Even *Bild* endorsed Draghi, calling him "the most German of all remaining candidates."

Draghi was also willing to use the power of the ECB. At one point, when his comic-opera countryman, Silvio Berlusconi, was clinging to power, Draghi let it be known that the Bank would stop buying Italian state debt until Berlusconi stepped down. This stance reportedly eased the transition to the new technocratic prime minister, Draghi's ally Mario Monti.

Within weeks of taking office on November 1, Draghi announced his package of three-year, 1-percent loans to European commercial banks. The banks could use state bonds and even mortgage-backed bonds as collateral. It was a disguised way of propping up public debt. The banks went ahead and put much of the new money into government bonds, buying time. But whenever Draghi has tried to move the ECB into more explicit and aggressive interventions comparable to those of the Federal Reserve, he has been stymied by Merkel and her allies on his own board.

As the summit gathered in Brussels on June 28, 2012, Merkel made her usual pronouncements that there could be no reversing the prohibition against direct lending to shaky banks or the quid pro quo of stringent budget discipline in exchange for aid. And then, after some fifteen hours of contentious negotiation, she appeared to back down on both issues. Sources at the meeting reported that Monti and Rajoy both dug in and refused to approve any agreement at all, until Merkel gave way on the two key points.

The deal provided that banks would be able to borrow directly from the still-to-be-ratified European Stability Mechanism, overturning what had been an inviolable German taboo. Secondly, states whose banks received such aid would not be subject to the humiliating supervision of the troika, reversing another key provision of Merkel's cherished fiscal pact before it was even formally implemented.

Once again, Merkel got a withering reception at home. "Merkel Buckles," *Bild*'s headline declared. She was characteristically unrepentant. At a press conference, she insisted: "We remain entirely within our prior formula: give and take, conditionality and control." Sure enough, as details were disclosed in the next few weeks, it became clear that Merkel had prevailed on the fine print: Spain would in fact be held to a rigid austerity formula after all, supervised by the European Commission rather than the troika.

Merkel had won again. Her operating formula, as it had been for the nearly three years of the deepening sovereign debt crisis, was unchanged: Dig in, refuse to budge. Then, when confronted with incipient disaster, make tactical accommodations that buy time but fail to solve the deeper problems. Lose on the headlines, win in the details. Both the deal and the long-delayed ratification of the now-weakened stability pact were approved by the German parliament by the required two-thirds vote, with the enfeebled Social Democrats voting in support. It's also significant what the deal did not do. There were no Eurobonds to refinance old debt at low interest rates, no Europe-wide deposit insurance, and no progress on policies to rein in financial speculation. The new €120 billion investment plan included in the package was better than nothing, but it represented just one-fourth of 1 percent of the EU's annual GDP. Nor did Merkel and the other leaders entertain a revisiting of the austerity terms for Greece, Portugal, and Ireland.

Not surprisingly, money markets were unimpressed. Despite appearances, the EU was not assuming responsibility for refinancing debts in a way that would allow new growth. The banking system was only taking on more debt. Speculation intensified against Spanish and Italian bonds, deepening the crisis.

On July 26, ECB president Draghi, desperate to reassure markets, threw a Hail Mary pass. Speaking off the cuff in London, Draghi vowed to do "whatever it takes" to save the euro and the European economy. The markets read his statement as a nervy and carefully staged declaration that the ECB would at last begin massive bond purchases, like the American Federal Reserve. Spreads narrowed, and stock prices rallied.

A week later, a chastened Draghi walked it all back. There would be no such purchases, he said, until governments did their part by getting their budgets under control. Violating the secretive norms of the ECB, Draghi made a rare public disclosure about the infighting that led to his reversal: Bundesbank Jens Weidmann, protégé of Angela Merkel and a powerful member of Draghi's board, had strenuously objected. And so the policy of relentless austerity, unbuffered by large-scale ECB interventions, continued. The market for Spanish and Italian bonds crashed again.

In early September, Draghi tried once again. After more than a month of consultations with his own board and national leaders, he declared that the ECB would make unlimited purchases of short-term government bonds, to keep borrowing costs low for struggling countries. He claimed "a massive majority of the [ECB] governing council for this concept." But the council member who mattered most, Bundesbank President Weidmann, remained adamantly opposed. The Bundesbank even issued a blunt statement warning that Weidmann "regards such [bond] purchases as being tantamount to financing governments by printing banknotes."

To mollify the hawks on his own governing board, Draghi repeated the conditions of his earlier failed effort: Governments that wanted help from the ECB would have to sign up for rescue funds from the EU and strict supervision of austerity budgets by the European Commission and the IMF. Nothing doing, said the leaders of Spain and Italy. Although there was a temporary stock market bounce in response to Draghi's offer of increased bond purchases, the larger impasse and deepening crisis continued.

In October 2012, a prominent French intellectual of the center-right, Alain Minc, published "An Open Letter to My Friends, the Financiers of America." The piece, which ran in the *New York Review of Books*, attempted to rally support for the European project and the euro. Minc wrote, "The European decision-making process may well be tortuous, clumsy, and hardly transparent to the public, but it works. . . . Who would have ever foreseen that, imbued with the culture of the Bundesbank, the European Central Bank would purchase sovereign debt and [make] large scale loans, greater in relation to GDP than the campaign of easing undertaken by the Fed? . . . . Who would have thought that Mario Draghi, the president of the ECB, with the support of German Chancellor Angela Merkel, would [pledge] to intervene as often, and as much as needed . . . to preserve the euro?"

But while this defense of the European ideal is admirable, Minc's analysis is wishful. The entire pattern of the ECB has been to encumber offers of aid to struggling nations with conditions that national leaders can't accept. The provisional financial-aid commitments of Draghi and Merkel invariably conceal a poison pill of deeper austerity. When weaker debtors such as Greece and Portugal have been compelled to accept the draconian terms, the consequence has been to drive them deeper into depression.

Despite suggestions in the press that the ECB was at last moving to become more like the Federal Reserve, two differences remain key. Under Ben Bernanke, the Fed has been entirely willing to pursue policies "tantamount to printing banknotes." And Bernanke has refused to be an agent of fiscal austerity. While Draghi was making his deal, trading more bond purchases for more fiscal restraint, Bernanke was giving a major speech at the Federal Reserve's annual summer conference at Jackson Hole, Wyoming, warning against too much fiscal restraint as Congress threatened to raise taxes and cut spending in a deep recession.

By late 2012, it was painfully clear that the austerity cure was only worsening the condition of Greece and all of Europe. The more that Greece cut spending and raised taxes in order to meet deficit targets, the more the economy shrank, revenues fell, and the deficit increased. In 2010, when the EC and ECB first agreed to exchange aid for austerity, they projected Greek GDP at 235 billion euros in 2013. The actual number will be about 183 billion, according to the Greek government. The debt was supposed to peak at just under 140 percent of GDP in 2012. It will be around 180 percent, rising to 190 percent in 2013. As spending in basic services was cut and cut again, human hardship kept increasing. Greek public health officials reported the first outbreaks of malaria since the 1950s. Unemployment exceeds 25 percent. The number of Greeks with jobs declined to just 3.7 million from 4.6 million in 2008. Austerity has put Greece on a treadmill that never leads to recovery.

In these circumstances, the unity of the troika began to crack. Senior IMF officials leaked word of contentious negotiations in which they pressed European leaders to lighten up on Greece. Austerity, the IMF feared, was feeding on itself; further belt-tightening would never allow Greece to hit its target of a reduced debt ratio of 120 percent of GDP by 2020. The IMF put forward several options, including cuts in interest rates on existing credits to the Greeks, write-downs for the ECB's own holdings of Greek bonds, and more direct aid to recapitalize Greek banks. All were summarily rejected by the ECB, the European Commission, and the German government. IMF leaders also resisted being used by the European authorities to provide a seal of approval for policies they considered excessively harsh. The IMF's own annual report on global economic conditions, published in October 2012, went so far as to admonish European leaders for imposing too much austerity. In November, IMF managing director Christine Lagarde openly broke with the EC over more debt relief for Greece, declaring at a joint news conference with Jean-Claude Juncker, the Luxembourg prime minister who serves as president of the Euro Group, "We clearly have different views."

One of the most ominous effects of the contagion of a crisis that could have been contained has been the fragmentation of European capital markets. The single market, Jacques Delors's great achievement of 1990, was intended to Europeanize the market for goods, services, capital, and labor. But as the sovereign debt crisis has spread, capital markets have retreated to their national boundaries. Between 2008 and 2012, according to the Bank for International Settlements, German banks reduced their exposure to five peripheral European countries (Italy, Spain, Portugal, Greece, and Ireland) by €301.8 billion, while French banks cut their exposure by €203.9 billion. Increasingly, Spanish banks are used to buy Spanish government bonds, and Italian banks to buy Italian ones. National central banks no longer print francs and lire, but they are still relied upon to advance euros to prop up their shaky domestic banks. An April report of the ECB warned of increasing "home bias" in the European banking system—the great exception being Germany, a "safe harbor" destination for investors from other countries. The glittering coach of a Pan-European capital market is turning back into a set of weak national pumpkins.

In one more sign of the limits of Mario Draghi's powers, by late 2012 much of the money advanced to Europe's commercial banks by the European Central Bank wound up being deposited right back in the ECB—over a trillion euros. In a deflated economy, commercial bankers could not find enough prudent and profitable lending opportunities, and were already too heavily invested in the bonds of EU member governments. The cold bath cure imposed on the most heavily indebted nations was not good for the rest of the Continent. In 2012, Europe went back into recession, suffering four consecutive quarters of negative GDP performance. Even relatively healthy economies with low debt loads lost ground. The Dutch economy, for example, shrank at an annual rate of 4.1 percent. Deeper recession is likely in 2013.

EUROPE'S CLOUDED FUTURE

In December 2011, the former German chancellor Helmut Schmidt (1974–1982), spry and witty at nearly ninety-three, delivered a keynote speech to the SPD's annual convention, using words that any active German politician would find difficult to utter. He recalled that a friend had asked him how long it would take for Germany to be a "normal" country. "I answered by saying that Germany would not be a 'normal' country in the foreseeable future. Standing in the path to normality is the enormous and unique burden of our history," Schmidt said. "In almost all our neighboring countries there still exists a latent distrust of Germans that will probably persist for many generations to come."

This sensitivity, once pervasive among the German governing elite, has now faded. The fact that Germany's war debt was written off by the victorious Allies in 1948 has vanished from the national memory. There is no compassion for the fact that Europe suffered an economic drag before the collapse in part because of Germany's lavish subsidies of its own eastern states. Nor is there any comprehension of the double standard reflected in the €2 trillion forgiven the former East Germany but the massive resistance against aid to fellow EU members. Germany, having tightened its own belt to help fellow Germans, is feeling self-righteous and willing to run roughshod over its neighbors.

German characterizations of Greece, in the press and in political speeches, range from patronizing to vicious—and they do not sound pretty in a German accent. One cosmopolitan German whom I know well, a man who has long lived in the United States, told me in 2012: "They should just dig a big hole, toss the Greeks in, and cover it over."

Given the widespread German attitudes, there is no serious opposition to Merkel's policies. The Social Democrats are led by men almost as fiscally conservative as Merkel's CDU. According to opinion polls, Merkel, who faces re-election no later than September 2013, is vulnerable—but because Germans fear she is too soft, not too tough, on the rest of Europe. The fact that if Europe collapses, Germany collapses too, seems lost on most German voters. Though Merkel plays the austerity role with particular relish, another German chancellor might not be so different. "Populism" is usually considered a disease of the far right or the far left, but in Germany Merkel stands for a kind of fiscal populism of the center. The more Merkel panders to public opinion on the subject of not rewarding the dissolute Mediterranean members of the EU, the more she reinforces it.

Germany acts in tandem with a deeply conservative European Commission permanent bureaucracy, with hedge funds as enforcers. In effect, without the broad consent or understanding of the European public, a huge amount of sovereignty has been transferred from nation-states to EU officials, who are beyond direct democratic accountability—and that authority is being used to enforce a perverse economic strategy. As the Nobel laureate Amartya Sen warned:

> If democracy has been one of the strong commitments with which Europe emerged in the 1940s, an understanding of the necessity of social security and the avoidance of intense social deprivation was surely another. Even if savage cuts in the foundations of the European systems of social justice had been financially inescapable (I do not believe that they were), there was still a need to persuade people that this is indeed the case, rather than trying to carry out such cuts by fiat. The disdain for the public could hardly have been more transparent in many of the chosen ways of European policy-making.

Though the EU was once a citadel of managed capitalism, both the Brussels ideology and the personal preferences of senior Commission officials today defer to markets. Europe's proud member states are now in the situation of supplicant Third World countries. As Greece's PASOK government learned, if complying with Commission demands leads to failed policies and a voter revolt, it is the local elected officials who lose their jobs, not the Brussels commissioners or their unelected staffs.

While the EU's governing machinery is strong enough to make national leaders clients of Brussels, it is too weak to address a deepening crisis. Under the Maastricht rules, key policy changes require unanimity. In the absence of a consensus on behalf of growth policies, the default position of the EU is for more austerity. While Merkel speaks grandly about turning the EU into a deeper "fiscal union," the EU spends only about 1 percent of European GDP, and there are only trivial mechanisms of income transfer from richer regions to poorer ones. That will not change any time soon. So her conception of fiscal union means nothing more than German budget policies for all.

Beyond the dysfunction of the EU and the unhelpful role of Germany, there are crucial differences between Europe and the United States that the sovereign debt crisis brought into relief. The U.S., still the provider of the world's most important currency, faced no runs on its government bonds. There was no possibility of a default, because America, unlike Greece or Portugal or Italy, still printed its own money. And the Federal Reserve had made clear that it would create as much money as necessary to weather the crisis. In theory (bad theory, in this case), recourse to the printing presses might run the risk of inflation. But in a deep recession, inflationary pressures are nil. One might think that investors would flee the dollar for stronger currencies, but given the weakness of Europe and Japan, and the currency manipulations of China designed to deter the renminbi's international use, there were no plausible alternatives to the dollar.

Moreover, unlike Europe, the United States is quite explicitly a "transfer union." Through a range of federal programs—including Social Security, Medicare, Medicaid, food stamps, and federal aid to education—as well as government contracts that the political process spreads around, America's richer states and taxpayers subsidize its poorer ones. Low income states like Mississippi and West Virginia get back from the federal government in public spending more than twice what they contribute in taxes. Between 1990 and 2009, just under $1 trillion of taxes collected in wealthy New York State subsidized the rest of America's fiscal union.

In addition, forty-nine of the fifty states are constitutionally prohibited from running deficits. So while some states have had severe budgetary crises, there have been few speculative attacks against state bonds because states don't run deficits. The federal government, however, *is* permitted to run deficits, so it provides the macroeconomic elasticity during downturns. The EU, by contrast, has a tiny common budget.

The debate in the U.S., as we saw in chapters 1 and 2, is precisely over whether Washington should use more or less deficit spending to lean against the prevailing winds. But in Europe, it is the constituent states that are pushed into deficit by recessions, while the weak central government (the EU) is too fiscally puny to even have a macroeconomic policy. So speculators attack the member states, while the central government stands idly by.

The form of bond purchases and of other rescues by the Federal Reserve has tempered the crisis in the United States, while the conditions attached to bailouts by the ECB and EU have exacerbated it in Europe. One can find fault with much that the Fed has done, most emphatically its failure to challenge the too-big-to-fail model in exchange for all the aid conferred on banks. However, the Fed has done one big thing right. When the Fed purchases the securities of the federal government or of banks, it does not demand disabling fiscal conditions. So its bond purchases serve as seals of approval and function to restore market confidence. By contrast, when one of Europe's rescue mechanisms pumps money into a wounded government or banking system, it signals to markets that the recipient is in grave trouble. The amount of the aid is invariably too little and too late, and the conditions attached only deepen the crisis and depress market confidence. The doling out of small sums of aid pending good behavior creates an aura of chronic near default.

It is now apparent that the metastasis of a fiscal imbalance in Greece into a general crisis of speculation against sovereign debt and serial runs on European banks and nations was a preventable tragedy. Perverse policy was rooted in fragmented institutions, flawed ideology, and asymmetries of power, but that doesn't excuse it. At each step of the way, policies were pursued with the primary goal of reassuring financial markets and punishing fiscal offenders, not of addressing underlying economic ills. The need to appease money markets—which often make systematic pricing errors—became an unquestioned article of faith.

As Greece teetered on the edge of collapse for the umpteenth time in mid-June 2012, U.S. Treasury secretary Tim Geithner, in a speech to the Council on Foreign Relations, warned, "If you wait to move on these things and you let the market get ahead of you, then you increase the cost of the solutions." Throughout the crisis, this view was the standard wisdom. One could cite any of hundreds of comments by political leaders, financial executives, or journalists expressing the same homily: Policy had to appease markets or suffer the consequences.

The excluded alternative is to appreciate that the folly is not in failing to stay ahead of the verdicts of markets, *but in allowing markets to define what's acceptable*. Markets, by definition, are hardly reliable.

After all, it was the failure of markets to accurately price securities that caused the collapse. Yet in the fifth year of the crisis, markets were still being permitted to define the correct price of sovereign bonds, and the self-fulfilling destruction of national credit systems by speculative markets was precluding a cure.

A serious recovery plan for Europe would require major policy changes. One is significant debt relief and restructuring for severely indebted member nations, and a respite from self-defeating austerity demands. Various proposals have been put forth for Eurobonds, meaning that the EU as a whole would refinance and guarantee old debts. Done properly, this policy would lower interest costs for heavily indebted nations, and reduce the capacity of money markets to destroy national economies. It would stop the speculative contagion.

A related need is for the ECB to be given the authority of a true central bank, including the ability to directly buy the bonds of member nations. That authority should be used, to demonstrate that speculating against European sovereign debt doesn't pay. The EU, like the United States, also needs much more stringent regulation of its banking system. The moves in late 2012 toward consolidated banking supervision are too weak. A new regulatory regime needs to compel bankers to revise and simplify their business model. A financial transaction tax, which would take the profit out of highly leveraged short-term trades, is a good place to start.

Fiscal limits, in the spirit of Maastricht, make sense in normal times but not in an economic depression. They should be waived until Europe is firmly on the road to recovery. Some European nations have very high debt-to-GDP ratios, but Europe's debt level as a whole is around 100 percent of GDP, well below the typical debt ratio at the end of World War II. Europe has much higher savings rates than the United States, and it is capable of financing this debt, if the cycle of speculation and crash can be broken and if Europe indeed becomes more of a transfer union. Bond-financed European recovery funds, well into the hundreds of billions of euros a year, would make an immense difference in restoring a virtuous circle of economic growth, employment, and increased revenues.

Assuring the survival of the euro, with or without Greece, has gotten a huge amount of attention. But while the collapse of the euro would intensify Europe's economic crisis, the sole focus on saving the single currency misses the larger point. The EU is pursuing a perverse theory of how to produce a recovery from a financial collapse. The problem is the policy, not the euro. Without a change in the strategy, tossing weaker nations out of the Eurozone will save neither the euro nor the promise of the EU.

In late 2012, despite a flow of cheap loans from the ECB, Europe's private-sector banks were sitting on an estimated €1.2 trillion in cash, and lending to business was declining. The Continent's crisis of deflation was worsening. The obsession among Europe's leaders with debt repayment rather than debt relief, and the protracted policy deadlock while the crisis worsens, are chillingly reminiscent of the 1920s. Unless the broader ideology of austerity for states and license for bankers is reversed, Europe will continue to lurch from crisis to crisis, and the Continent's institutions will face a generation of lost prosperity and lost legitimacy for its democratic governing institutions. Ironically, the whole point of the EU was to contain the dark forces of ultra-nationalism—which are being loosed again, from Norway to the Netherlands to neo-Nazis in Greece—by austerity policies imposed from Berlin. Europe, much less Germany, is not a good place to play with the social dynamite of prolonged depression.

PART THREE

Chapter 7

The Moral Economy of Debt

BY NOW, SEVERAL CONCLUSIONS SHOULD be evident. Reckless indebtedness leads to crisis. More often than not, the culprit is debt that results from the cycle of financial speculation and crash. After a crisis, debt relief is necessary for economic recovery. Avoiding moral hazard is a proper issue for averting the *next* crisis. Prevention of disabling debt is better achieved by adequate regulation of credit before the fact than by erecting prisons for the casualties of the last crisis. Intelligent people seem to have a very hard time grasping that paradox.

One reason for this myopia is that the pragmatic question of debt relief after a crisis is complicated by relations of power and privilege. Debt, as we have seen, is not just a means of financing investments or addressing public needs; it is part of a system for maintaining social relations or geopolitical advantage. In the collapse that began in 2007, the most toxic forms of debt were those incurred or promoted by banks. Banks, nonetheless, have retained the power to block debt relief for others. So have powerful nations. Today, entire economies are enlisted in the service of repaying old debts, even though debt relief would be far more efficient and far more socially just.

As we saw in the story of Daniel Defoe and the invention of modern bankruptcy, debt relief has been replete with double standards since its inception. Intermittent acts of mercy, case by case, were a poor substitute for national macroeconomic policies. As late as the nineteenth century, nations did not have the institutions or insights of modern economics. The banking system was badly regulated and chaotic. Only Britain had a central bank, and its bias was deflationary. Demands for respite from depression in the form of cheaper credit or bankruptcy reform were ad hoc and episodic. There was no coherent conversation about what today would be called countercyclical policy to temper the tendency of markets to overshoot on either the upside or the downside.

In the twenty-first century, governments have a modern arsenal of economic management institutions: central banks, instruments of fiscal and monetary policy, and highly refined tools of financial regulation and bankruptcy law. But they keep repeating the mistakes of the nineteenth century. What has not evolved with the institutions is the distribution of political power. If anything, financial elites enjoy far more concentrated influence than at any time since the Gilded Age. Thus the policy mistakes are not errors of judgment but the natural products of a lopsided politics.

DEBT AS SIN

Beginning with the statute of Queen Anne, the idea of a fresh start, of wiping away past debts, was for the merchant class, not for ordinary deadbeats. This distinction was intimately connected to the widespread belief among elites that too much kindness or charity would spoil the poor. In his celebrated work *The Fable of the Bees,* written in 1705, the very year bankruptcy reform was introduced in the English Parliament, Bernard Mandeville warned that the "proclivity to idleness" made relief of the needy a bad idea. The paupers' workhouse and the debtors' prison were twin emblems of that philosophy. Edward Bulwer-Lytton, an early nineteenth-century conservative critical of aid to the poor, wrote, "The Poor-laws were intended to prevent mendicants; they have made mendicancy a legal profession." Like the double standard in bankruptcy, this conservative view of debt relief and poor relief is enduring. When Charles Murray wrote in his best-selling 1984 critique of welfare policy, *Losing Ground,* "We tried to provide for the poor and produced more poor instead," he was channeling Mandeville and Bulwer-Lytton.

Curiously, the language of morality is seldom directed against the improvident *creditor*. Yet as applied to debtors, the earlier, moralistic view of unpaid debt as sin persisted alongside the more modern instrumental one. In a society heavily influenced by Calvinism, commercial success was given a moral free pass, while failure and debt suggested divine disgrace—a sign, as Cotton Mather put it, that the debtor was "most evidently called of God into a low and mean condition." Religious imagery and the language of social obligation are filled with metaphoric and literal references to debt. Our debt to God and to parents who brought us into the world are incalculable. When a felon serves out a prison sentence, he is said to have paid back his debt to society. Anthropologist David Graeber observes that in several ancient and modern languages, including Aramaic, Hebrew, and Sanskrit, debt, guilt, and sin are the same word. In modern German, *schuld* means both debt and guilt. The Lord's Prayer in the King James version based on the Gospel of Matthew (used by many Protestant denominations) asks God to forgive us our "debts," while the variation in Luke (and the Catholic liturgy) asks forgiveness for our "trespasses" or "sins." In purely market terms, Graeber notes, a debt is "an exchange that has not been brought to completion." One party received the goods; the other is owed a payment. To fail to honor a debt, therefore, is to be in a condition of guilt on both moral and economic grounds.

Before the invention of the modern banking system, finance was local. Debtors usually knew their creditors, and there was an intimacy to monetary obligations. Repayment was a personal and ethical obligation, and default was a moral failing. But as capitalism evolved into a system of impersonal financial intercourse, the immediate connection was severed. Thus the moral meaning of debt changed, at least for commercial transactions. Bad things sometimes happened to good entrepreneurs, and life needed to move on. An insolvency was often the consequence of a freely assumed business risk that went sour for reasons beyond the debtor's control. Investors were consenting adults. Settling the debt and allowing commerce to resume was in the general economic interest—even in the interest of creditors, who were better off getting some payment rather than merely enjoying the satisfaction of seeing the debtor suffer for his sins.

As debt became impersonal, it also became transferrable. Debt was so much paper. A merchant could sell it at discount, say 90 percent—the flip side of the buyer's 10 percent interest charge—to another merchant, or to a "factor" specializing in trading cash for accounts receivable, or to a bank. By the seventeenth century, the emerging banking system was already about creating, discounting, trading, and speculating in paper. This had enormous benefits for the expansion of commerce, but also risks. As debt collateralized further debt in a pyramid of paper promises, successful speculations depended on rising prices. When the bubble burst and prices abruptly fell, the pyramid came tumbling down. The severity of the crash was in direct proportion to the leverage.

Innocent bystanders got caught up in this chaos, and the system displayed scant compassion for the little people. John Dickens, a clerk in the Royal Navy Pay Office, was thrown into London's Marshalsea Prison in 1824 under the Insolvent Debtor Act of 1813. Dickens, with a large family and a small salary, was overwhelmed by several relatively modest debts. The immediate plaintiff was a baker, James Kerr, to whom Dickens owed forty pounds, ten shillings.

The bankrupt's son Charles was twelve at the time. In his 1858 classic, *Little Dorrit,* set in the same Marshalsea Prison in the 1820s, Charles Dickens offered this description of a bewildered debtor much like his father:

> The affairs of this debtor were perplexed by a partnership, of which he knew no more than that he had invested money in it; by legal matters of assignment and settlement, conveyance here and conveyance there, suspicion of unlawful preference of creditors in this direction, and of mysterious spiriting away of property in that; and as nobody on the face of the earth could be more incapable of explaining any single item in the heap of confusion than the debtor himself, nothing comprehensible could be made of his case. To question him in detail, and endeavour to reconcile his answers; to closet him with accountants and sharp practitioners, learned in the wiles of insolvency and bankruptcy, was only to put the case out at compound interest of incomprehensibility.

A ruined small bankrupt caught in a larger web of financial transactions inhabited a different universe from a corporate executive leaving the messy details of a Chapter 11 filing to the firm's lawyers and accountants. Today's unfortunates may not be literally in prison, but the nightmare experiences of homeowners trying to navigate the private banking bureaucracy in the hope of staving off foreclosure and eviction would be grist for a modern Dickens, if not a Kafka.

BANKRUPTCY, AMERICAN-STYLE

A century after Daniel Defoe's brush with debtors' prison, a similar scenario of widespread default and financial ruin played out in the aftermath of the American Revolution. All wars are costly, and there are only three ways to finance them: taxing, borrowing, or printing money that often loses value when the war ends. In 1776, with the populace suffering the privations of war, the legitimacy of the new government far from secure, and the entire conflict having been triggered by a revolt against taxation, a tax-financed rebellion against the British Crown was not practical. The Revolutionary War was underwritten mainly by printing vast sums and by borrowing more.

Between June 1775 and November 1779, the Continental Congress, in forty-two separate printings, issued notes known as Continental dollars, with a face value of $241.6 million. The states, during the same period, printed nearly another $210 million. These notes lost value almost as soon as they came off press, despite their nominal backing by precious metals. In 1780, the Continental Congress passed an act formally specifying that it took forty paper dollars to purchase a dollar of silver. The bonds issued during the war soon traded at deep discounts, and nobody knew whether they would be assumed and honored by the new national government or at what discount.

Like most wars, the American Revolution also produced a temporary economic stimulus, as fortunes were made supplying armies and speculating in products in short supply as well as in the bonds of the new government. But after the war ended, boom turned to bust. In 1785, the postwar depression and contraction of credit left states severely short of funds and farmers at risk of losing their homes to foreclosure. The Massachusetts legislature that year sought to meet its budget shortfall via more aggressive tax enforcement. But veterans of the War of Independence had not fought the British over illegitimate taxation only to have their lands seized by home-grown tax zealots.

In 1786, some 2,500 Massachusetts farmers under the leadership of Daniel Shays shut down local courthouses to prevent foreclosure proceedings. It took the state militia to break the rebellion. So the issues of currency, credit, and land policy were very much on the minds of the Founders as they gathered in Philadelphia.

Despite the ratification of the Constitution in 1789, these questions were still very much in contention. By 1792 another speculative boom in land and in the securities of the new nation had turned to bubble and then bust, sending high and low people alike to debtors' prisons, including some of the Republic's most prominent merchants, financiers, and statesmen. Robert Morris, the leading financier of the Revolutionary War and for a time America's wealthiest man, languished in Philadelphia's Prune Street Prison for three years, beginning in 1798. Prefiguring

Wall Street's conflicts of interest two centuries later, Morris not only underwrote and marketed Continental bonds but personally speculated in them, making and losing a fortune. A close associate of Morris and Alexander Hamilton, the aforementioned William Duer, secretary of the Board of the Treasury, speculated in various forms of paper, including federal government notes, land warrants, state securities, and bank debt. He financed his speculations with borrowed money.

With the collapse in March 1792 of the bubble in paper assets, partly pumped up by Duer himself, thousands of investors, large and small, were ruined, and America's first financial panic ensued. After fending off creditors for several years, Duer himself went to jail, owing upward of $3 million. James Wilson, a delegate to the Constitutional Convention and a sitting Supreme Court justice, died in a North Carolina debtors' prison.

On the eve of the crash, the states displayed a crazy quilt of bankruptcy laws, many left over from colonial times. Most favored creditors. Only Rhode Island allowed insolvent debtors to initiate a plea for relief and to keep 5 percent of their assets upon legal discharge.

Despite the explicit authority granted it by the freshly ratified Constitution to enact a comprehensive federal bankruptcy law, Congress remained deadlocked. Opinion was divided between Federalists, who were sympathetic to the merchant class, and Jeffersonians, who saw speculators like Morris and Duer as emblematic of a new aristocracy of wealth abhorrent to republican and agrarian principles. Complicating the debate was the shared premise that bankruptcy, as defined by the statute of Queen Anne, meant relief for merchants but not for the common man. This also offended the Jeffersonian soul.

The English model for American bankruptcy law empowered a creditor to organize an accounting of the assets of a cooperating debtor who sought discharge. Jeffersonians worried, not without reason, that this brand of bankruptcy reform could give creditors new legal rights to seize or attach the lands of farmers. The distinction between traders and common debtors was not as simple as the proposed law implied, argued Albert Gallatin, a leading Jeffersonian. "Go into the country," he warned in January 1799 in a debate on the House floor, "and you will scarcely find a farmer who is not, in some degree, a trader." Many state laws, he added, protected farmers from having their homesteads seized or attached. A federal bankruptcy law could sweep these laws away, altering the balance of power between creditors and farmers across rural America.

The federal bankruptcy statute finally enacted by Congress in March 1800 was modeled on the British law. The intended beneficiaries were commercial debtors. Only those with at least $1,000 of debt could file, and only creditors, not debtors, could initiate proceedings. Southern agrarians in the Senate proposed an amendment exempting "farmers, graziers, drovers, tavernkeepers or manufacturers," but the amendment failed, leaving the impact on country people unresolved. The law satisfied nobody. Jeffersonians were outraged that it served speculators; merchants were disappointed that it provided too little practical relief. Only about eight hundred cases were filed, and creditors ended up recouping about ten cents on the dollar. As one critic complained, "We saw rich men today, bankrupt tomorrow, and the next day in full business and great style, while the poor farmer or manufacturer . . . must suffer the penalties of the law in a jail." In 1803, with Jeffersonians in control of Congress, the law was repealed, two years before it was due to expire.

A pattern persisted throughout the nineteenth century. A periodic financial panic would lead to an epidemic of bankruptcies. In the absence of monetary or fiscal policies to temper recessions, relief of debtors was one of the few remedies available to policymakers. But the relief was understood to be temporary, and debates were charged with disputes over class and sectional interests. At the heart of the conflict was the issue of whether proceedings could be initiated by debtors or only by creditors, and whether bankruptcy protection was for common people or just for merchants and, later, corporations. These schisms prevented a general federal bankruptcy law from being enacted for most of the nineteenth century; the easiest consensus was to take no action.

The Panic of 1837 was followed by the short-lived Bankruptcy Act of 1841. In the 1840 election, the victorious Whig Party had made bankruptcy reform a central plank. Under the new act, bankruptcy, for the first time, did not require creditor consent. A debtor could petition for relief, cooperate with a court-appointed bankruptcy trustee, and receive a discharge. Some thirty-three thousand debtors obtained discharges before the law was repealed in 1843.

The Bankruptcy Act of 1867, which came during a period of mass economic turbulence following the Civil War, explicitly extended relief beyond the merchant class. It lasted eight years, providing for both voluntary and involuntary bankruptcy, but it did not prevent a massive shift into debt peonage among farmers afflicted by falling commodity prices. Not until a time when corporate power was ascendant did Congress enact a permanent general bankruptcy law. The Bankruptcy Act of 1898, of which more shortly, was heavily biased toward the commercial class and laid the groundwork for today's Chapter 11.

The states, meanwhile, had a hodgepodge of bankruptcy and debt collection laws, some of which were ostensibly friendly to debtors. Household goods and farm implements were typically placed beyond the reach of debt collectors. Virginia law required that creditors wait a year and a day before initiating collection proceedings in court. Several states, led by Texas, provided protections for homesteads. In principle, a farmer who defaulted on debts was protected from having his land attached and seized by creditors. But the concept of a homestead exemption is often misunderstood. It protects the home from being attached if a homeowner defaults on *other* debts. If a homeowner or farmer defaults on the mortgage, the creditor is free to seize the property.

In the absence of a federal law, state bankruptcy procedures were on balance pro-creditor. These state laws mostly allowed creditors to enforce contracts for a hundred cents on the dollar. The creditor who got to the courthouse first got first claim against the debtor. Discharges and fresh starts were rare. Creditors in many states could garnish as much as 100 percent of debtors' wages.

THE MONEY ISSUE

Americans have in the back of their minds from high school history courses a cartoon version of what our nineteenth-century forebears called "the money issue." Our ancestors, even those with little formal learning, were oddly obsessed with arcane questions of monetary policy. Andrew Jackson famously got into a feud with the Bank of the United States. Entire political parties, like the Greenback Party, were organized around the cause of paper money. The whole nation was evidently susceptible to the ideas of monetary cranks. It is worth looking beyond this caricature to sort out what our great-great-grandparents were really arguing about.

The early American economy suffered from a perennially unstable monetary system. The politics of bankruptcy were intimately connected with the politics of credit creation. The colonies and, later, the nineteenth-century republic were chronically short of so-called specie money—gold and silver—so they relied on paper, some of it locally created, some borrowed from abroad. The paper might be backed by land, or very partially by gold, or by other paper, or ultimately by nothing at all. Debt fueled commercial expansion, until the next bubble and panic left debtors unable to repay what they owed. As a consequence, the nature, availability, and control of credit became a central political preoccupation.

The authors of the Constitution explicitly gave the new nation's government exclusive power to coin money. Chastened by the inflationary experience with Continental dollars, they forbade the states and the federal government to create *paper* money. A draft clause empowering the new national government to "emit bills on the credit of the United States"—that is, to print paper money—was expressly stricken from the Constitution in the Philadelphia debates of 1787.

But if neither the states nor the federal government could print money, and with monetary precious metals scarce, where would the money necessary for commerce come from? Into this vacuum stepped banks, basically unregulated, able to create money almost at will, but leaving the entire system vulnerable to booms and busts. After 1781, states began chartering banks. As the nation grew, banking exploded. There were only 26 chartered banks issuing circulating notes in the 1790s. By 1815, there were nearly 200. By 1840, the number had risen to 711. And each bank was basically a law unto itself in the creation of credit.

In addition to notes and drafts written on banks, privately issued bills and notes became part of the money supply and were widely accepted as circulating currency, though often at discount. The typical American merchant, trader, artisan, or farmer was both a debtor and a creditor. Edward Balleisen, the historian of bankruptcy, wrote, "Manufacturers and urban importers depended on the remittances of wholesalers; wholesalers on timely collections from retailers and artisans; retailers and artisans on eventual payment from consumers; discounting banks and note brokers on disbursements by drawers of promissory notes and acceptors of bills of exchange; and endorsers on the pecuniary fidelity of friends or relatives." It was a highly unstable system, one that would be familiar to John Dickens, vulnerable to spinning into reverse in a downturn.

Ostensibly, banknotes were IOUs redeemable in gold or silver, but it was clear that there was not nearly enough specie to pay off claims should they ever be presented at the same time. Paper money soon became a system based mainly on trust that the paper would be generally accepted. The government sold paper to finance its own debt. Businessmen invested and accepted payment in notes. Farmers sold their crops for notes. Workers accepted payment of wages in paper. Counterfeit notes were widely mistaken for the real thing, which helped to provide a money supply adequate to expand commerce in a nation chronically short of precious metal coins. The dubious provenance of the fake notes was almost beside the point. In the era of "free banking" after 1838, when almost anyone could open a bank, the difference between outright counterfeiters operating with a clandestine printing press and sketchy state-chartered bankers producing notes backed by dubious collateral was only a matter of degree.

As John Kenneth Galbraith observed in his history of money, there was something splendidly democratic in this monetary anarchy: "The function of credit in a simple society is, in fact, remarkably egalitarian. It allows the man with energy and no money to participate in the economy more or less on a par with the man who has capital of his own. And the more casual the conditions under which credit is granted and hence the more impecunious those accommodated, the more egalitarian credit is."

Through the alchemy of banking, a deposit of $1,000 becomes collateral for a loan of $1,000. The depositor still has a credit of $1,000, but the borrower suddenly has a credit of a second $1,000, and the amount of "money" has abruptly doubled. In the modern era, regulators have imposed reserve requirements on this process. The banker can't lend the entire $1,000; he needs to keep, say, $100 as a reserve against losses. The reserve forms part of the bank's equity capital. This system is known as fractional reserve banking; banks still create money, but the reserve requirement limits their capacity to create it infinitely. The evil of twenty-first-century shadow banking was that unregulated financial firms could create money with no equity backstop. In Hamilton's day, gold backing served as a kind of reserve requirement, restricting willy-nilly credit creation.

But in the absence of a central bank as a lender of last resort, a general financial panic leads to a credit contraction. The leverage described by Galbraith goes into reverse: if a borrower defaults on his loan, the bank suddenly lacks the money to repay the depositor, and it calls in other loans. The entire credit system contracts just when it needs to expand. Unfortunately, the price that the young nation paid for its happy financial chaos was periodic panics. The question that vexed nineteenth-century Americans was how to devise a system of money so that credit was both plentiful and orderly—or "elastic," as a later generation of monetary reformers would term it.

Looked at logically (as opposed to historically), Alexander Hamilton's Bank of the United States, chartered in 1791, would seem to have solved the problem. As part of the process of consolidating monetary policy under the new federal government and promoting commerce, Hamilton's Bank assumed the debts of the states and the Continental Congress. It redeemed Continental notes at one cent on the dollar, actually a generous formula, since many speculators had bought up the bonds for far less. Hamilton sponsored the creation of a mint at Philadelphia to coin gold and silver, establishing specie as the basic money of the new nation. Notes issued by the Bank would be backed by gold or silver at a ratio of 3 to 1.

The Bank also served the monetary and regulatory function of facilitating the circulation of commercial banknotes, since its own notes were insufficient for the daily needs of a growing economy. In a process that prefigured the role of the Federal Reserve's discount window, which advances funds to member banks, Hamilton's Bank accepted the notes of commercial banks, but only those banks that exchanged paper for specie on demand. At a time when banknotes were mistrusted and often accepted only at discount, the Bank of the United States provided a seal of approval for private banks considered reliable.

Hamilton's Bank had much of the authority of a modern central bank, operating as the fiscal agent of the United States, lending to the government, and serving as the repository of taxes. It also advanced money to commercial banks and even competed with them, lending directly to merchants. Had the bank survived, the nineteenth century might have had a more stable, though probably more austere, monetary system.

But even before the Bank was chartered, it was a lightning rod for agrarian and anti-Federalist opposition. Jeffersonians were appalled at this centralization of monetary power in an institution with no democratic accountability. Jefferson himself, now President Washington's secretary of state, contended that the Constitution contained no authority for such a bank. The attorney general, Edmund Randolph, shared Jefferson's view. Though the charter was narrowly approved by a divided Congress, the president had enough doubts that he asked James Madison to prepare a veto message. In the end, Washington was convinced that the benefits outweighed the costs, and he signed the bill.

Jeffersonians detested the Bank on several counts. Not only did it represent the power of a rising "aristocracy of wealth" and a centralization of power that seemed antithetical to republican and agrarian principles, but it both displayed and invited corruption. When $8 million of the Bank's $10 million in capitalization was opened to public sale on July 4, 1791, many of the buyers of its securities were well-known speculators loathed by the Jeffersonians. The excesses of Hamilton's cronies in New York and Philadelphia triggered the panic of 1793; their speculative instruments included the Bank's own paper as well as state debt later assumed by the Bank. And the vaunted bank was largely powerless to remedy the depression that followed.

SORTING OUT THE MONEY DEBATE

The Jeffersonian and later Jacksonian agrarians found themselves whipsawed by the contradictory logic of money creation. On the one hand, they were congenitally distrustful of concentrated wealth. On the other hand, they wanted cheap and plentiful credit. As rural people, they profoundly mistrusted the eastern banks, both as emblems of wealth and as unreliable business partners. In the annual cycle of planting and harvesting, country banks typically relied on big-city banks to "discount" (accept for an interest charge) the paper they advanced to farmers and replenish their cash. When financial conditions grew tight, the country banks were the first to have their credit restricted by the eastern banks.

The remedy would have been a central bank biased toward generous credit creation, vigilant against speculative uses of credit, and under greater democratic control. This, in effect, was the demand of the populists in the 1880s and 1890s. The Federal Reserve, for a brief period in the 1930s and 1940s, was just that sort of institution. But a central bank responsive to the needs of small farmers and artisans was not on offer in the 1790s. The choice was Hamilton's Bank of the United States or no bank.

Most southern and western farmers, and their representatives in Congress, concluded that they'd be better off with no national bank. When they finally killed the bank in 1810, they settled for a system in which credit would be plentiful in good times. But for the most part, they failed to get one in which debt relief would be merciful in hard times.

In 1816, after the economic disruptions of the War of 1812, Congress chartered a second Bank of the United States, again for twenty years. It, too, was a lightning rod for agrarian and republican opposition. By the time Andrew Jackson became president in 1829, the antipathy to bankers was not just based on ideology and regional economic self-interest. It was deeply personal. This second Bank of the United States had a charter so broad that it placed the institution beyond political accountability—another harbinger of the Federal Reserve. After 1824, the Bank's president was Nicholas Biddle, who ran the institution like his own private financial preserve and political machine.

General Jackson distrusted banks, banknotes, and concentrated financial power. Biddle personified all three. Jackson was also convinced, with substantial evidence, that Biddle and the Bank had worked against his own election in 1828. Others in his circle, like the Jeffersonians before them, had a somewhat different rationale. They did not hate banks. Many were close to the independent state-chartered banks that chafed under Biddle's restraints. They just hated Biddle's Bank. Biddle explicitly viewed his bank as a force for a national currency, and said so. He wrote to a member of its governing board that his purpose was "to purify the currency by the substitution of the notes of the Bank for the notes of State banks." The state banks also coveted the government deposits that would be spread more broadly around the banking system if the Bank's twenty-year charter lapsed in 1836.

What is bizarre about the conflict is not that Jacksonians resisted the concentrated power of Biddle's Bank but that they associated their economic self-interest with a money system based entirely on gold and silver. If the previous half century had proved anything, it was that economic expansion required plenty of circulating paper money. The success of the Jacksonians in killing the Bank was an epic case of "Be careful what you wish for." With the demise of the Bank, gold and silver became scarce, largely unregulated bank paper proliferated, and so did the system's propensity for regular panics and depressions, beginning with the Panic of 1837.

For a time in the 1840s, agrarian antibanking sentiment was so extreme that three states, Texas, Arkansas, and Iowa, were admitted to the Union with absolute constitutional prohibitions against any form of banking. Thirty years later, interest-group positions reversed: eastern financial elites would demand a sound currency explicitly backed by gold, and agrarian radicals would clamor for paper money.

Reviewing events, one is struck by how muddled the lines of argument were. The availability of credit was the difference between prosperity and ruin, but class interests got all tangled up with regional claims and plain superstitions. Merchants and farmers regularly switched sides on the contentious issue of whether money should be metal or paper. Symbol frequently trumped substance. Citizens often found themselves passionately battling for policies that did not serve their interests.

Farmers—the vast majority of the common people—prized their economic autonomy. They hated banks in part because they hated to be vulnerable to creditors. As Bray Hammond, the dean of scholars of banking politics in early America, sagely observed, "The merchant borrowed eagerly because the credit enlarged his working capital and his profit. The farmer borrowed, if at all, because accident forced him to."

Specie, the opposite of paper, was revered by agrarians with a tenacity that one leading historian of the era, Irwin Unger, called almost fetishistic: "Banks seemed to violate natural economic law by attempting to supersede the money that God had provided. They were economic engines with the sinister and even blasphemous power of creating money out of nothing."

This muddle resulted in a stalemate that made credit intermittently plentiful but subject to periodic collapses in the first half of the nineteenth century and then led to a prolonged era of deflation and real harm to small farmers and factory workers in the half century after the Civil War. The stalemate on banking policy mirrored the deadlock on bankruptcy policy. In the aftermath of the panic and credit contraction of 1837, southern planters could neither profitably sell their crops nor pay their debts. Practical debt relief was often achieved not through the courts but by westward migration.

COMPASSION FOR THE SPECULATIVE CLASS

While credit was scarce for common farmers, it was plentiful for the rising business class. In America as in England, the middle and late nineteenth century was a period of vast speculation in land and in trans-portation endeavors. States, private merchants, and bankers invested massively in canals, harbors, turnpikes, and railroads. Many of these ventures overbuilt and went broke. As the law evolved, courts and leg-islators found ways to keep the wheels of commerce turning despite recurring panics and collapses. Most of these measures favored finan-cial elites. Only very occasionally did they provide relief for ordinary people. Though contracts are presumed sacrosanct and explicitly guar-anteed by article 1, section 10, of the Constitution, our legal system offers innumerable exceptions beyond the bankruptcy system.

One such mechanism was the expansion of the limited liability corpo-ration. In Anglo-American law, corporations were originally chartered for special purposes for a fixed period of time and required incorpo-rators to apply directly to legislatures. In 1809, the New York State legislature enacted the first general incorporation statute, intended to promote the growth of manufacturing companies. By 1815, more than a hundred new industrial corporations had been approved. Other legis-latures, fearing competitive disadvantage, soon followed.

In a partnership, as opposed to a corporation, each individual part-ner, such as the luckless Daniel Defoe or John Dickens, was personally liable for losses. With the growth of the general corporation came a doctrine not unlike bankruptcy. By incorporating, entrepreneurs and investors limited their financial exposure only to the money they had put into an enterprise. If the business failed, none of their other assets could be touched.

Long before the creation of modern bankruptcy relief under Chap-ter 11, limited liability provided financial protection for the expanding commercial class. It could be, and was, justified as facilitating a risk-taking society. By contrast, a small farmer who had a crop failure could wind up losing everything, evicted from his land or pushed into a debt peonage relationship with a larger merchant or landowner. His liability for personal debts was unlimited, bankruptcy was unhelpful, and state forbearance laws provided only limited and intermittent protection. By the late nineteenth century, corporations (and their cousins, trusts) con-centrated the distribution of wealth and political power in America. Both the common and statutory law ensured that despite reverses to particular individual investors, the corporate system would thrive.

A second form of corporate favoritism is the case of the railroad industry, recipient of massive public subsidy, object of endless private speculation, and beneficiary of legal favoritism. By 1880, federal and state governments had subsidized private development of the railroads by giving rail companies $700 million in cash and loans, as well as 155 million acres of public lands, an area equal to four times the size of New England. Some of these lands were used for actual rights-of-way, but far more of them were sold to raise cash. Not surprisingly, railroad ventures encouraged speculation. Railroad promoters often proved overly exuberant in their projections of rail usage and income and tended to go bust. Because of the massive capital needs involved, the railroads spawned the first generation of modern investment bankers, who advanced capital by selling securities to the public, often profiting hugely from conflicts of interest, since many of the bankers also controlled key rail companies. In effect, they lent the bank's money to themselves. The collapse of railroad securities was directly implicated in three of the nineteenth century's panics, in 1857, 1873, and 1893.

Faced with the dilemma of how to deploy illiquid railroad assets to satisfy claims of creditors, U.S. courts in the nineteenth century creatively used the common law to devise "receiverships" that looked much like twentieth-century bankruptcy proceedings. There wasn't much of a market for selling off pieces of a defunct railroad. Better to keep the line intact, write down the cost, and find a new buyer to carry it on. Economic necessity was the mother of a new judicial invention. A "receiver" could acquire the railroad intact.

Judicial receivership began in a relatively modest Georgia foreclosure proceeding in 1848. The Munroe Railroad and Banking Company, which owned about a hundred miles of track, went broke. The judge devised the novel remedy of ordering that all of the company's assets be sold as a package at auction, declaring that "disastrous consequences would have resulted if each judgment creditor had been permitted to seize and sell separate portions of the road." Within a generation, equity receivership became standard practice in the restructuring of insolvent railroad companies. Lawyers representing bondholders, often working with rail magnates seeking to pick up the pieces, worked with friendly judges. Receivership under the common law, and later Chapter 11, was more about advancing corporate interests than about providing fresh starts to common debtors, much less about macroeconomic relief after a crisis. Between 1872 and 1894, the number of railroad companies in receivership soared from 6 to 191.

Behind the invention of receivership was the same insight that informed the statute of Queen Anne before and Chapter 11 after. Assets could be returned to productive use, given an orderly process and a write-down of old debt. The Gilded Age is best known as a period of extremes in the concentration of wealth and political power; it was also an age of extremes in the access to credit and to debt relief.

THE QUEST FOR CREDIT

During the Civil War, paper bills popularly known as greenbacks were issued directly by the federal government under the Legal Tender Act of 1862. Eventually, the government printed some $450 million of them. After the war, in a period of falling prices, there was fierce conflict over whether greenbacks should be kept in circulation or even increased. But they were gradually withdrawn, and in his 1869 inaugural address President Ulysses S. Grant pledged to redeem every dollar of government debt for gold. In 1873, Congress passed legislation ending the free coinage of silver, another deflationary action, which its opponents referred to as the Crime of '73. By 1877, advocates of tight money controlled both parties.

The prolonged period of economic distress for small farmers eventually led to the populist revolt of the 1880s and 1890s, one of the most misunderstood movements in American history. Latter-day historians have depicted a blend of demagoguery, nativism, and crackpot monetary theory. But for the most part, populism was the political culmination of scattered efforts to liberate small farmers from the economic vise of falling prices, tight money, and perpetual debt. (See chapter 8.)

As the great historian of agrarian reform, Lawrence Goodwyn, wrote:

> Everywhere the farmer turned, he seemed to be the victim of strange new rules that somehow always worked to the advantage of the biggest business and financial concerns that touched his world. To be efficient, the farmer had to have tools and livestock that cost him forbidding rates of interest. When he sold, he got the price offered by terminal grain elevator companies. To get his produce there, he paid high rates of freight. If he tried to sell to different grain dealers, or elevator companies, or livestock commission agents, he often encountered the practical evidence of secret agreements between agricultural middlemen and trunk line railroads.

In these circumstances, frustrated farmers and kindred expansionists groped for a more reliable credit and marketing system. Some embraced a restoration of greenbacks; others clamored for the free coinage of silver. Beyond the debates over remedy, the widespread demand needs to be understood as a cry for the reversal of punishing deflation and for an end to marketing monopolies and as a general call for economic fairness for farmers and, later, factory workers. As it matured, populism as a movement aimed for broad structural reform of a capitalist system increasingly dominated by eastern bankers, land barons, railroad magnates, corporate monopolists, and financial speculators.

Populism had many tributaries, but Goodwyn dates its political beginning to September 1877 in Lampasas County, East Texas. There, in Pleasant Valley, at the farm of J. R. Allen, a group of farmers created the Knights of Reliance. From this modest beginning sprang county and state movements dedicated to rural self-help, plentiful credit, and broad antimonopoly reform. These were collectively known as the Farmers' Alliance and soon became the fastest-growing political organization in the South and the West.

At the 1885 Texas State Alliance meeting, addressing some 600 delegates from 555 sub-Alliances, a leader of the Erath County Alliance described a lumber cooperative with twenty-eight hundred Alliance members: "We can purchase anything we want through our agent, dry goods, and groceries, farm implements and machinery. We have a market for all of our wheat, oats and corn." He added, "We expect to build a cotton platform, weigh and load our own cotton and ship direct to the factories." Alliance warehouses and cooperative pooling of individual harvests (known as "bulking") allowed Alliance members to get fair prices, sometimes even premium prices, for their cotton crops. As news of these economic victories traveled, the Alliance movement expanded from Texas east into Louisiana, Mississippi, Alabama, Florida, Georgia, Tennessee, and the Carolinas; north into Arkansas, Missouri, Kansas, and Kentucky; and west to Colorado and the Dakotas. The word was spread by hundreds of traveling Alliance lecturer-organizers.

A self-taught economist and Alliance organizer named Charles Macune devised an ingenious credit and marketing plan called the sub-Treasury system. The federal government would issue paper currency, collateralized by farmers' production. The plan included government warehouses where farmers could store crops and a provision allowing

farmers to borrow up to 80 percent of the value of their crop in nego-
tiable certificates of deposit. This government credit would bypass the
whole system of merchants and bankers. Beyond the immediate value
to farmers, the notes issued by Macune's sub-Treasuries would be legal
tender, thus making credit more plentiful generally. The system would
free the money supply from the yoke of gold. But since it was rooted in
real productive wealth, it would not be inflationary. Macune's design
was one of the influences on the Federal Reserve System enacted by
Congress in 1913.

Alliance leaders had little sympathy for the cause of free coinage of
silver, which they viewed as a misleading distraction. Silver, after all,
was just another metal. Because recent discoveries had made it plentiful,
coinage of silver might be expansionary for the moment. But bimetal-
lism did not solve the underlying problem of unreliable credit. Macune's
sub-Treasury idea became a central plank of the new People's Party's
platform.

In North Carolina and a few other southern states where blacks had
not yet been totally disenfranchised, populists made tactical alliances
with Republicans. Outside the South, populists often went into coalition
with so-called Alliance Democrats, who embraced their program. In
1892, as the movement swelled, Colorado, Kansas, and North Dakota
elected Populist governors, and Populists held the balance of power in
several state legislatures. Four Populists went to the U.S. Senate. The
party nominated its own presidential candidate, James B. Weaver, who
carried four states, winning over a million votes, mainly at the expense
of Republicans. The Democrat, Grover Cleveland, won the presidency,
and Democrats enjoyed majorities in both houses for the first time since
the Civil War.

But after the Panic of 1893, the financially conservative Cleveland
concluded that foreign doubts about America's willingness to honor its
debts were a prime cause of the downturn. He successfully sponsored
the repeal of the Sherman Silver Purchase Act, binding money ever more
tightly to the gold standard. Domestic credit tightened. As the resulting
depression deepened, voters deserted the Democrats in droves, returning Republican majorities to both houses in 1894.

In this climate, the Populists were divided. One faction, hoping that
the People's Party would eventually displace the Democrats just as
Republicans had driven out Whigs after 1856, wanted to run a People's

Party candidate again in 1896. But pragmatists, seeing victory as an impossible long shot, argued that with Populist support the expansionist Democrats could take the party back from the gold bugs and Populists could share power. Two weeks after the Democrats nominated William Jennings Bryan in 1896, the People's Party endorsed him.

The move backfired. Bryan obsessively emphasized silver over a broader reform of credit policy and was trounced by the pro-business Republican William McKinley. The People's Party, though it limped along until 1908, never recovered.

The party's 1892 Omaha platform, the most comprehensive statement of late nineteenth-century agrarian radicalism, called for an elastic currency system based on Macune's sub-Treasury model; federal ownership of the railroads, telephone and telegraph systems; an income tax; and direct election of senators. As a gesture to its trade union allies, it incorporated several of their demands, including an eight-hour day and municipal ownership of local public utilities.

But the promised worker-farmer alliance never came together in the Gilded Age. The subcultures and political self-conceptions were too different. Farmers saw themselves as men of property who could not get a fair shake from the credit system. They, too, were small capitalists. Their sense of struggle was of the "simple people" who worked the land versus banks, merchants, and, later, railroads. The urban working class had a different imagery. Their struggle was labor versus capital.

As the social historian Norbert Wiley observed in a classic essay written in 1967, "The two streams of radicalism were at odds over membership, class interest, and therefore organizational and political programs. . . . The farmers lacked a clear interest in the labor market and the workers lacked interest in the credit market." Worse, the interests of the two underdog groups could directly collide: "Inflation, while it would have relieved farmer debt and increased farmer selling power, would have meant little more than increased commodity prices for urban workers."

These schisms were only compounded by race. In the absence of a coherent ideological or organizational structure, working people at the economic mercy of financial elites and random shocks are easy prey for right-wing populism, a trend that links "Pitchfork Ben" Tillman, Tom Watson, and other racist populists of the 1890s to Huey Long and Father Coughlin of the 1930s and the Tea Party of the twenty-first century. After the false start of the Progressive Era, it was not until the New Deal that the ideology, coalition, and many of the public policies sought in vain by the populists at last came together.

One thing can be said for the nineteenth-century debates about money. The common people paid attention because their livelihoods were at stake. Despite the confusion about paper versus specie, at bottom the issues were these: whether credit would be plentiful and reliable for ordinary farmers, artisans, and merchants; whether speculation would be allowed to overwhelm the real economy; whether debt relief would be forthcoming when the system experienced a panic; and whether financial elites would be permitted to prosper at everyone else's expense. Though yeoman farmers lost more often than they won, the issues were at least vividly in public contention. By comparison, though the underlying questions are the same enduring ones, the money debates of the early twenty-first century are wrapped in mystification, giving financial elites a free pass.

A CENTRAL BANK BY AND FOR BANKERS

With the Federal Reserve Act of 1913, the United States finally got the "elastic" central banking system for which the populists had clamored. But in an inversion of the reformist impulse, the new system was designed largely by bankers to be safely controlled by bankers.

In the three decades before Congress created the Federal Reserve, panics and depressions continued to break out with increasing frequency. Speculators often cornered the stock in a railroad company, borrowed against it, watered it down by issuing new shares, and cashed out before the price tumbled. Crash predictably followed bubble. In 1893, the Northern Pacific, the Union Pacific, the Santa Fe, the Erie, and the Philadelphia and Reading all went under. The financial firms that controlled them followed. By the end of 1893, nearly three hundred national banks failed. The stock market collapsed, and unemployment reached 20 percent.

The depression was compounded by the loss of confidence on the part of European investors and bankers, who were demanding gold for their U.S. securities. With no central bank, the Cleveland administration turned to J. P. Morgan.

The House of Morgan, respected in Europe, underwrote and marketed a successful bond issue that stemmed the run on gold. In 1894, and again in 1895, Morgan literally had to save the Treasury from defaulting on its debts to Europe. Depression conditions continued well into the late 1890s, when new discoveries of gold helped increase the money supply and propel a fragile recovery.

In 1898, with corporate insolvencies on the rise, business-oriented Republicans in control of the House and Senate, and the presidency under William McKinley, America finally got a permanent bankruptcy law. The major contribution of the Bankruptcy Act of 1898 was to systematize the process that later became Chapter 11, under the guidance of creditor committees and a rapidly growing bankruptcy bar serving mainly corporate clients. Like the equity receiverships of the common law, the new act was mainly intended to facilitate corporate restructurings. Explicitly excluded were farmers and laborers. And while it permitted states to provide homestead exemptions, the act was of no help to farmers who were in debt over their heads to landlords, merchants, bankers, and other middlemen. America's freeholders continued to be pushed into debt peonage in record numbers. The percentage of farmers working as tenants increased from 25 percent in 1880 to 38 percent by 1910. Two centuries after Daniel Defoe failed to qualify for the system of debt relief that he had invented, bankruptcy was, more than ever, for the benefit of capitalists. This bias would only widen in the twenty-first century.

Scarcely a decade later, an even more serious depression ravaged the economy. The Panic of 1907 was triggered by a run on banks set off by the collapse of the Knickerbocker Trust Company, New York's third largest, which had lost millions in copper speculation. On October 16, the highly leveraged stock of the United Copper Company collapsed. A week later, Knickerbocker was insolvent. Charles Barney, president of the besieged bank, sought Morgan's help. But Morgan had concluded that Knickerbocker was beyond redemption. Barney promptly shot himself. On October 23, two other major banks, the Trust Company of America and the Lincoln Trust Company, faced runs. Before the panic was over, 248 banks would fail. And once again, Morgan stepped into the breach.

Working with his club of New York bankers—including George F. Baker of First National, James Stillman of National City Bank, and Henry Davison of Bankers Trust and his young lieutenant, Benjamin

Strong—Morgan assembled a task force that anticipated Franklin Roosevelt's bank holiday of 1933 to determine which banks could be saved. He then cobbled together commitments of upward of $40 million from the strongest banks and the U.S. Treasury to deposit in the weaker ones. When this did not stem the bank run, Morgan called the presidents of all the major New York banks to his Italian Renaissance library on Fifth Avenue on the night of November 3, 1907, locked the doors, and extracted a commitment of another $25 million. The banking system held, but barely.

Congress concluded that it was no longer sufficient to rely on ad hoc rescues by J. P. Morgan. It created the National Monetary Commission, fittingly chaired by Senator Nelson Aldrich of New York, the richest man in a rich man's club. Meanwhile, in November 1908, Davison, now a Morgan partner, invited Aldrich to join him and four other influentials at a secret planning retreat on Jekyll Island, off the coast of Georgia, disguised as a duck hunting holiday.

For ten days, Aldrich, Davison, Strong, Paul Warburg of Kuhn Loeb, Frank Vanderlip of National City, and an assistant Treasury secretary, A. Piatt Andrew Jr., considered options. They returned with a plan to institutionalize what Morgan had been doing ad hoc. A proposed National Reserve Association would have the authority to issue currency and extend credit to member banks. It would have the functions of a central bank, but it would be owned and controlled as a bankers' cooperative, with the government given token representation on its board.

When this idea was made public as the Aldrich Plan, it provoked an immediate backlash. Progressives, Populists, Bryan Democrats, and most Republicans in Congress outside the Northeast wanted no part of it. In the debates that followed, key legislators were outraged that the plan left control of money in private hands and that short-term commercial notes could be presented for discount at the National Reserve banks but agricultural paper could not. In early 1913, President-elect Woodrow Wilson sided with congressional critics and called for a larger public role. So did his secretary of state, who happened to be William Jennings Bryan.

In the end, a compromise sponsored by Carter Glass, a conservative Democratic senator from Virginia, salvaged the plan by adding a modest role for the government. Renamed the Federal Reserve, Glass's variation created autonomous regional banks that were owned and controlled by local bankers and loosely governed by the Federal Reserve

Board in Washington. The regional autonomy appealed to southern and western interests, who were chronically suspicious of New York banks. The eastern banking elite was skeptical at first but gradually came to appreciate that the New York Reserve Bank would be more than first among equals—it would be the true central bank. This somewhat contradictory set of projections was enough to satisfy both progressives and conservatives, and Congress duly passed the Federal Reserve Act. Benjamin Strong was named the first president of the Federal Reserve Bank of New York.

Populists of the Charles Macune stripe had actually won one of their two major battles. Despite the nominal link to gold, the system was now based on fiat money, the nemesis of the hard currency forces. The new Federal Reserve notes, legal tender for all debts public and private, were created out of thin air. Public trust in their value would not reflect backing by precious metals but the competence of the central bankers, which would soon prove to be wanting. Macune's more fundamental battle had been lost. The new currency system, far from being democratically controlled, was firmly in the hands of the hated eastern financial elite, now armed with the further prestige of being a quasi-governmental institution created by Congress.

But in the 1920s, despite Strong's basic competence, the Fed made one misstep after another. These were not random blunders but rather reflected two basic structural biases that were second nature to the bankers who ran it: the natural preference of the creditor class for tight money and an indulgence of speculation. It was this seemingly anomalous pairing of opposites that made bankers rich.

As speculation burgeoned in the Roaring Twenties, Strong was torn between his need to keep interest rates low to help the debt-ridden Europeans and his concern that easy money was promoting unsustainable speculation at home. His conundrum had a solution that was largely beyond his ideological imagination and that of the dominant Republican Party and their corporate allies. In that laissez-faire era, with its bias against government regulation, it seldom occurred to the Fed that the answer was to couple low interest rates, on which European and American prosperity depended, with strict controls on pure speculation. As the stock market bubble swelled in 1928 and 1929, the weak Federal Reserve Board in Washington regularly called for tighter controls on margin, but the real power, the Federal Reserve Bank of New York, refused to comply.

That left monetary policy alone to bear the weight of the contradictory demands. Strong himself periodically expressed alarm, but he saw the Fed's role as superintending the overall economy, not regulating "the affairs of gamblers," as he characterized the less savory players on Wall Street. In 1925, he wrote to his friend Montagu Norman, head of the Bank of England, "It seems a shame that the best sorts of plans can be handicapped by a speculative orgy, and yet the temper of the people of this country is such that these situations cannot be avoided." Alan Greenspan—who pumped up the great bubble of the first years of the twenty-first century even as he warned of "irrational exuberance" while crusading against prudential regulation—could not have said it better.

When the bubble was too big to pop without triggering a crash, Strong belatedly changed his policies. Once again, it was mainly by means of the blunt instrument of interest rates. In early 1928, the Fed gradually raised rates from 3.5 to 5 percent. But it was too late. Between the late spring of 1928 and the early fall of 1929, the Dow sailed skyward, from 200 to around 380, based on expectations of further price increases and spurred by borrowed money. In October 1928, Strong, chronically ill from complications of tuberculosis, died at the age of fifty-five. His successor, George L. Harrison, acted to raise rates again. But so hot was the speculative fever and so primitive the regulatory levers that money kept pouring into New York.

When the inevitable crash finally came, neither the Federal Reserve nor New York's private bankers could pool enough buying power in the stock market, after the fashion of Morgan, to prevent the leveraged house of cards from collapsing. And if the adolescent central bank had failed to prevent the inflation of a stock market bubble on the upside, its policies compounded the damage on the downside. The Fed, believing with Treasury Secretary Mellon that a depression was the moment to purge the rottenness from the system, allowed banks to fail by the thousands, which further contracted the nation's money supply, and then it failed to loosen money for fear of inflation.

TWENTIETH CENTURY DEBT RELIEF

The exception to this saga of double standards was the New Deal era, a rare period when popular politics came together with a grave economic crisis and an insurgent president. Congress added new powers to the

Fed and enacted several laws to regulate financial markets and limit speculation. Roosevelt appointed the only progressive ever to chair the newly empowered Federal Reserve Board, Marriner Eccles. However, in a debt deflation, cheap money alone was not sufficient to achieve a recovery.

Congress also liberalized the Bankruptcy Act of 1898 in an effort to deal with the economic emergency and broaden the range of who could benefit from the bankruptcy laws. The Chandler Act of 1938 empowered the premier New Deal financial reform agency, the Securities and Exchange Commission, to play a prominent role in bankruptcy proceedings. The SEC's chairman, William O. Douglas, later a Supreme Court justice, had been a scathing critic of the private bankruptcy bar and the sweetheart deals for large corporations. Douglas's investigation documented a cozy club of lawyers and investment bankers favoring executives of failed companies at the expense of ruined shareholders.

With the 1938 reform, the SEC, representing the public interest, would be an intervenor in major bankruptcies. Instead of creditors' committees dominating proceedings, there would be an independent court-appointed trustee. Chapter 11 was added to the code, as a special provision for small firms. The Chandler Act also introduced for the first time the sort of provision that Daniel Defoe had pursued in vain, for the rehabilitation of individual debtors. With millions of Americans unemployed and overwhelmed by debts, personal bankruptcy was one part of the New Deal strategy of recovery from national debt deflation.

Like so much else about the FDR era, the Chandler Act would be the high-water mark of a more evenhanded treatment of corporations and citizens. In several postwar revisions to the bankruptcy laws, the role of the SEC was diminished, the ability of corporations to use bankruptcy was liberalized, and the barriers to individual debt relief were increased.

As personal bankruptcy filings rose from a low of 8,566 in 1945 to 191,729 by 1967, creditors clamored for changes in the law.

The 1978 revision, which introduced the current form of Chapter 11, gave more power to judges and removed the SEC from the process entirely. The law, passed by a Democratic Congress and signed by President Jimmy Carter, included several purely technical changes. But on balance, the effect was to make it somewhat easier for both corporations and households to file for bankruptcy. By making it easier for companies to emerge from bankruptcy, the legal changes made it more tempting for corporate executives to take their companies into bankruptcy. Judges were explicitly given the authority to modify prior contracts for all debts except mortgages. In the year after the law was enacted, filings increased by about 50 percent. This increase set off a lobbying campaign by bankers to raise hurdles to easy bankruptcy. But when the bankers finally succeeded in persuading Congress to tighten the law in 2005 (see below), the crackdown was directed mainly against consumers. Bankruptcy remained broadly available as a tool for corporations to shed debts.

MORAL HAZARD REVISITED

In a Chapter 11 bankruptcy, a corporation is reorganized under the supervision of the court-appointed trustee. The corporate managers, absent extreme malfeasance, can retain control. They are able to cancel contracts and renegotiate other debts. The company can obtain new loans that are protected from the bankruptcy proceeding. Creditors must vote to approve or reject the reorganization plan, but a bankruptcy judge can overrule them in a procedure popularly known as a cramdown. Eventually, the corporation emerges from bankruptcy with a nice, clean balance sheet. In recent years, Chapter 11 has been a favorite maneuver to escape labor contracts and pension obligations.

Bankruptcy has also become a key technique in one of the most abusive new forms of financial engineering: hostile takeovers, or leveraged buyouts. Beginning in the 1980s, what were then called corporate raiders used borrowed money to take control of a publicly traded company, with the company's own stock as collateral. After several scandals involving takeover artists who broke laws, including Michael Milken and Ivan Boesky, leveraged buyouts briefly went into well-deserved disgrace.

Then the industry rebranded itself as "private equity." The phrase nicely evokes a group of private investors who, like their venture capitalist cousins, pool their funds and put fresh equity capital into firms. Peter G. Peterson was one of private equity's pioneers. But a better name would be "private debt." Though they are advertised as superexecutives expert at turnarounds of underperforming companies, many private equity entrepreneurs get rich by loading up their target companies with new, tax-deductible debt. As companies whose shares are not publicly traded, private equity firms are exempt from most of the disclosure laws that have been the centerpiece of U.S. investor protection since the 1930s.

Private equity often attempts to cloak itself as a variant of venture capital, but in fact the two have little in common. Venture capitalists actually put their own money at risk. Some of the most notable technology start-ups, including Digital Equipment Corporation and Apple, received either initial funding or early money for expansion from genuine venture capitalists. Private equity entrepreneurs, by contrast, invest mostly in established companies and use the tax deductibility of borrowed money to profit from buying, restructuring, and selling them, often having paid themselves huge fees and special dividends along the way.

Private equity companies routinely use Chapter 11 after they bleed dry the operating companies they acquire, adding debt, extracting capital, and then declaring that, unfortunately, debts exceed assets. Once out of bankruptcy, the companies can be sold for more profit. Bain Capital, Mitt Romney's firm, pocketed hundreds of millions of dollars as special dividends from companies such as KB Toys, Dade Behring, Ampad, GS Technologies, and Stage Stores, all of which subsequently filed for bankruptcy. In late 2012, Hostess Brands, maker of products like Twinkies and Wonder Bread, went into liquidation, having been badly managed by a succession of owners. Well before Hostess filed for bankruptcy in 2012, executives in August 2011 simply stopped making contractually required pension contributions. When the company opted to go bankrupt, employees and retirees had no recourse. Lawyers even have a term for this situation. It's called "betrayal without remedy." The phrase nicely captures the double standards in bankruptcy law generally.

THE GREAT PENSION ROBBERY

In the steel, airline, auto, and other industries where good union contracts were once common, one of the biggest appeals of a Chapter 11 reorganization is that contractual pension and retiree health obligations can be swept aside. Pensions are debts that corporations owe to their employees. In the case of unionized companies, pensions are both the fruit of collective-bargaining contracts and legal obligations under federal labor law. Even in non-union firms, pensions are still legal liabilities—debts to employees that corporations may not unilaterally renounce. They are generally considered deferred wages.

But since the 1980s, America's corporations have come up with several creative ways of walking away from these debts to their employees and retirees. The shedding of pension debts—often nothing but transfers of wealth from workers to executives and shareholders—is one of the epic cases of the double standard in American debt relief.

Pensions were largely unregulated until Congress passed the Employee Retirement Income Security Act of 1974 (ERISA). Congress acted because several corporations had gone broke, leaving their pensioners high and dry. The act established rules for the prudent management of pension funds; and for cases where funds were mismanaged or ran short of assets, it also created a Pension Benefit Guarantee Corporation to pay pensions to former employees of companies that shut down with inadequate pension reserves. Before ERISA, ironically, there was no way for a corporation to dump its pensions and stay in business. But after ERISA, financial engineers were able to off-load pension obligations onto their workers and the PBGC. In the corporate takeover movement of the 1980s, more than two thousand corporations found ways of evading ERISA, usually by changing ownership in complex ways so that the successor company did not have the same pension obligations as the old one. The savings went into the pockets of the financial engineers. This wave of opportunistic termination of plans, including those of Revlon, LTV, and Occidental Petroleum, was seemingly reformed in 1990 when Congress passed a law requiring companies that terminated plans to pay a 50 percent excise tax on their windfall gains. But companies could avoid half of the tax if they put part of the proceeds into a "replacement" plan, such as a 401(k). The legal looting of pension plans led to mass conversions of traditional pensions to 401(k) plans, which are more lightly regulated and put all of the risks onto the retiree. A traditional pension plan typically costs the company about 5 to 8 percent of payroll. A 401(k) plan costs about half that.

Then a new strategy of pension looting became prevalent. In the booming 1990s, when the stock market was soaring, pension fund investments were increasing in value by roughly the same percentage as the stock market—around 20 percent per year. It was clear that the stock market could not keep rising indefinitely at more than triple the

rate of economic growth. Any prudent fiduciary should have appreciated that markets go down as well as up. But in the years of the stock
market bubble, corporate pension fund managers concluded that they
had roughly a quarter of a trillion dollars in "surplus" assets—in excess
of what they needed to pay out projected claims.

By 1999, at America's iconic companies the nominal surpluses were
prodigious: $25 billion at GE's pension fund, $24 billion at Verizon's,
and $20 billion at AT&T's. The corporate elite, their accountants
and lawyers, found several ways to divert these funds from retirees to
the corporation. Dozens of corporations did restructuring deals that
allowed pension reserves to flow back to the company. For example, in
1993 GE sold one of its aerospace units to Martin Marietta. The sale
included the transfer of employees and their pension fund. But since the
pension plan had a supposed surplus of $531 million, which would save
Martin Marietta that much money in future pension contributions, the
sale price paid to GE was $531 million more than it otherwise would
have been. Through this maneuver, GE captured more than half a billion dollars that otherwise belonged to its future retirees.

Thanks to ploys like this one, America's big corporations were able
to pare their pension fund reserves to the bone—just in time for the
stock market crash. According to Ellen E. Schultz, who covers pensions for the *Wall Street Journal*, GE resorted to dozens of similar deals,
siphoning billions from its pension plan. Then as stock market prices
plunged, the GE pension fund swung from a reported surplus (swollen
by the stock market bubble) of $24 billion in 1999 to a shortfall of
$6 billion by 2011.

Having taken tens of billions out of their pension funds and underfunded them on the premise of unsustainable stock market returns,
America's leading corporations then contended that they could no longer afford to subsidize funds that were now in deficit. This led to the
shift of even more traditional pension plans to 401(k)s.

A further maneuver used by corporations to divert pension money
is the creative use of Chapter 11. This can occur both in the context of
a leveraged buyout by a private equity company or corporate raider,
or by incumbent management. The executives of every major airline
have used the bankruptcy laws to shed pension debts to their employees
without losing control of the company.

Here's how it works. Because the airlines have been on such a financial roller coaster since they were deregulated in 1978, their creditors

have increasingly demanded liens on planes and other assets. So if an airline declares bankruptcy, the bank can seize its assets. But while banks that are parties to an airline bankruptcy proceeding are typically secured creditors—they have liens on assets—the pension plan is an unsecured creditor. So it is the last to get paid.

According to Joshua Gotbaum, who heads the Pension Benefit Guarantee Corporation, in the airline and steel company bankruptcies of the George W. Bush era, pension fund creditors got paid at approximately 5 to 10 cents on the dollar while other creditors got 50 or 60 cents on the dollar. Professor Teresa Ghilarducci, author of several books on pensions, describes these as "fake" or "sweetheart" bankruptcies, intended mainly to shed pension debts. Since the PBGC exists to guarantee pensioners that they won't lose out if a company with a pension plan goes broke, the basic strategy of these corporations was to off-load their liabilities on the government.

In the early 2000s, several major steel companies and airlines dumped their pension liabilities on the PBGC, including Bethlehem Steel, National Steel, Weirton Steel, Kaiser Aluminum, United Airlines, USAir, and Delta. Eight of the ten largest pension defaults in corporate history have occurred in the past decade. Because of the use of bankruptcies to dump pension costs on the government, the PBGC's own financial health went from a surplus of $10 billion in 2001 to a deficit of $11 billion just two years later. By September 2011, PBGC's own deficit was $26 billion—a classic case of the corporate sector shifting its debts to the government. Even so, the PBGC doesn't cover all of the costs, and is not obligated to cover collectively bargained health benefits for retirees.

In early 2012, American Airlines, the one large airline that had avoided Chapter 11, concluded that its competitors that had shed pension costs were enjoying a competitive advantage. So American filed for bankruptcy, proposing to transfer more than $9 billion in pension costs to the PBGC. This time, however, the PBCG, as one of the creditors in the bankruptcy case, concluded from its own extensive investigation that American did not require this degree of financial relief in order to assure its own survival. The judge in the case sided with the PBGC. In the end, American was able to freeze, but not terminate, its pension. The company saved less than $2 billion. Workers got a 401(k) plan that reduced their benefits going forward but didn't lose the past pension rights they had earned. But the American case was very much the exception to the pattern.

In 2012, Kodak became another iconic company to opt for Chapter 11. The financial press noted approvingly Kodak's discussions with JPMorgan Chase, Citigroup, and other banks to provide the company with new working capital. Citi eventually provided Kodak with $950 million in new operating capital, with UBS and JPMorgan Chase later providing additional new funding. The bankruptcy process protects Kodak's new creditors while management writes off its old debts—to bondholders and its own pension plan. Thanks to the doctrine of debtor-in-possession, the very executive group that drove the company into the ground keeps control and can incur fresh debts from lenders who figure that it won't go bankrupt again for a while. But these are the same banks that fiercely resist liberalization of the bankruptcy laws to allow homeowners to reduce the debts that are depressing the housing sector and, by extension, hampering the recovery.

Wall Street has convinced lawmakers that relief for ordinary people, even in a deflationary economic emergency, would result in unacceptable costs to banks and would promote moral hazard. There is indeed a moral hazard problem—in the increasingly promiscuous use of *corporate* bankruptcy.

The vaunted economic efficiency of Chapter 11 depends on a tacit balancing act between the expedient temptation to blow off your debts and the lingering shame attached to "going bankrupt." If Chapter 11 becomes too common, it ceases to be efficient because it courts reckless speculation and frightens off investors. The supposed shifting of norms, in which people no longer feared the stigma of bankruptcy, was the argument used by bankers in the 2005 legislative battle to make bankruptcy less available to ordinary citizens. It was an epic case of corporate America admonishing the citizenry: Do as I say, not as I do.

BACK TO DEFOE

In the last decades of the twentieth century, the financial industry concluded that what was freely available to corporations was too good for the common people. The ease of bankruptcy, supposedly, was inviting consumers to run up credit card debts and engage in other forms of profligate consumption. The usual business suspects—the U.S. Chamber of Commerce, the Business Roundtable, conservative think tanks, and above all bankers—lined up behind bankruptcy "reform."

Congress passed a harsh measure in 2000, but it was pocket vetoed by President Clinton.

Elizabeth Warren came to national prominence with her path-breaking research documenting that the charge of frivolous consumer bankruptcies was a red herring. As she demonstrated, most consumer bankruptcies were in fact driven by medical bills that overwhelmed family resources, by the death or disability of a breadwinner or another unforeseen financial calamity, or by the breakup of a marriage. Testifying before the Senate Judiciary Committee in 2005 against the bankruptcy bill, she noted that during the eight years that the financial industry was promoting a harsher consumer bankruptcy law, the number of bankruptcy filings actually increased by only a modest 17 percent, while credit card profits went up 163 percent, to $30.2 billion. Over that same eight years, in the run-up to the financial collapse, the escalating abuses were on the part of the financial industry, not consumers. Warren warned:

> Women trying to collect alimony or child support will more often be forced to compete with credit card companies that can have more of their debts declared non-dischargeable. All these provisions apply whether a person earns $20,000 a year or $200,000 a year.
>
> But the means test as written has another, more basic problem: It treats all families alike. It assumes that everyone is in bankruptcy for the same reason—too much unnecessary spending. A family driven to bankruptcy by the increased costs of caring for an elderly parent with Alzheimer's disease is treated the same as someone who maxed out his credit cards at a casino. A person who had a heart attack is treated the same as someone who had a spending spree at the shopping mall. A mother who works two jobs and who cannot manage the prescription drugs needed for a child with diabetes is treated the same as someone who charged a bunch of credit cards with only a vague intent to repay. A person cheated by a sub-prime mortgage lender and lied to by a credit counseling agency is treated the same as a person who gamed the system in every possible way.

However, with the election of George W. Bush and with Congress under Republican control, the banking industry redoubled its efforts to tilt the bankruptcy code against consumers, spending about $100 million in lobbying over eight years. The industry's bill passed and was signed into law by President Bush in 2005 as the Bankruptcy Abuse Prevention and Consumer Protection Act. The law's key provisions make it more difficult for consumers to file under Chapter 7, under which most debts are paid only out of existing assets and then forgiven, and requires instead filing under Chapter 13, which dictates a partial repayment plan over three to five years. The act introduced a means test by which only debtors with income below the state's median are exempt from the more onerous provisions of the law. If a citizen has above-median income, there is a "presumption" that abuse occurred, and future income is partly attached in order to satisfy past creditor claims, no matter what the actual circumstances. The law also partially overrides the homestead exemption that many states provide, limiting the value of the home that can be protected from creditor claims.

In promoting the law, financial executives testified that if losses could be reduced, savings would be passed along to the public in the form of lower interest rates. But after the law passed, the credit card industry intensified its efforts to market credit cards with high interest rates to consumers, including those with poor credit ratings. Adding insult to injury, the industry invented new fees. Thanks to the "reform," when overburdened consumers go broke, credit card companies now have far more latitude to squeeze them for repayment.

This penchant for condemning individual debtors but excusing corporate creditors and debtors has been rampant in the financial crisis that began in 2008. The corporate campaign to prevent debt relief from being offered to underwater homeowners has relied heavily on a rhetoric of morality. Representative Tom Price of Georgia, chairman of the Republican Study Committee, warned that extending bankruptcy protection to homeowners "rewards those who are living beyond their means," an argument seldom made about corporations that use Chapter 11.

The double standard continues to this day in the debate over mortgage relief. The banks that crashed the economy received over $700 billion in taxpayer aid and trillions more in Federal Reserve cash advances and bond purchases. The same financial elites who instrumentally rely on Chapter 11 to rearrange assets and shed debts warn of the shameful improvidence of families caught in a general downdraft of housing values. The strenuous effort of the big banks, with the aid of the U.S. Treasury, to deny more than token mortgage relief to homeowners is both a key double standard in the saga of debt relief and a key source of the extended economic slump.

Chapter 8

A Home of One's Own

IN THE UNITED STATES AND IN several European countries, including Britain, Spain, and Ireland, an overhang of housing debt continues to submerge both household net worth and bank balance sheets, deepening and prolonging the economic slump. The mortgage collapse triggered the broader financial crisis because a large fraction of the toxic securities that crashed the system in 2007 and 2008 were collateralized by highly leveraged debt that turned out to be nearly worthless. Those losses devastated the equity of the financial system. The problem was less the subprime borrowing per se than the pyramids of securities backed by the underlying mortgages. Had lenders simply held on to the loans, they would have made far fewer high-risk mortgages in the first place, and there would have been no (far more damaging) secondary crash.

The subprime affair is sometimes depicted as a case of unqualified borrowers taking out mortgage loans they could not afford, abetted by misguided government policies aimed at expanding homeownership. This picture, however, has the cause and effect backward. Most high-risk loans were made and then packaged into securities by financial entrepreneurs who had neither the mandate nor the motivation to help less affluent people buy homes. Originating and selling high-risk loans were simply ways for investment bankers and mortgage middlemen to maximize fees and trading profits. Much of the housing bubble in the United States and elsewhere was the result of low interest rates and lax lending standards bidding up property values to unsustainable heights. It had nothing to do with helping unfortunates.

Homeownership has an iconic place in the American experience, linking the democratic idea to the freeholder. Thomas Jefferson famously viewed the yeoman farmer as the social base of republican government. "The small landholders," he wrote to James Madison in 1785, "are the most precious part of the state." Senator Thomas Hart Benton in 1826 expressed the corollary: "Tenantry is unfavorable to freedom."

In Lincoln's day, the government dramatically broadened property ownership with the Homestead Act of 1862. By 1890, the United States already had owner-occupancy rates averaging close to 50 percent, and over 70 percent in some western farm states. Urban and small-town homeowners, meanwhile, benefited from building and loan associations, "thrift" groups dating to the 1830s that pooled savings and made revolving mortgage loans.

Homeownership, depressed in the 1930s, soared after World War II, from under 44 percent on the eve of the war to over 64 percent by the mid-1960s. But none of these gains relied on financial innovations of the commercial sector. Early freeholding was promoted by federal land and credit policies. The modern mortgage system was created by the New Deal.

In the 1930s, the government invented the long-term self-amortizing mortgage and then set up a secondary market to purchase these modern mortgages and ensure their acceptance in the marketplace. Roosevelt's suite of policies also included a central bank for thrift institutions, a government system for standardizing and insuring mortgages, and the Home Owners' Loan Corporation to refinance distressed mortgages.

Thrifts were mostly nonprofits. There were no layers of financial middlemen and no private securitization. Although the government made or insured loans with down payments as low as 3 percent (and subsequently zero percent under the Veterans Administration and the GI Bill), underwriting was careful. There were few defaults and infrequent bank failures—and no rewards for lending to unqualified borrowers. It all worked like a Swiss watch.

Once financial entrepreneurs got control of the home mortgage system, they ruined it. The regulatory lapses that led to the housing bubble of the early twenty-first century and the government's refusal to resolve the continuing drag of underwater mortgages add up to a catastrophic and needless policy failure. Housing prices remain depressed despite record low interest rates because underwater homeowners can't refinance, while prospective owners, unsure if housing is a good investment anymore, rent while they wait it out. That shortfall of demand causes a glut of supply that keeps housing prices depressed, and the cycle continues.

Against the history of Jefferson's republican land tenure policies, Lincoln's Homestead Act, Roosevelt's Home Owners' Loan Corporation, and Truman's GI loans, the lingering mortgage collapse was not just a financial calamity. It was a betrayal of a core republican ideal.

BORN UNEQUAL

The relationship of property to democracy is one of the great questions of political economy and political history. Whenever a revolution overthrows an old regime, land tenure is at the center of issues to be resolved. The most radical revolutions—France, Russia, and China being the classic cases—seize and redistribute the land of the nobility, either to the peasantry or to the state. Tamer revolutions oust regimes but leave property relations alone. The Nobel laureate James Meade, reviewing the diverse mechanisms for promoting an egalitarian society, such as a welfare state, progressive taxation, or strong trade unions, concluded that the most efficient strategy was a broad distribution of property to begin with.

European democrats envied revolutionary America because the New World had seemingly resolved this conundrum in advance. The United States, in the famous phrase of Alexis de Tocqueville, was "born equal." Unlike aristocratic Europe, the United States conveniently had vast public lands—seized from native tribes, bought from the French, annexed from Spain, or appropriated from Mexico—available to be distributed to the citizenry. Once America wrested its freedom from the British Crown, it could invent republican institutions from scratch and pursue property policies to match. Or so it seemed.

Though the housing policy debacle is central to the continuing crisis of debt overhang, the failure to defend the interests of small-property owners against speculators is far from historically unique. Despite the valorization of the freeholder in the saga of American republicanism, the record is decidedly mixed.

Pace Tocqueville, the Republic was not born equal. It was born colonial—with a partial legacy of feudalism and slavery. Key debates early in American history were about property ownership—whether to permit expansion of slavery into new territories and states, and whether land sales would favor large speculators or small freeholders. Policy and practice tacked back and forth, honoring the ideal of cheap land for small settlers but often favoring large landholders and pure speculators. After the Civil War, while some small farmers were staking claims under the Homestead Act, millions more were reverting to the status of sharecroppers. At a time when small freeholders had scant access to bank loans, there were railroad, timber, and coal speculators affiliated with banks who were awash in credit.

Yet even when it was poorly honored in practice, the conception of a republic of free citizens rooted in broad property ownership remained a potent and enduring ideal. America's actual practices on land tenure and credit amounted to a massive case of cognitive dissonance.

Beginning with the grant of the Virginia charter by King James I in 1609, settlers from the British aristocracy were given estates of thousands of acres to be maintained intact through English laws of primogeniture and entail. The cultivation of tobacco and cotton by slaves reinforced the plantation system. In New England, by contrast, both the laws of landholding and the absence of large cash crops and slavery created a more democratic pattern of ownership and, later, citizenship. Beginning in 1634, Massachusetts provided for the orderly creation of townships, six miles square, to be settled by sixty families, with a common church and school, and prohibitions against large aggregations of land. Enthusiasts praised the system for creating "little republics."

As the Ohio Valley was opened for settlement in the decades before the Revolution, there were intrigues at court in London and fierce battles within the colonial legislatures over whether the new lands would be sold to large speculators or reserved for small settlers. Many plantation owners "planted in the east and speculated in the west," as the saying went. Among the issues that led to the War of Independence was colonial resistance to the king's several attempts, culminating in the Quebec Act of 1774, to limit western encroachments by land companies that led to costly battles with Indians.

Though Thomas Jefferson hailed from aristocratic Virginia and owned thousands of acres and hundreds of slaves, his views on land tenure were more like those of freeholding Massachusetts. Almost a century before Lincoln signed the Homestead Act, Jefferson's draft of the Virginia Constitution provided that "every person of full age neither owning nor having owned 50 acres of land shall be entitled to an appropriation of 50 acres." This remarkably radical proposition did not become part of the final document, but Jefferson was more successful in resisting the sale of western lands to large speculators, at least in principle.

The original royal charters left seven states with lands extending westward all the way to the Mississippi River. Virginia was the biggest of these. But after the War of Independence, the six other states without such lands, led by Maryland, successfully demanded that the largely unsettled western lands be turned over to the new national government as public property.

As ratified in 1781, the Articles of Confederation provided that the original colonies would cede the western lands to the nation, rather than selling tracts wholesale to private land companies. Under the Ordinances of 1784, 1785, and 1787, substantially Jefferson's handiwork, these western territories, comprising over 236 million acres, could be carved into new states, with the same rights as the original thirteen, as the population expanded and local governments were established. They later became Kentucky, Ohio, Indiana, Illinois, Wisconsin, and parts of five other states.

However, just as the new nation was awkwardly born half slave, half free, the Republic's desperate need for revenue and the legacy of pre-Revolutionary law led to a mixed land distribution system—part freeholder, part speculator. The land ordinances were a compromise between the New England system and that of the southern states. Sales to large land companies were widespread, at prices as low as twelve and a half cents an acre. In one of the first, the United States sold 822,900 acres to the Ohio Company in 1787.

Since prospective settlers seldom had ready cash or access to credit, there was extended conflict over the financing of land purchases. In the Land Acts of 1796 and 1800, Congress authorized the government to sell land directly to settlers for 5 percent down, the balance to be paid off in one to four years. The idea, according to an authoritative history, was "to prevent large scale speculators from taking advantage of the poorer settlers." But even these generous terms proved beyond the means of most small farmers.

As president, Jefferson promoted policies to enable freeholders to benefit from his 1803 purchase of the Louisiana Territory from Napoleon. "How much better," he wrote Albert Gallatin in 1807, "to have every 160 acres settled by an able-bodied militia man, than by [slave-holder] purchasers with their hordes of Negroes." Yet during Jefferson's lifetime, Louisiana, Arkansas, and Missouri were carved from his purchase and entered the Union as slave states.

The General Land Office was created by Congress in 1812 to survey, manage, and sell federal public lands to settlers, a noble idea that was soon corrupted. Politically connected land speculators found that they could borrow down payments from lightly regulated state banks, then borrow the rest from the new government agency. Edward King, son of the Federalist senator Rufus King of New York, purchased large tracts entirely on credit. So did the former governor of Virginia, Wilson Cary Nicholas. By 1819, the General Land Office had lent over $22 million, much of it in large tracts to speculators. It placed no limits on buyers, other than their ability to make the first payment. As long as farm prices held up and land could be subdivided and sold off, the pyramid worked. But after the collapse of prices in the Panic of 1819, some 20 percent of the land purchased on credit by the Land Office was forfeited between 1820 and 1824.

It was a classic bubble: a crash in speculative land values followed by an extended deflation, interacting with cascading bank failures. In the early nineteenth century, the government lacked the tools and economic insights for dealing with the aftermath of a bubble. There is far less excuse in the early twenty-first century.

FREEDMEN, HOMESTEADERS, AND DEBT PEONS

The several contradictions in America's land tenure policy came to a head with the Civil War—and then only intensified. Lincoln's Homestead Act offered setters 160 acres of free land; once they had worked the land for five years, they would own it. This and successor acts eventually conveyed 270 million acres of public lands, about 10 percent of the land area of the United States, to 1.6 million farm families. As late as 1986, you could still apply for homesteads in Alaska.

Lincoln had had a long-standing interest in the democratization of landholding. After he finished his sole term in Congress in 1849, he had been encouraged by President Zachary Taylor to apply to be commissioner of the General Land Office, but the appointment never came through. Under Lincoln, homesteading was part of a postslavery strategy both to expand free farming in the West and to anchor the economic liberation of former slaves in a radical land redistribution program.

By late 1864, the Union Army controlled millions of acres of abandoned or seized plantation land. Tens of thousands of black refugees were streaming into the Union lines. In January 1865, General William Tecumseh Sherman issued a field order setting aside an initial four hundred thousand acres along the Georgia coast, known as the Sherman Reservation, for ten thousand black families, who would each get "a plot of not more than 40 acres of tillable ground." The victorious army, no longer needing so many pack animals, would also provide each family with a mule. On March 3, 1865, Congress passed a bill creating the Freedmen's Bureau, which was responsible for an extension of Sherman's policy throughout the former Confederacy. In a parallel to the national homesteading policy, former slaves who worked the land for three years would be awarded title.

A second pillar of Lincoln's intended postwar Reconstruction was the political quarantine of those who had served the Confederacy and the extension of citizenship to former slaves. In 1862, and again in 1865, Congress approved measures requiring officeholders to swear an "Ironclad Test Oath" that they had never taken up arms against the United States nor served in any office of the Confederacy. Educated freedmen and blacks who had served in the Union Army were to be given the vote. When both reforms were aborted by Lincoln's assassination, the reverberations affected not just the civil rights of freed slaves but the entire system of land tenure and credit.

Vice President Andrew Johnson, a unionist Democrat from slaveholding Tennessee, had been put on the Republican ticket in 1864 as a unity gesture. Once sworn in as president, however, Johnson immediately set about destroying Lincoln's Reconstruction program. One of his first acts was to pardon plantation owners and force some forty thousand freedmen off their land, often at bayonet point. As federal authority withdrew from the former Confederacy, the planter class regained power. "Redeemer" governments replaced Reconstructionist ones. Land tenure policies intended to repress freed slaves combined with a long period of depressed farm prices to push increasing numbers of white farmers, as well as blacks, into debt peonage.

FROM EMANCIPATION TO FEUDALISM

At the heart of the farmers' distress was the crop-lien system. Small farmers without independent access to markets or credit relied on local furnishing merchants for supplies and cash advances to plant their crops. The merchant, who was sometimes also the landlord, obtained a mortgage, or lien, on the crop. At settling-up time, the tenant farmer usually learned that his crop had failed to "pay out" against his debt. The merchant would then agree to carry the farmer through the winter in exchange for a new note.

Once in perpetual debt to a merchant, the farmer could not qualify for bank credit. The republican ideal of a yeoman farmer class was being slowly crushed by permanent debt. As the historian of southern land tenure Harold D. Woodman has written, "The new system was even more pernicious than the old, for it enthralled not only the blacks but a majority of the white farmers as well."

William Faulkner, in his 1940 novel *The Hamlet,* describes Will Varner, a furnishing merchant who was also a local judge: "He owned most of the good land in the country and held mortgages on most of the rest. He owned the store and the cotton gin and the combined grist mill and blacksmith shop in the village proper and it was considered, to put it mildly, bad luck for a man of the neighborhood to do his trading or gin his cotton or grind his meal or shoe his stock anywhere else."

The legal basis of the new feudalism was reinforced by legislatures and courts. Consider one representative case. In the spring of 1871 in southwest Georgia's Early County, the freedmen Stephen Odom and John Mozee contracted with a landowner named A. J. Mercier to grow corn and cotton. At harvest time, the laborers were to be compensated with half the crop. In the meantime, they needed seed, fertilizer, food, and other provisions. They got $200 worth of supplies on credit from a local furnishing merchant, Thomas K. Appling, who got a lien against their share of the crop.

When autumn came, the furnishing merchant and the landowner fought over who was to get paid first. The case went all the way to the Georgia Supreme Court. The justices held that the landowner took priority over the merchant, who in turn superseded the croppers. Odom's share—five bales of cotton—was seized by the sheriff.

The court used this case to overturn long-standing doctrines of landlord-tenant law. Before the Civil War, tenant farmers had rights. These included the right of "quiet enjoyment" of the land they rented. Without an elaborate eviction process for cause, tenants could not be thrown off as long as they paid the rent. Nor could landlords control how tenants disposed of their crops. But in the context of plantation owners seeking to restore financial control over former slaves, a pre–Civil War doctrine of rights devised for white tenants provided far too much economic independence for blacks. In *Appling v. Odom*, the Georgia Supreme Court held that sharecroppers had only the rights of contract workers, not the historic rights of free tenants. All over the South after the Civil War, as more small farmers became sharecroppers, the rights of croppers were similarly narrowed by both legislatures and courts. Among blacks and whites alike, Jeffersonian yeoman farmers were a dwindling breed. Despite liberalization of the homesteading laws, freeholding was in retreat. By 1880, 36 percent of southern farms were operated by tenants; by 1900, fully half were. And 55 percent of tenant farmers were white. Nationally, rates of homeownership stagnated at around 45 percent.

The Jim Crow system kept black and white small farmers from uniting around common economic interests. Landowners sometimes evicted white tenants and replaced them with blacks, who were more desperate, had less bargaining power, and were easier to control. This risk of displacement helped poison relations between black and white tenants, a by-product that the landed elite noted with satisfaction.

The declining crop prices, meanwhile, were part of a general deflationary period of tight money caused by banker influence on both parties. This trend was compounded by increasing agricultural productivity and competition from abroad. Cotton fell from eighteen cents a pound in 1871 to nine cents by 1883 and just four and a half cents by 1894. Wheat, not a slave crop, declined in tandem, from a dollar a bushel in 1870 to eighty cents in 1885 and sixty cents in the 1890s; many farmers received as little as thirty-five cents. Corn followed a similar trajectory, from forty-five cents a bushel in 1870 to a dime by 1889. Real wages also fell. It was this combination of debt and declining prices that led to the abortive populist revolt described in chapter 7.

Farmers did enjoy a brief decade of prosperity during and right after World War I. But in the years before and during the Great Depression, prices declined again, triggering an epidemic of foreclosures. Between 1929 and 1932, the price of a bushel of wheat fell from $1.03 to thirty-eight cents. Hog prices dropped from $11.36 a head to $4.31. In 1932 alone, 8 percent of Iowa farms suffered forced sales.

With escalating foreclosures came radical politics, demands for forbearance, and the election of progressive legislatures and governors. The long-deferred populist moment came back around. An Iowa organizer named Milo Reno, with roots in the agrarian revolt of the 1880s, helped found the Farmers' Holiday Association, a mass movement that called for a freeze on foreclosures, a farmers' strike, and the withholding of crops from market. Under Reno's leadership, farmers blocked the roads to auction sales and bid a dollar at the auction site so that they could purchase the foreclosed farm for next to nothing and return it to its owner.

In the early 1930s, radical governors were elected in several midwestern states. Minnesota's populist governor Floyd Olson issued a decree creating a one-year moratorium on farm foreclosures. In February 1933, Iowa's newly elected Democratic governor, Clyde Herring, signed a law freezing foreclosures and providing that farmers delinquent on mortgage payments could pay fair market rent (much reduced because of falling land prices) to their bankers and keep their farms.

Minnesota's legislature quickly gave statutory form to Olson's moratorium decree. The law led to one of the most surprising Supreme Court decisions of the early 1930s, confirming Mr. Dooley's dictum that the Supreme Court follows the election results. Until 1937, a very conservative Court overturned several key pieces of New Deal legislation, leading an exasperated Roosevelt to make his disastrous attempt to pack the High Court with additional judges. After this skirmish, the Court began upholding the New Deal. But in a landmark ruling well before the court-packing affair, *Home Building and Loan Association v. Blaisdell (1934)*, the justices upheld the Minnesota Mortgage Moratorium Act as a necessary exercise of emergency state power, despite the fact that it plainly violated the contracts clause of the Constitution. In the Depression years, twenty-seven state legislatures enacted emergency foreclosure moratorium legislation.

A NEW DEAL FOR DEBTORS

At the federal level, as defaults and foreclosures spread from farmers to other homeowners, the Roosevelt administration literally reinvented the entire mortgage system. Before Roosevelt, the typical mortgage was an interest-only short-term renewable note, with the entire principal due and payable at the end of the term, which was generally two to eleven years. In the melodramas about farmers losing their homesteads because they couldn't pay "the mortgage," the sum in question was not a monthly payment or two. It was the entire principal.

The loan seldom covered more than 60 percent of the purchase price, and the homebuyer often borrowed part of the down payment in the form of a second or even a third mortgage at punishingly high interest rates. In normal times, the farmer or homeowner could expect that the note would be rolled over by the bank. In a depression, when the deflated value of the collateral was less than the value of the mortgage and banks were failing, mortgages frequently could not be refinanced and the home was lost. By the spring of 1933, half the mortgages in America were in default, and foreclosures were averaging about a thousand a day. This was the human meaning of a debt deflation.

The government's response was as exemplary in the 1930s as it is feeble today. In July 1932, late in the Hoover administration, Congress created the Federal Home Loan Bank System, modeled on the Federal Reserve. Like the Reserve, which serves commercial banks, it is a system of twelve regional banks that can make advances to its member thrift institutions. But as the Depression deepened, just as the Federal Reserve could not cure deflation with cheap money or cash advances, the home loan banks proved helpful but far from sufficient.

In July 1933, Congress created the Home Owners' Loan Corporation to refinance distressed mortgages. The HOLC sold more than $3 billion worth of bonds at the government borrowing rate of 2.5 to 3 percent and used the proceeds to make direct loans. It was a retail operation, with 458 local loan offices and nearly twenty-one thousand employees throughout the country. By 1937, the HOLC held about 14 percent of the value of all mortgages in the United States. The equivalent today would be around $1.5 trillion. It saved an estimated one million homes from foreclosure. When the HOLC finally went out of business in 1951, after housing markets had normalized, it returned a small profit of $14 million to the Treasury.

Even with the HOLC, housing prices were still falling in many areas. Foreclosures had slowed but not ceased. Roosevelt's next innovation was the National Housing Act of 1934, which created the Federal Housing Administration. By offering mortgage insurance on loans to people who had less than 20 percent to put down, the FHA could expand the pool of buyers. Initially, it insured loans to qualified buyers with down payments as low as 7 percent of the home's appraised value. This was cut to 3 percent in 1957. The FHA also began insuring mortgages with terms as long as thirty years. These terms largely eliminated the need for second mortgages to cover down payments. Because the FHA carefully evaluated the creditworthiness of loan applicants, its earnings from premiums more than covered its losses.

With the FHA, the Roosevelt administration invented the long-term, fixed-rate, level-payment self-amortizing mortgage that we take for granted today. The New Deal idea was an ingenious variation on a century-old repayment plan, used by some building and loan associations, in which mortgages, for a term of up to twelve years, were interest-only, but with a requirement that the mortgage holder gradually accumulate savings in a separate account so that when the note came due, the savings would be sufficient to pay it off.

In the version pioneered by the New Deal, interest and principal repayments are combined in the same mortgage. Early in the mortgage term, the monthly payment is mostly interest. As the principal is paid down, the payment gradually becomes slightly less interest (on a reduced debt) and slightly more principal, until the debt is totally paid off.

One more government innovation completed the new mortgage system. Banks and thrifts were primarily local institutions. When local demand for mortgage loans exceeded the supply of savings, there would be a bottleneck in the production of mortgages. The solution was a national "secondary market." A government corporation, the Federal National Mortgage Association, was created by Congress in 1938 to purchase FHA-insured mortgage loans from approved lenders, replenishing their cash to enable them to make more loans. It was privatized in 1968 and rebranded as the for-profit corporation Fannie Mae, which after 2005 helped facilitate the collapse. As a public entity, FNMA had been scandal-free.

This basic system organized and defined America's housing market from the mid-1930s through the 1970s. Homeownership rates, which had fallen from nearly 50 percent in the late 1920s to below 40 percent in the pit of the Depression, rebounded to new highs of 55 percent by 1950 and almost 62 percent by 1960.

WALL STREET TO THE RESCUE

What killed this highly effective home loan system was a combination of random circumstance, bad economic theory, shifts in the distribution of political power, and financial innovations from hell. Instead of a straightforward, transparent, publicly anchored system to serve homeowners, mortgage finance became a speculative circus to enrich middlemen.

The circumstance was an increase in inflation triggered by the Vietnam War, the collapse of the Bretton Woods system, and the OPEC oil price increases. The inflationary 1970s were lethal for long-term fixed-rate loans. The coup de grâce was Paul Volcker's announcement on October 6, 1979, that the Federal Reserve would be deliberately raising interest rates in order to stem inflation. Savings and loans were now hemorrhaging money, paying higher rates to attract demand deposits than they were earning on long-term fixed-rate mortgage loans. Two remedies emerged, one from an increasingly deregulated financial industry, the other from Congress. Both set the stage for the collapse that followed.

In the late 1970s, Lewis Ranieri, head of the mortgage bond department at Salomon Brothers, was experimenting with new products and trading strategies. His vehicle was mortgage-backed securities. Investment banking houses like Salomon, realizing that these securities were too lucrative to leave to staid old Fannie Mae, began to issue their own "private label" securities that didn't involve Fannie or FHA and were less subject to government scrutiny.

As the thrift industry bled money by having to lend long and borrow short, lenders became frantic to unload mortgages to replenish cash. While S&Ls were in a panic to sell, Ranieri was on a buying spree, often getting bargains of around eighty cents on the dollar. The industry feared that interest rates would keep rising. Ranieri suspected that they had peaked. He was wagering, correctly, that eventually Volcker would break the back of inflation and let rates decline. By 1982, he was proved right, and he would make a fortune for himself and Salomon in the bond market rally that followed.

In the meantime, banks and S&Ls needed strategies to make up their losses. At the dawn of the Reagan era, this need comported nicely with the new doctrine that markets could do no wrong. One by one, New Deal financial regulations and provisions were watered down or repealed. In commercial banking, this sequence of events led to the erosion and eventual repeal of Glass-Steagall in 1999. In the thrift industry, it led to the Garn–St. Germain Depository Institutions Act of 1982, which in turn triggered the first of the serial financial collapses of the past three decades: the savings and loan disaster.

Garn–St. Germain freed the thrift industry to venture far afield from home mortgage loans, into everything from fast-food franchises to commercial real estate gambles and high-risk securities. Deposit insurance was increased so that S&Ls could attract more savings. Industry-friendly regulators also weakened capital standards. Tiny, highly leveraged S&Ls could suddenly become giants, because they were able to bid for deposits in the national market by offering returns slightly above the going rate. They then had to find higher-yield (and higher-risk) investments to finance the higher interest rates they were paying to attract savings. This was also the period when many nonprofit thrifts converted to for-profit status and executives began paying themselves seven-figure salaries and bonuses.

The S&L disaster was the result of more than just risky gambles. It included plenty of corruption. Industry influence led several states to relax their standards for state-chartered S&Ls, putting pressure on Washington to weaken rules for federal charters. Charles Keating, head of the infamous Lincoln Savings and Loan Association, the product of a hasty acquisition binge, used his campaign contributions and political contacts to get examiners off his case. Before the S&L collapse was over, Keating and more than a thousand other industry executives went to prison.

The speculative spree led to what was the most serious financial collapse since the Great Depression. Between 1986 and 1995, no fewer than 1,043 thrift institutions with over half a trillion dollars in assets went broke. The crash cost the FDIC at least $143 billion, which seemed like a lot of money at the time. The entire industry lost some $29 billion in equity capital and had to be rebuilt. Reform legislation in 1989 limited speculative activities by S&Ls, but financial entrepreneurs soon figured out how to use derivative securities and subprime loans for new speculative strategies, bypassing regulated S&Ls in favor of unregulated mortgage brokers.

Meanwhile, legislation enacted in 1968 had turned the Federal National Mortgage Association into a private corporation. The intent was to get its $7 billion loan portfolio off the government's books while retaining its social mission of providing liquidity to the mortgage market. By the 1990s, however, executives were treating Fannie like just another for-profit business and even got caught falsifying its accounting in order to maximize the value of their stock options.

Ranieri's mortgage-backed bonds at Salomon Brothers were straightforward compared with what was coming. In 1983, Larry Fink, the head of mortgage trading at rival First Boston, created the collateralized debt obligation, or CDO. Unlike simple mortgage bonds, CDOs sliced securities into separate bonds, or tranches (from the French word for slice), according to their supposed degree of risk.

The financial engineers soon split mortgage pools into as many as twenty different tranches, some of which might provide interest-only payments and others might use flows of principal-only. Wall Street began marketing these bonds to foreign buyers. As the inimitable Michael Lewis described in *Liar's Poker*, his 1989 memoir of his life as a bond trader, "The homeowner didn't know it, but his interest payments might be destined for a French speculator and his principal payments for an insurance company in Milwaukee."

Then Wall Street added yet another twist, *recombining* interest payments from one set of mortgages with principal flows from others to create securities even further removed from the underlying loans. An essentially unregulated multitrillion-dollar synthetic market had been created, with middlemen taking a cut at each stage and having the insider knowledge to make even more money by betting on market trends. The argument was that all this added "liquidity" to the mortgage market. But mainly it added complexity, opacity, and the risk of a catastrophic collapse. Nobody envisioned what might occur if it all blew up.

Under pressure from financial interests, both political parties colluded in policies to prohibit regulation of derivative securities. This increasing regulatory capture freed investment bankers such as Goldman Sachs and J.P. Morgan to create even more complex and opaque forms of derivative securities, including "CDOs squared," which were derivatives made up of packages of other derivatives, and "synthetic" CDOs, which were not actually backed by mortgages at all but were merely vehicles to place bets on market trends.

Supposedly, all of this was good for homeowners. But between 1970, when mortgage-backed securities were invented, and 1990, by which time they were ubiquitous, the national rate of homeownership crept up by just 1.3 percentage points. And because the enhanced complexity increased opportunities for insiders to tack on fees at every stage, net costs to borrowers actually rose.

All of these financial innovations created the preconditions for the scam that finally crashed the economy and prolonged the agony afterward: subprime mortgage loans. The subprime story has been told by many writers, including this one, but here is the pertinent essence.

With S&Ls partly re-regulated after the debacle of the 1980s, the action shifted to unregulated mortgage brokers. Brokers had traditionally been a relatively small corner of the mortgage industry. But by 2000, unregulated brokers were originating over half of all mortgages. The number of brokerages ballooned to over fifty thousand. The brokers created variable-rate products for borrowers, offering a low "teaser" rate of, say, 3 percent, which would be reset at perhaps 9 percent after two years. Variable-rate mortgages had been around since the 1970s, but their interest rates fluctuated with prevailing rates and were capped. Subprime mortgages, by contrast, automatically increased to far higher rates and monthly payments. Borrowers were led to believe that they could keep refinancing as housing prices rose, but when the music stopped, they were locked in.

Often such mortgages required no documentation of creditworthiness. These were coded "Alt-A" by the industry and were colloquially known as NINJA loans ("No Income, No Job or Assets"). New Century Mortgage Corporation, one of the worst offenders, combined these products into a so-called 80-20 loan, where 80 percent was the first mortgage and 20 percent the second mortgage, meaning that the buyer put no money down whatever.

A broker could make money on a loan with a large risk of default because the fees were high and someone else was taking the loan off his hands. The game of pass-the-risk included at least seven different layers of middlemen: the mortgage broker who made the loan, the local bank that forwarded it to Wall Street, the investment banker who purchased it, the sometimes different investment banker who packaged and sold it, the lawyers who created the trust to hold the underlying mortgages, the proprietors of an industry-wide electronic database designed to keep track of the whole affair, the credit rating agency that blessed packages of highly risky loans as triple-A securities, and issuers of credit default swaps who insured the bonds against default. Each of these middlemen took a cut. All this was celebrated as the efficient ingenuity of the free market.

In one case study by the Financial Crisis Inquiry Commission, mortgage brokers provided 3,433 loans to New Century, which in turn sold them to Citigroup to be packaged into nineteen tranches and sold to investors. The average fee collected directly by the broker from the borrower was 1.81 percent of the loan amount. On top of that, brokers got another roughly 1 percent on the spread. No wonder the net cost to homeowners increased rather than decreased.

At the end of the line was an unlucky buyer looking for safe, high returns who naively trusted the triple-A rating. The investor might be a California pension fund, a German development bank, or a Norwegian township. These investors—and U.S. homeowners, who stood innocently by as $9 trillion in home equity was lost—were left holding the bag.

By 2005, even Fannie Mae, which had at first rejected subprime loans as overly risky, was buying them and their near relations, no-documentation Alt-A loans, in order to maintain its market share. This seal of approval from once-reputable Fannie further increased the market for sketchy mortgage paper. When Fannie had to be taken over by the government in September 2008, subprime losses were heavily implicated.

Housing prices ceased rising in 2007, and the entire pyramid started to totter. Trillions of dollars' worth of securities held for sale by major investment bankers became unmarketable, and the chain of bank failures and the collapse in housing values began. For our purposes in understanding the destructive role of a debt overhang, the more important part of the story is what happened afterward.

A DOOMSDAY MACHINE

As housing prices fell and subprime mortgages began to reset, millions of Americans found themselves at risk of default or foreclosure. Sixty-one percent of subprime loans made in 2006 were in default by early

2010. One home in four, including many with conventional mortgages, was worth less than the outstanding principal on the loan. The housing bubble had produced a glut of speculative new construction. Now the millions of foreclosed or vacant homes added to the oversupply and depressed housing values generally. The declining housing values, in turn, put assets in the portfolios of banks underwater. These two parts of the great housing deflation fed on each other.

It was a far more convoluted mess than the one that confronted Roosevelt. When the New Deal created the Home Owners' Loan Corporation in 1934 to refinance mortgages, FDR faced a similar downward spiral of falling housing prices, defaulting homeowners, and wounded banks. But Roosevelt, unlike the Obama administration, was willing to restructure the banking system and its entire business model. The government also compelled banks to recognize their losses. In one of Roosevelt's first acts, the bank holiday of March 1933, the FDIC assessed which banks were sound enough to open, and closed (or merged) the rest. Roosevelt was not fearful of breaking up the big banks; his Glass-Steagall Act did so deliberately. And when the government helped recapitalize some banks through the Reconstruction Finance Corporation, it got a say in running them.

By contrast, when Obama became president, he inherited from the Bush presidency the new Troubled Asset Relief Program, whose purpose was to shore up rather than break up large banks. This program, developed in close collaboration with the Fed, was substantially the handiwork of the former president of the Federal Reserve Bank of New York, Timothy Geithner. That same Geithner was now Obama's Treasury secretary and was not about to repudiate his own strategy for containing the crisis.

Propping up the big banks required colluding with them in creative accounting to reassure the public that they were essentially sound. That goal made it unattractive to compel the banks to book large losses in their portfolio of mortgages. This premise in turn killed the appetite for any program of broad refinancing.

In Roosevelt's day, there was no securitization to complicate the challenge. So government refinancing of a mortgage was simplicity itself. The HOLC paid off the mortgage and created a new one. Full stop. But by 2009, most mortgages were no longer held directly by banks or thrifts. They had mutated into securities, and many had been split into separate streams of interest and principal. Turning them back into mortgages was technically tricky and politically fraught.

When a borrower fell behind in the monthly payments, the interests of the servicer and the bondholder diverged. The servicer kept getting paid for collection efforts, while it might be in the interest of the investor to reach an accommodation. Prolonged delinquencies actually maximized servicer fees. Conversely, when some servicers did offer relief, they were sometimes threatened with lawsuits by investors who didn't want to recognize the accounting loss.

In these circumstances, turning underwater securitized loans back into whole mortgages, then refinancing them so that the homeowner might keep the home, was an imperative goal of macroeconomic policy. But it seemed a legal and logistical impossibility. Thus the lucrative invention of securitization, compounded by ever more complex derivatives and then by subprime, did more than cause the financial collapse. It created a doomsday machine that made recovery from the collapse seemingly unattainable.

HAMP, HARP, AND HYPE

Once the Obama administration decided neither to require banks to book losses from underwater mortgages nor to tamper with the Frankenstein system of securitization, it was left with a series of feeble second-bests. The core weakness was that any program had to be voluntary to the bankers—who had no incentive to refinance.

Obama's program, called Making Home Affordable, was unveiled on February 18, 2009. Its centerpiece was a cumbersome scheme with a clunky name to match: the Home Affordable Modification Program. It was budgeted at $75 billion of TARP money; to date, just $3 billion has been spent. Under HAMP, the government offered lenders incentive payments totaling as much as $4,500 per loan if they would reduce monthly payments to no more than 31 percent of a borrower's gross monthly income. But this was voluntary, and many banks wouldn't play.

One provision of Obama's relief bill actually had some teeth. Bankruptcy judges were authorized to alter the terms of mortgages. That provision was fiercely opposed by the financial industry, and Geithner quickly spread the word to Congress that it was not an administration priority. Twelve Senate Democrats who did not wish to offend their bankers joined Republicans in voting against the provision, and it died.

The Obama program was aimed at homeowners who were only moderately underwater. But in much of inner-city America, and in states such as Nevada, Florida, Arizona, and California, half of homes had mortgages of 30 to 50 percent more than the value of the home. In these states, declining prices created a downward vortex. As homeowners walked away, local governments lost property tax revenues; neighbors with conventional mortgages and unblemished credit records lost all of their home equity, too. HAMP did little or nothing for the most damaged areas. The problem was not "unqualified" borrowers but a collapse of housing values generally.

HAMP created an added layer of gratuitous complexity. Rather than a simple refinancing, the relief was initially to be in the form of "trial modifications," a category invented by Treasury bureaucrats to minimize risks to the banks. To qualify a borrower for relief, the servicer would perform tests based on a complicated formula that included the market value of the house and the borrower's capacity to pay. According to TARP's inspector general, the Treasury modified the formula nine times in 2009 alone. Only if the borrower met the terms of the trial modification and stayed current on loan payments for six months could the modification be made permanent.

Obama's Treasury set an initial goal of five hundred thousand loan modifications by December 2009, but only about seventy thousand had been achieved by year-end. Servicers had been caught unprepared by the February announcement. The entire system of securitization was designed to minimize costs and operate like an assembly line. Loan originators with little training took applications, checked them against a formula, got underwriter sign-off, and approved the mortgages. That worked fine during the boom. But after the bust, restructuring mortgages was a very labor-intensive enterprise that entailed carefully assessing the capacity of the borrower to pay and the likely market value of the house, as well as complying with detailed government requirements to get the bonus payment. In corporatespeak, it was a cost center. Lenders were unwilling to allocate enough staff to do the job properly. An August 2010 survey by ProPublica found that the servicer bureaucracy was so inefficient that a homeowner applying for a loan modification under HAMP had to submit the same documents an average of six times.

In October 2010, the Treasury reported some 700,000 failed trial modifications, compared with about 460,000 successful ones. And an estimated half of borrowers who received successful modifications fell back into default because either the relief was too shallow or the deeper problems of the recession, namely unemployment, were impairing their capacity to pay.

An underwater borrower mainly needed reduction in the principal amount of the loan. This straightforward approach, however, was unacceptable to the administration because it would have required the bank to book the loss. The inspector general for TARP, source of the funding for HAMP, issued a scorching report in March 2010 criticizing the Treasury's failure to include principal reduction. The very next day, Treasury officials responded to this and other pleas by announcing a new $14 billion principal reduction program, to be run by the Department of Housing and Urban Development, intended to help one and a half million homeowners avoid foreclosure. Known as the Home Affordable Refinance Program, it was a bureaucratic maze designed to keep banks from having to book losses. By the end of 2011, only 646 homeowners had gotten relief.

Because the existing mortgage could be worth no more than 115 percent of the home, the vast majority of underwater homeowners did not qualify. Few lenders were willing to participate. In 2012, the administration sought to jump-start HARP by asking Fannie Mae to purchase mortgages with reduced principal. Fannie Mae, however, was still a ward of the government, and this initiative was blocked by Fannie's regulator, Ed DeMarco, who feared that many people would just stop paying their mortgages in order to qualify for relief. His concern was overblown, since a refinancing process would determine whether an applicant was proceeding in good faith. But even assuming Fannie's cooperation, the program was far from sufficient. DeMarco's agency calculated that only between 74,000 and 248,000 homeowners would be eligible for principal reduction through Fannie Mae and that fewer would actually get it. Simple refinancing by a modern-day HOLC would be a far better strategy.

According to the Treasury's most recent documents (from late 2012), about 1.3 million homeowners have received loan relief though HAMP and its variants such as HARP. Roughly half of these are expected to go back into default. This compared with the 10.8 million who owed more on their mortgages than their homes were worth, representing some

22.5 percent of all mortgages. In Nevada, the figure was 67 percent. In California, it was 32 percent. About five million families have already lost their homes to foreclosure, and at least another five million are in serious default and in some stage of the foreclosure process. Over a million of these homes belong to banks, and millions more are vacant, subject to vandalism and dragging down the property value and security of their neighbors' homes. With this immense downdraft in the housing market, and with falling wages and rising unemployment, it is hard to see how housing prices can recover in weaker markets.

A better approach was proposed by Sheila Bair, the head of the FDIC. In the case of small and medium failed banks taken over by the FDIC, the process is both rigorous and straightforward. The agency performs a thorough audit. It fully guarantees insured deposits, pays off depositors who want their money back, writes off losses, and temporarily takes over the insolvent bank. The bank is then reopened as a healthy smaller bank, merged into a bank that acquires its assets, or it is shut down.

One failed bank, California's IndyMac, gave Bair a chance to try out an ingenious strategy for dealing with underwater mortgage loans. When the FDIC took over IndyMac in 2007, in an early harbinger of the mortgage bust, the agency analyzed the entire loan portfolio to see which loans were good candidates for modification or refinancing. IndyMac, as run by the FDIC, modified thousands of loans, sparing homeowners from foreclosure. Bair's strategy was to ignore the temporarily depressed value of the collateral if the homeowner could make payments on a reduced principal. This was the process that Bair recommended to Geithner. But the model was rejected because the Treasury secretary was unwilling either to have the government temporarily take over insolvent large banks or to undertake direct refinancing, Roosevelt-style. And so the mortgage crisis dragged on and on, sandbagging the recovery and the dream of homeownership.

In the absence of more robust remedies, the government was left with only one policy: the Fed's strategy of very low interest rates. This helped homeowners with good credit and positive equity, but it did not cure the debt overhang. Between 2001 and 2012, the spread between lenders' cost of money and average mortgage rates widened by a full point, as fees became ever more of a profit center. When borrowers complained, lenders cited the cost of complying with new regulations—which were necessitated by their own propensity to excess! The remedy of cutting the Gordian knot by vastly simplifying the system or making direct government loans was off the table.

NO EXIT

Two further episodes in 2011 and 2012 provide deeper insights on the policy prison created by complex securitization. The first was a legal mess of the industry's own making.

As the bonanza for middlemen in the origination, packaging, and sale of mortgage bonds accelerated after 2000 thanks to subprime, the industry created an assembly line that cut a lot of corners. Under the laws of every state, a mortgage is a loan collateralized by real property: your house. When you close on the mortgage, you sign two key documents: a note promising to repay the loan; and a lien, or legal claim against the property, giving the bank the right to take the house in the event that you fail to pay. The lien is duly recorded at the local recorder of deeds. In the event that the mortgage is sold (as all are when loans are securitized), the note and lien are supposed to be signed over to the new owner, and the transfer of ownership recorded as well. This is known as the chain of title.

But in their haste to securitize, loan originators and their investment banker sponsors did not always have time for these legal niceties. To keep track of the whole daisy chain and speed up loan processing, the financial industry created an electronic database known as the Mortgage Electronic Registration Systems (MERS). Since its founding in 2005, it has registered more than sixty-six million mortgages. MERS was meant also to be the owner of record of the mortgage, with the right to foreclose or to pass that right along to the loan servicer. This worked fine on the upside, but as mortgages fell into foreclosure, some glitches emerged.

In the rush to process foreclosures, the nation's largest bankers had employed human "robo-signers." One such employee, Jeffrey Stephan of GMAC Mortgage, testified in a lawsuit that he processed on average about one document a minute. In these documents, he attested to the fact that he had personally verified mortgage payment histories—something not remotely possible in a minute.

As courts, Congress, and the press looked deeper into the high-speed foreclosure mills, it turned out that in the securitization stampede, documents were often forged or backdated or they misrepresented the actions of the signatory. Many mortgage transfers had not been properly recorded in the first place. If MERS does not have proper title to the note and the deed of trust, its designee cannot foreclose.

A bankruptcy court in New York ruled in November 2010 that the Bank of New York could not foreclose on a mortgage that it had purchased from Countrywide because MERS had failed to transfer the proper documentation. If similar rulings became the norm, supposedly securitized packages of loans would be collateralized by nothing whatever—and major banks would be insolvent. This fear set off a scramble for a quick fix. But state attorneys general quickly grasped that the court rulings gave them leverage against the banks to deliver more mortgage relief in exchange for a general settlement of the legal quagmire.

A key attorney general, Eric Schneiderman of New York, held out not only for better terms but for intensified criminal prosecutions against senior bank executives. Most of the trusts that held the mortgages had been created under New York law. Schneiderman had broad authority under the state's Martin Act to prosecute bankers for various forms of misrepresentation and fraud. What he lacked was the investigative manpower that only the federal government could provide.

In February 2012, after more than a year of jockeying, the Justice Department and forty-nine attorneys general, including Schneiderman, announced the long-awaited master settlement. In exchange for cleaning up the legal mess that was clogging the foreclosure machinery, the attorneys general and the federal government got the major banks to part with $25 billion, to be used for principal reductions and payments to people wrongly foreclosed on. There was a lot of double counting in the settlement, and not more than $10 billion of the $25 billion was new money. The banks, without admitting wrongdoing, agreed to reform a variety of practices, robo-signing and fast-track foreclosures among them. Federal and state law enforcement retained the right to bring criminal cases.

As part of the deal, Schneiderman was named codirector of an interagency task force on criminal prosecutions that was to get a lot of federal manpower. If prosecutors ever decided to throw the book at bankers, there were plenty of ways, starting with tax fraud, wire fraud, and postal fraud. Schneiderman's hope, expressed to me and other journalists, was that if large numbers of legal, accounting, and investigative people were pooled from several agencies, including the Internal Revenue Service, the U.S. Postal Inspection Service, the Justice Department, and the SEC, the distribution of power could drastically change. Not only would some senior executives finally go to jail for massive frauds, as had happened in the S&L scandal of the 1980s, but the threat of possible criminal prosecutions could produce mortgage relief of a whole other order of magnitude—in the hundreds of billions rather than the low tens of billions.

But as of this writing, it looks as though the financial industry got the better of the deal. As of September 2012, of the nominal settlement, just $2.5 billion has found its way to principal-reductions for some 22,000 homeowners. Legal leverage that might have been used to drastically change the foreclosure process and obtain far more financial relief from banks was bargained away for a relative song. Defaults and foreclosures continue. The interagency task force nominally cochaired by Schneiderman has been given only a few dozen additional people. No major new criminal cases have been launched. Neither the Justice Department nor the Treasury has the appetite for major prosecutions of senior bankers.

One other intriguing initiative that might have broken the foreclosure logjam was also repeatedly aborted, again because it would have been too costly or too inconvenient for the banks. In 2008, as the mortgage crisis deepened, several legal scholars proposed that the government use the power of eminent domain to convert packages of securitized mortgages back into whole loans. Eminent domain, recognized in the Constitution and repeatedly upheld by the Supreme Court, allows the government to condemn private property for public purposes, with due process of law and just compensation.

In this case, the government would take securitized mortgages on underwater homes, which were typically trading at around fifty or sixty cents on the dollar. It would compensate the investor at the reduced market value, convert the securities back into mortgages, and pass along the savings to the homeowner. A $400,000 mortgage might thus be reduced to a $200,000 mortgage. Ideally, this would have required a new Home Owners' Loan Corporation, but it could have been done by the Treasury, using TARP funds as the initial capital for the first round of takings. This option was fiercely opposed not only by the banks but by the Treasury and Fannie Mae for fear of the impact on bank balance sheets.

In the spring of 2012, a group of investment bankers, lawyers, and policy activists who happened to be liberal Democrats tried to run with the eminent domain idea, using a private for-profit company as middleman. Calling itself Mortgage Resolution Partners, the group was led by Steven Gluckstern, a venture capitalist and the founding chair of the left-wing Democracy Alliance. Even if one takes Gluckstern at his word that the group's purpose is to serve the public interest, MRP's odyssey speaks volumes about the mess the securitizers made.

The typical underwater mortgage locked up in a securitization trust includes a second mortgage as well as a first. If the first mortgage were taken by eminent domain and written down to the property's actual (much reduced) value, the second mortgage would be worthless. Most second mortgages are owned by large banks. So, out of the gate, MRP faced the opposition of the large banks and the investment banks that dominated the business of securitization, both of whom shared an interest in pretending that the mortgage-backed bonds were worth their face value.

In the summer of 2012, MRP caught the interest of several distressed communities, including San Bernardino County, California, where the collapse in housing values had so severely cut property tax revenues that the county had to declare bankruptcy. MRP offered to provide the county with legal expertise and to find investors to capitalize the eminent domain seizures. The county, as a government body, would exercise its right of eminent domain and hold the properties as they went through the legal process. Then, once titles were obtained, new mortgages with reduced principal would be written and insured by the FHA.

Note, however, the several disadvantages of relying on yet another set of financial industry middlemen rather than on a one-stop government agency such as Roosevelt's HOLC. For starters, MRP braced itself for massive litigation from Wall Street. Its legal advisers concluded that it would need a war chest of at least $25 million to get a case to the Supreme Court affirming this use of eminent domain and that even if it prevailed, individual eminent domain claims could be contested one by one. A new HOLC, by contrast, would have pockets deep enough to fend off litigation, as well as explicit public authority.

MRP also needed investor capital to finance its purchases. One of its principals told me that it was offering investors a return of 20 to 30 percent—money that under a public program would go to homeowners.

MRP quickly found that the loans that most readily lent themselves to its strategy were underwater mortgages on which borrowers were current in their payments, or so-called performing loans. But in depressed neighborhoods in the real world, one house might be in foreclosure, another owned by a bank, a third abandoned, a fourth occupied by a homeowner who's behind in payments, and a fifth underwater but "performing." By focusing on performing loans, MRP addressed only the low-hanging fruit, which was just a fraction of the total ecology of distressed communities. At this writing, MRP has made little headway, but it has rekindled the interest of the Federal Reserve in trying to use eminent domain in a refinancing strategy.

The attempt by arguably public-minded private financiers to break the logjam of distressed mortgages locked up in securitized trusts demonstrates just how byzantine was the knot created by the geniuses on Wall Street. Unraveling it is simply beyond the capacity of other market actors, no matter how well intentioned. The housing collapse will continue to drag down the economy until the government musters the nerve to compel banks to recognize losses, to blow up rather than protect the securitization machine, to convert Fannie Mae back into a nonprofit public entity, and to vastly simplify the entire dysfunctional system. The Federal Reserve has bought nearly a trillion dollars' worth of mortgage-backed securities as a way of getting these toxic securities off the books of banks. The Fed should pressure banks to reduce the principal value of underwater mortgages. It could do so by limiting its future purchases of such securities to those whose mortgages have been given principal write-downs.

BLAMING THE VICTIMS

Readers may dimly recall the origin of the Tea Party movement. It happened on February 19, 2009, on the cable network CNBC, when a former commodities trader and on-air reporter named Rick Santelli went on a now-famous rant about "losers" who had taken out high-risk mortgages. Santelli, speaking from the floor of the Chicago Board of Trade to whoops and cheers from nearby traders, attacked Obama's just-released HAMP plan, accused the government of "promoting bad behavior," and called for a "Chicago Tea Party" to protest policies that caused irresponsible mortgage borrowing. Irresponsible *lending* was not part of Santelli's rant, and Wall Street came in for no blame. The organizing of local Tea Parties followed, backed by a lot of right-wing billionaire financing.

It is fitting that the Tea Party movement began, of all places, on the floor of a financial exchange and that it started with a former trader blaming the victims rather than the perpetrators of the most damaging financial scam in nearly a century. But such is the pseudopopulism and inverted responsibility that characterizes the politics of the continuing economic collapse. Santelli was echoing a conservative counternarrative about the roots of the financial crisis. Free-market ideologues could not very well admit that the crisis was caused by a catastrophic failure and corruption of private financial markets. It had to be the government's fault.

In this far-fetched counter-narrative, the housing collapse occurred because politicians, mostly Democrats, had put pressure on banks and thrifts to lend to unqualified borrowers, many of them minorities. It supposedly began with the Community Reinvestment Act of 1977, which required federally regulated lenders to serve low- and moderate-income communities as well as affluent ones. The pressure increased under the Clinton administration, with its programs of affordable home finance. Even George W. Bush fanned the flames with his vision of an "ownership society" to turn more low-income Americans into homeowners.

This story line was disseminated in papers by think tanks such as the American Enterprise Institute and repeated endlessly on right-wing talk radio and Fox News and in speeches by Republican congressmen. Peter Wallison of the AEI, in his dissent to the report of the Financial Crisis Inquiry Commission, contended that the U.S. government, through the Community Reinvestment Act and other means, "sought to increase homeownership in the United States through an intensive effort to reduce mortgage underwriting standards." As a consequence, he added, lenders and secondary market institutions such as Fannie Mae "were compelled to compete for mortgage borrowers who were at or below median income in the areas in which they lived. This competition caused underwriting standards to decline, increased the number of weak and high-risk loans . . . and contributed importantly to the 1997–2007 housing bubble."

But everything about this story is untrue. First, the preponderance of subprime loans were originated by mortgage brokers, *who are not covered by the Community Reinvestment Act,* which requires sound underwriting standards. Most community banks and thrifts covered by the act maintained normal standards, stuck with conventional mortgages, and had far lower default rates. A research study by the Federal Reserve, no less, found that in 2006, at the peak of the subprime madness, only 6 percent of high-yield, high-risk (subprime and Alt-A) loans were made by institutions covered by the act.

Second, the investment bankers and mortgage brokers who dreamed up subprime had no government mandate to increase low-income homeownership and could not have cared less about it. The subprime scam was simply a way to maximize the profits of lenders and middlemen. Indeed, studies have found that roughly half of the borrowers who were persuaded to take out high-profit subprime loans could have qualified for conventional loans. African American loan applicants were especially targeted for subprime loans, and many borrowers were refinancing paid-up mortgages in order to meet the expenses of old age. They were manipulated into taking on loans whose risks they didn't comprehend.

Third, the legitimate programs to expand homeownership had high underwriting standards and exemplary records. President Clinton, impressed by the work of the South Shore National Bank, a pioneering lending institution serving small businesses and homeowners in a depressed Chicago neighborhood, sponsored legislation in 1993 to create other "community development financial institutions" to meet the needs of those whom banks tend to avoid. These institutions carefully evaluate the resources of low-income loan applicants and give them extensive and ongoing counseling. Studies of one such model institution, the Center for Community Self-Help, based in Durham, North Carolina, found that while subprime borrowers with adjustable-rate mortgages suffered default rates of about 40 percent, Self-Help borrowers with comparable economic characteristics had default rates of only 8.5 percent, and many of those defaults were due to the recession.

America's history of homeownership is punctuated by broken promises to African Americans: the failure to block the extension of slavery to states carved out of the Louisiana Purchase, the forty-acres-and-a-mule that never materialized after Emancipation, the replacement of slavery with something more like serfdom. Against that history, the steady increase in black homeownership rates in the late twentieth century was a rare, if aborted, success.

Black homeownership peaked in 2004 at 49.1 percent, some twenty-two points below white rates, but then started falling. By 2012, the black rate had dropped by nearly six points, while the white rate had declined by just two points. But that only begins to convey the devastation in black America. Among black and Latino households, one in four had either lost their homes to foreclosure or were seriously in default, compared with one in eight for non-Hispanic whites.

The gap between black and white wealth has long been far greater than the income gap. Financial assets are crucial to economic success because they provide a cushion against reverses, the wherewithal to become entrepreneurs, savings for retirement, and a legacy for children. As a consequence of the lingering aftereffects of slavery and segregation, most blacks did not get on the ladder of asset ownership until well into the twentieth century.

Between 1984 and the boom year of 1995, the black-white wealth gap slowly declined from a ratio of 12 to 1 to a (still-extreme) low of 7 to 1. But all of the recent progress was obliterated by the housing collapse. To a much greater extent than whites, black net worth is concentrated in home equity. Most blacks simply do not have the discretionary income to accumulate substantial financial wealth. In just the four years between the homeownership peak in 2005 and the bottom of the recession in 2009, the black-white wealth gap nearly doubled. In 2004, the ratio of white to black median household wealth was 11 to 1. By 2009, it had increased to 20 to 1.

Blacks lost more than half of their net worth. In 2009, median white net worth was $113,149. Median black net worth was just $5,766, and one black household in three had negative net worth. Whites, with more wealth in financial holdings such as stocks, mutual funds, pensions, and 401(k) plans rather than in housing, lost only 16 percent. For Hispanics, two-thirds of whose net worth was in home equity and who are concentrated in states hardest hit by the housing collapse, including Florida, Nevada, Arizona, and California, the loss was even worse.

The devastation of African American communities extended to the financial institutions that served them. The South Shore National Bank, founded in 1973, did not go in for subprime lending. In the predominantly black South Side of Chicago, the bank made conventional fixed-rate loans, and it had very low default rates. Renamed ShoreBank in the 1980s, it was hailed as a national model of how to serve low-income communities and maintain high standards. When the subprime collapse hit, ShoreBank refinanced $32 million worth of local subprime mortgages with fixed-rate "rescue loans." But as the crisis deepened, housing values in the community it served plummeted. Unemployment rates rose. In 2008, the bank was profitable. By 2009, many of its loans, which had been perfectly sound before the recession hit, were in trouble. The bank booked a $100 million loss on the year, about half of its equity capital.

ShoreBank applied for TARP assistance. It needed $72 million in aid from the Treasury, a pittance compared with the hundreds of billions that the government found for Wall Street's biggest banks. At the request of regulators, the bank enlisted investors to pump in what eventually totaled an additional $146 million in new capital, exceeding the initial target. Though its prime regulator, the FDIC, voted to approve the TARP assistance, the Treasury refused to concur, and on August 20, 2010, ShoreBank closed its doors.

Citigroup, Bank of America, and Goldman Sachs, which had underwritten the subprime debacle, were too big to fail and received hundreds of billions in government aid. But exemplary ShoreBank was too small to matter. The government's failure to support this pioneering bank serving responsible low-income borrowers was one more emblematic double standard in the politics of debt and property.

Chapter 9

The Third World's Revenge

FOR A BRIEF PERIOD AFTER World War II, the global financial system was geared toward generous credit creation combined with constraints against reckless speculation. The 1940s were also a period of debt defaults and generous debt restructurings. Then, in the late twentieth century, the rules of the world economy turned harshly against debtors. The World Bank and later the International Monetary Fund became prime agents of debt collection. This inversion of their original role reflected the resurgence of business and free-market ideology and the influence of the fund's largest shareholder, an increasingly market-oriented United States. "Keynes," as Joseph Stiglitz observed, "would be rolling over in his grave to see what happened to his child."

Beginning in the 1980s, the IMF and World Bank promoted a set of views known as the Washington Consensus, a reference to the D.C.-based Fund, Bank, and U.S. Treasury, as well as to local friendly think tanks. This model held that developing countries needed to have tight fiscal policies, keep their exchange rates and labor costs competitive, privatize state ventures, reduce or eliminate subsidies, and above all open their financial markets to foreign capital flows. In commending open markets, the Washington Consensus did not distinguish between short-term speculative money and long-term direct investments.

The IMF, in its annual reviews of national economies, promoted these policies not just in crises but in all seasons. When a nation got into a balance-of-payments problem, or a run on its bonds or currency, the approved remedy was to intensify the formula: more budget balance, more labor market discipline, a more open market, less government involvement. Loans from the Fund and Bank were typically conditioned on a "structural adjustment" package built on such policies.

It took two decades of intermittent crises for the IMF to acknowledge that this one-size-fits-all guidance often worsened recessions and did not improve the target nation's capacity for recovery. Had the formula been applied to Western nations at early stages of their own development, it would have prohibited many of the government-assisted strategies that the West used to industrialize and to surmount periodic financial panics and depressions.

The past quarter century, however, has seen two counter-reversals. First, several major developing nations attained very high levels of growth by rejecting the key tenets of the Washington Consensus. Japan, South Korea, Brazil, and later China developed mainly with their own capital. They used a neomercantilist formula of incubating and protecting their industries, relying on government-business cartels, limiting speculative money flows, and negotiating the terms on which foreign suppliers and investors could participate—all to advantage their domestic producers. Taiwan, generally considered more of a market-oriented country, built its dominance in microelectronics exports with a government industrial policy and subsidies.

None of these nations trusted their development to free markets, least of all to global capital markets dominated by Western banks. This formula, the opposite of the one commended by the United States and surrogate international agencies, produced annual growth rates of between 7 and 10 percent over several decades—faster than anything in the West. A report on the "East Asian Miracle" reluctantly prepared by the World Bank in 1997, under pressure from the Japanese, acknowledged that the world's fastest-growing economies violated much of the Washington Consensus. Latin America, which had bent to the neoliberal formula in the 1980s and suffered a lost decade of growth, pursued a more heterodox path in the new century.

In a second startling reversal, the leading emergent nation to reject the neoliberal development recipe became America's prime banker. Standard economic theory says that money should flow from richer nations to poorer ones, but by the turn of the twenty-first century China was already the world's biggest creditor nation, and the United States was the largest debtor. This inversion continues to be a source of vulnerability for the United States and the global financial system. China, rather like Germany within Europe, is using its financial power as a surrogate for explicit political power but not acknowledging its systemic responsibilities except as creditor. Beijing continues to manipulate its currency, both to keep the renminbi undervalued to promote exports and to prevent its use as a global reserve currency.

Unlike the obsession with domestic deficits and debts that has diverted attention from practical solutions to the current economic crisis, America's debt to China is a genuine problem. The debt is the bill for an escalating trade imbalance that reflects America's industrial displacement. Over time, the huge reliance on loans from Beijing (see below) will give China increasing diplomatic leverage to resist Washington's rather feeble efforts to attain a more balanced trade relationship. But there are no high-level panels like the Bowles-Simpson commission demanding urgent action on the U.S.-China situation.

There is one further ironic inversion. For more than a decade, the IMF has been moderating its rigid policy of using austerity as the all-purpose remedy for Third World debt crises. But in the meantime, twenty-first-century Europe's policies for its heavily indebted members embrace the fund's discarded playbook.

DELUSIONS AND DEFAULTS

In 1817, a Scottish adventurer named Gregor MacGregor arrived in London promoting investment in the Central American nation of Poyais, of which MacGregor had been appointed viceroy. He sold £600,000 worth of Poyaisian bonds to British banks and investors and distributed maps, local currency, and even a 350-page book describing the new nation, with its rich mineral wealth, fertile farmland, and friendly English-speaking locals. The bond issue was oversubscribed, and bonds soon traded at a premium. In 1823, nearly two hundred emigrants sailed from the port of Firth on the merchantman *Kennersley Castle* for their new homeland, bearing enough provisions for a year, the local currency, and the green-and-white flag of Poyais.

But the country did not exist. It was an invention of MacGregor and his confederates. His fantastic tale of Poyais was borrowed from the actual history of the nearby British enclave of Belize. When Poyais was revealed to be a fraud, there was no government of Poyais to occupy, sue, or negotiate with. The nimble MacGregor managed to evade prosecution until his death in 1845.

The Poyais affair was only the most extreme case of a speculative overseas investment frenzy that infected London in the 1820s. London was obsessed with the promise of South America, a land of gold, silver, agricultural riches, liberation struggles, and exotic natives. Between 1824 and 1825, some forty-six companies recognized by the London Stock Exchange raised £17 million to invest in the newly liberated colonies of Spain and Portugal, about three-quarters of all the capital for foreign governments raised in London during that period.

South America's struggle with Spain, from 1809 to 1824, was popular in the English press. Stimulated by the French invasion of Spain in 1808, the independence wars of the Spanish colonies raged over two decades. France invaded again in 1823 to displace a liberal Spanish government and restore an absolute monarchy. Britain, longtime rival of both nations, feared French influence in South America and formally recognized the secession of Spain's former colonies in 1825, prompting British foreign secretary George Canning's famous remark that he "called the New World into existence to redress the balance of the Old."

In addition to underwriting new governments, funds flowed to silver and gold mining ventures, land companies, canals, and, slightly later, railroads. The first such issue was a £2 million twenty-year loan to the government of the new nation of Gran Colombia in 1819. It carried the unheard-of interest rate of 6 percent. The loan had to be floated in Paris by a British syndicate, in an early case of offshoring to evade regulation, since the yield violated the Bank of England's usury ceiling. A £1.2 million loan to Chile with a 6 percent interest rate shortly followed.

The loans to new governments were closely linked to the desire of British investors to win concessions for gold and silver mining, as well as to the government's wish that its naval fleet get a friendly reception in South American waters. The New Brazilian Mining Company, launched in 1824, counted eight members of the British Parliament on its twelve-person board of directors.

Gran Colombia and Chile defaulted on the bond issues in 1826, along with Peru. In all, some £25 million worth of South American loans suspended payments that year. It was soon revealed that interest and dividends had been paid out of principal, a practice later disparaged as a Ponzi scheme but indulged when the purpose was to satisfy creditors. By mid-1828, eleven of twelve nations that had raised capital in London defaulted, the sole exception being Brazil. Venezuela set the record, with six defaults between 1826 and 1898. Yet new generations of British bankers kept striking new investment deals.

Waves of defaults and fresh bond issues were closely linked to cycles of euphoria and collapse in Britain. A financial panic in London in late 1825, following a bust of commodity prices and failures of leading banks, caused financiers to turn cautious, abruptly halting the flow of new funds to South America. It was a pattern that would be repeated over two centuries. The next great foreign lending bonanza began in the 1850s and 1860s, as trade with South America picked up. Bankers underwrote over £120 million in new bonds, mainly for government military expenses, the railway boom, and the refinancing of old debt.

The practice of creditors' cartels, or "clubs," had begun in 1827, when the London Stock Exchange refused to list new bonds by debtors that were in default on old issues. The London creditors' cartel was formalized as the Corporation of Foreign Bondholders, which shared information and spearheaded joint negotiations for debt restructuring. Its board of twenty-one notables included bankers, substantial bondholders, and representatives of the London Chamber of Commerce.

Restructurings of bonds in default typically included either reductions in the outstanding principal or cuts to the interest owed. In the 1840s and 1850s, Argentina, Chile, Ecuador, Peru, and Venezuela received new loans at interest rates of 3 percent so that they could resume payments on old loans. It took until 1872 for Colombia's 1826 loan of £6.75 million to be reduced to £2 million. Mexico's loans from that era were almost totally written off.

By 1870, about £300 million worth of bonds to Latin American and peripheral European countries such as Greece, Turkey, and Portugal were in default. Negotiated restructurings reduced this to about £25 million by 1906. The revised terms typically included longer repayment periods, interest and principal reductions, additional credits, and temporary repayment moratoriums. In some cases, creditors managed to get control of a revenue stream, such as customs receipts, or a property transfer, such as a concession to operate the national rail system.

One scholarly review of fifty-seven debt settlements between the mid-nineteenth century and World War I found that only seventeen included revenue or property diversions. These included a guano concession in Peru and control of railways in Colombia, as well as seizure of specific revenue streams by a debt administration council for brief periods in

Greece, Egypt, Tunisia, and the Dominican Republic, among others. But most settlements relied entirely on debt reduction and rescheduling. For example, agreements between the British creditor committee and Argentina in 1891 and 1893 included a new £15 million loan to help Argentina service its old debts, followed by a cut in interest payments and an eight-year suspension of principal payback.

Two conclusions are evident from this history. First, debt crises in peripheral nations originate in the fads, fashions, and panics of *creditor* countries. They are less the consequence of good or bad policies in debtor nations than of boom and bust cycles in London or New York capital markets. This pattern only intensified in the twentieth century, as technology enabled ever shorter-term investment flows.

Second, a review of the sheer randomness of international debt negotiation in the nineteenth century suggests that debt policy, if anything, has gone backward over the past 150 years. While the nineteenth century was a period of explicit colonialism in Africa and Asia, as well as of extensive mineral, mining, and land concessions to Western corporations in Latin America, its debt collection system, paradoxically, was less draconian and more flexible than its late twentieth-century successor.

In any given case, the particular restructuring plan was mainly a function of the debtor nation's capacity to pay and power to resist. There was no IMF functioning as a gatekeeper and insisting on budget austerity as quid pro quo for new loans (though creditor nations occasionally sent gunboats). Even a potent creditors' cartel representing the world's leading suppliers of capital in London recognized that private investors in far-off speculations were consenting adults who had knowingly taken a risk and that some debtors simply could not pay. The cartel did not expect that investors would always recoup all of what was owed.

During the 1930s, when the bottom fell out of the global economy, debt nonrepayment became the norm. A study of defaults in that decade found that investors lost 37 percent of their capital lent to Colombia, 62 percent to Peru, 69 percent to Chile, and 92 percent to Bolivia. Of all the nations that borrowed money from the United States during the World War I era and the Depression, only Finland, famously, paid the debt in full. During the war, Washington was generous with debt relief toward Latin America to keep hemispheric nations tied to the Western Alliance. None of this relief prevented a robust postwar recovery, and in fact contributed to it.

In the 1970s and 1980s, after the Bretton Woods interlude, the dynamics of sovereign debt financing and debt collection underwent a drastic change to the advantage of creditors. The most dramatic immediate impact was on Latin America, but the effect was to alter the entire system.

INVERTING THE IMF

When the World Bank and the IMF were created in 1944, a paramount goal was to free nations to pursue domestic policies of high growth and full employment, insulated from the caprices and deflationary pressures of speculative international money markets. As Keynes observed, "The whole management of the domestic economy depends on being free to have the appropriate rate of interest without reference to the rates prevailing elsewhere in the world. Capital controls is a corollary to this." The intellectual fathers of Bretton Woods distinguished between productive and speculative capital. Harry Dexter White, Keynes's American co-architect of Bretton Woods, shared the belief that speculative cross-border financial flows produced costs in the form of instability and deflation that outweighed the benefits of unregulated access to foreign private capital. The World Bank was established as an alternative source of patient public development capital.

This thinking was not the product of economic theorizing in a historical vacuum. In the 1920s and 1930s, abrupt inflows and outflows of foreign capital had been profoundly destabilizing, creating upside bubbles and downside busts and runs on currencies. Misguided efforts to retain investor confidence had led to crippling and futile measures to raise interest rates in a deepening depression, as well as bouts of competitive devaluation.

The original Bretton Woods system permitted controls on both capital inflows and outflows. The legacy of the war, when ordinary commerce had virtually ceased, meant that very tightly regulated capital markets were the starting point. The policy challenge was to permit enough liberalization to promote growth without allowing speculation to swamp the real economy. Explaining the IMF agreement to the House of Lords, Keynes said, "Not merely as a feature of the [postwar] transition, but as a permanent arrangement, the plan accords to every major government the explicit right to control all capital movements. What used to be a heresy is now endorsed as orthodox."

The right of nations to regulate cross-border capital movements was codified not just in the IMF's Articles of Agreement of 1945 but also in the European Economic Community's Treaty of Rome of 1956 and in the documents of the OECD. As we saw in chapter 5, the postwar economic system thrived on these controls on capital movements. With a fixed-rate currency regime, an entire category of speculative foreign exchange transactions did not exist. In 1973, as the fixed-rate system was shifting to floating rates, however, daily foreign exchange transactions rose to an alarming $15 billion. In 2007, on the eve of a crash driven by speculative trades, the daily figure was $4 trillion.

By the 1970s, most Western countries had lifted controls on long-term foreign investment capital as wartime relics, though some controls on short-term financial capital flows remained until 1990. Automakers like Ford and General Motors built plants in Europe rather than exporting from America. The United States in the early postwar era had a huge trade surplus. Policymakers liked the idea of American multinationals creating jobs in Europe. With the exception of Japan, Korea, and other explicitly mercantilist nations, developed and developing countries alike welcomed long-term direct foreign investment. But when it came to *short-term* capital flows, many developing nations recognized the risks of opening their financial markets and retained controls. Even advanced countries limited the exposure of their financial systems to foreign bankers. The German banking system was strictly German, and the French system emphatically French. American financiers could neither buy control of European banks nor set up retail domestic banking operations.

By the 1990s, however, the ideological counterrevolution was in full swing. Keynes had spoken too soon. The old orthodoxy had returned with a vengeance and capital controls were now heresy once again. The 1994 Uruguay Round of trade negotiations, sponsored by the United States, went well beyond the GATT's traditional franchise of negotiating reciprocal reductions in tariffs and called for relaxation of trade in "services," including financial services. This was a polite way of demanding the end of capital controls and full access for Western bankers to Third World domestic financial systems. Some smaller nations, such as Colombia, insisted on retaining regulation of cross-border financial flows. But when a nation came to the IMF for emergency aid, relaxation of capital controls was usually one of the quid pro quos.

The IMF, meanwhile, executed a parallel 180-degree reversal from the original conception of 1944. At the September 1997 annual joint meetings of the IMF and the World Bank, the Fund, under heavy prodding from the U.S. Treasury, fully embraced the neoliberal view of financial flows. The IMF's Interim Committee, a policymaking body made up of finance ministers and heads of central banks, declared:

> It is time to add a new chapter to the Bretton Woods agreement. Private capital flows have become much more important to the international monetary system, and an increasingly open and liberal system has proved to be highly beneficial to the world economy. By facilitating the flow of savings to their most productive uses, capital movements increase investment, growth and prosperity. Provided it is introduced in an orderly manner, and backed both by adequate national policies and a solid multilateral system for surveillance and financial support, the liberalization of capital flows is an essential element of an efficient international monetary system in this age of globalization.

This policy was not formally adopted by the IMF, thanks to pushback from Third World countries, but it continued to be the goal of the financial industry and key Western governments. Crises were used by the U.S. government and the IMF to promote further capital liberalization. But the economic assumptions and policies reflected in that declaration would soon be catastrophically refuted by events. Hot capital flows did not prove "highly beneficial." After the East Asian crisis of the late 1990s, developing nations, painfully aware that IMF aid was a poisoned chalice, increasingly avoided the Fund. By 2007, on the eve of the crisis, the IMF loan portfolio was down to a three-decade low of just $20 billion.

Even in the United States, the shift to full liberalization of short-term financial flows was controversial. During the Clinton administration, the Council of Economic Advisers, especially Joseph Stiglitz and Alan Blinder, supported direct foreign investment by Western corporations but cautioned about the destabilizing effects of short-term financial flows on small economies. On the other side was the Treasury, led by Robert Rubin and Larry Summers. Rubin, former cochairman of Goldman Sachs and future senior executive of Citigroup, saw huge opportunities for Wall Street. Summers, then Treasury undersecretary for international economic affairs, supported Rubin on grounds of free-market theory: capital should be free to flow to its most profitable uses. The Treasury won the internal debate and became a relentless advocate within the international system for more financial market liberalization. The United States, as a source of dollars, largest stockholder in the IMF, and principal guarantor of the peace, had immense leverage over IMF policy.

The Fund also acted as a gatekeeper for other sources of international lending, such as the World Bank, the Inter-American Development Bank, and complementary credits by wealthy member nations. Only when the IMF certified a recovery package as sound did other funds flow from what was a creditors' cartel led by the United States.

But in the new era of liberated financial flows, a nation with sound internal fiscal balances often found itself subject to abrupt foreign investor panic. Sometimes this attack had nothing to do with fiscal fundamentals; it was merely the result of herd instincts exacerbated by newly open financial markets. A recession engineered by IMF austerity conditions only widened budget deficits. A devaluation made it more expensive for local corporations and banks to pay their hard currency debts, weakening rather than strengthening the local economy. Far from stabilizing the situation, the IMF package often made it worse.

THE CREDITORS' BALL

Some Third World countries invited their own problems with corrupt governments and reckless finances. Typically, alliances between local political and financial elites and foreign bankers led to inefficient uses of capital. The costs of debt repayment, however, were imposed on the entire nation.

Yet the economic forces that did such damage to developing regions in the 1980s and 1990s mostly originated in events and policies far beyond these nations' control. In the United States, two fateful financial trends that converged in the 1970s would have devastating effects on developing countries. First, bank profits were squeezed by inflation, leading to pressure for deregulation to enable bankers to pursue new, often riskier sources of earnings. This raised the curtain on the speculative and overleveraged epoch that ended with the collapse of 2008.

Second, the same inflation, triggered by a quadrupling of oil prices, sent windfall profits to oil-exporting countries. Between 1972 and 1977, OPEC's annual revenues increased from $14 billion to $128 billion. By 1978, OPEC nations had some $84 billion on deposit in U.S. banks, most of it in offshore branches. In that era, long before "sovereign wealth funds" invested petroleum earnings directly, Western leaders and bank executives hammered out a rough bargain with oil-exporting nations, notably Saudi Arabia. The West, which really didn't want an oil war with the Arabs, would allow the price increases to stand. But in return, the OPEC nations would give Western banks the lucrative business of "recycling," in the contemporary term, trillions of dollars in swollen oil profits.

The idea was that the OPEC deposits would be lent to developing countries to pay their increased bill for oil and, more wishfully, to help them develop. The deal seemingly accomplished multiple goals. It produced a kind of face-saver for the West, which had been humiliated politically by the Arabs and the loss of cheap oil. Recycling kept the West tied to key Arab allies like Saudi Arabia by linkages of finance. It kept Western control of massive inflows of new money, preserving U.S. hegemony over the global monetary system. And it gave the beleaguered banks a huge source of new profitability: deposits from the OPEC nations, which would in turn be lent to oil-scarce developing nations. That, at least, was the theory. Unfortunately, the grand bargain had huge perverse effects, first on Latin America, then on U.S. banks, and finally on the global system of debt and debt collection.

In the postwar era, despite bouts of political instability and corruption, most Latin American nations had enjoyed solid economic growth. As an exporter of primary goods, Latin America piggybacked on rising demand in wealthier nations. Some countries, including Brazil, also pursued successful programs of industrialization. Fixed exchange rates and tight financial regulation provided a stable monetary environment. As late as the 1970s, the real annual growth rate in Latin America for the decade was 5.9 percent, and the average national budget deficit was just 1.1 percent.

By 1980 all of this changed. As the price of petroleum quadrupled and global growth slowed, the terms of trade turned against Latin America.

It took relatively more wheat, beef, coffee, or copper to buy a barrel of oil or an automobile. Trade deficits of non-oil-exporting nations swelled dramatically.

For a time, the OPEC recycling project disguised this underlying weakness. Capital inflows, most for relatively short terms, massively increased. In 1970, Latin America's total foreign debt was $29 billion. By 1978, it had increased to $159 billion. By 1982, it had doubled again, to $327 billion, over ten times what it had been a decade earlier. Debt servicing costs more than tripled between 1978 and 1980 alone. After 1979, new loans went mainly to pay the increased interest on old loans.

In this inflationary environment, lenders sought to protect themselves by making floating-rate loans. The maturity was typically seven years, but with interest rates adjusted every three to six months. The interest rates were based on a spread of so many points above the best interbank lending rate (Libor*), depending on the perceived risk. The rates were attractive to the borrowers, but only as long as the credits could be rolled over at comparable rates when the loan came due.

Since the loans were usually in dollars, the debtor nation was taking a double risk: that exchange rates would worsen, which would require it to come up with more local currency to service the dollar-denominated debt, and that prevailing interest rates would rise. Both things happened, at a scale far beyond the imagination of creditors or debtors. The fatal premise, as Citibank chairman Walter Wriston memorably put it in 1982, was that "countries don't go out of business." But they do frequently default—at least 250 times since 1800, according to one exhaustive compilation.

A new, more complex form of bank lending made the crisis more intractable, foreshadowing the subprime crisis and its aftermath four decades later. Large Wall Street banks increasingly syndicated shares of loan deals to other banks. To sweeten the package, secondary creditors were given legal rights that in effect allowed them to veto any restructuring, making a debt relief plan far more difficult to negotiate.

What caused this house of cards to collapse was the United States' abrupt turn in 1979 to tighter money, Paul Volcker's strategy for breaking inflation. Very high interest rates in the United States raised the

* The London Interbank Offered Rate

value of the dollar against other currencies, causing a ripple effect of higher interest costs worldwide, as other nations defensively increased their own interest rates. The tight money also triggered a global recession, decreasing the demand for primary products and reducing the real prices of Third World exports to their lowest level since the Depression.

All three trends were lethal for Latin America. From 1975 to 1977, Latin debtor nations were paying interest rates averaging 6 to 8 percent. By 1981, the figure was nearly 18 percent. (Because of the high inflation of the period, the real interest rate was more like 7 percent, still a punishing rate. And in the low-inflation decade of the 1990s, Latin America was made to pay even higher real rates.) It is noteworthy that all of these trends originated outside the region most deeply affected. The rise in the price of oil, the worsening terms of trade, the spike in interest rates, depressed global demand, and rising debt service costs had nothing to do with how Latin American nations were managing their economies. This followed the same pattern set in the 1820s, when the boom-bust cycle of credit for developing nations originated with trends in London.

This has been the pattern of Third World development generally for nearly two centuries. Crises tend to spread from the powerful nations that dominate the global financial systems to smaller peripheral countries. The most successful developing nations, appreciating the risk of being at the mercy of forces and trends they don't control, have sought to manage their own development and to limit their reliance on foreign capital. Most have also endeavored to shift from dependence on exports of primary products, whose prices in global markets tend to be highly volatile and to decline relative to industrial goods over time. All of this flies in the face of the Washington Consensus.

This is not to say, of course, that developing nations are free of blame for their own instability. But one needs to differentiate between the people and their leaders, especially in nations that are not democracies. A nation with a corrupt or autocratic political system often finds that foreign investment goes into the pockets of dictators and crony capitalists, leaving the rest of the nation to bear the debt.

The Latin American leaders of the 1970s were complicit in one respect: they increased their international borrowing, though bankers were fairly begging them to take out more loans. In normal times, Third

World finance ministers came hat in hand to bankers. In the 1970s, bankers wined and dined finance ministers.

But in the 1980s, the psychology and loan flows went into reverse. Foreign capital provision to Latin America swung from a net inflow of $26.4 billion in 1981 to a net outflow of $34.7 billion in 1985. The trend was compounded by private "capital flight," as local elites, exercising their rights to unfettered capital flows, moved their money out of the country. In crises, flight capital outflows often exceeded IMF-sponsored inflows.

On August 12, 1982, the Mexican government announced it would not be able to meet the August 16 payment obligation on its $80 billion foreign debt. Mexico was soon followed by Brazil and Argentina. By October 1983, twenty-seven countries were in arrears by some $239 billion. Four large Latin American nations—Mexico, Brazil, Venezuela, and Argentina—accounted for $176 billion of this debt.

The Latin American debt crisis led to a much harsher debt collection environment. By 1981, the roughly $50 billion owed by Latin American nations to the eight largest U.S. banks amounted to 263.9 percent of the banks' capital and reserves, according to the FDIC. If the bonds were accurately marked down to their current depressed trading value, as accounting rules required, every money center bank in New York would have been insolvent. The entire banking system was at risk, and rescuing it was a far higher priority than alleviating the pain of Third World debtors.

The Federal Reserve and the Treasury responded on several fronts. First, they informally suspended the accounting rules, permitting the wounded banks to fictitiously carry their bonds at book value. Second, the government helped the bankers find new sources of equity capital to rebuild required equity ratios. And the creditors got much tougher about squeezing every possible nickel from the debtors, through a creditors' cartel organized by the U.S. Treasury. Their instrument, paradoxically, was the International Monetary Fund.

The IMF, reflecting the new neoliberal thinking, had embraced the idea that if a nation was facing international financial troubles, it must have "lived beyond its means." The cure was a variety of belt tightening and market-opening measures to reassure foreign investors. The effect was to deepen recessions.

This remedy, coming on top of the damage already caused by trends entirely beyond the control of the target countries, cost Latin America a decade of growth. Two debt restructuring plans sponsored by the U.S. Treasury secretary, James Baker, failed to solve the problem because the proposed relief was too small and the terms required excessive austerity. In 1989, after several failed efforts to advance nations new loans to keep current on old debts, Baker's successor, Nicholas Brady, came up with a plan to belatedly require creditors to share some of the losses. Most observers attributed the long delay to Washington's concern for rescuing the banks first. Debt forgiveness was out of the question until the banks were given time—almost a decade, in this case—to rebuild their own capital.

The much-lauded Brady Plan traded short-term debt for long-term debt. Using a complex swap of Third World sovereign bonds for zero-coupon U.S. Treasury securities, it also allowed the banks to modestly reduce their exposure. It was really a series of more than twenty different plans for different countries, and negotiations dragged on, well into the 1990s. Eventually, restructurings under the aegis of the Brady Plan relieved the burden of the indebted nations by something like thirty cents on the dollar. But as in the case of Weimar Germany and twenty-first-century Greece, the protracted pressure to repay in the meantime did massive damage.

ASIAN FLU

The East Asian financial crisis that broke out in the late 1990s contradicted the IMF's assumptions of what got a nation into trouble. Yet the Fund stuck to its austerity recipe and needlessly worsened the downturn. Between the late 1960s and the 1990s, Thailand, Indonesia, Malaysia, the Philippines, Taiwan, Singapore, and South Korea had become export champions, with annual growth rates of 7 to 12 percent.

In line with the prevailing wisdom and pressure from Washington, in the late 1980s and early 1990s they opened their capital markets, and a lot of Western money poured in. This liberalization typically included removal of limits on foreign ownership of stocks, bonds, and local financial institutions and permission for domestic banks and corporations to borrow overseas at will. The new capital inflows, in turn, led to some overbuilding in many sectors. They also caused local banks to pursue riskier ventures to generate high returns, and increased indebtedness to foreigners in hard currencies, mostly dollars.

By the eve of the crisis, the five countries most severely affected had a total debt exposure in hard currency of $274 billion, of which nearly two-thirds was short-term money that could vanish almost overnight. That equaled about 30 percent of their collective GDP. In the same five nations, private international capital swung from a net inflow of $92.8 billion in 1996 to a net outflow of $12.1 billion in 1997, as lenders ceased renewing short-term loans. When the money poured out, these nations did not have enough dollars both to defend their currencies and to service their debts.

The Asian crisis began in July 1997, when the Thai government announced that it would no longer defend the fixed rate of its currency, the baht, at roughly twenty-five cents to the dollar. Thailand, building up its exports of shoes, textiles, electronics, and other goods, had enjoyed an extraordinary decade, growing at annual rates of more than 9 percent a year between 1985 and 1996. As the nation liberalized its financial markets, its banks borrowed abroad and invested in far-flung ventures at home. The fixed exchange rate, coupled with low inflation and high returns, made Thailand a very attractive place for investors. But by 1996, the inflows had stimulated increasing overcapacity in real estate and industry, and growth was slowing. Banks and lightly regulated finance companies reported large increases in nonperforming loans. To add to the problem, the Federal Reserve was raising interest rates for reasons that had nothing to do with Thailand, causing the dollar to gain value. Since Thailand's baht was linked to the dollar by a fixed exchange rate, Thai exports became more expensive and less competitive. This, in turn, worsened Thailand's trade imbalance.

Hedge funds and other short-term sources of finance, sensing a devaluation, began shorting the baht, which only compounded the pressure. The Thai central bank used complex swap agreements to obtain dollars, disguising its vulnerability and delaying a day of reckoning. But by July 1997, the bank was fast running out of its dollar reserves. Foreign bankers smelled blood in the water and stopped rolling over routine loans except at punitive rates. IMF officials urged the Thais to let the baht fluctuate within a wider trading band, but this only intensified the pressure. At that point, the government let the currency float downward. Far from stemming the crisis, the new policy compounded it.

With a weaker currency, Thai banks and corporations that owed dollars to foreign lenders, suppliers, and investors had to spend more baht to obtain the needed dollars, deepening the downturn. Not knowing how far the baht would sink, foreign investors pulled back even further.

With no alternatives, the Thai government in August agreed to accept an IMF loan package of $17.2 billion. In return, the Fund demanded a wrenching austerity that was not required by the situation on the ground. Thailand's budget was in surplus. The crisis was the result of an investment bubble triggered by massive foreign capital inflows followed by abrupt outflows. Nonetheless, the Fund asked for and got tax increases and spending cuts equal to 3 percent of GDP, pushing Thailand deeper into recession and sending its currency even lower, despite IMF support. In a 1999 internal review unearthed by the *Washington Post* reporter Paul Blustein, IMF staffers admitted that the policy had been wrong. Blustein wrote that they "took their colleagues to task for underestimating the weakness of the Thai economy, a mistake that would be repeated in Indonesia and Korea." Eventually, Thailand recovered, no thanks to the IMF.

Having taken down the baht, speculators next turned on the Indonesian rupiah. With a population of two hundred million, Indonesia had a far larger economy than Thailand. It ran a big trade surplus, and its central bank had huge dollar reserves of around $20 billion. But with the financial liberalization and increased flows of hot money, it had the same new vulnerabilities as Thailand.

Indonesia was governed by an autocrat, General Suharto, who was seventy-six years old in 1997. Relying on the advice of Western-trained economists, he liberalized the economy in the late 1980s and opened it to foreign capital flows. Unlike Thailand, Indonesia had sizable elements of corruption, and Suharto's cronies and relatives got favored treatment from banks and government lending and contracting agencies. Foreigners investing in local enterprises often had to partner with Suharto allies. Even so, Indonesia managed real growth in excess of 7 percent a year, and it was regularly cited as a success story by the IMF and World Bank.

As financial flows were liberalized, foreigners invested heavily in Indonesian banks and corporations, attracted by the nation's rapid growth rate and stable currency. The rupiah was not pegged, but the Indonesian central bank carefully managed a slow, predictable rate of decline against the dollar. But as traders took a closer look in the aftermath of the crash of Thailand, they suspected that Indonesia's currency would also have to be devalued and began betting heavily against it.

Once again, the IMF devised a loan package and austerity plan that made a bad situation far worse. As in the case of Thailand, the IMF threw together a crisis team with little knowledge of Indonesia. According to reporter Blustein, the director of the emergency mission, an Iranian American economist named Bijan Aghevli, had not been to Indonesia in years. The austerity plan was based on the standard formula. A $33 billion loan package was traded for budget cuts, higher interest rates, and other austerity measures.

Supposedly, the deeper crisis was caused by misallocation of resources, and the necessary cure, though painful, included "structural reform." Some 140 changes in the structure of the Indonesian economy were specified in excruciating detail, down to the level of eliminating such agencies as the Clove Marketing Board. The IMF team took the opportunity to demand the end of favoritism to Suharto's family and friends. Some of these changes were salutary over the long term; others trespassed on a largely successful homegrown growth model. But they went well beyond the IMF's franchise and knowledge and were carried out in a way that added to the economic carnage.

A central element of the Fund's program was a hastily concocted reform of the banking system, which required the closing of sixteen shaky Indonesian banks, several of them linked to Suharto's family and cronies. The plan had only minimal provision for deposit insurance for very small savers. IMF staffers, citing "moral hazard," had argued strenuously against deposit guarantees for the rest of the banking system. The result was a general run on Indonesian banks, which deepened the crisis.

Not only did the IMF stabilization plan fail to halt the speculative attacks on the rupiah, which declined against the dollar by 85 percent within six months, but the austerity led to the worst depression in Indonesia's history, an economic contraction of 14 percent in 1998, causing mass unemployment and a decline in wages of 30 to 40 percent. By applying a standard formula to a situation whose primary cause was not fiscal imbalances but speculative attacks on the local currency, the Fund had worsened the collapse. The IMF itself, in an internal evaluation report leaked to the press, concluded that its program was worse than nothing: "In Indonesia . . . the depth of the collapse makes it difficult to argue that things would have been worse without the IMF."

Most shocking was the spread of the contagion to Korea. In the years since the Korean War, South Korea had been Asia's standout success story. It had gone from impoverished peasant nation to industrial powerhouse, relying on a system of government-bank-industry interlocks via conglomerates known as chaebol. As a strategy of development, South Korea's was the antithesis of the free-market system recommended by the IMF, the U.S. Treasury, and conservative economists everywhere.

South Korea, under Park Chung-hee until 1979, was also a near dictatorship. But, as economists liked to say, its "fundamentals were sound." South Korea had high savings rates, a balanced budget, and a careful monetary policy. Its entire national debt was just 3 percent of GDP. Its people had a fierce work ethic and a devotion to education. These conventional measures of strength allowed the IMF and its brethren to discreetly avert their eyes from the heresies of a state-led semicapitalist economy. The world's consumers provided a free-market reality check for highly competitive made-in-Korea goods, never mind their dubious origins in government industrial policy.

An economy like South Korea's, however, is like a Calder mobile: if you lop off one of its elements, you throw the whole affair out of kilter. The bank-industry interlocks and the tight government management of finance were one such element. A major aspect of Seoul's development strategy was state direction of capital flows from banks or official development agencies to the auto, shipbuilding, steel, petrochemical, microelectronics, and other preferred industries. South Korean corporations could operate with cheap capital and high leverage ratios thanks to the government direction. Insulation from global speculative finance was essential for the strategy to work.

South Korea had thrived by going its own way for three decades. But in the 1990s, the United States had two major sources of leverage: North Korea was making menacing noises, and South Korea was protected by some thirty thousand American troops. Also, as a developing nation that had arrived, South Korea was eager to be admitted to the rich nations' club, the OECD.

Under heavy pressure from the United States, South Korea was persuaded to open its capital markets, and this shift destabilized the entire system. South Korean banks and corporations were able to borrow in dollars at higher interest rates. In turn, they needed higher-yield sources of investment. Suddenly two financial systems were operating side by side: the proven system of government-directed and carefully monitored channeling of low-interest capital to priority industries using the domestic currency, the won, and a Wild West exposure of South Korean corporations and banks to speculative money markets using dollars.

In the hot-money craze of the 1990s tolerated by a new government in Seoul, chaebol bent on expansion borrowed in short-term global money markets. Some of this exposure was disguised because the debts were incurred outside South Korea by offshore branches or affiliates of South Korean banks and conglomerates. As Western financiers pulled back from exposure to other Asian currencies, they noticed the similarities between Korea, Indonesia, and Thailand. Foreign banks stopped rolling over routine extensions of short-term credits. Traders began shorting the won.

The IMF followed the usual script. When the Korean government appealed for help, the Fund eventually offered over $55 billion. In exchange for this huge loan package, it required not only the usual austerity measures but a remaking of the South Korean industrial and financial system in the image of free-market Western capitalism. By now, many in the IMF were wary of this demand, chastened by the failures of the rescue programs for Thailand and Indonesia. The insistence that no rescue program could go forward without broader changes in the South Korean system came from Robert Rubin and Larry Summers at the U.S. Treasury, without whose approval no IMF package could be extended.

The IMF's program did not stabilize the won, which sank further in global money markets. But it did deepen South Korea's worst postwar recession. What finally helped stabilize the Asian currencies hit by the self-fulfilling speculative attacks was a partial reversal of IMF policy, under pressure from the IMF's Japanese and European members and by some of its own staff. The idea was that the same Wall Street bankers who had been driving these currencies into the ground with their short-term trades should provide some respite by agreeing as a group to exchange short-term credits for longer-term ones. The IMF's chief economist, Michael Mussa, who devised the strategy, termed it a "bail-in." Rather than the Fund bailing out sinking countries, creditor banks would join the rescue effort.

But this would require the help of the Federal Reserve. Following much debate within the Fund and the U.S. Treasury, with South Korea sinking further into depression, the president of the Federal Reserve Bank of New York, William McDonough, called an emergency meeting with the chief executives of six of Wall Street's largest banks just before Christmas 1997. McDonough convinced them that they had a better chance of recouping their money if they converted Korea's exposure to long-term bonds. After a month of negotiation, the banks agreed to a very sweet deal. They would exchange $22 billion in short-term credits to banks and corporations (which were becoming more unpayable by the day) for one- to three-year bonds guaranteed by the government in Seoul (and implicitly by the IMF and the Treasury). These bonds would pay the banks a premium of 2.25 to 2.75 percentage points over the short-term interbank lending rate and would be a sure thing.

As Paul Blustein, now a fellow at the Brookings Institution, observed in his authoritative and evenhanded account of the Asian crisis, "In a sense, the international banks got away with murder. They had foolishly injected billions of dollars of short-term loans into a country with a shaky financial system, yet they were suffering no losses." On the contrary, the banks were ending up with guaranteed above-market returns.

But the losses for the affected nations were devastating. Between 1997 and 1998, GDP per capita in dollar terms declined by 42.3 percent in Indonesia, 21.2 percent in Thailand, and 18.5 percent in South Korea. In terms of local purchasing power, the decline was less severe but still substantial. In real terms, per capita GDP declined 14.3 percent in Indonesia, 6.3 percent in South Korea, and 11.6 percent in Thailand. Unemployment rose in Indonesia for seven years before gradually subsiding. East Asia's worst setback resulted from following the advice of the U.S. Treasury and the IMF to fling open its markets to short-term finance.

LESSONS LEARNED (AND NOT LEARNED)

The affected economies of East Asia eventually recovered. Annual per capita income growth rebounded to an average of 8.2 percent in dollar terms between 1999 and 2005. For East Asia, the main takeaway was to avoid the IMF and revert to their successful model of state-directed, export-led development and careful regulation of finance. Their common regional strategy was to "self-insure" against speculative attacks on currencies by assembling massive war chests of hard currency reserves. Foreign exchange holdings quadrupled in the five crisis countries between 1997 and 2005, and by 2007 totaled around $500 billion. (Had such reserves existed in 1997, the nations could have withstood the speculative attacks and thumbed their noses at the IMF.) Once these nations had repaid the Fund, they rejected much of its advice and continued to follow their own development paths. Inflows of foreign capital rebounded, but these governments tightened bank regulation to discourage hot money. Governments also required that bank and corporate debts in hard currency be substantially hedged so that shifts in exchange rates would not be ruinous.

In Malaysia, another small nation that had suffered the effects of currency speculation, Prime Minister Mahathir Mohamad rejected the advice of the IMF and resorted to direct capital controls. This was ridiculed by Western experts as a mark of economic illiteracy, yet the strategy worked beautifully. The central bank used controls mainly to kill the offshore speculative market in Malaysia's currency, the ringgit. Outside Malaysia holders of the ringgit had to wait a year before converting the currency. Long-term investment was still welcome.

The policy enabled little Malaysia to do what Roosevelt had accomplished for the United States in 1933—to break the link between foreign and domestic interest rates so that the government could use low interest rates to stimulate a recovery without crashing the currency. Despite a chorus of orthodox scorn, which included a downgrading of Malaysia's bonds by the ever-helpful credit rating agencies, the policy was vindicated. Growth, having declined during the speculative panic by 7.4 percent in 1998, rebounded to 6.1 percent in 1999 and 8.2 percent in 2000. It was the most rapid recovery of any of the affected Asian nations.

In early 2007, facing exchange rate instability, the Thai government also resorted to capital controls. It first restricted sales of short-term bonds to foreigners. Then it required that 30 percent of inflows be placed in a zero-interest account, refundable after a year. The Chilean government successfully pursued similar policies, as did Colombia in the 1990s and again in 2007.

In South Korea, which suffered a needless recession, once the IMF missions went home the chaebol system of bank-corporate interlocks and state direction continued pretty much as before. The system violated free-market conceptions of the supposed efficiency of unregulated commerce, but it more than compensated by producing the growth of strategic export industries. The South Koreans, using subtle forms of administrative guidance, managed to keep key industries in local hands and used regulatory constraints on banks and corporations to prevent hot-money contamination from destabilizing its financial markets. By the turn of the new century, South Korean growth rates were back to 7 or 8 percent, and this high rate of growth continued even in the global financial crisis that began in 2007. Indeed, so intact was the country's industrial-financial system that Washington began negotiating the United States–Korea Free Trade Agreement in 2007, aimed at reducing Korea's still-stubborn barriers to foreign capital and American exports. The deal was ratified in 2012, but nobody expects it to fundamentally alter Korea's system of state-led development anytime soon.

Reviewing the East Asian crisis of the late 1990s, it is clear that it was a dress rehearsal for the broader crisis that followed a decade later. For the most part, the right lessons were not learned. The U.S. government did not rein in the financial excesses that put the whole system at risk. Rather, the Treasury and the Fed resorted to ad hoc restructuring deals that favored creditors and left debtors to bear the pain. These bailouts of large banks relied on ever-lower interest rates but scant regulations—thus inviting the next crisis.

The IMF did become somewhat more heterodox. A succession of chief economists challenged the conventional view, from Michael Mussa, who devised the "bail-in" strategy that belatedly helped South Korea, to Kenneth Rogoff, who acknowledged the inevitability of debt relief in a best-selling 2009 book, and Simon Johnson, who became a fierce critic of the excesses of deregulation. These officials and others served as internal counterweights to the orthodoxy. The Fund's internal evaluation unit could be scathing in its criticisms of one-size-fits-all. During the brief tenure of Dominique Strauss-Kahn, the Fund's top leadership came down on the side of growth rather than austerity. Yet when a crisis of speculative attack against sovereign debt hit Europe in 2009, European Community officials and their allies among the IMF senior staff behaved as if they were stuck in a time warp.

DON'T CRY FOR ARGENTINA

For the most part, Third World nations began boycotting the IMF and rejecting the neoliberal counsel of orthodox Western economists. The world's largest nations, China and India, had never taken Western orthodoxy seriously. Even after it was admitted in 2001 to the World Trade Organization—the club of nations that agree to trade according to free-market rules—China clung to its highly successful mercantilist strategy. India partly liberalized its product markets but kept tight control of its financial system. Both nations initially avoided the direct effects of the Western financial collapse, though the protracted slump is depressing the market for their exports.

I happened to be at a conference at the United Nations in the winter of 2008, when all hell was breaking loose in financial markets, and one of my fellow panelists was Yaga Reddy, who had just retired as governor of India's central bank. I asked him how India was faring, and he replied casually that India's growth rate was around 8 percent in 2008 and that he expected the same in 2009. Somewhat astonished, I pressed him on how India had dodged the bullet. He explained that he had used reserve requirements to keep India's banks from speculating in the kind of securitized derivatives that crashed Western economies. "We are a poor developing country," he said with a smile. "We don't understand these complex financial securities, so we don't permit our banks to use them. We leave them to the advanced countries like you."

Despite the claim that these products are too opaque to regulate, it was not difficult to nip them in the bud, given political will. Reddy simply required India's banks to deposit reserves at the central bank to offset their exposure to complex derivatives. Hiding the exposure in off-balance-sheet affiliates was prohibited. These requirements made the entire strategy unprofitable.

Latin America eventually emerged from its lost decade. And when it did, its leading nations displayed great skepticism of the neoliberal recipe. In the 1990s and 2000s, leftist presidents were elected in Peru, Bolivia, Argentina, Brazil, Chile, Ecuador, and Venezuela, and one might have been elected in Mexico in 2007 but for an election marked by extensive fraud. In Brazil, the government of Luiz Inácio Lula da Silva combined careful fiscal and monetary policies and other elements of economic orthodoxy with strong elements of state-led development, limits on short-term capital flows, and an expansion of the welfare state. Brazil emerged from crisis in 2004 and soon ended its relationship with the IMF.

Argentina may be the most instructive and improbable story. Between the late nineteenth century and the Great Depression, it was one of the world's wealthiest countries. Thanks to exports of beef and grains, Argentina's per capita income in the early twentieth century exceeded that of France and Germany. It was a favored destination of European immigrants, and the elegant boulevards of Buenos Aires looked like a cross between Paris and Rome. As late as 1929, it had the world's fourth-highest GDP. But after the Depression hit, Argentina entered an era of political instability and economic decline.

For most of the period between 1930 and 1983, Argentina was ruled by the military, with only brief and weak democratic interludes. From 1946 to 1955, the country's elected president was a populist strongman, General Juan Domingo Perón. The Peronist party continues to be a major force as Argentina's left-nationalist governing party. A vicious military dictatorship ruled in the years between 1976 and 1983, a period when thousands of people critical of the regime were "disappeared." Argentina's economy was famously mismanaged during the postwar era, and the country suffered from reduced living standards during a period when most of its neighbors were prospering. After the restoration of democracy, Argentina fell victim to the same external forces that crashed the rest of Latin America in the 1980s.

The Argentine version of the lost decade ended with a bout of hyperinflation in 1990 and 1991. A new economy minister, Domingo Cavallo, embraced a drastic solution. He tied the Argentine peso explicitly to the U.S. dollar, a strategy to halt inflation and reassure investors once and for all. Anyone could exchange one peso for one dollar anytime. The IMF counseled against the scheme. But the policy, after three years of depressed output, produced stability and growth. In April 1993, Argentina finally negotiated a debt reduction deal under the Brady Plan, exchanging short-term loans for long-term bonds, and growth returned. Soon Argentina was hailed by the IMF for its good fiscal balance, sound currency, high growth rates, and open capital markets.

But the memory of bankers is short. In the mid-1990s, both Argentina and the money center banks repeated the policy disaster of the late 1970s. Massive sums of foreign money flowed in, lured by Argentina's link to the dollar, its IMF seal of approval, and its good economic performance. Then, in the wake of the East Asian crisis of the late 1990s, money flowed out just as fast. Now the link to the dollar backfired, as Argentines and foreigners exercised their right to exchange pesos for dollars. The recession worsened.

Finally, in November 2001, the government did the unthinkable. It announced a selective default on its $100 billion foreign debt. Like it or not, bondholders would take a substantial loss. About 75 percent of the defaulted bondholders reached an agreement to be paid about 30 cents on the dollar. This was done without the consent of the IMF. Because Argentina was not following the conditions of a stabilization package negotiated in 2000, the Fund soon suspended disbursement of loan payments. As the government, desperate to pay its bills, seized assets and tightened restrictions on bank account withdrawals, riots broke out. Just before Christmas 2001, the government declared martial law. Protesters burned government buildings, and dozens were killed in the chaos. The president, Fernando de la Rúa, resigned, followed by his vice president. The Peronist opposition, with a majority in the Chamber of Deputies, named a successor. In January, the new government bowed to the inevitable and broke the dollar link, letting the peso float downward.

What followed defied the orthodoxy. Argentina, largely shut out of international credit markets, enjoyed Latin America's most robust economic boom. The devaluation of the peso restored the competitiveness of Argentina's exports. Without the international money markets or the IMF to appease, the government was freed to promote a domestic recovery. Defying predictions of deeper catastrophe, the Argentine economy grew at an annual rate of 9 percent between 2002 and 2007, and has managed to grow at rates in excess of 8 percent for most of the crisis that began in 2008. Contrary to a lot of disparaging commentary, this success was not a lucky break based on a boom in commodity prices, which rose only modestly during this period. The vast majority of Argentina's recovery was driven by increased domestic demand.

In 2005, the government offered a take-it-or-leave-it debt swap, over the objections of the IMF, that traded short-term loans for long term bonds, leaving creditors with a 65.6 percent "haircut." Most took the deal, though some so-called vulture funds—like Dart Management, which had bought Argentine debt at discount and hoped to redeem it at par—continued to hold out for a better deal. In October 2012, one of the funds, Elliott Associates, managed to get a court order in New York and temporarily impounded an Argentinean naval vessel, the ARA *Libertad,* that happened to be stopping in Ghana. The failure of the global system to have clear rules for Third World debt relief leaves nations open to such opportunistic raids and almost random patterns of retribution. But despite these skirmishes, Argentina on balance seems to be getting away with its unilateral debt policy.

The combination of a write-down of foreign debt and far higher growth vastly improved Argentina's total debt-to-GDP ratio, which fell from a peak of 166 percent in 2002 to just 44 percent by 2012. Had Argentina been forced to embrace an austerity program, Greek-style, slow growth would have kept pushing the debt burden upward. Had Greece been granted the kind of relief that Argentina was able to pull off, the Greeks would not be mired in prolonged depression.

Where did Argentina get the capital it needed for expansion? Most of it was generated internally. In 2005, Argentina repaid its entire remaining IMF debt, and President Néstor Kirchner took the opportunity to declare, "We're leaving behind an irresponsible model of indebtedness that did nothing but isolate us." By November 2010, Argentina's unpaid foreign debt was down to $7 billion, and the government began consultations with creditors to reduce it to zero. The IMF was explicitly kept out of the negotiations.

Argentina continued to have Latin America's highest growth rate, 8.9 percent, in 2011, though that is projected to decline to under 3 percent in 2012 and in the range of 3 to 4 percent in 2013. Controversy has also erupted over allegations that the government was manipulating its inflation statistics. The official inflation rate in 2012 was just under 10 percent, while outside economists put it at around 25 percent. Wage settlements tended to be based on unofficial tabulations, suggesting that inflation is higher than the official rate. Argentina is far from a general role model. Its propensity to corruption and political instability remains, but debt restructuring has made an immense difference in its capacity for renewed growth and prosperity.

A PATIENT DRAGON

In early September 2012, while Bill Clinton was nominating Barack Obama for a second presidential term, Hillary Clinton was not in attendance. The secretary of state was on a mission to Beijing, where the Chinese leadership was openly uncooperative. Issues included U.S. displeasure at Beijing's support for Syrian president Bashar al-Assad, Beijing's refusal to be helpful in international crises from North Korea to Iran, China's increasingly aggressive land claims to small islands in the East China Sea, and long-standing conflicts over Beijing's manipulation of its currency, the renminbi. Clinton returned home empty-handed.

Treasury Secretary Tim Geithner had similarly failed to gain traction in his repeated efforts to pressure the Chinese to deliver on their promises to allow the renminbi's value to be set by market forces. Yet despite the requirements in U.S. trade law that the government identify and punish nations that rig currencies for trade advantage, Washington has refused to label Beijing a currency manipulator, sparing the United States from having to impose sanctions.

The contention that the value of China's renminbi is set by market forces is laughable. If that were the case, China's currency would be worth substantially more against the dollar, as befits a country with a chronic trade surplus. But the Chinese government regularly intervenes in currency markets to keep the renminbi depressed, both to advantage Chinese exports and to discourage its use as a global reserve currency.

Though China employs a state-led strategy of development, the United States has also declined to pursue major trade complaints, either bilaterally or through the WTO. Its occasional moves, against China's tire, solar panel, and other egregiously subsidized industries, are narrowly targeted and carefully designed not to challenge Beijing's development system or the broader relationship. The U.S.-China Trade Commission estimates that half of China's industry is still owned by the state, directly or indirectly, and that most of the other half is subject to mercantilist rules that favor Chinese-owned companies. The trillion-dollar China Development Bank, directed and subsidized by the state, now competes head to head with private commercial banks throughout Asia. Though China practices a brand of semicapitalism, the terms on which foreign companies can enter its markets are strictly controlled. Companies such as Intel and General Electric, which have invested tens of billions of dollars in production in China, are subject to technology deals with Chinese partners imposed on them by the Beijing government. The terms of where and how they can sell are also determined by the state. For the most part, foreign firms are welcome to the extent that they manufacture in China for export. Domestic sales are largely reserved for Chinese companies.

The U.S. government plays hardball to promote free-market capitalism through the IMF, the WTO, the OECD, and its own diplomacy, but Washington indulges China's lapses. Why the gentle treatment by Republican and Democratic administrations alike? You don't mess with your largest creditor. As of June 2012, China held $1.16 trillion worth of U.S. Treasury securities. China is gradually diversifying its portfolio of foreign sovereign debt, but at a slow pace that keeps the market for U.S. Treasuries stable.

The U.S. tolerance of Chinese mercantilism produces a massive trade deficit (just under $300 billion in 2011). China finances the deficit by lending the United States money. Both sides seem to benefit. Orthodox economists insist that China's immense trade surplus cannot be the result of its mercantilism because protectionism doesn't work; and that U.S. trade deficits must be the consequence of its low savings rate because structural differences in economies ultimately don't matter. But the same economists warn that the huge imbalances can't continue; eventually, the dollar has to crash.

However, the Chinese government doesn't take such economists seriously. Chinese civilization has been around for millennia, and Beijing takes the long view. The strategy of lending the United States massive sums of money while China displaces U.S. industrial leadership works just beautifully for the Chinese. It serves Beijing's interest for the dollar to remain as the world's primary reserve currency. Beijing has also been very gradual and calibrated in the way it expands its influence regionally and globally, avoiding anything that would threaten a vital American national security interest or provoke a confrontation. And the U.S. government, giving finance priority over industry and national defense priority over national economic self-interest, has been content to watch investment and employment migrate to China.

Unlike the domestic red ink that is the obsession of the budget hawks, foreign deficits and debts are grave problems. America's chronic trade deficit with China is a mark of its diminishing economic performance, which will eventually translate into reduced living standards. As interest rates rise to more normal levels, this large external debt will become a serious drag. When I studied economics, we were taught that our national debt was not a major problem "because we owe it to ourselves." Today, we increasingly owe it to China, Japan, Korea, OPEC, and Russia—with almost half of our foreign debt owed to China. Borrowing from abroad allowed the United States to outspend its own national income between 2000 and 2008 by $4.3 trillion. To the extent that this money financed long-term investment, some economists could defend it (though not with poorer countries as the lenders). But since most of the net foreign lending financed chronic trade deficits, this pattern is not sustainable.

The United States faces a huge diplomatic challenge. On the one hand, America needs to respect the fact that China's development system, despite flagrant violations of standard Western economics, works well for China. It represents the most significant alleviation of global poverty of the past quarter century—six hundred million souls lifted from destitution to minimally decent living standards. The percentage of the Chinese population living below the poverty line (using the spartan definition of poverty as earning less than $1.25 a day) fell from 60 percent in 1990 to 15 percent in 2005. This represents about 75 percent of global poverty reduction. At the same time, to the extent that China violates trade rules that ostensibly guarantee equal market access, China is taking advantage and the United States needs to assert its national interests (which are not the same as U.S. corporate interests) before American dependency on China grows even more extreme.

The European Union has been less shy than the United States about contesting Chinese mercantilism. Though Europe as a whole has balanced trade accounts and has not been reliant on Chinese loans, the sovereign debt crisis has given Beijing new leverage. When the crisis hit, China was quick to offer the EU bond purchases. In exchange, Beijing insisted that Europe ease its trade complaints. This diplomatic dance is still playing out, but it will end with Europe having less political ability to resist unfair trade practices. Before very long, China will be able to exercise explicit global political influence more commensurate with its new economic power—and the system that Beijing champions bears little resemblance to Western parliamentary democracy or to Western idealized free-market capitalism.

THE SOUTH RISES

In November 2001, Jim O'Neill, an economist at the London office of Goldman Sachs, coined the acronym "BRIC" to refer to Brazil, Russia, India, and China. These nations, he declared, stood to be the growth champions of the next decade. Sometimes a catchphrase creates its own reality. Not only did the term pass into the popular lexicon, but in 2008 the BRIC countries and South Africa (thus making it BRICS) decided to establish a membership organization. Their leaders now meet regularly, and they could easily become a trading bloc with economic views and interests dramatically different from those of the neoliberal West. Trade among the developing nations of the "Global South" is now the fastest-growing category of global commerce.

O'Neill was right. The economic performance of the BRICS countries far surpassed European and North American growth rates in the decade before the crash, and they have done better at maintaining their performance during the crisis, though their growth is expected to slow in 2013.

Despite the popularity of the label, however, the BRICS countries seemingly have little in common. Russia is a crony autocracy with state-protected pseudocapitalist billionaires. China is a one-party dictatorship. India and South Africa have fragile parliamentary systems, and Brazil is a robust, contentious democracy. What unites these diverse countries, who have just under half of the world's population and almost a quarter of its GDP, is that they reject the Western development model, with its conceptions of free speculative capital markets and its notions of austerity as the remedy for recession. To the extent that the West clings to these policies, it stands to be displaced.

In March 2012, the presidents of the BRICS nations met in New Delhi to create a BRICS bank, described as a "South-South development bank." Such a bank would be independent of the pressures of the Washington Consensus and could give financial support to heterodox development policies.

In the East Asian crisis of the late 1990s, Japan was unhappy with America's hostility to the Asian development model and the gratuitous damage wrought by clumsy IMF stabilization demands. One of the most bitter sources of contention between the United States and Japan in that era was Japan's abortive effort to set up an Asian monetary fund, independent of Washington's monetary hegemony. The United States, led by the Treasury, crushed the idea. But as nations that reject the Washington Consensus grow stronger, independent sources of global finance will soon give them more capacity to go their own way. It would be child's play for China, sitting on trillions of dollars in reserves, to underwrite a counter-IMF. Beijing desists for now, not for lack of money but only because of its policy of not provoking Washington while China grows stronger. Time, however, is on the BRICS countries' side.

One mixed success that benefits the Third World has been a debt relief initiative for the world's poorest countries long promoted by civil society organizations working through a coalition called Jubilee 2000, named for the debt forgiveness traditions of the ancient Hebrew kings. *
This plan, known as the Heavily Indebted Poor Countries initiative, was embraced in a watered-down form by the heads of the IMF and World Bank in 1996, endorsed by President Bill Clinton and British prime minister Tony Blair in 1999, and carried out beginning in 2002. It writes off most of the foreign debt of nations whose debt service payments far exceed their capacity to pay or their export earnings. The nations must then allocate that money to domestic poverty alleviation. As of 2011, thirty-six of forty eligible countries had qualified. Together, they received about $100 billion in debt relief, reducing their combined debt burden from about 5 percent to 1 percent of GDP. During the same period, poverty reduction outlays in these nations have increased by about three percentage points, so the grand bargain of less debt servicing for more antipoverty spending broadly works, though it will take a great deal more support and economic growth in these nations to alleviate extreme poverty.

The acknowledgment that it was self-defeating to squeeze very poor countries for money they could never repay sidestepped the usual qualms about moral hazard. Many of these countries, after all, had histories of corruption and wildly inefficient uses of foreign loans, though much of that corruption was facilitated by international banks and multinational corporations that paid bribes. The remedy, however, was not to keep these countries in debtors' prison indefinitely but to couple debt relief with reform and increased development aid. But significant development aid has been very slow in coming.

Under HIPC, commercial banks absorbed only about 6 percent of the loss. Most of it was borne by public development banks, such as the World Bank and the Inter-American Development Bank, which diverted funds that otherwise would have gone for economic assistance. Still,

---

* Every fifty years, a Jubilee was proclaimed and debts were forgiven. This was not done consistently but depended on the mercy of a particular king.

the IMF and World Bank policies toward Africa's poorest (and often most corrupt) nations have been more enlightened than the EU's policy toward Greece. In the decade since the world's poorest nations received debt relief, their performance has improved. Even sub-Saharan Africa, long written off as a hopeless case, managed a quite respectable growth rate of 5.7 percent before the global crash in 2008 and grew at about 5 percent in 2012. Though sponsors of the Washington Consensus would like to credit this improvement to economic liberalization, in reality the Global South uses a broad range of development strategies and is mostly wary of opening its capital markets to short-term trading.

The most rapidly growing developing nations, of course, face their own challenges. In both China and India, exports have far outstripped infrastructure. Even relatively middle-class neighborhoods in India lack reliable power grids and water and sewer systems. An article published in 2010 vividly titled "Excremental India" startled Western readers by pointing out that more than half of the Indian population, including many city dwellers, defecate outdoors—not in latrines but in alleyways, railroad rights-of-way, and parks. Russia continues to be a blend of autocracy and kleptocracy, far too reliant on international oil prices for its prosperity. As the Western world has fallen into a protracted economic slump, China has kept its production machine humming despite faltering global demand, leading to massive inventory pileups. China in particular will need to shift to a reliance on internal demand, meaning higher wages for its own people.

And this whole transition must be accomplished in a fashion that acknowledges the limited carrying capacity of the planet. Growth, increasingly, must be green growth. It is essential that we reconcile better living standards with a lower environmental toll through technology and reduced carbon emissions. Air-conditioning a room uses ten times the amount of electricity in Mumbai that it does in Chicago. If India and China were to attain Western levels of consumption at Western levels of pollution, our environment would be destroyed.

In sum, it is in the interest of both the BRICS nations and the West to surmount the global economic crisis, but conventional attitudes and policies toward debt repayment are a key obstacle to recovery. One sound idea, long proposed by Third World leaders and dissenting economists such as Joseph Stiglitz, would be a Chapter 11 process for indebted nations. Surprisingly, this idea was also embraced by the then first deputy managing director of the IMF, Anne Krueger, a conservative economist selected in 2001 for the job by the George W. Bush administration. In Stiglitz's version, old debt would be substantially written down, and new financing for growth and development would be insulated from the demands of old creditors, just as in a Chapter 11 corporate workout. By contrast, under most IMF loan agreements for Third World nations and EU programs for European debtor nations, the workouts typically use new money to pay interest on old debts. No new money flows to development. The premise is that debt repayment will somehow reassure foreign investors so that they will pump in more speculative capital. But that entire approach has been utterly discredited by events.

The current economic crisis originated in the West. More precisely, it originated in the U.S. financial sector. The nations that rejected the Western development model and Western demands to open their capital markets to what proved to be toxic contagion have been best insulated from the global crisis. The West itself rejected that model in promoting its own industrialization. A little humility from the world's largest debtor nation and a little more respect for heterodox paths to development would be in order.

Chapter 10

Back to the Future

THE READER WILL HAVE NOTICED that at several points in the story we invoke events in the middle third of the twentieth century, a time when finance was kept in its proper place and debt was not permitted to destroy possibility. Relief from war debt was conferred on Europe. The financial system was cleaned up and its speculative tendencies were contained. Depressed mortgages were refinanced and reinvented. The global monetary system was biased in favor of growth. Domestic economies got a constructive burst of public investment. The growth in wages tracked the growth in productivity. All of this was possible because of leadership, intellectual breakthroughs, happenstance, and, most important, a different constellation of political power.

This book has criticized the current system, which caused the financial collapse and now prolongs a depressed aftermath, as one that gives free rein to speculative finance and is obsessed with budgetary austerity. The alternative is a set of rules that would harness finance in service of the real economy, contain its destructive tendencies, and prioritize balanced growth and full employment. Fortunately, this alternative model is not an idealized hypothetical. It existed in the period after World War II, with exceptional results for both economic performance and broadly distributed prosperity.

When war came, democracies had the huge challenge of financing it at affordable interest costs, as well as containing the inflationary tendencies that wars, with their production bottlenecks and opportunities for profiteering, usually produce. The United States did remarkably well on all counts.

Wars, especially mass mobilizations, invariably entail public borrowing; taxes cannot finance the entire cost, and exorbitant taxes are politically unpopular at a moment when leaders are seeking to rally public opinion. In terms of the twin challenges of war finance and noninflationary war production, the United States entered World War II with a few advantages. It had a popular and politically astute president in Franklin Roosevelt, who had just won an unprecedented third term in November 1940. The lingering depression meant that the economy had a large number of idle workers and production capacity that could be devoted to the war effort. This, in turn, bought time to ramp up military industries without creating civilian shortages and price pressures, giving the United States several months in early 1942 in which to devise a surprisingly successful system of wartime rationing, as well as wage and price controls.

Most important to our story, the ideological disgrace of the crash of 1929, followed by the financial reforms of the New Deal in the eight years prior to the outbreak of war, had gone a long way toward containing speculative finance. Thus it was not a huge leap to get capital markets to finance the war at the lowest possible interest rates.

In the Second World War, despite the government's best efforts, there was some profiteering in war production. But thanks to tight controls, there was virtually none in the *financing* of war debt. World War II was unique in this regard. Wars ordinarily produce huge windfalls for the bankers who help governments market their war bonds and, as insiders, are positioned to speculate in public debt. This was the case in every American war from the Revolution to World War I.

The story is told in more detail below, but here is the essence of the radical break that World War II financing brought: The Treasury and the Federal Reserve, under White House direction, agreed to a pact in which the war debt would be financed by bonds carrying very low fixed interest rates. The government would print as much money, and the Fed would purchase as many bonds, as necessary to achieve this goal. Inflation—which ordinarily soared during wars—would be contained with wage and price controls and rationing. Citizens were urged to buy war bonds as a patriotic act.

THE GREATEST ACCIDENTAL RECOVERY PROGRAM EVER

World War II cost the United States about $296 billion. That was about a third of its GDP once full mobilization was attained. It equals more than $4.2 trillion in today's dollars. Of that amount, the government borrowed an astonishing $185.7 billion in war bonds. More than two-thirds of Americans bought bonds. The general public bought some $40 billion worth; the rest was bought by banks, corporate pension funds, insurance companies, and the Federal Reserve, whose aggressive purchases kept interest rates low.

The tax base was broadened and deepened. Loopholes were closed, enforcement was stepped up, and marginal tax rates on high incomes were increased to a maximum of 94 percent. Executive pay was capped at $25,000. The basic tax rate on working people was kept at a low 13 percent. Even with these increases, taxes covered only about 41 percent of war spending. The rest had to be raised by borrowing. Public spending, most of it for the war effort, peaked at 45 percent of GDP, and deficits during the four war years ranged from 24 to 29 percent.

Wage and price controls and rationing suggest privation. There was certainly enormous sacrifice on the part of America's sixteen million GIs, of whom 670,846 were wounded and 405,399 lost their lives. But on the home front, life was a lot better for most Americans than it had been during the Depression. After the attack on Pearl Harbor, full employment returned in a matter of months. Some seventeen million new jobs were created during the war. GDP increased by about 15 percent per year during the war.

With rationing, luxury goods were hard to come by, and purchases of meat, sugar, butter, shoes, gasoline, and other staples were restricted. Production of new cars was deferred until after the war so that factories could make tanks, ships, warplanes, and artillery. Even so, civilian living standards were a lot higher in 1944 than in 1934—or in 1940, for that matter. Despite the fact that about a third of national output was devoted to the war during the three peak war years, by 1944 the total value of goods and services available to *civilians* was higher than it was in 1940. Household income in 1942 was at least 50 percent above its level of 1938. Some six million new jobs for women were created, and wages of women production workers rose by roughly half. Even with wage controls and rationing, civilian consumption increased by about 15 percent, while the civilian savings rate exceeded 20 percent for the four war years, peaking at 25 percent in 1944. In a splendid rendezvous of supply with deferred demand, a lot of those war bonds were cashed in when peacetime returned, helping to power the postwar boom.

Four months before Pearl Harbor, Roosevelt had created by executive order the Office of Price Administration. The European war was already creating some shortages and price pressures, and it was clear that the United States would eventually be pulled in. A balky Congress reluctantly passed the Emergency Price Control Act in January 1942. In an era before computers, it took several months for the system to become fully operational. In 1942, inflation was over 9 percent. But once price control became effective, the consumer price index rose by just 8.7 percent between October 1942 and September 1945, when the war ended, a remarkable inflation record of less than 3 percent a year for most of the war.

World War II was a national emergency, and few would suggest that wage and price controls, rationing, and a top tax rate of 94 percent are sensible policies for ordinary times. However, the controls on finance are another story, and they have a lot to teach about good financial regulation in peacetime.

Most of the wartime economic regime was dismantled within a year of V-E Day. Wage and price controls were phased out at the insistence of Congress more abruptly than many of Roosevelt's old team had advised, leading to a modest outbreak of inflation in 1946. Rationing was gradually terminated, and all wartime controls were finally ended in November 1946. War production was quickly restored to commercial control. In a process known as reconversion, the auto assembly lines that had been shifted to production of tanks, jeeps, and aircraft in 1942 were returned to civilian use in time for Detroit's 1946 model year.

But because of the need to finance the lingering war debt, which peaked at over 120 percent of GDP, the pact between the Treasury and the Fed was not lifted until 1951. This meant that there was no speculation in government bonds. Thus the accumulated war debt did not limit the government's capacity to pursue a recovery. By contrast, after the collapse of 2008, the overhang of debt, the national obsession with reducing it, and worries about "bond vigilantes" bidding up interest rates hobbled the government's ability to implement recovery policies.

When it came to public finance, the banking system of the 1940s was treated as a public utility. The New Deal constraints on speculation, most notably the Glass-Steagall Act of 1933, also continued. As a result of these several controls—some of which were deliberately legislated as a progressive reaction to the crash of 1929, others fortuitously improvised as a response to war—the United States entered the postwar era with a regulatory regime in which private finance was compelled to serve the rest of the economy, public and private, rather its own interests. That rare set of constraints, in turn, undergirded the postwar boom.

A SERVANT, NOT A MASTER

In the policy set by the Roosevelt administration in 1941, interest rates on government debt were pegged at three-eighths of 1 percent for ninety-day debt and a maximum of 2.5 percent for long-term debt. The Fed was simply required to purchase bonds at a quantity sufficient to maintain those rates. In an order of March 1942, the Fed's board of governors formalized the policy, directing its banks to purchase all Treasury bills offered to them whenever the market interest rate reached 0.375 percent. As part of the understanding, long-term rates were maintained at 2.5 percent. Britain had a similar policy, though the target rate on long-term bonds was 3 percent. In March 1951, as the arrangement was about to end, the Treasury locked in the low rates by converting some of its short-term tradable bonds to twenty-nine-year nontradable ones.

The experience of the war and early postwar era blows a huge hole in one of the bedrock premises of orthodox economic theory. Conservative economics holds that large public deficits do—and logically should—produce higher interest rates. Government borrowing allegedly "crowds out" private credit demands. The risk of rising rates is considered the market's way of disciplining government. This dynamic clearly kicks in at some point—government can't borrow infinite amounts without debasing the currency and triggering inflation. But the experience of the war and postwar era shows that government has a lot more latitude than is commonly thought in combining substantial borrowing with low interest rates. Whether government is prevented from pursuing these salutary policies is largely a function of how much license is granted to private financial speculation. Contrary to conservative theory, large deficits did not produce high interest rates in the quarter century after World War II.

Wartime annual deficits, as high as 29 percent of GDP, were more than double the level that led to a run on Greek sovereign debt and nearly triple the recent peak annual deficits in the United States. But these war deficits were accommodated by private savings, public borrowing, and the creation of money by the Fed. Had private financial markets during the war and postwar years been permitted to set interest rates, the war would have been prohibitively expensive, money would have been diverted from the war effort into the pockets of bankers, and capital costs would have risen sharply for industries involved in war production. It also turned out that preventing markets from speculating in government debt ensured that the postwar recovery would not be stunted by speculative pressures to raise interest rates.

"In time of war the duty of the Federal Reserve, as of everyone, is to support the country's war effort." That's the Fed's own description of what occurred. No legislation was required to enlist the Federal Reserve in the war effort. Once the democratically elected branches of government had determined the amount and character of government borrowing, according to the Fed's official history of the war years, it was the Fed's job "to see to it that the banking system is in a position to absorb any public debt essential for war expenses that is not purchased by investors other than banks." Since the Fed was prohibited from raising interest rates as a tool for managing the debt and controlling the risk of inflation, it had to rely "on selective rather than general methods of control." According to the legal scholar Timothy Canova's study of the Fed-Treasury pact, this constraint meant that the Fed

> used selective credit controls to channel credit away from private consumption and speculation, particularly by imposing interest rate ceilings and high margin requirements (such as minimum down payment requirements) on private borrowing for housing, autos, consumer durable goods, and corporate securities. These margin requirements resulted in the rationing of credit away from private sub-prime borrowers while ensuring the public borrowing would remain prime by facilitating the Federal Reserve's efforts to set yields and prices on Treasury securities. This paradigm was the polar opposite of today's Federal Reserve, which uses only one policy instrument—short-term interest rates—to slow the economy without any selective credit controls to prevent speculative bubbles from developing.

The Treasury-Fed pact was long gone when I worked as chief investigator of the Senate Banking Committee in the 1970s, but its constraints were part of the Fed's institutional memory. I vividly remember the

Federal Reserve resisting any efforts by Congress to have it selectively allocate credit by setting standards, reserve or margin requirements, or down payments for different categories of loans. In the conventional view, only markets can efficiently allocate credit. But catastrophic failures of market valuation and market conflicts of interest suggest otherwise. As the collapse of 2008 demonstrated, greater Fed vigilance over credit standards and leverage ratios is necessary policy, and it was sorely lacking in the run-up to the crash. Only now are such policies again considered desirable, but they are next to impossible to carry out given how needlessly complex the financial system has been permitted to become.

Though standard accounts of central banking treat this period of pegged interest rates as entirely anomalous and regrettable in the history of the Federal Reserve, it should be seen as the one period when the Fed was brought under democratic control to serve public purposes. Before and after that ten-year exception during the Roosevelt-Truman era, the Fed was largely captured by the private banking industry. The design of the Fed was primarily the work of a committee of bankers. The boards of the Fed's regional banks were and are accountable to bankers; most members appointed to its national board of governors come from the banking industry. Until the Dodd-Frank Act of 2010 injected a little sunlight, Fed operations were for the most part conducted in secret. This was all justified as insulating monetary policy from political pressure. But in practice, it meant that the Fed's primary constituency was private finance.

In the exceptional decade that ended in the early 1950s, not only was the Fed under democratic control, but the financial system bequeathed by the New Deal and World War II was simple enough to be well regulated. In midcentury America, commercial banks provided short-term financing to corporations and local businesses. Nonprofit savings and loan associations and mutual savings banks provided mortgages to ordinary people and offered them a convenient place to save. And investment bankers underwrote stock issues.

Some exotic financial devices hadn't been invented yet, and most of those that had been devised in the speculative 1920s were prohibited by the reforms of the New Deal. There were no off-balance-sheet subsidiaries of banks, no shadow banking system, no hedge funds, no credit derivatives, no securitization of mortgages except in transparent form by a government agency (the original FNMA). Salaries in finance were relatively modest, except in investment banking, where partners put their own capital at risk and did not expect to be bailed out by taxpayers if they miscalculated. Margin was well regulated, as were the leverage ratios of commercial banks. The system was not perfect. There was a lot of jousting over what needed to be publicly disclosed under SEC rules, as well as contention over such potential conflicts of interest as stock brokerage firms trading for their own accounts. But on the whole, there were no gross abuses, and the financial part of the economy did its job of supplying credit to the real economy.

To hear the orthodox account of the past three decades, in which each new financial "innovation" was described as a great gain for economic efficiency and hence GDP growth, you'd think that the tight limits on finance in the postwar era had suppressed the genius of markets and the health of the economy. Yet the postwar boom was the most successful economic period of American history. With a well-regulated financial sector, the real economy thrived, growing at a real rate of 3.8 percent a year for twenty-seven years. Business had no trouble finding capital—or customers. For this was also the rare era when wages rose in tandem with productivity. As the economy prospered, it actually became more equal.

People did not need to go into debt in order to finance consumption because their wages were rising. Companies did not need to outsource production or make deals with low-wage countries because domestic demand was high. Despite claims about the value of increased trade for economic growth, as late as 1960 only 5 percent of American GDP was in exports or imports, and Americans consumed nearly all their output at home.

The agreement between the Federal Reserve and the Treasury was ended in March 1951, and money markets gradually began to set rates on government securities. Nonetheless, the legacy of that era of much tighter constraints on private finance continued for almost another three decades. Not until the late 1970s did the effort to dismantle much of the New Deal system of financial regulation take off.

ORTHODOXY AT ODDS WITH HISTORY

The actual experience of the 1940s is so at odds with the conceits of conservative economics that it is worth pausing to unpack the claims and counterclaims. Some contend that it was only normal that the

United States experienced an explosion of growth after World War II because of the deferred demand from the Depression and the war and the temporary suppression of competition from Europe. But if this were true, there would have been a durable consumer boom after World War I, a period when the United States was the supreme creditor nation, new industries like aircraft, auto, and radio had been stimulated by the war spending, farmer and worker wages had been depressed for a generation, and competition from Europe was in eclipse. Yet no such durable boom occurred. What actually occurred was a postwar recession, followed by a brief and unstable boom based on speculation, widening income inequality, and financial engineering—a bubble economy like that of the early 2000s. The difference between the two postwar eras is that the economy of World War II and its aftermath benefited from sensible government policies and that of World War I did not.

Among economists, there are long-running debates about whether governments can improve on the decisions of markets in developing processes and products. The argument over government promotion of innovation deserves its own book, and several such books have been written. But whatever you think of government's role in product markets, *financial* markets are a whole other story. The combination of well-disciplined capital markets and low real interest rates is good for the real economy. Industry needs relatively cheap and reliable capital in order to grow. In principle, one can imagine a highly regulated financial system coexisting with either a relatively managed or a relatively laissez-faire approach to nonfinancial industry. (Though as a matter of politics, periods of managed capitalism tend to be applied to both the financial and the real economy, and the liberation of finance tends to act as a solvent on other forms of regulation.)

In the period of financial deregulation that began in the late 1970s and culminated in the great collapse of 2008, real interest rates rose and capital was diverted from productive uses to the financial sector itself. GDP growth slowed, unemployment rose, and the economy became more unequal. By contrast, the period of tighter financial regulation corresponded with better economic performance and broader prosperity.

Some conservative economists and politicians also contend that during the World War II years, inflationary pressures were merely deferred, not contained, and that we paid for that deferral in the subsequent inflation of the 1970s. But that contention, too, is not borne out by the record. With the abrupt lifting of price controls in 1946, there was a brief outbreak of inflation. It was soon contained in the late 1940s, resurged somewhat during the Korean War, when the government used a limited form of price controls. But by the mid-1950s, the United States settled back into a period of price stability, and any deferred price pressures left over from World War II were long gone. Between 1954 and 1966, the average annual inflation rate was just 1.2 percent. This price stability even coexisted with record levels of unionization—but the wage increases were earned by productivity increases, and finance remained well constrained.

Not until the twin events of the collapse of Bretton Woods and the economic overheating of the Vietnam War did inflationary pressures break out again, fifteen years after the Korean conflict. Vietnam was surely not inevitable. Bretton Woods as a surrogate for the dominance of the U.S. dollar was destined to change. On the other hand, a truly international monetary system in the spirit of the original Bretton Woods design of 1944 could well have endured longer.

The entire postwar financial regime is best understood as a comprehensive system. The combination of tight regulation of domestic finance in the United States, the lingering European capital controls left over from World War II, and the Bretton Woods international monetary rules meant that global financial flows were even more tightly restricted than domestic ones. There was no speculation in currency movements and no regulatory arbitrage—the playing of one nation off against another to batter down financial regulation generally. The Cayman Islands were an obscure tourist destination, not a tax and regulatory haven.

While the tight regulation of U.S. domestic finance reflected a mix of deliberate New Deal policies and wartime improvisations, the controls on international capital blended the legacies of wartime disruption with a Keynesian design. From the vantage point of the early twenty-first century, it is difficult to remember the mind-set that was dominant in 1944. The architects of the postwar financial and monetary regime were painfully aware of the role of currency instability and financial speculation in the destruction of the interwar economy. Their goal was to restart financial flows in a manner that preserved the autonomy of nations to pursue high growth and full employment. That required not just a stable monetary system but controls on international capital movements.

THE GREAT REPRESSION

What can the experience of the war and immediate postwar era teach us as we confront today's high debt levels and austerity programs? Above all, the lesson seems to be that to attain reliable prosperity, we need to relieve debts, constrain speculative finance, and reinvest in the real economy. And support for containment of finance comes from surprising quarters.

In 2009, as the impact of the financial crash was unfolding, the economists Carmen Reinhart and Kenneth Rogoff published an unlikely best seller. Their book, titled *This Time Is Different: Eight Centuries of Financial Folly,* is an encyclopedic history of defaults on public debt, replete with hundreds of tables and charts. Economic recoveries, they demonstrated, tended to take far longer after a financial collapse than following an ordinary cyclical recession. Reinhart, a Harvard economist and former senior IMF economist affiliated with the Peterson Institute for International Economics (yes, that Peterson), and Rogoff, a professor at Harvard and former chief economist of the IMF, are about as mainstream, eminent, and technical as it gets. Their ironic title is taken from an aphorism attributed to David Dodd, coauthor of a famous text on investing: "The four most dangerous words in the English language are 'This time, it's different.'" Dodd's point is that self-deception is endemic to financial bubbles—if something seems too good to be true, it invariably is.

As Reinhart and Rogoff made clear, each bout of financial excess reflected the same blind euphoria, similar market mispricings of risk, and comparable dashed hopes. However, the details of how defaults were resolved were in fact quite different. Sometimes nations were kept in debtors' prison for a prolonged period; other times, like Daniel Defoe and United Airlines (but not Greece), they either negotiated their way out of crushing debt or just defaulted. As technical economists, Reinhart and Rogoff had little to say about the *politics* of which nation got what sort of debt relief, which ones were made to pay in full, and why.

In passing, they mentioned an intriguing concept: *financial repression.* Under a regime of financial repression, they wrote in a disparaging tone, "governments force local residents to save in banks by giving them few, if any, other options. They then stuff [government] debt into the banks via reserve requirements and other devices. This allows the government to finance a part of its debt at a very low interest rate." Financial repression, they added, was a disguised form of tax.

In fact, the book's characterization of financial repression was something of a straw man. There are few real-world cases of governments limiting savings options to local bank accounts, except in totalitarian regimes. Even during the period of highly regulated finance in Europe and America, people were free to invest their savings in, for example, corporate stocks or annuities.

Reinhart subsequently published several papers that offered a much richer and more sympathetic account of financial repression. Maybe, even to some mainstream economists, financial repression is the least bad of the alternatives available in the current circumstances.

As Reinhart explains in a 2011 paper she wrote with M. Belen Sbrancia, when governments find themselves overwhelmed by debts, whether from wars, depressions, or failed grand projects, faithful servicing and repayment at par value can be disabling to the larger economy. The alternative is to find ways of "liquidating" (Reinhart's term) the debts, so that the real economy can recover. In Reinhart's analysis, repression of the influence of private finance turned out to be a key aspect of debt liquidation not just during World War II but for more than three decades afterward.

The paper points out a few basic ways that the government can repress finance for the sake of tempering the overall burden of prior debt. It can require its central bank and commercial banking system to finance public debt at very low interest rates, which the United States did between 1941 and 1951. It can limit the ability of capital markets to set interest rates by putting ceilings on rates paid and charged by banks, as the United States did from the 1930s until the 1970s and as several states used to do with usury laws. Government can require or incentivize "captive domestic audiences" such as pension funds to buy government securities. It can promote high rates of growth, so that the value of past debt fades relative to GDP. And it can tolerate moderate inflation to reduce the real value of the debt. Contrary to widespread myth, mild inflation almost never turns into hyperinflation.

Moderate inflation combined with low interest rates, of the sort that prevailed in the three decades after World War II, does, however, function as a hidden tax on creditors. As Reinhart and Sbrancia note, in the period between 1945 and 1980 in both the United States and Britain, the rate of inflation was often higher than the interest rate on public debt. So for both countries during that period, "the annual liquidation of debt via negative real interest rates amounted on average from 3 to 4 percent of GDP a year." Thanks to low interest costs (and high real growth rates), the debt-to-GDP ratio in the United States was reduced from 116 percent in 1945 to 66.2 percent in 1955. For Britain, the figures were 215.6 percent and 138.2 percent. If speculation had been permitted in government bonds, debt costs would have been far higher and the reduction of the debt overhang far lower.

Moreover, they report, real interest rates were significantly lower from 1945 to 1980 than in the freer capital markets before World War II and after financial liberalization: "This is the case irrespective of the interest rate used—whether central bank discount, treasury bills, deposit, or lending rates and whether for advanced or emerging markets." For all advanced countries, the inflation-adjusted interest rate on short-term government Treasury bills was a −1.6 percent. But the flip side was the rapid liquidation of government debt and low capital costs for industry.

In short, the three-decade postwar period was great for the real economy and terrible for the bond market. Investors in bonds had negative rates of return. Adjusted for inflation, total stock market returns in the 1960s and 1970s were barely positive.

The increasing equality of income and wealth that characterized the quarter century after the war is partly a reflection of strong unions and rising real wages but also of the fact that the investor class on average did not enjoy high returns, whether in bonds or stocks. While some bonds were held by widows, orphans, pension funds and small savers, the typical household in the bottom three-quarters of the income distribution had very little financial savings other than home equity.

That the investor class lost out during America's greatest boom era defies a core premise of orthodox economics. Presumably, if we want increased savings, investment, and growth, we need to reward investors. That has been the premise of every conservative president since Reagan and the goal of Republican tax and budget policy. It makes a certain amount of intuitive sense. Yet the postwar boom was one in which investors on average did poorly—and the economy delivered broadly distributed prosperity. There was plenty of capital to finance industry's needs—much of industry was, in fact, self-financed by retained earnings—and plenty of consumer purchasing power to buy the products. Low capital costs, modest inflation, and tight financial regulation were just the ticket to fuel the real economy.

So maybe there is something beneficial about financial repression for the rest of the economy. Financial repression is, in effect, a close cousin to Keynes's older concept of the euthanasia of the rentier.

FROM REPRESSION TO LIBERATION

The period from 1945 to 1980 was not quite the single era that Reinhart describes, except in the statistical sense that it was a time of generally negative real interest rates. But there were major institutional differences between the early and later postwar periods. The key breakpoint was 1971, the year the Bretton Woods system collapsed and inflation became a serious problem. Prior to 1971, real interest rates were mostly negative, but inflation was well controlled and the financial system was well regulated. After 1971, international monetary anarchy returned and serious inflation broke out, triggered both by a weaker dollar and emphatically by the OPEC oil shock. This financial instability, in turn, set in motion economic and political trends that led to the liberation of finance.

As the 1970s wore on, inflation worsened. In 1979, Paul Volcker, then the newly appointed chairman of the Federal Reserve, decided to tame inflation once and for all by putting interest rates through the roof. Today, Volcker is something of an improbable hero to critics of financial excess because he is relatively public minded and relatively pro-regulation. He was a public servant most of his working life, he never became part of the financial old boys' club resisting regulation, and he has been an advocate of Glass-Steagall restoration, a position resisted by Wall Street and embraced only in watered-down form by the Obama administration in its invention of the "Volcker rule."

But in 1979, Volcker was no hero. As one who believed that markets should allocate credit, he resolved to slay inflation using the bluntest of instruments—raising short-term interest rates, to a peak of 20.5 percent. Contemporary critics of Volcker urged him to pursue narrower-gauge strategies instead. Much of the inflation of the 1970s was in fact sectoral rather than macroeconomic. It was the result not of general economic overheating but of a convergence of price pressures in key sectors. Energy prices rose not because of excess demand but because of the OPEC cartel. Medical costs rose because the new Medicare system paid whatever doctors and hospitals billed. Food prices rose because of coincidental droughts and shortages. Housing costs rose—in circular fashion—because the rising interest rates used to battle inflation produced more expensive mortgages. Labor costs rose because inflation triggered cost-of-living clauses. Dealing with these distinct drivers of inflation at their origin as a microeconomic or regulatory problem, rather than using very tight money as an all-purpose macro-cure, could have spared the nation the deep recession that resulted from Volcker's cold-bath monetary policies.

Those dissenting voices were unheeded. The Volcker recession helped elect Ronald Reagan. And Reagan ushered in an era in which finance escaped its salutary shackles. After 1980, interest rates turned positive—extremely positive. The rate of inflation came down much faster than the prevailing interest rates. So real interest rates averaged a positive 7 percent in the 1980s. If the third of a century after the war was a grim period for the bond market, the third of a century after 1980 was a rentier's paradise. Disinflation was also very good for the stock market. There is a mechanical relationship between the general rate of inflation and the general price of shares. The lower the rate of inflation, the higher multiple of earnings can be justified as a share price. Returns to capital soared beginning in the 1980s, just as returns to labor diminished. An economic shift and a political shift proved to be mutually reinforcing and cumulative. By the presidency of George W. Bush, labor was losing even more of the national income and was even weaker politically. And capital was king.

In the three decades that began in 1981, private finance clawed back the license that it had lost in the New Deal, the war, and the early postwar period. What goes under the heading of "deregulation" really has three distinct forms. Some laws—including the Glass-Steagall Act, the strict constraints on the underwriting of mortgages, state usury statutes, the Federal Reserve's Regulation Q limiting interest rates, and federal securities laws giving investors broad rights to sue in cases of fraud—were literally repealed.

Other laws were simply not enforced well, or their enforcement was corrupted. The SEC had plenty of tools to prevent the accounting fraud that enabled the Enron scandal, but its chairman at the time, Harvey Pitt, was formerly a chief lobbyist for the accountants' trade association. The federal regulatory agencies took no action against the gross conflicts of interest in which stock analysts supposedly representing consumers were actually touts for companies whose underwriting business the analysts' firms were seeking. Enforcement fell to New York's attorney general.

A third form of regulatory capture was the studied incuriosity of regulators and of Congress as financiers kept inventing opaque and often deceptive new products that put the entire system at risk. Innovation, by definition, was held to be positive. By the eve of the financial collapse, a new generation of toxic products with the potential to crash the entire system lay beyond the purview of regulators.

In the 1970s, two concepts devised by free-market economists were embraced by financial entrepreneurs as a rationale for deregulation. These were the efficient market hypothesis and the doctrine of maximizing shareholder value. The former, first propounded by the University of Chicago economist Eugene Fama in 1970, is really Adam Smith applied to financial markets. By definition, the market price of a security must be right. Hence, the price of a stock or bond is "informationally efficient" because it is based on all available information. If you accepted that (tautological) premise, it logically followed that the duty of financial markets was to shake off regulatory constraints and maximize shareholder value.

All power to the shareholder was the radically libertarian solution to a dilemma most famously identified by A. A. Berle, Jr., and Gardiner Means in 1932—that managers had too much power relative to owners. But if the rules of finance were changed so that stock prices and shareholders were kings, superior efficiencies would supposedly follow. Another leading free-market economist, Henry Manne, proposed that if there were an unregulated "market for corporate control," the direction of corporations would pass into the hands of the best-qualified managers.

This intellectual apparatus undergirded the shift to financial deregulation and the boom in leveraged buyouts. The hostile takeover artist merely appeared to be capturing windfalls as a middleman; a bidding war for control of a corporation was actually doing the Lord's work by allowing markets to set the correct share price (often a temporarily inflated one) and installing superior managers (often interested only in a quick killing).

All of these theories, which have been demolished by the collapse of 2008, were very useful to the financial opportunists who persuaded Congress and several administrations to dismantle the regulatory apparatus of the New Deal era. The slow growth and declining competitiveness of the 1970s gave the crusade credibility. Presumably, if markets were liberated from corporate oligopolies, capital would flow to newer and more productive uses and better managers. But the ills that lent credibility to this ideological shift in fact worsened. U.S. industry continued its competitive slide, America's trade imbalance widened, and the nations that made competitive gains at America's expense, as we saw in chapter 9, were those that kept tight controls on their financial markets.

Even the boom in the technology sector, America's crown jewel in the late twentieth century, had little to do with shifts in financial markets. The technological innovations depended heavily on government-funded research. The rapid growth of computer hardware and software companies was mostly either self-financed or underwritten by fairly conventional issues of stock, not by leveraged buyouts or other financial razzle-dazzle. Venture capitalists, whose rise had nothing to do with the radical deregulation of money markets, did provide financing to several early start-ups, though the venture capital industry peaked on the eve of the tech bust of 2000–1 and has never recovered from it. The application of radically free-market concepts to finance added to the complexity, opportunism, and extreme leveraging of money markets. Far from producing accurate or efficient prices, these concepts allowed prices of stocks, bonds, and mortgages to wildly diverge from economic fundamentals, setting up a crash of both the economy and the theory.

THE CASE FOR A NEW REPRESSION OF FINANCE

After the publication of Reinhart and Rogoff's book, several conservative commentators noticed the brief reference to financial repression and branded it a very bad idea. Bill Gross of PIMCO, who runs the world's biggest bond fund, warned of financial repression for years to come as the Federal Reserve made huge bond purchases to keep interest rates low. Kevin Warsh of the Hoover Institution, a former Federal Reserve governor, wrote in *The Wall Street Journal* that policymakers "are finding it tempting to pursue 'financial repression'—suppressing market prices that they don't like. But this is bad policy, not least because it signals diminished faith in the market economy itself."

Some presidents of the Fed's regional banks, such as Richard Fisher in Dallas and Jeffrey Lacker in Richmond, fretted that Ben Bernanke's policy of buying trillions of dollars' worth of public and private debt to keep interest rates low as a form of stimulus was only delaying an inflationary day of reckoning. At some point, the huge deficits would have to cause interest rates to rise.

Sooner or later (later unless we drastically revise prevailing assumptions and policies), recovery will occur. And at that point, the Fed will indeed allow rates to rise. Investors locked into the low-rate long-term bonds of the Bernanke era will share the same fate as their counterparts in the 1950s and 1960s: they will have negative real rates of return. But there are worse things than a period of negative real interest rates. One is a prolonged depression.

A key question today is whether gradual liquidation of government debt using the several strategies of repressing finance is better than the alternative of prolonged economic suffering. Though the rentier class paid a hidden tax in the decades after World War II, the real economy thrived; and, on balance, the rising tide soon lifted even the yachts.

What would a deliberate policy of financial repression include today? The low interest rates and purchases of government debt being pursued by central banks are necessary, but hardly sufficient. As we saw in the discussion of Europe's sovereign debt crisis, the failure to regulate speculation means that hedge funds and other shadow banks play cat and mouse with central bankers, destabilizing debt markets and raising the public costs of maintaining solvency for banks and nation-states. No sooner do the European Central Bank and the European Commission come up with large sums to support bank capitalization than speculators find ways to undermine the strategy.

Most important, as we saw in chapters 5 and 6 on the European crisis, we need complementary strategies to discourage private speculation in sovereign debt. The idea that this particular genie cannot be put back in the bottle because of the Internet or globalization is just plain wrong. The 1920s saw all manner of speculation against government bonds. The information traveled at the same speed of light; it just went over telephone and telegraph copper wires rather than fiber-optic cables.

We also had laissez-faire globalization in the 1920s. But the experience of the Great Depression and the Second World War persuaded citizens and leaders to opt for a managed form of capitalism that contained speculation—or repressed finance, to use Reinhart's term.

In this debate about financial repression, an important distinction tends to get lost. Different people have used the term to mean different things. To a Bill Gross or a Kevin Warsh, the Fed's policy of pursuing very low interest rates can be considered repression of a sort because it denies investors in bonds the higher returns that logically accompany high public deficits, according to conventional theory.

However, the Fed's current engineering of low interest rates is only one form of financial repression. As we have seen in the years since the crash of 2008, very low rates, though alarming to some conservative critics, have not been sufficient to end the depression. Broader forms of financial repression are also necessary to keep financial speculation and the narrow self-interest of banks from blocking the recovery policies that the economy needs. Financial markets in the immediate postwar era were, above all, simple. They were simple enough to regulate. Simple also meant that it was harder to hide plain corruption. Simple meant government could resolve to keep interest rates low and make the policy stick. It also meant that bankers made modest returns channeling capital to the real economy and did not make the kind of mischief that put the real economy at risk.

Going forward, we face the two interlocking questions of how to drastically simplify finance and how to limit the capacity of money markets to make accumulated debts drag down recovery. The answers to these questions have similar fundamentals but different specifics in the United States and Europe. Interestingly, many developing economies have a head start because they never entirely bought into the free-market theories of development or the drastic financial deregulation. And they have had better than two decades of pushback against the excessive austerity policies of the IMF.

THE ROAD FROM HERE

It is not my purpose to close by offering a detailed manifesto. But here are some basic principles. The remedy comes in two parts: undoing the damage of the last crash and preventing the next one.

Recovery of the economy requires both debt relief and public outlay to compensate for the damage to banks and the shortfall of private purchasing power. In the United States, one central need is a program for reducing the principal on underwater mortgage loans and refinancing them. This can be done most efficiently with a new Home Owners' Loan Corporation, which would use the government's own low borrowing rate. To the extent that some banks suffered losses that pushed them close to insolvency, they would need to be recapitalized and reorganized, with government playing an active rather than a passive management role. We already have a model for this process in the FDIC's procedures for failed smaller banks. Even if Congress refuses to enact a new HOLC, the executive branch has plenty of authority to run such a program through the Treasury or FHA, or through Fannie Mae, which is now government-owned.

The Federal Reserve could be a major player in a strategy of mortgage debt relief. At a time when much of the rest of official Washington is obsessed with the wrong part of the debt crisis, namely the government debt, Chairman Bernanke, a student of the Great Depression, has stayed focused on the private debts that are sandbagging the recovery.

In 2012, the Fed surprised its critics by turning its attention to the deflationary effects of the continued housing drag. William Dudley, president of the New York Federal Reserve Bank, gave a major speech calling for more aggressive government action to provide mortgage relief. He urged Fannie Mae and its quasi-public enterprise, Freddie Mac, to write-down balances on mortgages that they hold. Federal Reserve governor Sarah Bloom Raskin worked with Chairman Bernanke and enlisted the Fed staff to write a white paper on the larger economic consequences of the housing bust. The staff paper explicitly called for reductions in principal.

If the rest of the government fails to act, there is much more that Bernanke could do. The Fed, relying on emergency powers legislated in 1933 that give the central bank the right to take extraordinary measures in an economic emergency, has been buying up securities to the tune of trillions of dollars. In 2012, the Fed announced the third such program since 2008, to purchase $40 billion worth of mortgage-backed securities every month. The Fed has been pursuing this strategy both to pump money into the economy in order to keep interest rates very low, and to help sop up toxic securities that still clog banks' balance sheets.

But this extraordinary program has failed to stimulate a robust recovery, because banks can't find enough uses for the money. The homeowners who need relief the most can't get it because their homes are too far underwater. Using its emergency authority (which under the Dodd-Frank Act now requires the concurrence of the Treasury), the Fed could simply launch its own direct loan program, and refinance mortgages with reduced principal at very low interest rates. By agreeing to create enough money to finance the war debt at very low interest rates after World War II, the Fed made possible the postwar boom.

In December 2012, for the first time ever, the Federal Reserve announced that it would give priority to bringing down unemployment rather than stabilizing prices. But in setting an unemployment target of 6.5 percent, Bernanke kept the official inflation target at 2.5 percent, far too low to have much impact on the debt burden. The ECB, meanwhile, has kept its inflation target at 2 percent or below, and doesn't even have an unemployment target, while unemployment rates in the Eurozone are now in excess of 11.4 percent and heading higher.

Professor Kenneth Rogoff, the former IMF chief economist, has shocked his colleagues by calling for an annual inflation target in the range of 4 to 6 percent, to reduce the real burden of the accumulated debt. This would be "financial repression," par excellence. In addition, a higher inflation target would allow the Federal Reserve to run an even more expansive monetary policy to restore GDP growth and employment before slamming on the monetary brakes for fear of inflation.

Alan Blinder, former vice chairman of the Federal Reserve, points out that the risk is not that the Federal Reserve might succeed in achieving higher inflation. He is more concerned that the economy is so deflated that the Fed might *fail* to generate higher prices even if it tried, thus impairing the central bank's credibility. While central banks could do more, there is no substitute for more aggressive fiscal policy—public borrowing and investing. Yet most officials of both parties, when they raise the issue of fiscal policy, still have in mind deficit reduction, not stimulus.

Public policy also must find ways to give relief to the other private debts that are depressing demand and holding back recovery. Central among them are student debts, whose interest and principal payments leave young Americans hard-pressed to buy life's necessities. A Student Loan Forgiveness Act has been introduced in Congress. It forgives loans after ten years of payment, reduced to five years if the

debtor is working in a public service job; and it caps the interest rate at
3.4 percent.

There is still a huge, deferred agenda of financial reform. The largest
players in the financial system are not just too big to fail. They are too
complex to regulate. The crisis of the past five years has demonstrated
conclusively that the complexity did not add to economic efficiency; it
only added risk and the potential of a catastrophic crash. So we also
need a restoration of the Glass-Steagall Act and a breakup of the largest banks. Study after study has found that after a bank reaches a size
of about $100 billion, there are no further efficiency gains to be reaped
from sheer scale. Today's $2 trillion banks are about executive pay and
bonuses and the capacity to evade regulation and supervision, not about
economic efficiency. Complexity also conceals corruption.

I've urged Congress to create an expert commission that would study
all of the financial innovations of the past three decades and report
back on which ones truly added economic efficiency and which ones
added only risk and middleman profit. A vastly simplified financial system whose purpose is to serve the rest of the economy should be the
national policy goal. That would have the additional benefit of reducing
the bankers' political power.

The larger economy is now stuck in a cycle of very slow growth and
debt overhang. As we've seen, it was the massive spending of World
War II that finally cured the Great Depression. Today, the counterpart
would be both debt relief and a public investment program aimed at
modernizing America's decaying public infrastructure and investing in
sustainable energy.

As noted in the introduction, Hurricane Sandy called attention to
the urgent need to invest hundreds of billions of dollars in protecting
coastal cities from surges that will only increase as the oceans rise and
storms become more intense. Quite apart from the issue of whether all
of the climate change is man-made (which is increasingly settled by the
evidence), there is no doubt whatever that sea levels will continue to
rise. This new reality creates a need not just for physical barriers of the
sort that the Dutch have used for centuries, but for upgraded and better
protected water and sewer systems, power stations, bridges, tunnels,
and transit systems.

Some advocates of a drastic strategy for reversing climate change and
mitigating its effects bridle at the idea that we need to restore some-

thing called "growth." Surely, our climate crisis results from too much emphasis on growth when we should be emphasizing sustainability and just distribution of income and wealth. But it is possible—and necessary—to square this circle. A debt overhang creates a depressed economy with under-utilized productive and human capacity. People need jobs and income, and the economy should realize its potential. A World War II–scale green investment program could simultaneously pull the economy out of its deep hole and allow better living standards at lower cost to the planet.

The European variant also requires a shift from austerity to debt relief and new investment. The same kind of constraints on speculative finance and the same drastic simplification of the banking system are needed on both sides of the Atlantic. Because of the pressure on government bonds in Europe's more vulnerable nations, there is no good alternative to Pan-European assumption of old debt. To make that feasible, the European Central Bank would have to be given the powers of the U.S. Federal Reserve and act on them. This would lower interest costs throughout the Continent.

Seemingly, a public investment program as a recovery strategy is more difficult for Europe than for the United States because Europe has higher tax rates and many of Europe's most vulnerable economies already have large deficits and debts. But the debt ratio of Europe as a whole is not much higher than that of the United States. Both economies have room for fiscal expansion—if speculative pressures on bonds can be contained. Europe, though highly taxed, also has room for selective taxes on financial transactions. This would be good policy in its own right—it would discourage speculation—and it would produce revenues so that not all of an expansionary investment program would rely on borrowing. This general strategy also requires the Europeanization of fiscal and investment policy, but not the deflationary sort envisioned by Chancellor Merkel. Either Europe will go forward to a true federation or it will stay mired in deepening depression and perhaps break up. And on both sides of the ocean, moderately higher inflation rates would be a tonic, both to expand economic activity and to reduce the burden of debt.

This view of the current crisis and its necessary remedy is far from the center of political debate in 2013. That is not because these proposals are radical or utopian. In the mid-twentieth century, they were mainstream. The fact that they are not today has nothing to do with inexorable trends of technology or with efficient markets supplanting clumsy states. The change in the mainstream view simply represents shifts in political power. So if we want these ideas to be taken seriously in politics, their sheer logic is not sufficient. We need to take the power back.

Today, one encounters two forms of pessimism. The first holds that the economy is doomed to a generation of depression and that all we can do is share sacrifice until confidence returns. The other holds that the economics in fact could and should be drastically different but that our politics will not allow us to get there from here. The latter pessimism is the more disabling. We must begin by reclaiming democratic politics.

Acknowledgments

This book began as an inquiry into the role of debt in economic crises and the political forces promoting austerity. That exploration took me across several fields of history, politics, economics, and finance. It could not have been written without a great deal of generous help from colleagues and associates.

The editors at Knopf served as proxies for the reader and kept reminding me that the story needed to be a compelling narrative as well as a technically precise economic analysis. Thanks especially to editor Andrew Miller and associate Mark Chiusano, as well as my agent, Ike Williams.

Colleagues at *The American Prospect* and Demos encouraged this research, some of whose earlier products took the form of policy papers and articles. Relatively short portions of this text are variations of material that has appeared in the *Prospect*. The germ of the book originated in a column published in May 2011 also titled "Debtors' Prison." Thank you to Kit Rachlis, Miles Rapoport, Amelia Warren Tyagi, Harold Meyerson, Paul Starr, Tamara Draut, Wally Turbeville, Heather McGhee, Sue O'Brian, Christen Aragoni, and Gabe Arana, among many others.

The incomparable Emma Stokking functioned as my principal research assistant and was miraculous at tracking down impossible-to-find documents in several languages.

The Rockefeller Brothers Fund provided a travel grant for research in Europe, as part of my ongoing work for Demos on the challenges of global governance. Thanks to program officer Tom Kruse and President Stephen Heintz.

I appreciate the generosity of several European friends and colleagues who helped with insights and contacts. They are too numerous to mention but particular thanks to European Parliament leaders

Pervenche Berès, Ieke van den Burg, and former Danish prime minister Poul Nyrup Rasmussen, to Frans Becker of the Wiardi Beckmann Stifting, Ernst Stetter of the Foundation for European Social Progress, former EU commissioner and Swedish finance minister Allan Larsson, and to Wiemer Salverda at the University of Amsterdam and AIAS, where I was a visiting fellow in 2011. I gratefully count all of these as friends.

One of my heroes, the late Albert Hirschman, called himself a trespasser, for his habit of venturing into far-flung disciplines in order to capture insights wherever he might find them. As a lifelong trespasser, I often turn to mentors when I am on unfamiliar ground. In this book, I was fortunate to have generous mentors including the legal historian of bankruptcy Bruce Mann, who is married to another mentor and hero, Senator Elizabeth Warren. Others who helped by deepening my understanding or introducing me to new literatures, concepts, and people were Joseph Stiglitz, José Antonio Ocampo, Bob Pollin, Thierry Philipponat, Suzanne Berger, Bruce Kogut, Robert Litan, Rob Johnson, and Damon Silvers.

Special thanks to several people who read portions or drafts of the entire book: Richard Parker, Arthur Goldhammer, Peter Gourevitch, José Antonio Ocampo, Rick Valelly, Rob Johnson, and Bob Pollin. My wife, Joan Fitzgerald, to whom this book is dedicated, read multiple drafts.

Others who helped in innumerable ways included Michel Aglietta, Phil Angelides, Gerry Arsenis, Sheila Bair, Dean Baker, Jared Bernstein, Marc Blecher, Alan Blinder, Andreas Botsch, Pia Bungarten, Tim Canova, Peter Coldrick, Andrea Coles-Bjerre, John Evans, Charles Goodheart, Michael Greenberger, Pierre Habbard, Jacob Hacker, Peter Hall, Margaret Hallock, Will Hutton, Simon Johnson, Sony Kapoor, Louka Katseli, Dennis Kelleher, Bruce Kogut, Mike Konczal, Katerina Lambrinou, Robert Lawless, Neal Lawson, Adam Levitin, Kathie Jo Martin, Henning Meyer, Larry Mishel, Leif Pagrotsky, Yannis Palaiologos, Joachim Palme, Vassilis Papadimitriou, Jean Pisani-Ferry, Frank Portney, Yaga Reddy, Carmen Reinhart, André Sapir, Anya Schiffrin, Sherle Schwenninger, Janet Shenk, David Smith, Yves Smith, Katherine V. W. Stone, Nicolas Véron, Jelle Visser, Andy Watt, Mark Weisbrot, Sofka Zinovieff, and Martha Zuber.

My family deserves a different sort of thank you. When I am in book mode, I tend to disappear into a zone of deep concentration and composition. This routine has come to be familiar in my house, probably a little too familiar. Now that this opus is done, I look forward to spending more relaxed time with Gabe, Jess, Shelly, and their spouses, with Owen, James, Eli, Amaryah, and Alex, who will not be nine, five, four, four, and three forever, and above all with Joan.

Notes

INTRODUCTION

3 ON OCTOBER 29, 1692: Michael Quilter, "Daniel Defoe: Bankrupt and Bankruptcy Reformer," *Journal of Legal History* 25, no. 1 (2004): 54.

4 "THE WILLFUL AGENT": Daniel Defoe, *Robinson Crusoe* (New York: Simon and Schuster, 2001, 1719), 56.

4 "IT BEGGARED DEBTORS": Bruce Mann, *Republic of Debtors: Bankruptcy in the Age of American Independence* (Cambridge, Mass.: Harvard University Press, 2002), 18.

5 A REFORMIST PAMPHLET: John C. McCoid II, "Discharge: The Most Important Development in Bankruptcy History," *American Bankruptcy Law Journal* 70 (Spring 1996): 179.

5 "AFTER A DEBTOR": Quilter, "Daniel Defoe," 59.

7 LEGAL HISTORIANS HAVE OBSERVED: See Mann, *Republic of Debtors,* especially chapters 2 and 3.

10 "FOR THOUSANDS OF YEARS": David Graeber, *Debt: The First 5,000 Years* (Brooklyn, N.Y.: Melville House, 2011), 8.

1: AGONY ECONOMICS

18 "THE EUTHANASIA OF THE RENTIER": John Maynard Keynes, *The General Theory of Employment, Interest, and Money* (New York: Harcourt, 1964, 1936), 322.

19 "LIQUIDATE LABOR": Herbert Hoover, *Memoirs*, vol. 3, *The Great Depression, 1929–1941* (New York: Macmillan, 1951), 30.

21 PUBLIC STATE UNIVERSITIES: See http://projectonstudentdebt.org/pub_home.php.

21 AVERAGE STUDENT DEBT: Ibid.

22 "THE PLASTIC SAFETY NET": Tamara Draut, *Strapped: Why America's 20- and 30-Somethings Can't Get Ahead* (New York: Doubleday, 2006), 12.

22 THE RATIO OF DEBT TO INCOME: Edward N. Wolff, "Recent Trends in Household Wealth in the United States: Rising Debt and the Middle Class Squeeze—an Update to 2007" (Working Paper 589, Levy Economics Institute, Annandale-on-Hudson, N.Y., March 2012, http://www.levyinstitute.org/pubs/wp_589.pdf).

22 CREDIT CARD DEBT: Ibid., 13.

23 MEDICAL DEBT: Elizabeth Warren and Amelia Warren Tyagi, *The Two-Income Trap: Why Middle-Class Mothers and Fathers Are Going Broke* (New York: Basic Books, 2003).

23 RATIO OF DEBT TO HOUSEHOLD INCOME: David Rosenberg, "Credit Bust Scars Will Take Years to Heal in Aftershock Era," *Financial Times,* August 2, 2012.

24 "THE LINE SEPARATING SPECULATION": Edward Chancellor, *Devil Take the Hindmost: A History of Financial Speculation* (New York: Farrar, Straus and Giroux, 1999), xi.

24 "FORECASTING THE PROSPECTIVE YIELD": Keynes, *General Theory,* 132.

25 GOVERNMENT BOND FUTURES: Chancellor, *Devil Take the Hindmost,* 7–8.

25 OFF-BALANCE-SHEET VEHICLES: Steve Fraser, *Every Man a Speculator: A History of Wall Street in American Life* (New York: HarperCollins, 2005), 5–8.

25 "SOLD THE SKIN": Ibid., 46.

25 ISAAC LE MAIRE: Chancellor, *Devil Take the Hindmost,* 13.

25 AGENCY HOUSES: Scott Nelson, *A Nation of Deadbeats: An Uncommon History of America's Financial Disasters* (New York: Alfred A. Knopf, 2012), 103.

26 CALL LOANS: Chancellor, *Devil Take the Hindmost,* 157.

29 "THIS ISSUE": See http://www.iousathemovie.com/additionalresources/.

31 HOMEOWNERSHIP RATE FOR PEOPLE: Draut, *Strapped,* 133.

31 THE WORK OF THE HARVARD PEDIATRIC RESEARCHER: Jack P. Shonkoff et al., "The Lifelong Effects of Early Childhood Adversity and Toxic Stress," *Pediatrics,* December 26, 2011, http://pediatrics.aappublications.org/content/early/2011/12/21/peds.2011-2663.full.pdf+html.

31 ONLY ABOUT A QUARTER: Ife Finch and Liz Schott, "TANF Benefits Fell Further in 2011 and Are Worth Much Less Than in 1996 in Most States," Center on Budget and Policy Priorities, November 21, 2011, http://www.cbpp.org/cms/?fa=view&id=3625.

2: THE GREAT DEFLATION

35 "OUT OF MAYBE 13": *The Financial Crisis Inquiry Report: Final Report of the National Commission on the Causes of the Financial and Economic Crisis in the United States* (New York: Public Affairs, 2011), 354.

36 INCLUDING ONE OF MINE: Robert Kuttner, *The Squandering of America: How the Failure of Our Politics Undermines Our Prosperity* (New York: Alfred A. Knopf, 2007).

37 A CLASSIC ARTICLE: Irving Fisher, "The Debt-Deflation Theory of Great Depressions," *Econometrica* 1, no. 4 (October 1933), http://fraser.stlouisfed.org/docs/meltzer/fisdeb33.pdf.

37 SECONDARY PYRAMID OF SECURITIES: See analysis of Ben S. Bernanke, "Some Reflections on the Crisis and the Policy Response" (speech at the Russell Sage Foundation's conference Rethinking Finance, New York, April 13, 2012, p. 3 of prepared text).

37 THE TOTAL VALUE OF RESIDENTIAL REAL ESTATE: *Flow of Funds Accounts of the United States,* Federal Reserve Board, Washington, D.C., June 7, 2012, http://www.federalreserve.gov/releases/z1/20120607/z1.pdf.

38 SINCE THE PEAK IN HOUSING VALUES: Census data cited in Teresa Tritch, "Still Crawling Out of a Very Deep Hole," *New York Times,* April 8, 2012.

38 THROUGHOUT 2011: Standard & Poor's/Case-Shiller index, http://www .standardandpoors.com/indices/sp-case-shiller-home-price-indices/en/us/ ?indexId=spusa-cashpidff—p-us—.

40 STATE AND LOCAL GOVERNMENTS CUT SPENDING: Phil Oliff, Chris Mai, and Vincent Palacios, "States Continue to Feel Recession's Impact," Center on Budget and Policy Priorities, June 27, 2012, http://www.cbpp.org/cms/index .cfm?fa=view&id=711.

40 SINCE AUGUST 2008: Lawrence Mishel, Josh Bivens, Elise Gould, and Heidi Shierholz, *The State of Working America,* 12th ed. (Washington, D.C.: Economic Policy Institute, 2012).

41 THE ECONOMY GREW: Office of Management and Budget Historical Tables, http://www.whitehouse.gov/omb/budget/Historicals.

41 THE PRESIDENT'S BUDGET FOR THE FISCAL YEAR 2011: Office of Management and Budget, *Budget of the U.S. Government, Fiscal Year 2011* (Washington, D.C.: Government Printing Office, 2010), 146, http://blackburn.house .gov/UploadedFiles/FY_11_Budget.pdf.

42 IN THE PRESIDENT'S BUDGET FOR FISCAL YEAR 2013: Office of Management and Budget, *Budget of the U.S. Government, Fiscal Year 2013* (Washington, D.C.: Government Printing Office, 2012), 247, http://www.whitehouse .gov/sites/default/files/omb/budget/fy2013/assets/budget.pdf.

42 ECONOMIC RISKS THAT HAD BEEN BORNE: See Jacob S. Hacker, *The Great Risk Shift: The Assault on American Jobs, Families, Health Care and Retirement and How You Can Fight Back* (New York: Oxford University Press, 2006).

42 THIS TREND WORSENED: Mishel et al., *The State of Working America.*

43 THE PERCENTAGE OF ADULTS WORKING: Chad Stone, "Economic Recovery Watch," Center on Budget and Policy Priorities, April 6, 2012, http://www .cbpp.org/cms/index.cfm?fa=view&id=3742.

43 ACCORDING TO THE ECONOMIST: Andrew Sum, Ishwar Khatiwada, Joseph McLaughlin, and Sheila Palma, "The 'Jobless and Wageless' Recovery from the Great Recession of 2007–2009: The Magnitude and Sources of Economic Growth Through 2011 and Their Impacts on Workers, Profits, and Stock Values," Center for Labor Market Studies, Northeastern University, Boston, Mass., May 2011, http://www.employmentpolicy.org/sites/www .employmentpolicy.org/files/field-content-file/pdf/Mike%20Lillich/Revised %20Corporate%20Report%20May%2027th.pdf.

45 A PAPER GIVEN: Ben S. Bernanke, "The Great Moderation" (address to meeting of the Eastern Economic Association, Washington, D.C., February 20, 2004, http://www.federalreserve.gov/boarddocs/speeches/2004/20040220/default .htm).

46 IN 2002, AS THE BIG BANKS: Michael T. Snyder, "10 Banks Own 77% of U.S. Banking Assets," Seeking Alpha, July 19, 2011, http://seekingalpha.com/ article/280289-10-banks-own-77-of-u-s-banking-assets.

46 FULLY 97 PERCENT: See FDIC data and Robert Kuttner, "The Costs of Financial Favoritism," *American Prospect,* March 2012.

47 "NO EXAMINER": Quip to the author.

3: THE ALLURE OF AUSTERITY

51 "TO PUT THE MATTER BLUNTLY": Peter G. Peterson, "Social Security: The Coming Crash," *New York Review of Books,* December 2, 1982, http://www.nybooks.com/articles/archives/1982/dec/02/social-security-the-coming-crash/?pagination=false.

53 "PAYING [WALKER] THROUGH": Ryan Grim and Paul Blumenthal, "Peter Peterson Spent Nearly Half a Billion in Washington Targeting Social Security, Medicare," *Huffington Post,* May 15, 2012, http://www.huffingtonpost.com/2012/05/15/peter-peterson-foundation-half-billion-social-security-cuts_n_1517805.html.

55 THAT YEAR, THE ACTUAL BUDGET: Office of Management and Budget, *Budget of the U.S. Government, Fiscal Year 2013: Historical Tables* (Washington, D.C.: Government Printing Office, 2012), table 1.1, http://www.whitehouse.gov/sites/default/files/omb/budget/fy2013/assets/hist.pdf.

55 THE 2012 TRUSTEES' REPORT: 2012 *Annual Report of the Trustees of the OASDI Trust Funds* (Washington, D.C.: Government Printing Office, 2012), 97.

55 SOCIAL SECURITY IS FINANCED: Ibid., 158.

56 "WE SUFFER": *I.O.U.S.A.* transcript at http://www.iousathemovie.com/additionalresources/.

56 A SHARP DETERIORATION: Office of Management and Budget, *Budget of the U.S. Government, Fiscal Year 2013: Historical Tables,* table 1.1.

56 THROUGH HIS FOUNDATION: Peterson Foundation Form 990 filings with the IRS for 2009, 2010, and 2011.

57 THE VERY FIRST STORY: Elaine S. Povich and Eric Pianin, "Support Grows for Tackling Nation's Debt," *Washington Post,* December 31, 2009, http://www.washingtonpost.com/wp-dyn/content/article/2009/12/30/AR2009123002576.html.

58 A NATIONAL POETRY CONTEST: Ian Wilhelm, "Foundation Invites Poetry About National Debt," *Chronicle of Philanthropy,* November 11, 2009, http://philanthropy.com/blogs/giveandtake/foundation-invites-poetry-about-national-debt/10361.

58 AT A MAY 2011 "FISCAL SUMMIT": The 2011 Fiscal Summit: Solutions for America's Future, http://www.pgpf.org/FiscalSummit.aspx.

60 "I KNEW": Lori Montgomery, "Stumping for Attention to Deficit Disorder," *Washington Post,* June 21, 2007, http://www.washingtonpost.com/wp-dyn/content/article/2007/06/20/AR2007062002342.html.

61 "SEN. KENT CONRAD": Lori Montgomery, "Kent Conrad's Last Stand on Debt," *Washington Post,* March 16, 2012, http://www.washingtonpost.com/business/economy/kent-conrads-last-stand-on-debt/2012/03/08/gIQABudYGS_story.html.

61 HIS LAUDATORY ANALYSIS: James B. Stewart, "For All the Furor over Ryan's Plan, It's a Place to Start," *New York Times,* April 6, 2012, http://www.nytimes.com/2012/04/07/business/lots-of-accolades-but-little-action-on-budget-plan-common-sense.html?pagewanted=all.

62 "IF WE CONFRONT": See http://www.whitehouse.gov/assets/blog/Fiscal_Responsibility_Summit_Report.pdf.

63 "FAMILIES ACROSS THE COUNTRY": See http://www.huffingtonpost.com/
2010/01/27/state-of-the-union-2010-full-text-transcript_n_439459.html.

64 IN RECENT YEARS, BOWLES: See http://www.theracetothebottom.org/executive
-comp/2011/6/20/the-director-compensation-project-morgan-stanley.html.

65 THE ECONOMIC ADVISERS: Author's interviews.

66 AN EFFUSIVE WASHINGTON POST COLUMN: Steven Pearlstein, "CEOs and
Simpson-Bowles 3.0," *Washington Post*, July 21, 2012, http://www.washington
post.com/business/ceos-and-simpson-bowles-30/2012/07/20/gJQAMLfpoW
_story.html.

67 THE CONGRESSIONAL BUDGET OFFICE CALCULATED: Congressional Budget
Office, *Economic Effects of Reducing the Fiscal Restraint That Is Scheduled
to Occur in 2013* (May 2012), http:www.cbo.gov/sites/default/files/cbofiles/
attachments/FiscalRestraint_0.pdf.

67 IN HIS FIRST WEEKLY ADDRESS AFTER THE ELECTION: http://www
.whitehouse.gov/the-press-office/2012/11/09/weekly-address-extending
-middle-class-tax-cuts-grow-economy.

69 I PROPOSED THE FOLLOWING: Robert Kuttner, *Obama's Challenge: America's Economic Crisis and the Power of a Transformative Presidency* (White
River Junction, Vt.: Chelsea Green, 2008), 177–78.

71 BECAUSE OF THE LATER RETIREMENT AGE: See Alicia Munnell and Annika
Sunden, *Coming Up Short* (Washington, D.C.: Brookings Institution, 2004).

71 SEVENTY-FIVE-YEAR SHORTFALL: Congressional Budget Office, *CBO's Long-
Term Projections for Social Security: 2009 Update* (August 2009), http://www
.cbo.gov/ftpdocs/104xx/doc10457/08-07-SocialSecurity_Update.pdf.

71 THAT WAS INCREASED: Kathy A. Ruffing, "What the 2011 Trustees' Report
Shows About Social Security," Center on Budget and Policy Priorities, May 24,
2011, http://www.cbpp.org/files/5-24-11socsec.pdf.

4: A TALE OF TWO WARS

77 "IF GERMANY": Robert Skidelsky, *John Maynard Keynes,* vol. 1, *Hopes
Betrayed, 1883–1920* (New York: Elisabeth Sifton Books/Viking, 1986), 355.

77 IRONICALLY, THE MAN: Ibid., 175.

78 "MELT THE RESERVE": Ibid., 292.

80 "WE MUST NOT ALLOW": Margaret MacMillan, *Paris 1919: Six Months
That Changed the World* (New York: Random House, 2002), 163.

80 "OUR FIRST TASK": John Maynard Keynes, *The Economic Consequences of
the Peace* (Hamburg: Management Laboratory Press, 2009), 83.

80 "I DO NOT BELIEVE": Ibid., 82.

81 "THE GERMANS": Ibid., 85. Other writers have slightly different versions of
this quote.

81 "SHORTLY AFTER THEIR ARRIVAL": Ibid., 86.

81 GERMAN ANNUAL GDP: Liaquat Ahamed, *Lords of Finance: The Bankers
Who Broke the World* (New York: Penguin Press, 2009), 105

82 THE FRENCH FINANCE MINISTER: Skidelsky, *John Maynard Keynes,* 358.

83 "GERMAN DEMOCRACY": Keynes, *Economic Consequences,* 117.

83 "DEAR PRIME MINISTER": Skidelsky, *John Maynard Keynes,* 375.

83 "YOU CANNOT RESTORE": Keynes, *Economic Consequences,* 33.

84 "THERE CAN SELDOM": Ibid., 36.

84 THE FRENCH BUDGET WAS ABOUT $4.4 BILLION: Ibid., 141.

84 "SO LONG AS SUCH STATEMENTS": Ibid., 126.

84 "GERMANY WAS THE BEST CUSTOMER": Ibid., 22.

85 KEYNES TALLIED UP: Ibid., 101.

85 "BUSINESS LOSES ITS GENUINE CHARACTER": Ibid., 140.

85 "SPECULATORS MAY DO NO HARM": John Maynard Keynes, *The General Theory of Employment, Interest, and Money* (New York: Harcourt, 1964), 159.

85 "THE POLICY OF REDUCING": Keynes, *Economic Consequences*, 121.

86 ADDING TO THE IMPENDING: Amos Elon, *The Pity of It All: A History of the Jews in Germany, 1743–1933* (New York: Henry Holt/Picador, 2002), 356–57.

87 "THE DAMAGE TO GERMANY": Timothy W. Guinnane, "Financial *Vergangenheitsbewältigung:* The 1953 London Debt Agreement" (Center Discussion Paper 880, Economic Growth Center, Yale University, New Haven, Conn., 2004), 8, http://www.econ.yale.edu/growth_pdf/cdp880.pdf.

87 "THE REALLY PERNICIOUS EFFECT": Ahamed, *Lords of Finance*, 144.

88 AS THE ECONOMIC HISTORIAN: Charles P. Kindleberger, *The World in Depression: 1929–1939* (Berkeley: University of California Press, 1973), 28.

92 CHURCHILL WAS INITIALLY SUPPORTIVE: Alec Cairncross, *The Price of War* (London: Basil Blackwell, 1986), 55.

92 BUT THE STATE DEPARTMENT: Robert Skidelsky, *John Maynard Keynes: Fighting for Freedom* (New York: Viking, 2000), 362–65.

93 DIRECTIVE 1067 OF THE JOINT CHIEFS OF STAFF: Barry Eichengreen, *The European Economy Since 1945: Coordinated Capitalism and Beyond* (Princeton, N.J.: Princeton University Press, 2007), 57.

93 AT THE POTSDAM CONFERENCE: Hans-Joachim Braun, *The German Economy in the Twentieth Century* (London: Routledge, 1990), 148.

93 THIS IDEA WAS SUPPORTED: Alan S. Milward, *The Reconstruction of Western Europe, 1945–51* (London: Methuen, 1984), 28.

93 THE ALLIES AND THEIR TAXPAYERS: Tony Judt, *Postwar: A History of Europe Since 1945* (New York: Penguin Press, 2005), 123.

93 "IT SEEMS MONSTROUS": Cairncross, *The Price of War,* 100.

94 GERMAN LIVING STANDARDS: John Gimbel: *Origins of Marshall Plan* (Stanford, Calif.: Stanford University Press, 1976), 69.

94 THE SOVIETS, MEANWHILE, HAD REMOVED: Henry Ashby Turner Jr., *Germany from Partition to Reunification* (New Haven, Conn.: Yale University Press, 1992), 13.

94 860 CALORIES: Judt, *Postwar,* 21.

94 JAMES BYRNES GAVE A SPEECH: Braun, *German Economy,* 150.

95 AN EGG SOLD FOR: Eichengreen, *European Economy,* 62.

95 MANY AMERICAN GIS MADE: Judt, *Postwar,* 86.

95 THE MOST REMARKABLE ASPECT: André Piettre, *L'Économie Allemande Contemporaine (Allemagne Occidental), 1945–1952* (Paris: Editons M.-Th. Génin, Librarie de Médicis, 1952), 44, 191.

95 HITLER RAN UP A PUBLIC DEBT: James MacDonald, *A Free Nation Deep in Debt: The Financial Roots of Democracy* (Princeton, N.J.: Princeton University Press, 2006), 475.

96 THE HOLE IN THE RESERVES: Eichengreen, *European Economy,* 71.

96 "EUROPEAN INTEGRATION": Ibid., 69.

98 THE WEST GERMAN CHANCELLOR: Guinnane, "Financial *Vergangenheitsbe-wältigung*," 24–26.

98 WHAT OF THE REST: MacDonald, *Free Nation*, 458.

99 A QUARTER OF ITS TOTAL NATIONAL WEALTH: Richard N. Gardner, *Sterling-Dollar Diplomacy* (Oxford: Oxford University Press, 1956), 178.

99 "THE MOST UNSORDID ACT": Ibid., 170.

100 "THE UNITED STATES WANTS": Ibid., 171.

101 IN 1949, THE POUND WAS DEVALUED: MacDonald, *Free Nation*, 469.

5: EUROPEAN DISUNION

105 EUROPEAN CIVIL WAR: John Maynard Keynes, *The Economic Consequences of the Peace* (Hamburg: Management Laboratory Press, 2009), 16.

105 "THERE WILL BE NO PEACE": See http://www.historiasiglo20.org/europe/monnet.htm.

113–14 THEORY OF HEGEMONIC STABILITY: Charles P. Kindleberger, *The World in Depression: 1929–1939* (Berkeley: University of California Press, 1973). Kindleberger originated the concept, but it was formalized as a theory by later scholars drawing on his work.

114 "EXORBITANT PRIVILEGE": Barry Eichengreen, *Exorbitant Privilege: The Rise and Fall of the Dollar and the Future of the International Money System* (Oxford: Oxford University Press, 2011), 4.

114 "MR. BLAIR": Told to the author by an aide to Blair.

115 40 PERCENT MORE THAN THE EURO: David Bocking, "The High Price of Abandoning the Euro," *Spiegel Online*, November 29, 2011, http://www.spiegel.de/international/europe/preparing-for-the-worst-the-high-price-of-abandoning-the-euro-a-800700-3.html.

116 THE TRIFFIN DILEMMA: Robert Triffin, *Gold and the Dollar Crisis* (New Haven, Conn.: Yale University Press, 1960).

118 A CONVERSATION CAUGHT: Nixon Presidential Library, Watergate Tapes, June 23, 1972, http://www.nixonlibrary.gov/forresearchers/find/tapes/watergate/wspf/741-002.pdf.

120 "YOU WILL NOT STOP": David Marsh, *The Euro: The Politics of the New Global Currency* (New Haven, Conn.: Yale University Press, 2009), 137.

121 A POLITICAL MODEL NOT EASILY TRANSPLANTED: See Robert Kuttner, "The Copenhagen Consensus," *Foreign Affairs*, March–April 2008, 78–94.

124 FULLY 61 PERCENT: Wiemer Salverda, Maarten van Klaveren, and Marc van der Meer, *Low Wage Work in the Netherlands* (New York: The Russell Sage Foundation, 2008), 14.

125 "I SUCCEEDED": To the author.

126 "SOCIETY OF INSIDERS AND OUTSIDERS": Bruno Palier, *A Long Goodbye to Bismarck* (Amsterdam: University of Amsterdam Press, 2011).

127 ONE RECENT DECISION: Andreas Bücker and Wiebke Warneck, *Viking–Laval–Rüffert: Consequences and Policy Perspectives* (Brussels: European Trade Union Institute, 2010), http://www.etui.org/Publications2/Reports/Viking-Laval-Rueffert-consequences-and-policy-perspectives.

129 THE DEMOCRATIC STATE: A good discussion of this paradox is Colin Crouch, *The Strange Non-Death of Neo-Liberalism* (London: Polity Press, 2012).

129 "CERTAIN ECONOMIC POWERS": Friedrich A. Hayek, "The Economic Conditions of Interstate Federalism," in *Individual and Economic Order* (Chicago: University of Chicago Press, 1948), 255–72.

131 IN THE INITIAL ROUND OF MASSIVE INTERVENTION: "Measures Designed to Address Elevated Pressures in Short-Term Funding Markets," press release, December 12, 2007, http://www.ecb.int/press/pr/date/2007/html/pr071212 .en.html.

132 "WE WERE THE FIRST": Jean-Claude Trichet, "Supporting the Financial System and the Economy" (speech at a conference organized by the Nueva Economía Fórum and *Wall Street Journal Europe,* Madrid, June 22, 2009, http://www.ecb.int/press/key/date/2009/html/sp090622.en.html).

132 AT THE G-20 SUMMIT: London Summit Leaders' Statement, http://www.imf .org/external/np/sec/pr/2009/pdf/g20_040209.pdf.

133 A SPECIAL SERIES: Nicholas Dunbar and Elisa Martinuzzi, "Goldman Secret Greece Loan Shows Two Sinners as Client Unravels," Bloomberg News, March 6, 2012, http://www.bloomberg.com/news/2012-03-06/goldman-secret -greece-loan-shows-two-sinners-as-client-unravels.html.

6: A GREEK TRAGEDY

138 THE GOVERNMENT DEFAULTED: Carmen M. Reinhart and Kenneth S. Rogoff, *This Time Is Different: Eight Centuries of Financial Folly* (Princeton, N.J.: Princeton University Press, 2009), 12–13.

141 4 TO 5 PERCENT OF GERMAN GDP: Jennifer Hunt, "The Economics of German Reunification" (McGill University, 2006), http://www.rci.rutgers.edu/ ~jah357/Hunt/Transition_files/german_unification.pdf.

141 HARTZ REFORMS: Jochen Kluve and Lena Jacobi, "Before and After the Hartz Reforms," IDEAS, http://ideas.repec.org/p/rwi/dpaper/0041.html.

142 MERKEL'S DOMESTIC PRIORITY: "Tie Your Hands, Please: Is Germany's Fiscal Straitjacket an Example for Others?" *Economist,* December 10, 2011, http://www.economist.com/node/21541459.

142 HER VEHICLE: See http://en.wikisource.org/wiki/Treaty_on_Stability, _Coordination_and_Governance_in_the_Economic_and_Monetary_Union.

142 THE MACROECONOMIC IMBALANCE PROCEDURE: See http://europa.eu/ rapid/pressReleasesAction.do?reference=MEMO/12/388.

143 A NEOLIBERAL HAMMER: See http://ec.europa.eu/economy_finance/economic _governance/macroeconomic_imbalance_procedure/index_en.htm.

143 A DETAILED REPORT WARNING: European Commission, "Macroeconomic Imbalances—France," July 2012, http://ec.europa.eu/economy_finance/ publications/occasional_paper/2012/pdf/ocp105_en.pdf.

143 "THOUSANDS OF FINANCIAL TRADERS": Helmut Schmidt, "Germany in and with and for Europe" (speech to SPD, December 4, 2011, http://library .fes.de/pdf-files/id/ipa/08888.pdf).

143 HE ALSO PLEDGED THAT FRANCE: William Horobin, "France Pledges to Meet Deficit Goals Despite Ailing Growth," *Wall Street Journal,* June 14, 2012, http:// online.wsj.com/article/SB10001424052702303734204577466100245388694 .html.

144 THE IFO INSTITUTE IN MUNICH PUTS: IFO Institute and Leibniz Institute for Economic Research at the University of Munich, "The Exposure Level,"

July 10, 2012, http://www.cesifo-group.de/ifoHome/policy/Haftungspegel
.html.

145 MEETING WITH EUROPEAN LEADERS: Terence Roth and Brian Blackstone,
"Trichet Pegs Euro's Future to Tighter Fiscal Management," *Wall Street Journal,* May 16, 2010, http://online.wsj.com/article/SB1000142405274870461
42045752461917460291 22.html.

145 TOTALED €750 BILLION: Council of the European Union, press release 9596/
10, May 9–10, 2010, http://www.consilium.europa.eu/uedocs/cms_data/docs/
pressdata/en/ecofin/114324.pdf.

146 THE GERMAN PRESS: German press characterizations quoted in Wolfgang
Priossi, *Why Germany Fell Out of Love with Europe* (Brussels: Bruegel Institute, 2010), 32.

146 IN EXCHANGE FOR THE RESCUE: International Monetary Fund, "Greece:
Request for Stand-by Agreement" (IMF Country Report, Washington, D.C.,
May 2010), http://www.imf.org/external/pubs/ft/scr/2010/cr10111.pdf.

146 "WE WANT TO MAKE SURE": Marcus Walker, "How a Radical Greek Rescue
Plan Fell Short," *Wall Street Journal,* May 10, 2012, http://online.wsj.com/
article/SB10001424052702304203604577393964198652568.html.

147 POSITIVE GDP GROWTH OF 1.1 PERCENT: European Commission, *The Economic Adjustment Programme for Greece,* May 2010, http://ec.europa.eu/
economy_finance/publications/occasional_paper/2010/pdf/ocp61_en.pdf.

149 "THERE WAS NO ECONOMIC LOGIC": Author's interview.

149 "PRIVATE SECTOR INITIATIVE": "Merkel, Sarkozy Back 'Voluntary' Private-
Sector Involvement in Greek Rescue," *EU Observer,* June 17, 2011, http://
euobserver.com/economic/32507.

150 A SHOUTING MATCH: Charles Forelle, David Gauthier-Villars, Brian Blackstone, and David Enrich, "As Ireland Flails, Europe Lurches Across the Rubi-
con," *Wall Street Journal,* December 27, 2010, http://online.wsj.com/article/
SB10001424052748703814804576035682984688312.html.

151 "THE FAR-REACHING AND AMBITIOUS": European Commission, *The Economic Adjustment Programme for Portugal,* December 2011, http://ec.europa
.eu/economy_finance/publications/occasional_paper/2012/pdf/ocp95_en.pdf.

152 IN A KEYNOTE SPEECH: See http://www.conservatives.com/News/Speeches/
2009/04/The_age_of_austerity_speech_to_the_2009_Spring_Forum.aspx.

152 "TRIPLE-DIP" RECESSION: Institute for Public Policy Research, "Economic update—December 2012: Triple-dip Ahead?" http://www.ippr.org/
articles/56/10049/economic-update--december-2012-triple-dip-ahead.

153 THE BIG BANKS HAD CREATED: Gillian Tett, *Fool's Gold* (New York: Free
Press, 2009), 26.

154 EVEN DEEPER AUSTERITY: "Europe Slashes Greek Debt by 50 Percent," *Spiegel
Online,* October 27, 2011, http://www.spiegel.de/international/europe/agreement
-in-brussels-europe-slashes-greek-debt-by-50-percent-a-794278.html.

155 UNLESS GREECE MET: Stephen Brown and Noah Barkin, "Merkel, Sarkozy
Press for Quick Greek Solution," Reuters, January 9, 2012, http://www
.reuters.com/article/2012/01/09/us-eurozone-idUSTRE80809C20120109.

156 DART GOT PAID: Landon Thomas Jr., "Bet on Greek Bonds Paid Off for
'Vulture Fund,' " *New York Times,* May 15, 2012, http://www.nytimes.com/
2012/05/16/business/global/bet-on-greek-bonds-paid-off-for-vulture-fund
.html.

157 "WILL BE IMPOSED": Jonathan House, Matina Stevis, and Gabriele Stein-

hauser, "Spain to Request EU Aid for Banks," *Wall Street Journal,* June 9, 2012, http://online.wsj.com/article/SB10001424052702303753904577456044240154190.html.

158 MARIO MONTI OF ITALY: Mario Monti, remarks to the Foundation for European Progressive Studies conference, Rome, May 3, 2012.

159 "THE MOST GERMAN": Nikolaus Blome, "So Deutsch Ist der Neue EZB-Chef," *Bild,* April 29, 2011, http://www.bild.de/geld/wirtschaft/mario-draghi/ist-neuer-ezb-chef-17630794.bild.html.

159 DRAGHI WAS ALSO WILLING: Martin Neal Baily and Natalie McGarry, "European Macroeconomic Policy," in *Europe's Economic Crisis,* ed. Robert M. Solow and Dennis S. Hamilton (Baltimore: Johns Hopkins University Cournot Center, 2011), 17.

159 "WE REMAIN ENTIRELY": "Politicians Demand Delay in German Bailout Vote," *Spiegel Online,* June 29, 2012, http://www.spiegel.de/international/germany/angry-politicians-call-for-delay-in-euro-vote-a-841769.html.

160 "WHATEVER IT TAKES": James Wilson, Robin Wigglesworth, and Brian Groom, "ECB 'Ready to Do Whatever It Takes,'" *Financial Times,* July 26, 2012, http://www.ft.com/cms/s/0/6ce6b2c2-d713-11e1-8e7d-00144feabdco.html.

160 DRAGHI WALKED IT ALL BACK: Transcript of Draghi press conference, August 2, 2012, http://www.ecb.int/press/pressconf/2012/html/is120802.en.html.

161 "REGARDS SUCH [BOND] PURCHASES": "Weidmann Isolated as ECB Plan Is Approved," *Financial Times,* September 7, 2012.

161 IN OCTOBER 2012: Alain Minc, "An Open Letter to My Friends, the Financiers of America," *The New York Review of Books,* October 25, 2012, 23–24.

162 BERNANKE WAS GIVING: Ben S. Bernanke, "Monetary Policy Since the Onset of the Crisis" (speech at the Federal Reserve Bank of Kansas City Economic Symposium, Jackson Hole, Wyo., August 31, 2012, http://www.federalreserve.gov/newsevents/speech/bernanke20120831a.htm).

162 THEY PROJECTED GREEK GDP: Charles Forelle and Marcus Walker, "Fixing Greek Debt Remains Elusive Euro-Zone Target," *The Wall Street Journal,* November 2, 2012.

162 ALL WERE SUMMARILY REJECTED: Matthew Dalton and Costas Paris, "IMF Pushes Europe to Ease Greek Burden," *Wall Street Journal,* August 6, 2012, http://online.wsj.com/article/SB10000872396390443517104577573302911904824.html?mod=googlenews_wsj.

163 BETWEEN 2008 AND 2012: "Convergence in Reverse," *Financial Times,* September 4, 2012.

163 "HOME BIAS": European Central Bank Frankfurt, "Changes in Bank Financing Patterns," April 2012.

163 MUCH OF THE MONEY ADVANCED TO EUROPE'S COMMERCIAL BANKS: David Enrich, "Large European Banks Stash Cash," *Wall Street Journal,* November 13, 2012.

164 DELIVERED A KEYNOTE SPEECH: Helmut Schmidt, "Germany in and with and for Europe."

165 "IF DEMOCRACY HAS BEEN": See http://artgoldhammer.blogspot.com/2012/08/amartya-sen-considers-europe-question.html.

166 MOREOVER, UNLIKE EUROPE: "The Red and the Black: America's Fiscal Union," *Economist,* August 1, 2011, http://www.economist.com/blogs/dailychart/2011/08/americas-fiscal-union.

167 "IF YOU WAIT": Council on Foreign Relations, "A Conversation with Timothy F. Geithner," transcript, June 13, 2012, http://www.cfr.org/economics/conversation-timothy-f-geithner/p28509?cid=rss-americas-a_conversation_with_timothy_f.-m061312.

7: THE MORAL ECONOMY OF DEBT

174 IN HIS CELEBRATED WORK: See http://files.libertyfund.org/files/846/Mandeville_0014-01_EBk_v6.0.pdf.

174 "THE POOR-LAWS WERE INTENDED": Quoted in Albert O. Hirschman, *The Rhetoric of Reaction: Perversity, Futility, Jeopardy* (Cambridge, Mass.: The Belknap Press of Harvard University, 1991), p. 29.

174 "WE TRIED TO PROVIDE": Charles Murray, *Losing Ground: American Social Policy, 1950–1980* (New York: Basic Books, 1984), 9.

174 "MOST EVIDENTLY CALLED": Quoted in Bruce Mann, *Republic of Debtors: Bankruptcy in the Age of American Independence* (Cambridge, Mass.: Harvard University Press, 2002), 40.

175 "AN EXCHANGE": David Graeber, *Debt: The First 5,000 Years* (Brooklyn, N.Y.: Melville House Publishing), 121.

176 "THE AFFAIRS OF THIS DEBTOR": Charles Dickens, *Little Dorrit* (New York: Penguin Classics, 2003, 1857), 75.

177 BETWEEN JUNE 1775 AND NOVEMBER 1779: John Kenneth Galbraith, *Money: Whence It Came, Where It Went* (Boston: Houghton Mifflin, 1975), 58.

178 WITH THE COLLAPSE IN MARCH 1792: Steve Fraser, *Every Man a Speculator: A History of Wall Street in American Life* (New York: HarperCollins, 2005), 5–7; Mann, *Republic of Debtors,* 101–4, 202–3; and Scott Nelson, *A Nation of Deadbeats: An Uncommon History of America's Financial Disasters* (New York: Alfred A. Knopf, 2012).

178 ONLY RHODE ISLAND: Mann, *Republic of Debtors,* 60.

178 "GO INTO THE COUNTRY": Quoted in ibid., 209.

179 SOUTHERN AGRARIANS: Ibid., 218.

179 "WE SAW RICH MEN": Charles Warren, *Bankruptcy in United States History* (Washington, D.C.: Beard Books, 1999), 20.

179 THE LAW WAS REPEALED: Nelson, *A Nation of Deadbeats,* 57.

179 SOME THIRTY-THREE THOUSAND DEBTORS: Edward J. Balleisen, *Navigating Failure: Bankruptcy and Commercial Society in Antebellum America* (Chapel Hill: University of North Carolina Press, 2001), 124.

180 100 PERCENT OF DEBTORS' WAGES: Catherine S. M. Duggan and Alexander F. Roehrkasse, "Negotiating Trust: Borrowers, Lenders, and the Politics of Household Debt" (Harvard Business School Paper N-9-710-048, February 24, 2010).

181 AS THE NATION GREW: Stephen Mihm, *A Nation of Counterfeiters: Capitalists, Con Men, and the Making of the United States* (Cambridge, Mass.: Harvard University Press, 2007), 3.

181 "MANUFACTURERS AND URBAN IMPORTERS": Balleisen, *Navigating Failure,* 31.

182 "THE FUNCTION OF CREDIT": Galbraith, *Money,* 71.

184 THOUGH THE CHARTER: Bray Hammond, *Banks and Politics in America* (Princeton, N.J.: Princeton University Press, 1957), 118.

184 WHEN $8 MILLION: Ibid., 123.

185 "TO PURIFY THE CURRENCY": Mihm, *A Nation of Counterfeiters*, 128.

186 "THE MERCHANT BORROWED": Hammond, *Banks*, 32–33.

186 "BANKS SEEMED TO VIOLATE": Irwin Unger, *The Greenback Era* (Princeton, N.J.: Princeton University Press, 1964), 32.

188 BY 1880, FEDERAL AND STATE GOVERNMENTS: Fraser, *Every Man a Speculator*, 118.

188 JUDICIAL RECEIVERSHIP BEGAN: David A. Skeel Jr., *Debt's Dominion* (Princeton, N.J.: Princeton University Press, 2001), 57.

188 BETWEEN 1872 AND 1894: Ibid., 53.

189 ULYSSES S. GRANT PLEDGED: James MacDonald, *A Free Nation Deep in Debt: The Financial Roots of Democracy* (Princeton, N.J.: Princeton University Press, 2006), 395.

189 "EVERYWHERE THE FARMER TURNED": Lawrence Goodwyn, *Democratic Promise: The Populist Moment in America* (New York: Oxford University Press, 1976), 116.

190 "WE CAN PURCHASE": Ibid., 43.

190 AS NEWS OF THESE ECONOMIC VICTORIES: Ibid., 91.

191 MACUNE'S DESIGN: Elizabeth Sanders, *Roots of Reform: Farmers, Workers, and the American State, 1877–1917* (Chicago: University of Chicago Press, 1999), 242–51.

192 "THE TWO STREAMS": Norbert Wiley, "America's Unique Class Politics," *American Sociological Review* 33 (August 1967): 534.

193 IN THE THREE DECADES: Fraser, *Every Man a Speculator*, 161–62.

194 THE PERCENTAGE OF FARMERS: Goodwyn, *Democratic Promise*, 544.

194 248 BANKS WOULD FAIL: Galbraith, *Money*, 111.

194 CLUB OF NEW YORK BANKERS: Fraser, *Every Man a Speculator*, 181.

195 MORGAN ASSEMBLED A TASK FORCE: Ron Chernow, *The House of Morgan: An American Banking Dynasty and the Rise of Modern Finance* (New York: Atlantic Monthly Press, 1990), 127.

195 WHEN THIS IDEA: Sanders, *Roots of Reform*, 233–44.

196 IT WOULD BE THE TRUE CENTRAL BANK: See discussion in Sanders, *Roots of Reform*, 240–44; William Greider, *Secrets of the Temple: How the Federal Reserve Runs the Country* (New York: Simon and Schuster, 1987), 268–82; and Gabriel A. Kolko, *The Triumph of Conservatism* (New York: Free Press of Glencoe, 1963), 217–54.

197 "IT SEEMS A SHAME": Liaquat Ahamed, *Lords of Finance: The Bankers Who Broke the World* (New York: Penguin Press, 2009), 277.

198 AS PERSONAL BANKRUPTCY FILINGS: Skeel, *Debt's Dominion*, 137.

199 FILINGS INCREASED BY ABOUT 50 PERCENT: Duggan and Roehrkasse, "Negotiating Trust."

200 BAIN CAPITAL: Josh Kosman, *The Buyout of America: How Private Equity Will Cause the Next Great Credit Crisis* (New York: Portfolio, 2009), 107.

201 A TRADITIONAL PENSION PLAN TYPICALLY COSTS: Fran Hawthorne, *Pension Dumping* (New York: Bloomberg Press, 2008), 28.

202 THE NOMINAL SURPLUSES WERE PRODIGIOUS: Ellen E. Schultz, *Retirement Heist: How Companies Plunder and Profit from the Nest Eggs of American Workers* (New York: Penguin, 2011), 9.

202 GE SOLD ONE OF ITS AEROSPACE UNITS: Ibid., 16–17.

203 PBGC'S OWN FINANCIAL HEALTH: Hawthorne, xvii.

205 TESTIFYING BEFORE: Elizabeth Warren, Testimony before the Senate Judiciary Committee, February 10, 2005, http://www.judiciary.senate.gov/hearings/ testimony.cfm?id=e655f9e2809e5476862f735da100f836&wit_id=e655f9 e2809e5476862f735da100f836-1-7.

206 "REWARDS THOSE WHO ARE": Republican Study Committee, Legislative Bulletin, February 25, 2009, http://rsc.jordan.house.gov/UploadedFiles/LB _022509_Homes.pdf.

8: A HOME OF ONE'S OWN

207 "THE SMALL LANDHOLDERS": Benjamin Horace Hibbard, *A History of the Public Land Policies* (Madison: University of Wisconsin Press, 1965), 143.

208 "TENANTRY IS UNFAVORABLE": Erika Doss, *Benton, Pollock, and the Politics of Modernism: From Regionalism to Abstract Expressionism* (Chicago: University of Chicago Press, 1991), 20.

208 HOMEOWNERSHIP, DEPRESSED IN THE 1930S: U.S. Department of Commence, Bureau of the Census, Historical Census of Housing Tables, http:// www.census.gov/hhes/www/housing/census/historic/owner.html.

209 THE NOBEL LAUREATE: James Meade, *Efficiency, Equality and the Ownership of Property* (London: Routledge, 1964).

210 PROHIBITIONS AGAINST LARGE AGGREGATIONS: Milton Conover, *The General Land Office: Its Histories, Activities and Organization* (Baltimore: Johns Hopkins University Press, 1926), 9.

210 "LITTLE REPUBLICS": Hibbard, *History*, 36.

210 "PLANTED IN THE EAST": Roger G. Kennedy, *Mr. Jefferson's Lost Cause: Land, Farmers, Slavery, and the Louisiana Purchase* (New York: Oxford University Press, 2003), 64

211 ARTICLES OF CONFEDERATION: Frank Bourgin, *The Great Challenge: The Myth of Laissez-Faire in the Early Republic* (New York: George Braziller, 1989), 110.

211 822,900 ACRES: Conover, *The General Land Office*, 143.

211 "TO PREVENT LARGE SCALE SPECULATORS": Ibid., 15.

211 "HOW MUCH BETTER": Kennedy, *Mr. Jefferson's Lost Cause*, epigraph, ii.

212 ENTERED THE UNION AS SLAVE STATES: Ibid., 26–27.

212 POLITICALLY CONNECTED LAND SPECULATORS: Scott Nelson, *A Nation of Deadbeats: An Uncommon History of America's Financial Disasters* (New York: Alfred A. Knopf, 2012), 69–70.

212 IT PLACED NO LIMITS: Conover, *The General Land Office*, 20.

212 SOME 20 PERCENT OF THE LAND: Nelson, *A Nation of Deadbeats*, 70.

212 AFTER HE FINISHED: Thomas Ewing, "Lincoln and the General Land Office, 1849," *Journal of the Illinois State Historical Society* 25, no. 3 (October 1932): 139–53.

213 "A PLOT": Richard M. Valelly, *The Two Reconstructions: The Struggle for Black Enfranchisement* (Chicago: University of Chicago Press, 2004), 25.

213 FORMER SLAVES WHO WORKED THE LAND: James M. McPherson, *The Negro's Civil War* (New York: Vintage Books, 1993), 303–4.

213 "IRONCLAD TEST OATH": Valelly, *The Two Reconstructions*, 26.

213 FORCE SOME FORTY THOUSAND FREEDMEN: McPherson, *The Negro's Civil War*, 304.

214 THE CROP-LIEN SYSTEM: Lawrence Goodwyn, *Democratic Promise: The Populist Moment in America* (New York: Oxford University Press, 1976), 26–27.

214 "THE NEW SYSTEM": Harold D. Woodman, *New South, New Law: The Legal Foundations of Credit and Labor Relations in the Postbellum Agricultural South* (Baton Rouge: Louisiana State University Press, 1995), 93. For a general discussion of how the Civil War changed the cotton production and marketing system, see also Woodman's *King Cotton and His Retainers: Financing and Marketing the Cotton Crop of the South, 1800–1925* (Lexington: University of Kentucky Press, 1968).

214 "HE OWNED": William Faulkner, *The Hamlet* (New York: Random House, 1994), 30.

215 IN APPLING V. ODOM: The *Appling* case and the changes in law and custom that it represented are treated at length in Jonathan M. Bryant, *How Curious a Land: Conflict and Change in Greene County, Georgia, 1850–1855* (Chapel Hill: University of North Carolina Press, 1996), 147–82.

215 BY 1880, 36 PERCENT: Woodman, *King Cotton*, 313.

215 COTTON FELL: Goodwyn, *Democratic Promise*, 38.

215 CORN FOLLOWED: Ibid., 114.

215 BUT IN THE YEARS: John L. Shover, *Cornbelt Rebellion: The Farmers' Holiday Association* (Urbana: University of Illinois Press, 1965), 12.

216 IN 1932 ALONE: Ibid., 78.

216 BUT IN A LANDMARK RULING: Richard M. Valelly, *Radicalism in the States: The Minnesota Farmer-Labor Party and the American Political Economy* (Chicago: University of Chicago Press, 1989), 92–93.

217 THE HOLC SOLD: Dan Immergluck, *Foreclosed: High-Risk Lending, Deregulation, and the Undermining of America's Mortgage Market* (Ithaca, N.Y.: Cornell University Press, 2009), 30; see also Alex F. Schwartz, *Housing Policy in the United States: An Introduction* (New York: Routledge, 2006), 53–54.

217 RETURNED A SMALL PROFIT: Pollock, "Crisis Intervention."

218 HOMEOWNERSHIP RATES: U.S. Department of Commerce, Historical Census of Housing Tables.

220 THE S&L DISASTER: William K. Black, *The Best Way to Rob a Bank Is to Own One: How Corporate Executives and Politicians Looted the S&L Industry* (Austin: University of Texas Press, 2005).

221 "THE HOMEOWNER DIDN'T KNOW IT": Michael Lewis, *Liar's Poker* (New York: Coronet Books, 1989), 163.

222 THE NATIONAL RATE OF HOMEOWNERSHIP: U.S. Department of Commerce, Historical Census of Housing Tables.

223 IN ONE CASE STUDY: *The Financial Crisis Inquiry Report: Final Report of the National Commission on the Causes of the Financial and Economic Crisis in the United States* (New York: Public Affairs, 2011), 91.

226 THE TREASURY MODIFIED THE FORMULA: Neil Barofsky, *Bailout: An Inside Account of How Washington Abandoned Main Street While Rescuing Wall Street* (New York: Free Press, 2012), 134.

226 ONLY ABOUT SEVENTY THOUSAND: Ibid., 194.

226 AN AUGUST 2010 SURVEY: Paul Kiel and Olga Pierce, "Homeowner

Questionnaire Shows Banks Violating Gov't Program Rules," ProPublica, August 16, 2010, http://www.propublica.org/article/homeowner-questionnaire-shows-banks-violating-govt-program-rules.

227 IN OCTOBER 2010: U.S. Department of the Treasury, *Troubled Asset Relief Program: Two-Year Retrospective* (Washington, D.C.: Government Printing Office, 2010), 75.

227 ONLY 646 HOMEOWNERS: Barofsky, *Bailout*, 196.

227 IN 2012, THE ADMINISTRATION: Edward J. DeMarco, letter to Congress on the use of principal forgiveness by Fannie Mae and Freddie Mac, FHFA, July 31, 2012, http://www.fhfa.gov/webfiles/24110/PF_LettertoCong73112.pdf.

227 ACCORDING TO THE TREASURY'S: *Financial Crisis Inquiry Report,* 402–5.

228 FEES BECAME EVER MORE: Peter Eavis, "With Rates Low, Banks Increase Mortgage Profit," *New York Times,* August 8, 2012, http://dealbook.nytimes.com/2012/08/08/with-rate-twist-banks-increase-mortgage-profit/.

229 ONE SUCH EMPLOYEE: Deposition of Jeffrey Stephan, http://4closurefraud.org/2010/03/22/full-deposition-of-jeffrey-stephan-gmacs-assignment-affidavit-slave-10000-documents-a-month/.

230 A BANKRUPTCY COURT IN NEW YORK: *Financial Crisis Inquiry Report,* 407.

231 SEVERAL LEGAL SCHOLARS PROPOSED: "Jackson Says the Treasury's Bailout Plan Should Target Bad Loans, Not Burned Investors," *Harvard Law School News,* September 25, 2008, http://www.law.harvard.edu/news/2008/09/25_jackson.html.

234 "SOUGHT TO INCREASE": *Financial Crisis Inquiry Report,* 444, 445.

235 A RESEARCH STUDY BY THE FEDERAL RESERVE: Glenn Canner and Neil Bhutta, "Staff Analysis of the Relationship between the CRA and the Subprime Crisis" (memo of the Board of Governors of the Federal Reserve System, Washington, D.C., November 21, 2008,. http://www.federalreserve.gov/newsevents/speech/20081203_analysis.pdf).

235 STUDIES OF ONE SUCH MODEL INSTITUTION: Alyssa Katz, "A Needless Housing Collapse," *The American Prospect,* May 2011, http://prospect.org/article/needless-housing-collapse.

236 BLACK HOMEOWNERSHIP PEAKED: "Wealth Gaps Rise to Record Highs Between Whites, Blacks, and Hispanics," Pew Research Center, July 26, 2011, http://www.pewsocialtrends.org/2011/07/26/wealth-gaps-rise-to-record-highs-between-whites-blacks-hispanics/.

236 AMONG BLACK AND LATINO: "The Changing Face of Homeownership in Large Metro Areas," Diversitydata.org, May 2012, http://diversitydata.sph.harvard.edu/Publications/Homeownership_brief_final.pdf.

236 BETWEEN 1984 AND THE BOOM YEAR: "Wealth Gaps Rise."

237 SHOREBANK APPLIED FOR: James E. Post and Fiona S. Wilson, "Too Good to Fail," *Stanford Social Innovation Review,* Fall 2011, http://www.ssireview.org/images/articles/Fall_2011_Case_Study_Too_Good_to_Fail.pdf.

9: THE THIRD WORLD'S REVENGE

238 "KEYNES WOULD BE ROLLING OVER": Joseph Stiglitz, *Globalization and Its Discontents* (New York: W. W. Norton and Company, 2002), 13.

238 WASHINGTON CONSENSUS: The term "Washington Consensus" was coined

in 1989 by John Williamson of the Peterson Institute for International Economics.

239 TAIWAN, GENERALLY CONSIDERED: Dan Breznitz, *Innovation and the State: Political Choice and Strategies for Growth in Israel, Taiwan, and Ireland* (New Haven, Conn.: Yale University Press, 2007).

239 THE WORLD'S FASTEST-GROWING ECONOMIES: Stiglitz, *Globalization and Its Discontents*, 91.

240 IN 1817, A SCOTTISH ADVENTURER: David Sinclair, *The Land That Never Was: Sir Gregor MacGregor and the Most Audacious Fraud in History* (Cambridge, Mass.: Da Capo Press, 2004).

240-41 A SPECULATIVE OVERSEAS INVESTMENT FRENZY: Carlos Marichal, *A Century of Debt Crises in Latin America: From Independence to the Great Depression, 1820–1930* (Princeton, N.J.: Princeton University Press), 13–14.

241 "CALLED THE NEW WORLD": George Canning's Address on the King's Message Respecting Portugal, *Hansard*, XVI [N.S.], 390–98, 1826, http://www.historyhome.co.uk/polspeech/portugal.htm.

241 VIOLATED THE BANK OF ENGLAND'S: Sinclair, *The Land That Never Was*, 59–61.

241 THE NEW BRAZILIAN MINING COMPANY: Carlos Marichal, *Century*, 24.

241 GRAN COLOMBIA AND CHILE: Federico Sturzenegger and Jeromin Zettelmeyer, *Debt Defaults and Lessons from a Decade of Crises* (Cambridge, Mass.: MIT Press, 2006), 7–8.

241 INTEREST AND DIVIDENDS HAD BEEN PAID: Edward Chancellor, *Devil Take the Hindmost: A History of Financial Speculation* (New York: Farrar, Straus and Giroux, 1999), 116.

241-42 VENEZUELA SET THE RECORD: Carmen M. Reinhart and Kenneth S. Rogoff, *This Time Is Different: Eight Centuries of Financial Folly* (Princeton, N.J.: Princeton University Press, 2009), 91.

242 THE NEXT GREAT FOREIGN LENDING BONANZA: Marichal, *Century*, 96.

242 THE PRACTICE OF CREDITORS' CARTELS: Sturzenegger and Zettelmeyer, *Debt Defaults*, 11–13.

242 IT TOOK UNTIL 1872: Marichal, *Century*, 59.

242 NEGOTIATED RESTRUCTURINGS REDUCED: Sturzenegger and Zettelmeyer, *Debt Defaults*, 12.

242 ONE SCHOLARLY REVIEW: Christian Suter, *Debt Cycles in the World Economy: Foreign Loans, Financial Crises, and Debt Settlements, 1820–1990* (Boulder, Colo.: Westview Press, 1992).

243 AGREEMENTS BETWEEN THE BRITISH: Sturzenegger and Zettelmeyer, *Debt Defaults*, 15–16.

243 A STUDY OF DEFAULTS: Erika Jorgensen and Jeffrey Sachs, "Default and Renegotiation of Latin American Foreign Bonds in the Interwar Period," in *International Debt Crises in Historical Perspective*, ed. Barry Eichengreen and Peter H. Lindert (Cambridge, Mass.: MIT Press, 1989), 48–83.

244 "THE WHOLE MANAGEMENT": John Maynard Keynes, "National Self-Sufficiency," *Yale Review*, June 1933.

244 "NOT MERELY": Quoted in Rawi Abdelal, *Capital Rules: The Construction of Global Finance* (Cambridge, Mass.: Harvard University Press, 2007), 7.

245 DAILY FOREIGN EXCHANGE TRANSACTIONS: Ibid., 2.

246 "IT IS TIME": Paul Blustein, *The Chastening: Inside the Crisis That Rocked*

the Global Financial System and Humbled the IMF (New York: Public Affairs, 2001), 49.

246 EVEN IN THE UNITED STATES: Joseph E. Stiglitz, *The Roaring Nineties: A New History of the World's Most Prosperous Decade* (New York: W. W. Norton, 2003), 222.

248 BY 1978, OPEC NATIONS: FDIC, "An Examination of the Banking Crises of the 1980s and Early 1990s" (undated), 192.

248 AS LATE AS THE 1970S: Manuel Pastor Jr., "Latin America, the Debt Crisis, and the International Monetary Fund," *Latin American Perspectives* 16, no. 1 (Winter 1989): 96.

249 IN 1970, LATIN AMERICA'S TOTAL FOREIGN DEBT: FDIC, "Examination," 198.

249 "COUNTRIES DON'T GO OUT OF BUSINESS": IMF, "Debt and Transition," https://www.imf.org/external/np/exr/center/mm/eng/mm_dt_01.htm.

249 AT LEAST 250: Reinhart and Rogoff, *This Time Is Different*, 34.

250 FROM 1975 TO 1977: Pastor, "Latin America," 89.

251 FOREIGN CAPITAL PROVISION: Ibid., 94.

251 ON AUGUST 12, 1982: FDIC, "Examination," 193.

251 263.9 PERCENT OF THE BANKS: Ibid., 197.

252 THE MUCH-LAUDED BRADY PLAN: John C. Clarke, "Debt Reduction and Market Reentry Under the Brady Plan," *FRBNY Quarterly Review* (Winter 1993–94): 38–62.

253 BY THE EVE OF THE CRISIS: Mark Weisbrot, "Ten Years After: The Lasting Impact of the East Asia Crisis," Center for Economic and Policy Research, 2007, http://www.cepr.net/documents/publications/asia_crisis_2007_08.pdf.

254 "TOOK THEIR COLLEAGUES": Blustein, *The Chastening*, 82.

255 THE IMF THREW TOGETHER: Ibid., 85.

256 "IN INDONESIA": David E. Sanger, "IMF Reports Plan Backfired, Worsening Indonesia Woes," *New York Times*, January 14, 1998.

256 AN ECONOMY LIKE SOUTH KOREA'S: Alice H. Amsden, *Asia's Next Giant: South Korea and Late Industrialization* (New York: Oxford University Press, 1989).

258 "IN A SENSE": Blustein, *The Chastening*, 202.

258 BUT THE LOSSES: See http://www.adb.org/publications/key-indicators-asia-and-pacific-2012.

258 ANNUAL PER CAPITA INCOME GROWTH: Janet L. Yellen, "The Asian Financial Crisis Ten Years Later: Assessing the Past and Looking to the Future" (speech to the Asia Society of Southern California, Los Angeles, February 6, 2007, http://www.frbsf.org/news/speeches/2007/0206.htmlhttp://www.adb.org/publications/key-indicators-asia-and-pacific-2012).

259 FOREIGN EXCHANGE HOLDINGS: Ibid.

259 BY 2007 TOTALED AROUND $500 BILLION: Weisbrot, "Ten Years After," http://www.cepr.net/documents/publications/asia_crisis_2007_08.pdf.

259 THE POLICY ENABLED: Abdelal, *Capital Rules*, 186–188. Rawi Abdelal and Laura Alfaro, "Capital and Control: Lessons from Malaysia," *Challenge* 46, no. 4 (2003): 36–53.

259 IN EARLY 2007: Yellen, "Asian Financial Crisis."

260 SOUTH KOREAN GROWTH RATES: See http://www.adb.org/sites/default/files/pub/2012/ki2012.pdf.

263 FINALLY, IN NOVEMBER 2001: Paul Blustein, *And the Money Kept Rolling In (and Out): Wall Street, the IMF, and the Bankrupting of Argentina* (New York: Public Affairs, 2005).

263 WHAT FOLLOWED DEFIED: Weisbrot et al., "The Argentine Success Story and Its Implications," Center for Economic and Policy Research, October 2011, http://www.cepr.net/index.php/publications/reports/the-argentine-success -story-and-its-implications.

264 "WE'RE LEAVING BEHIND": Eliana Raszewski and Andrew J. Barden, "Argentine Peso Tumbles as IMF Payment Raises Inflation Concerns," *Bloomberg News,* December 15, 2005, http://www.bloomberg.com/apps/news?pid =newsarchive&refer=latin_america&sid=aN2Sgudfr6O4.

264 GOVERNMENT WAS MANIPULATING ITS INFLATION STATISTICS: "The Price of Cooking the Books," *The Economist,* February 25, 2012.

265 THOUGH CHINA EMPLOYS: *2011 Report to Congress of the U.S.-China Economic and Security Review Commission* (Washington, D.C.: Government Printing Office, 2011).

266 CHINA HELD $1.16 TRILLION: See http://www.treasury.gov/resource-center/ data-chart-center/tic/Documents/mfh.txt.

266 EVENTUALLY, THE DOLLAR HAS TO CRASH: See discussion in Barry Eichengreen, *Exorbitant Privilege: The Rise and Fall of the Dollar and the Future of the International Money System* (Oxford: Oxford University Press, 2011).

266 "BECAUSE WE OWE IT": Lawrence R. Klein, *The Keynesian Revolution* (New York: Macmillan, 1966), 182.

267 BORROWING FROM ABROAD: *Perspectives on Global Development: Shifting Wealth* (Paris: OECD, 2010).

267 COINED THE ACRONYM: James O'Neill, "Building Better Global Economic BRICs" (Global Economic Paper 66, Goldman Sachs, November 2001, http://www.goldmansachs.com/our-thinking/topics/brics/brics-reports-pdfs/ build-better-brics.pdf).

269 THIS PLAN: "HIPC Initiative and MDRI Initative: Status of Implementation," International Monetary Fund, Washington, D.C., November 2011, http://www .imf.org/external/np/pp/eng/2009/091509.pdf.

269 AS OF 2011: "HIPC Initiative and MDRI Initiative: Status of Implementation" (Washington, D.C.: International Monetary Fund, Washington, D.C., November 2011,) http://siteresources.worldbank.org/INTDEBTDEPT/ProgressReports/ 23063134/HIPC_MDRI_StatusOfImplementation2011.pdf.

270 EVEN SUB-SAHARAN AFRICA: "Perspectives on Global Development."

270 AN ARTICLE PUBLISHED: Malise Ruthven, "Excremental India," *New York Review of Books,* May 13, 2010.

270 ONE SOUND IDEA: Joseph E. Stiglitz, "Sovereign Debt," in *Overcoming Developing Country Debt Crises, ed.* Barry Herman, José Antonio Ocampo, and Shari Spiegel (Oxford: Oxford University Press, 2010), 58.

10: BACK TO THE FUTURE

273 WORLD WAR II COST: Stephen Daggett, "Costs of Major U.S. Wars," Congressional Research Service, Washington, D.C., June 29, 2011, page 2, http:// www.fas.org/sgp/crs/natsec/RS22926.pdf.

274 EVEN SO, CIVILIAN LIVING STANDARDS: John Morton Blum, *V Was for Victory: Politics and American Culture During World War II* (New York: Harcourt, Brace, and Jovanovich, 1976), 71.

274 THE CIVILIAN SAVINGS: See http://wiki.dickinson.edu/index.php?title =Economy_of_the_US_during_WWII and http://eh.net/encyclopedia/article/ tassava.WWII.

275 IN 1942, INFLATION: See http://wiki.dickinson.edu/index.php?title =Economy_of_the_US_during_WWII. See also John Kenneth Galbraith, *A Theory of Price Control* (Cambridge, Mass.: Harvard University Press, 1980).

276 IN THE POLICY: Barry M. Eichengreen and Peter M. Garber, "Before the Accord: U.S. Monetary-Financial Policy, 1945–51," in *Financial Markets and Financial Crises,* ed. R. Glenn Hubbard (Chicago: University of Chicago Press, 1991), 181, http://www.nber.org/chapters/c11485.pdf.

277 "IN TIME OF WAR": Board of Governors of the Federal Reserve System, *The Federal Reserve System: Purposes and Functions,* 2nd ed. (Washington, D.C.: Board of Governors of the Federal Reserve System, 1947), 105, 107.

277 "USED SELECTIVE CREDIT CONTROLS": Timothy Canova, "Public Finance, Agency Capture, and Structural Limits on Fiscal Policy" (unpublished paper, May, 2010), 14–15.

279 THERE WAS A LOT OF JOUSTING: See Joel Seligman, *The Transformation of Wall Street: A History of the Securities and Exchange Commission and Modern Corporate Finance* (New York: Aspen Publishers, 2003).

281 BETWEEN 1954 AND 1966: U.S. Department of Labor, Bureau of Labor Statistics, Consumer Price Index, ftp//ftp.bls.gov/pub/special.requests/cpi/ cpiai.txt.

282 AN UNLIKELY BEST SELLER: Carmen M. Reinhart and Kenneth S. Rogoff, *This Time Is Different: Eight Centuries of Financial Folly* (Princeton, N.J.: Princeton University Press, 2009).

282 "THE FOUR MOST DANGEROUS": See http://encycl.opentopia.com/term/ David_Dodd.

282 "GOVERNMENTS FORCE": Reinhart and Rogoff, *This Time Is Different,* 143.

283 AS REINHART EXPLAINS: Carmen M. Reinhart and, M. Belen Sbrancia, "The Liquidation of Government Debt" (Working Paper 16893, National Bureau of Economic Research, Cambridge, Mass., March 2011, http://www.imf.org/ external/np/seminars/eng/2011/res2/pdf/crbs.pdf).

283 THE PAPER POINTS OUT: Ibid.

284 "THE ANNUAL LIQUIDATION": Ibid.

284 THANKS TO LOW INTEREST COSTS: Ibid.

284 FOR ALL ADVANCED COUNTRIES: Ibid.

287 THE EFFICIENT MARKET HYPOTHESIS: See Eugene Fama, "Efficient Capital Markets: A Review of Theory and Empirical Work," *Journal of Finance* 25, no. 2 (1970): 383–417.

287 MAXIMIZING SHAREHOLDER VALUE: See William Lazonick and Mary O'Sullivan, "Maximizing Shareholder Value: A New Ideology for Corporate Governance," *Economy and Society* 29, no. 1 (2000): 13–35.

287 ALL POWER TO THE SHAREHOLDER: A. A. Berle and Gardiner Means, *The Modern Corporation and Private Property* (New York: Commerce Clearinghouse, 1932).

287 ANOTHER LEADING FREE-MARKET ECONOMIST: Henry Manne, "Mergers

and the Market for Corporate Control," *Journal of Political Economy* 73 (1965): 110–20.

288 BILL GROSS: Wes Goodman, "Pimco's Gross Predicts 'Repression' with Additional Easing," *Bloomberg Businessweek,* January 26, 2012, http://www.businessweek.com/news/2012-01-26/pimco-s-gross-predicts-repression-with-additional-easing.html.

289 "ARE FINDING IT TEMPTING": Kevin Warsh, "The 'Financial Repression' Trap," *Wall Street Journal,* December 6, 2011, http://online.wsj.com/article/SB10001424052970204770404577080181384917926.html.

289 SOME PRESIDENTS OF THE FED'S REGIONAL BANKS: Richard W. Fischer, "Comments to the Harvard Club of New York City on Monetary Policy" (September 19, 2012, http://www.dallasfed.org/news/speeches/fisher/2012/FS120GIG.cfm).

291 GAVE A MAJOR SPEECH: William C. Dudley, "The Recovery and Monetary Policy," October 15, 2012 http://www.newyorkfed.org/newsevents/speeches/2012/dud121015.html.

292 STUDENT LOAN FORGIVENESS ACT: See Library of Congress: http://thomas.loc.gov/cgi-bin/query/z?c112:H.R.4170.IH.

293 I'VE URGED CONGRESS: See http://prospect.org/article/alarming-parallels-between-1929-and-2007.

Index

ALSO BY
ROBERT KUTTNER

THE SQUANDERING OF AMERICA

The American economy is in peril. It has fallen hostage to a casino of financial speculation, creating instability as well as inequality. Tens of millions of workers are vulnerable to layoffs and outsourcing, while health care and retirement burdens are increasingly being shifted from employers to individuals. Here Robert Kuttner debunks alarmist claims about supposed economic hazards and exposes the genuine dangers: hedge funds and private equity run amok, sub-prime lenders, Wall Street middlemen, and America's dependence on foreign central banks. He then outlines a persuasive, bold alternative, a new model of managed capitalism that can deliver security and opportunity, and rekindle democracy as we know it.

Economics